Duke

Duke

The Life and Image of John Wayne

By Ronald L. Davis

UNIVERSITY OF OKLAHOMA PRESS : NORMAN

Also by Ronald L. Davis

A History of Opera in the American West (New York, 1965)
Opera in Chicago (New York, 1966)
The Social and Cultural Life of the 1920s (New York, 1972)
A History of Music in American Life (New York, 1980–82)
(with Paul Boller) *Hollywood Anecdotes* (New York, 1988)
Hollywood Beauty: Linda Darnell and the American Dream (Norman, 1991)
The Glamour Factory: Inside Hollywood's Big Studio System (Dallas, 1993)
John Ford: Hollywood's Old Master (Norman, 1995)
Celluloid Mirrors: Hollywood and American Society since 1945 (New York, 1997)

Library of Congress Cataloging-in-Publication Data

Davis, Ronald L.
  Duke: the life and image of John Wayne / by Ronald L. Davis.
    p.   cm.
  Filmography: p.
  Includes bibliographical references and index.
  ISBN 0-8061-3015-6 (cloth)
  ISBN 0-8061-3329-5 (paper)
    1. Wayne, John, 1907–1979.   2. Motion picture actors and
actresses—United States—Biography.   I. Title.
PN2287.W454D38   1998
791.43′028′092—dc21
[B]   97-42059
                                                                            CIP

4 5 6 7 8 9 10 11 12 13

For Jan and Hank,
my family

Contents

Illustrations

Preface

In a 1995 Harris Poll, sixteen years after his death, John Wayne still ranked as America's favorite movie star, ahead of Clint Eastwood, Mel Gibson, Denzel Washington, Kevin Costner, and Tom Hanks. More than a Golden Age film actor, John Wayne has become a legend, a cultural phenomenon whose stature grows with the passage of time. Enhanced in memory and invigorated to meet the turmoil of a modern world, Wayne's image stands as a reminder of America's frontier past. His death brought to a close an era in Hollywood's history, but his spirit lingers as a popular icon. For millions, the Duke remains emblematic of strong, silent manhood, of courage and honor in a world of timidity and moral indifference. On the screen his monochromatic characters rescue the wounded, trounce scoundrels, and salvage a blemished society—all this with no compromise to personal integrity. Not long after Wayne's death his screen persona had grown to overshadow his private identity, and soon the composite came to represent America itself.

A man's ideal more than a woman's, John Wayne soared to popularity on the silver screen without becoming either a great actor or an established sex symbol. Not flirtatious by nature, Duke did his share of philandering during his early life, but his female admirers saw him more as a protector than as a paramour. In his performances he seemed uncomfortable in love scenes, innocent and shy about women, far more natural when brawling or bonding with rugged masculine types.

Wayne's biggest success came in Westerns, although he wasn't an expert horseman and was a product of small-town America rather than the raw frontier. Studio publicists claimed that he had gotten his first experience in riding the range on his family homestead near the Mojave Desert, that he had bunked in a real ranch house, learned to corral horses and steers, and tasted the life of a cowboy in his youth. Such reports were pure fiction; even Wayne found them amusing. Yet his image became that of the dauntless cowpoke—honest, principled, as independent as he was loyal. While the star's war movies proved immensely popular and while he also played in other genres, his reputation is linked to the Old West. "Anytime you put guys like Duke in civilian clothes," veteran director Raoul Walsh remarked, "they're dog meat."

During World War II, Wayne came to symbolize patriotic ideals, although he didn't participate directly in the war. He inched his way up from the bottom of a competitive industry and perhaps embodied the work ethic more visibly than anyone else in the business. Wayne learned efficiency and how to drive a hard bargain; he developed an aptitude for giving his public what they wanted and expected. "Duke is one of the greatest action men we have ever had in this business," said Chuck Roberson, the star's longtime double. Unlike most actors, Wayne was not afraid to risk hazards that might have resulted in injury. A methodical person, he built a production company that operated years after his death. "He was something special," Duke's son Michael declared, "and he built something special. Very few movie companies have lasted as long as his."

For his admirers John Wayne was not so much a performer as a folksy personality they could identify with and embrace. "He was the most charismatic actor I've ever known," makeup artist Dave Grayson said. "He was really quite irresistible." For many that was true of Duke on-screen and off. Wayne loved people and mixed easily with most kinds. In return he expected devotion and demanded it of those closest to him, even though he had trouble sustaining intimacy himself.

Wayne was a man of simple ideas; he had an uncomplicated outlook. When asked once to name the good things in life, he listed first "the sound of a kid calling you Dad for the first time." He wanted to be a better family man than time and a demanding career permitted. He prided himself on his candor, rarely tried to be more than he was, and did his best to live a decent existence. Duke's hero of heroes was Winston Churchill. "After all," Wayne said, "he took a nearly beaten nation and kept their dignity for them." Dignity in the face of adversity was basic to John Wayne's credo, and he faced severe adversity himself during his final years.

Like all public figures, Wayne had his detractors, many of whom spoke with passion against his conservatism, his militarism, his bigotry, and his chauvinism. When Jimmy Carter awarded John Wayne the Medal of Freedom, former Democratic strategist Frank Mankiewicz was nonplussed that a movie star should be hailed as a great American. "Wait a minute!" Mankiewicz said. "John Wayne wasn't a great American. He wasn't even a great actor. He just played great Americans." But the heroes Wayne brought to the screen were central to the nation's mythic tradition, and in time Duke's public came to see themselves in the image he projected.

For John Wayne himself the matter was less clearly defined. To begin with, he wasn't John Wayne, but Marion Morrison, a "sissy's" name he came to hate, even though he was never comfortable answering to John. While he grew into a giant of a man who could take care of himself, he didn't care for horses and never rode except when work demanded. Under a tower of brawn dwelt a person of enormous sensitivity—idealistic, insecure, easily hurt. While he enjoyed stardom, his ego was never so great that he deliberately sought the heroic stature his public foisted on him. Instead, he became a magnet that drew the cultural ideals and popular attitudes of the nation into an agreeable figurehead. "It was like John Wayne was inside Mount Rushmore," said former child actress Diana Serra Cary, "and Duke was carrying this load of rock around."

Duke: The Life and Image of John Wayne aims to cut through the mythic hero without destroying his importance. My intent has been to tell a sustained life story, not to engage in detailed film analysis that would undermine the thread of a biographical narrative.

Somewhat to my surprise, since we come from different points on the political spectrum, the deeper I probed the more I came to respect John Wayne. His conservatism became understandable in light of his background and his long struggle for recognition. Wayne cherished his country and fans and was determined to be what they expected of him, keeping his personal conflicts hidden.

For millions, Duke still today nurtures the inner child that even mature adults harbor, feeds youthful reveries, and lends the strength to confront a complex world. For countless males, he represents what they would like to be—or feel they should be. For women, Wayne's impact is more problematic; his persona can be seen as a monument to sexism, and many feminists rage at what he symbolizes.

Yet myth serves a purpose, stabilizes a society, illuminates existence, and adds zest to lives. "Myths," psychoanalyst Rollo May declares, "are essential to the process of keeping our souls alive and bringing us new meaning in a difficult and often meaningless world." For his army of fans John Wayne is an anchor, an ally out of the past who animates their faith in justice and moral certainty, their belief that solutions exist in a turbulent global community; he restores their confidence in themselves. Such is the function of myth. John Wayne, America's ubiquitous hero, rerun on television week after week, is for millions a regenerative force, steadfast and brave, a shared legacy for successive generations in search of an ethical foundation.

"I can't understand why they want to puncture the myth of the Old West," said Wayne. "The American people accept the cowboy as their folklore. I see no reason to try and smash it and belittle a period of our history that was so adventurous and so alive with incident that more has been written about it than anything else." For John Wayne the old values were the true values, the ones his country had been founded on. He accepted honored axioms from the past and was impatient with concession and ambiguity. Even when he suspected that his country was going soft, Wayne continued to believe in its destiny. "I'll always be optimistic about the future of America," he said in 1976, "right up until the time we stumble and fall down."

Any biographer of John Wayne faces problems. Members of Wayne's first family continue to withhold personal papers and business records and are unresponsive to requests for interviews when those interviews are to focus on Duke himself. Michael and Patrick Wayne were forthcoming and generous with their time when I was researching my biography of John Ford. Both discussed their father at that point, but neither responded to my request for a later interview once I announced my intention of writing a book on their father. With the Wayne papers unavailable, oral history remains the major source for reconstructing Duke's life and career. Fortunately I was able to talk with many of the people who helped shape that story.

My twenty-five years of work in oral history have produced a multitude of rich experiences and incurred as many debts of gratitude. Interviewees who shed particular light on the life and career of John Wayne include Julie Adams, Gene Autry, Hall Bartlett, Charles Bennett, Budd Boetticher, Steve Broidy, Red Buttons, Harry Carey, Jr., Diana Serra Cary, Linda Cristal, Donald Curtis, Laraine Day, Edward Dmytryk, Ann Doran, Joanne Dru, Harry Essex, Dale Evans, Douglas Fairbanks, Jr., Charles FitzSimons, Dan Ford, Kathleen Freeman, Leone "Mike" Goulding, Coleen Gray, Henry Hathaway, Earl Holliman, Roy Huggins, Marsha Hunt, Martha Hyer, John Ireland, Ben Johnson, Martin Jurow, Burt Kennedy, Pauline Kessinger, Anna Lee, Janet Leigh, Mary Anita Loos,

James Lydon, Adele Mara, Andrew McLaglen, Catherine McLeod, Walter Mirisch, Mildred Natwick, Lloyd Nolan, Darcy O'Brien, Gil Perkins, Stefanie Powers, Ella Raines, Cesar Romero, Martha Scott, James T. "Happy" Shahan, Melville Shavelson, Dean Smith, R. G. Springsteen, Robert Stack, Charles Starrett, Linda Stirling, Peggy Stewart, Milburn Stone, Marshall Thompson, Claire Trevor, Hal B. Wallis, Michael Wayne, Patrick Wayne, Elmo Williams, Marie Windsor, and Hank Worden. I welcome this opportunity to thank all of them.

Pilar Wayne and Maureen O'Hara, from different perspectives, humanized John Wayne for me more than all the rest put together. Without their insight, the man might have remained obscured by his legend. I met Pilar Wayne at a showing of her paintings in Wimberley, Texas, then spent an afternoon with her at her home in Laguna Beach, California. "I was his favorite wife," she proudly announced early in our conversation. "I was with John Wayne longer than anybody." Hers was a mixed portrait—full of love and regret, but with no trace of bitterness. Maureen O'Hara, Duke's favorite leading lady, knew Wayne for almost forty years, considered him "a bloody good actor," and cherished him as a friend she could depend on. We spent four hours talking about Duke in her home in Los Angeles two days after she had arrived there from Ireland. Her loyalty was steadfast. The John Wayne she knew had no insecurities; he was strong, spoke his mind, and always did what he believed to be right. The two of them had worked hard and had fun together, being careful to avoid any mention of politics. "We talked kids, family, grandchildren, old friends, old times, and John Ford," O'Hara said.

The longer an author researches a subject the greater his or her obligations become. Mine are far-reaching, beginning with my secretary, Claudia Erdmann, and a perceptive coterie of early readers, especially Eleanor Solon, R. Hal Williams, John Lenihan, and Judy Mason. All of us who write film history know and treasure the generosity of Ned Comstock and the staff of the Doheny Library at the University of Southern California, Sam Gill and his colleagues at the Margaret Herrick Library of the Motion Picture Academy of Arts and Sciences, and the courteous workers in the Mayer Library at the American Film Institute. For me the Lilly Library at Indiana University was particularly valuable, as were the oral history collection at Columbia University, the special collections library of Brigham Young University, the Wisconsin Center for Film and Theater

Research, the Theater Collection in the Humanities Research Center of the University of Texas at Austin, the Arizona State Historical Society, the Hamon Arts Library at Southern Methodist University, the Madison County Historical Society in Winterset, Iowa, and the public libraries in both Glendale and Lancaster, California.

My personal gratitude also extends to June Beck, Judy Bland, Paul Boller, Kay Bost, Carol Bruce, Tony and Ghada Colom, Lennie Draper, John Drayton, Jane Elder, Richard Etulain, Kathryn Lang, John Marrs, Gideon Ong, Mildred Pinkston, Craig Schoenfeld, Lizabeth Scott, Walter and Mickey Seltzer, Beverly Todd, Leah Whittington, my colleagues in the History Department at Southern Methodist University, and a university administration that provides time and resources for faculty to engage in research and writing.

Duke

American Icon

On June 12, 1979, an elderly gentleman sat at a breakfast table in the Cafe de Paris in Monte Carlo reading an Italian newspaper with tears streaming down his cheeks. Lilia Garcia, a Hispanic teenager from south Texas caught a glimpse of the headline and started to cry too. "Il Duke e Morti" (The Duke Is Dead), the newspaper announced. That same day, halfway around the world, the Lima, Peru, *Noticias* declared in bold letters, "Adios, Vaquero" (Goodbye, Cowboy). Movie actor John Wayne had died at age seventy-two.

"Growing up on a ranch," Lilia Garcia said later, "it was easy for me to relate to John Wayne. Now that I've reached the ripe old age of twenty-six, he brings back the belief I had as a child—the conviction that if you ride high in the saddle, you can accomplish anything. Thanks to John Wayne, I'll never turn loose of those dreams."

Craig Schoenfeld, a wealthy undergraduate from Florida, bought cowboy boots and a Stetson soon after arriving in Texas for his freshman year of college. He returned to his dormitory and asked a friend to take his picture in front of a life-sized poster of the Duke he had taped to his door. "I've always had a picture of John Wayne in my room," Schoenfeld said. "When I was a teenager and my father and I didn't agree on *anything*, there were two things we could do together: watch sports events and John Wayne movies on television."

A thirty-seven-year-old clerk at a small-town Wal-Mart claimed in 1993 that she sold more John Wayne videos than any others. "I've been watching John Wayne movies all of my life," she said; "I can't imagine the world without him." A vacationer in Provo, Utah, declared with pride a year later that whenever he finds a Wayne film while channel surfing at a television set, he stops cold. "In our house the Duke rules," he said.

The Mexican grandfather of Isidro Aguirre, a graduate student at Southern Methodist University, suffered from cataracts and never *saw* a John Wayne film. He became a fan of "Juan Wayne" just from hearing the voice and from his grandson's description. A young father of modest means, his wife, and their small child detoured to visit the John Wayne birthplace in Winterset, Iowa. No detail about his idol was too insignificant for this young man to investigate. Asked why Wayne was his favorite movie star, the fellow replied, "For me the Duke is the only one."

"When I was growing up," Lilia Garcia said, "most girls liked Donny Osmond, but I was in love with a big, weather-beaten man over sixty years my senior. I was fascinated that Wayne married three Hispanic women, a unique facet to this American icon. I prefer to think that he complemented his American individualism with an earthy, passionate Latin flavor." Jane Elder, a working wife and mother of two preschool children, admires Wayne's strength on the screen and his willingness to act on his beliefs. "He reminds me of my father, who didn't take any nonsense from the corporate structure," she said. "John Wayne represents the kind of man you'd like to have around in a time of crisis."

Years after Wayne died, a young man told Duke's daughter Aissa that he had suffered child abuse at the hands of his alcoholic father. From the earliest time he could remember through adolescence the youth had a recurring dream that John Wayne appeared, beat up his father, and protected him against further mistreatment.

President John Kennedy watched Western movies and liked Randolph Scott, but John Wayne was his screen hero. Hong Kong–born filmmaker Wayne Wang, director of *The Joy Luck Club*, was named after John Wayne. So were executed serial killer John Wayne Gacy and dismemberment victim John Wayne Bobbitt. A decade and a half after the Duke's death, bumper stickers still proclaim, "God Bless John Wayne," while advertisements for The Gap assure readers that "John Wayne wore khakis." Visitors to Knott's Berry Farm can visit the John Wayne Theater, where stills and memorabilia of the star serve as a tribute. If one wished to order a John Wayne .45, the pistol could be purchased in 1987 for a deposit of $79, plus four monthly installments of the same amount.

Molly Haskell, a liberal journalist with feminist leanings, found herself in awe of the Duke when she interviewed him on the set of *The Shootist*, his last picture. "I never expected the sight of him to wipe me out," Haskell wrote. But when she saw Wayne in person, looking larger than life, she desperately wanted him "to take me in his arms, to tell me that everything is all right. . . . That he is not going to leave me. That it is all right for me to be a little girl sometimes." Novelist Joan Didion in 1965 summarized his impact for millions: "When John Wayne rode through my childhood, and very probably through yours, he determined forever the shape of certain of our dreams."

Selden West, a film biographer, wife, and mother, sees Duke as a "masculine, masculine, *masculine* character. Not much education, but smart, big and strong. Tough and in control. Kind, with a sort of innocence. Never much self-doubt—just on the move and in action. John Ford may have thought Wayne had a 'fairy walk,' but I can assure you no woman ever did. When I was a little tomboy, I wanted to *be* John Wayne."

Wayne became Hollywood's all-time box-office draw, remaining the nation's top screen star for five years during his lifetime and ranking among the top ten for another fourteen. In a career that spanned half a century he made nearly two hundred movies and starred in seventeen of the highest-earning films in motion picture history. At the time of his death Wayne's movies had grossed $700 million, and his lasting popularity around the world marks him as the most enduring star in the Hollywood galaxy. Dismissed by the eastern intelligentsia and belittled by critics, Wayne's films have earned more money than those of any actor or actress of his generation. Yet John Wayne represents more than a successful movie star; he has become a folk hero, a symbol of America, a reminder of a time when his country had a mission.

"To the people of the world," actress Maureen O'Hara said before a congressional subcommittee a month before Duke's death, in an appearance in which she urged representatives to award her friend a special medal, "John Wayne *is* the United States of America. He is what they believe it to be. He is what they hope it will be. And he is what they hope it will always be." For countless fans Wayne embodies virility and courage; flinty resolution and moral purpose; steadfastness, dignity, and strength; fearlessness and action in the face of danger. His life came to exemplify hard work, upward mobility, and economic success. Wayne was a survivor, motivated by an inner code, consistent in his beliefs, always ready to stand up and be counted. He projected a friendly demeanor, yet his power made clear that he could be headstrong and combative when the need arose. Wayne's values, grounded in American mores of the nineteenth century, coincided with the traditional ethos of his nation. He stood for virtues many Americans aspired to and wanted to believe were typical of their country.

The equation was made simple by Wayne's ardent patriotism. "I am proud of every day in my life I wake up in the United States of America,"

5

he often said. He genuinely believed that sentiment; America had been good to him, and he would remain its defender. Duke "loved this land of ours," said Pilar Wayne, his third wife, "and his movies reflected that love." As his life took on mythic proportions, John Wayne came to be viewed almost as an extra star on his country's flag or an eagle that kept alive a legendary past. "I was America to them," Duke said of his fans.

More specifically, John Wayne personified for millions the nation's frontier heritage. Eighty-three of his movies were Westerns, and in them he played cowboys, cavalrymen, and unconquerable loners extracted from the Republic's central creation myth. Wayne's Western heroes are men of decision, unburdened by family ties, obsessed with a mission, placing duty before love or personal tranquility. Skilled in violence, they nonetheless possess a vulnerability that tempers their overriding toughness. Anti-intellectual, solitary, sometimes rebellious, Wayne's frontiersmen shoot first and talk afterwards. But ultimately his frontier heroes are the force that make order and civilization possible.

The conquest of the West has long been accepted as a unique aspect of American history, and the cowboy is still viewed by many as a chivalrous knight upholding justice on the last frontier. "My father became the symbol of the cowboy," said Michael Wayne, Duke's oldest son. "He wasn't a cowboy, but people saw him that way." Wayne knew the difference but was malleable enough to fit the image that earned him fame. A far better actor than most critics acknowledged, he disciplined himself to play a role the public expected. Yet he seldom mistook the movies and his professional persona for real life.

Wayne's image was a personification of a figure that had already become mythical through dime novels, Wild West shows, silent movies, and comic books. John Wayne breathed new life into the lore of the cowboy and made his men on horseback indestructible examples of what Americans imagined their heroes should be. "The cowboy is gone," Wayne said. "He lived only a hundred years [in reality, decades less], yet there is more folklore about him than any other figure of any nation. The cowboy, like all legendary heroes, symbolized the basic things of life—love, anger, hate, joy. He was always easily understood. He had no nuances. He lived healthily, loved healthily, hated healthily, laughed healthily, and fought healthily. And, of course, he was never a coward."

John Wayne's screen impersonations were a throwback to an earlier time, while his Westerns could be seen as morality plays. For Americans, the saga of the Old West is comparable to the Greek *Iliad*, the Robin Hood legends of England, the Wagnerian *Ring des Nibelungen*, or stories of the Japanese samurai. Wayne's imaginary West is a place of hope, where heroes are in control and men have integrity and purpose. While the characters Wayne played so persuasively are flawed and commit mistakes, audiences know that the Duke, whatever his role, has done the best he could and will be man enough to admit his shortcomings.

As he grew older, Wayne became the eternal father figure, revealed a deepening genius for screen acting, and layered his characters with subtle complexities that are manifest in his aging face. His scenes with children are especially touching, as he portrays the loving patriarch teaching life's lessons to the young. With women half his age, he was able to project sexual tension without direct suggestions of physical involvement.

The older he got, the more Wayne embodied the American past. Always a man's man, he turned into more of a loner, estranged but still fighting the good fight, often using unorthodox means to achieve his ends, yet winning battles that would keep his society great. Katharine Hepburn, who worked with Duke toward the end of his career, admired both his independence and his skill as a film actor. For Hepburn, Wayne was "the style of man who blazed the trails across our country" and "who reached out into the unknown." He was the kind of man who was "willing to live or die entirely on [his] own independent judgment."

In addition to his work in Westerns, John Wayne also portrayed stalwart heroes of World War II, even though he was never in the armed forces and never fought in any war. Still, the Wayne persona was strengthened by his roles as a tough military man who shows superhuman courage under fire and teaches those serving under him the meaning of being soldiers. The Duke's war heroes are fearless, incorruptible, and exaggerated, though tempered by rough good humor and the hint of human weakness.

When Bob Crane was establishing the title character of television's *Hogan's Heroes* (1965–71), the producer insisted that Hogan not be played strictly for laughs. He and his buddies in the Nazi prison camp had to have a heroic dimension as well. After much thought, the actor decided to play him a bit like John Wayne. "That's it! John Wayne!" three guys in the crew yelled when Crane announced his solution. "If you want to be a hero, think John Wayne."

More than any other movie star, John Wayne became a role model for young American males, and millions the world over viewed him as their masculine ideal. In his book *Born on the Fourth of July*, Vietnam veteran Ron Kovic recalls how as boys he and a buddy sat watching the Duke in *Sands of Iwo Jima* charge up a hill and get killed just before reaching the top. They both cried when they saw the marines in the film raise the American flag on Iwo Jima. From then on John Wayne was their hero, their concept of what the American man should be. "Nobody ever told me I was going to come back from this war [Vietnam] without a penis," said Kovic. "Oh God, I want it back! I gave it for the whole country. . . . I gave [it] for John Wayne."

"People actually thought of Wayne as a great hero," screenwriter Roy Huggins said, "and, of course, John Wayne was just an actor. He was never in any armed service, never saw a war, never even saw a gun fired that actually had lead in it. To me that is an incredible comment on American society. It says something about the confusion in the American people between reality and myth." For men who secretly felt less masculine than the John Wayne prototype, the confusion often produced guilt and emotional complexes. For others it built a basic unreality into their relationships and into their concepts of life and danger. When an American officer during the Vietnam War realized that his unit was trapped in a Vietcong ambush, he reportedly rallied his troops by yelling, "Don't worry, it's only a John Wayne movie!"

Yet maintaining such a powerful image on occasions gave even Wayne himself problems. "Like so many American men of his generation," Duke's daughter Aissa said, "my father believed if a man was to call himself a man, he must wear a kind of armor, male and indestructible, that concealed his fears and deepest feelings from his family." In truth Wayne was a sensitive man, insecure in some areas and in need of constant love and affirmation. Underneath a genial, guarded exterior was a complicated personality—torn by conflict, driven by pride, haunted by a troubled boyhood and a failed first marriage. While he could be chilling in personal encounters, given to dictatorial stances and angry rages, he was also warmhearted, generous, and sentimental. Above all he was forthright and honest. "If he told you tomorrow's Christmas," his colleague Ben Johnson said, "you could get your stocking ready. He was that kind of person."

"I think the world should know that this was a human being," one of

Wayne's friends, director Budd Boetticher, declared. "He wasn't a lower-case God, he wasn't Eisenhower running an army, he wasn't all the things he played in the movies. He was a human being that made a hell of a lot of mistakes. Duke was either very bad or very good; he was never down the middle. He did some really wonderful things, but I'll tell you—sometimes he was despicable." Actress Kathleen Freeman agreed: "Wayne was not a bender, never subtle. He could be a martinet and cut your head off, yet there was a vulnerable streak in him that ran deep."

Despite the laurels and public acclaim, Wayne was a lonely man, living in a black-and-white world, with little room for compromise or accommodation. His wife Pilar attested to the fact that Duke did not understand nor know how to treat women, and he freely admitted that they "scared the hell" out of him. "I've always been afraid of women," he said. In private Wayne was essentially the man's man he played on the screen, baffled by women and relaxed in the company of men. His leisure activities—sailing, hunting and fishing, poker, chess, and drinking—were mainly enjoyed with male friends. While never an alcoholic, he could outdrink most of his cronies without appearing drunk, and he swore without realizing it. "Like Ford, it was impossible for him to say two sentences without using words that would put a dockworker to shame," actor Henry Fonda maintained.

An outdoorsman who had been a football player in his youth, Duke continued to think of himself as an athlete. He placed little trust in his intellect, except where his career was concerned, nor was he given to introspection. "I can't picture the cowboy in his long underwear lying on a psychiatrist's couch," said Wayne. "The menace in the cowboy's life came from the seasons, the weather, the land. Not from interior sparks." Like the heroes he played, Wayne shied away from nuances—and from psychoanalysts' couches.

Much of Duke's ability to merge a screen image with his own person came from his physical makeup—his height and bulk, his deep voice, his macho swagger. No one else walks the way John Wayne did—that long, rolling, slightly pigeon-toed stride that became his trademark, as graceful as it was athletic. Nor does anyone deliver dialogue the way he did—slow and rhythmic, broken by unexpected pauses for emphasis. "I see him right now," said Coleen Gray, who played the sweetheart Duke left behind in the early scenes of *Red River*, "and I think of the expanse of his chest, the broad shoulders, the way he stood with his feet like they were ground into the soil. He was a pillar of strength."

And there was an innocence about him that audiences continue to find enchanting. The fact that he wasn't a ladies' man and didn't relish love-making on the screen makes him attractive to many of his female fans. To them he doesn't seem like an actor; he seems like a real man, awkward and naive when it comes to women. "I suppose my best attribute, if you want to call it that, is sincerity," Duke said. "I can sell sincerity because that's the way I am."

A significant factor in Wayne's success was the way he affected people he met throughout his life. He possessed a magnetism that endeared him to diverse types. Because of his deliberate, outspoken nature, people knew where he stood and responded to his common touch. Conservative police officers who spent a few days with Duke worshiped him; liberal reporters who spent time with him ended up adoring him, despite the gap in their politics. "Everyone thinks I'm a neighbor," said Wayne. His folksy demeanor simply humanized his heroic image. "He was big, he was strong, . . . he was a man of his word, [and] he was a man of conviction," said Bill McKinney, who worked with Wayne on *The Shootist*. "There is something very deep inside all of us which responds to that. That deep core inside everybody that says, 'Here is a guy I can trust. I can lean on him. He will lead and will stand by his word.'"

For colleagues in the film business Wayne was the consummate professional who knew his craft and insisted on being a team player. "Sometimes kids ask me what a pro is," said actor Steve McQueen. "I just point to the Duke." Seldom part of the Hollywood social scene, Wayne disliked large parties and hated the phoniness of his profession. Although he strove for excellence in his work, he considered himself more a screen personality than an actor. He knew that eastern critics held his performances in low regard, but that rarely bothered him. "My business is stardom," Wayne said, and he enjoyed the rewards. Duke denied the contention that he merely played himself on the screen. "Nobody's natural in front of the camera," he said; the trick is to *act* natural. In retrospect, most film enthusiasts view Wayne as a better actor than contemporaries suggested. "The camera loved John Wayne," Coleen Gray maintained, "because he was sparse in his acting and left more to the imagination."

With fame, Duke exercised firm control over his career, selecting roles that suited his image and abilities. "I think he recognized that he was a movie actor with a certain range," said John Ford's grandson Dan. "He couldn't play anything; he was a type-cast guy." In later years Wayne worked with writers in shaping his parts, aware that audiences expected his movies to be uncomplicated and the characters he played to demonstrate certain traits. "Audiences could relax because they knew the good guys were going to win," said actress Julie Adams. "It would be tough going, but Duke knew what was right and would win."

Wayne's magic lay in convincing his public that he *was* the image he projected on the screen. Like other established stars of the Golden Age, Duke was not free to invent himself anew with each role. "If you fool [audiences] or try to be cute, you won't be the man they came to see," he explained. "I read dramatic lines undramatically and react to situations normally. . . . This is not as simple as it sounds. I've spent a major portion of my life trying to learn to do it well." Wayne worked at honing his craft, seasoning his screen persona until it became immortal.

"Duke stood for values that many of us hold dear," said Coleen Gray, "and he survived in this town long enough to become an institution." He has also survived changing times and wholesale shifts in social values. John Wayne's America was based on white, middle-class, capitalist supremacy. The California he knew as a youth was relatively nonethnic, except for the Hispanic element, which Wayne embraced in three marriages. Native Americans, blacks, and Asians, on the other hand, have reason to accuse the Duke of racism, and many have. His films are sexist and politically abhorrent by current standards. Duke's characters are often iron-willed, stubborn, and fanatic to the point of obsession—maladjusted and ruthless, iconoclasts on a rampage against the corporate structure, not reluctant to employ illegitimate means to achieve their concept of order. His heroes are frequently repressed, celibate, and sometimes brutal. Yet Wayne's impact persists, out of sync with the ethics of modern urban society, although his popularity is by no means restricted to rural and underdeveloped areas.

Wayne's politics were notoriously reactionary throughout his later career. Yet many liberals admire him as a person and as a performer, probably because he was so open about his views. "His politics I never could stand," said screenwriter-director Melville Shavelson, "but whatever Wayne did, he felt he was doing for America." Few doubted his motives, even when they found his position indefensible. "Duke believed everything he said," Budd Boetticher maintained; "there was nothing phony about the guy." Wayne thought his views were fundamental to the American system. "All I'm for," he said with characteristic simplicity, "is the liberty of the individual."

In a complex, factionalized world, where confusion and ambiguities abound, the romantic hero who determines his own code and lives by his own standards has insistent appeal. In an age of permissiveness and antiheroes, when most characters in drama are realistically flawed if not downright weak, the Duke continues to loom as the invincible victor, no longer limited by time, a constant in an unsteady world. Younger generations have grown up watching his movies on television, since John Wayne retrospectives appear week after week on cable and local channels. Jimmy Stewart once claimed that Duke was "like a mountain"; he's there for us, etched against the sky, and we know what to expect from him. "I'm not the sort to back away from a fight," said Wayne. "I don't believe in shrinking from anything. It's not my speed. I'm a guy who meets adversities head on." That's America's Duke—the kind of man who doesn't talk much but does plenty.

Clint Eastwood, often considered Wayne's heir in screen entertainment, was one of millions who grew up watching the Duke's films. Although their approach is different, the two actors appeal to similar audiences. "Clint Eastwood is only the afterglow of John Wayne," said Darcy O'Brien, son of movie actor George O'Brien. "Both fulfill America's frontier ideal of itself."

For many American males, the Duke remains part of their youth. They cling to him as a reminder of their lost innocence, a time they remember as happy and carefree, filled with limitless possibilities. They revere John Wayne as the man who defined for them the parameters of masculine behavior, the surrogate father who made their world safe, enabling them to explore and discover themselves.

Women frequently voice less enthusiasm, insisting that John Wayne represents a sexist, macho point of view they find offensive. Most women say that what they want in a man is respect, sensitivity, and a partner secure enough to show tenderness in love. To some, Wayne represents a masculine cult that demeans women as sex objects and places male bonding above mature heterosexual relationships between equals. Not only do extreme feminists revile the Duke, they reject with vehemence what he stands for. The more militant may become exasperated at their husbands when they watch Wayne reruns on television with such obvious joy.

For more sympathetic women, John Wayne seems less a sex symbol than a father or grandfather figure. Molly Haskell pointed out that father figures "have gotten a bad name" from some feminists, yet movies are full of fathers who nurture "heroines of the most spirited kind." Like Selden West and other "liberated" women, Haskell's affection for Wayne goes back to when they "were flat-chested adolescents, tree-climbers with dirty faces and with more rats-and-snails than sugar-and-spice," to when little girls went to movie theaters and identified with the heroes rather than with their sweethearts. More extreme feminists tend to view Duke's masculinity as hollow, playacting at best. They reject the man himself as dishonest for posturing as a war hero when he was not, masquerading as Mr. Macho to disguise what they suspect is latent homosexuality.

Although Wayne was no homosexual, he was timid around women, a residue that remained from tensions with his mother. Duke resolved the problem through constructive male bonding and by marrying outside his culture. His three Hispanic wives were diverse personalities, yet none resembled his fretful mother, whose personality produced restraint and feelings of rejection in her famous son.

The public knew little about the troubled, tormented side of John Wayne and preferred to focus on his heroic image. The fact that he appeared to have beaten cancer in 1964 merely enhanced the legend of indestructibility. "Good old Duke didn't just destroy villains," his wife Pilar maintained, "he faced down death itself." It was at that point, more than any other, that Wayne became a national institution, at precisely the moment when American values were making a dramatic break with tradition. "I'm just the big tough boy on the side of right," Duke said, and a maturing America, emotionally shattered by supersonic transformations on multiple fronts, ignored his dark side and lionized him as an emblem of vanishing ideals.

Along with other liberals, Marsha Hunt, Wayne's leading lady in *Born to the West*, one of the countless budget Westerns he made before *Stagecoach*, puzzled over Duke's position as an American icon. "As he often admitted when we worked together in 1937, he was surely no actor," said Hunt, "although he grew into a highly proficient performer. And I don't know that anyone ever considered him handsome. Rugged, outdoorsy, virile, but never handsome. Could I have just named some of the very qualities that won America's heart? He seemed so ordinary, so unexceptional, that many an average man might picture himself in Wayne's place, identifying with him. John Wayne was just the personification of an ordinary, quick-tempered, big lug, who found himself doing heroic deeds."

Duke's view of life was external and commonplace. "He got up every morning determined to do his best," Pilar Wayne said. "Though the results varied, the effort never did. He believed that hard work, sweat rather than talent, was what it took to succeed." John Wayne endures as perhaps the last noble hero, Superman with the heart of a child. "I'll tell you what I enjoyed most about my father," Duke's son Michael said. "My father knew what space he occupied. But what was refreshing about him was that he used to tell me, 'Michael, when you start believing your own bullshit, that's when you're in trouble.' He had a great philosophy of life, and he had a sense of humor about himself, but he also knew exactly who he was."

"Nobody should come to the movies unless he believes in heroes," said Wayne, who never anticipated becoming the most lasting star in screen history. While Gable, Tracy, Cooper, Fonda, and others from Hollywood's Golden Age are remembered with fondness, John Wayne has become an American treasure. Like Joan of Arc, he is best understood in terms of his heroic reputation rather than in terms of his deeds. Wayne mirrors his culture's expectations of heroism; he is a cultural receptor successive generations can remake to meet the requirements of their changing society.

The Trek West

John Wayne was born on May 26, 1907, in a simple white-frame house in Winterset, Iowa. The name given on his birth certificate is Marion Robert Morrison, although the name was changed to Marion Michael when his brother Robert was born four years later. The future actor was brought into the world by Dr. Jesse Smith, a woman physician and family friend. The baby had blue eyes and weighed thirteen pounds at birth. His parents, Mary and Clyde Morrison, had been married by a justice of the peace in Knoxville, Iowa, on September 29, 1906, and since Marion was born just eight months after their wedding, tongues in Winterset were set wagging.

Clyde Morrison was a darkly handsome, charming man of medium height, gentle and intelligent, but a tad on the irresponsible side. His Scotch ancestors had moved from Ohio to Illinois, where they were farmers and staunch members of the Presbyterian Church. Clyde's father, Marion Mitchell Morrison, for whom Duke was named, had fought with the Eighty-third Illinois Infantry in the Civil War and had been wounded in a skirmish on the Tennessee River. After the war the elder Morrison returned to his farm near Monmouth, Illinois, where Clyde was born in 1884.

A few years later the family moved to Iowa, and Duke's grandfather became a real estate agent. In 1899 he was elected treasurer of Warren County. Clyde therefore grew up in Iowa, attended Simpson College in Indianola on a football scholarship, and studied pharmacy there. Eager to move on with his life, Clyde left school before graduating and served an internship as a pharmacist in Waterloo, Iowa. There he met his future wife, Mary Alberta Brown, a telephone operator from Des Moines.

Redheaded, blue-eyed Mary Brown was of Irish descent and had the temper to prove it. She was born in 1885 in Lincoln, Nebraska. Her family moved to Iowa when Mary's father, Robert Emmett Brown, became a proofreader for a Des Moines newspaper. Tiny and vivacious, Mary was a rather plain young woman and morally straight-laced. When a writer pointed out later that John Wayne's parents had married less than nine months before their first son's birth, Duke said, "If my mother were still alive, she would have horsewhipped him down Main Street."

Shortly after Clyde and his bride's nuptials, the groom took a job as a pharmacist's clerk at M. E. Smith's drugstore on the south side of the square in Winterset, the seat of Madison County. At the time of their first son's birth, the Morrisons lived at 224 South Second Street in a four-room house, built in the 1880s, with a wide front porch and stained-glass windows. Winterset would become famous for two reasons—as John Wayne's birthplace and for the area's covered bridges that novelist Robert James Waller immortalized in his best-selling novel *The Bridges of Madison County* (1992). Surrounded by rich farmland, Winterset now boasts a central thoroughfare named John Wayne Drive. In 1907 the town had less than three thousand residents and espoused the provincial values of the American heartland.

The streets of Winterset were not paved in those horse-and-buggy days and frequently were muddy. Alice Miller, a neighbor of the Morrisons, remembered "the big ditches along the streets and how people would put big wooden planks across the ditches to get to the street." She also recalled how Mary Morrison, whom friends called Molly, would push her baby carriage with little Marion inside up to the town square and home again.

But Mary and Clyde were incompatible personalities, and there were soon marital problems. He was amusing and easygoing, quick to trust others; she was ambitious and impatient with the ineffectual Clyde. Mary was by far the stronger personality, and she came to dominate her husband, as she would her sons. "[My mother] was the first women's libber," an adult Duke said. "She was the first woman I ever saw smoke." A dynamic force, Mary was full of anger. "I get my hot temper from her," Duke said.

With Mary's help, Clyde saved enough money to make a down payment on his own pharmacy in nearby Earlham. The Morrisons moved there in 1910, when Marion was three. They bought a bigger house at 328 Ohio Street in Earlham, where their second son, Robert Emmett, was born on December 8, 1911. "The only vivid memory I have of Iowa," Duke said later, "was when my brother was born and I was put out for the day at a dentist's, who was a friend of my father's." Named for Mary's father, Robert became the apple of his mother's eye, and she doted on the boy far more than she ever had on Marion. Duke resented her preferential treatment and grew closer to his father. "The happiest part of Duke's childhood ended the day his brother was born," Pilar Wayne maintained.

In time, young Marion grew antagonistic. Feeling unloved by his mother, he became strongly independent. He spent as much time as possible outside the house and liked exploring the countryside. Sometimes he gave his parents anxious moments by disappearing. The Morrisons' house was near the railroad tracks that ran through Earlham. One day Marion noticed an empty boxcar in the freight yard; he crawled inside and went to sleep. When he awakened, the car was several miles down the track.

A neighbor remembered Marion as the best-dressed boy in town, particularly in his blue sailor suit and matching cap. When the lad went for a haircut, the barber would put lather on his face, then remove it with the back of a razor, causing the youngster to laugh with delight. The family attended the Presbyterian Church in Earlham, although it was almost impossible for Marion to stay still during the service. He often crawled under the seats, sitting with people in different pews when he came up.

The Morrisons had a one-horse shay and a horse named Sadie, which was usually tied to a hitching post behind Clyde's drugstore. Clyde, whom customers called Doc, was quite popular around town and active in local affairs. He possessed a fine baritone voice and maintained his compact, sturdy physique by continual workouts. He helped train the Earlham Academy football teams in 1911 and 1912 and occasionally refereed games. He spent most of his leisure hours with Marion, teaching his son how to pass a football and tackle. "My father was the kindest, most patient man I ever knew," Duke would recall. The boy admired his father and considered him his best friend, while he found his mother's world suffocating and trivial.

As soon as Robert could walk, he tried to be his brother's shadow, but Marion rebuffed him. Hurt by the love and attention his mother showered on Bobby, Duke for years spurned his brother, much to Mary's dismay. While Bobby was her darling, Marion irritated her. Duke's curiosity and inquisitive nature taxed Mary's patience, and her older son's growing alliance with Clyde served to aggravate her.

Mary was a complainer, and her nagging of Clyde distressed Marion; his security was undermined by their constant bickering. Mainly they argued over how to manage the pharmacy. Convivial man that he was, Clyde found pressing customers for payment of bills difficult, whereas the cynical Mary tended to think the worst of people and demanded that her husband become more aggressive. She objected to his policy of easy credit and complained about the scant income. Night after night, Marion lay in his bed listening to Mary berate Clyde for his shortcomings. The boy would drift off to sleep, only to be awakened by their angry voices.

As Duke's world became increasingly edged with anxiety, he turned more and more to his father for emotional support. He found talking to his mother frustrating, sensed her indifference to him, and retreated into fantasies. Growing up on the Iowa prairie he heard tales of covered wagons, buffalo hunters, and stagecoach robberies, all of which sparked his imagination. Lore of the recently conquered West helped the boy forget his own discomfort and loneliness. "He never admitted his deepest fears or hurts, not to his mother or father in his childhood," Pilar Wayne declared. "By choosing not to reveal his feelings, Duke formed a habit that lasted a lifetime."

In addition to his parents' quarrels, Marion had to contend with his name, which made him an easy target for town bullies and neighborhood pranksters. They called him a little girl, asked why his mother dressed him in pants rather than skirts, and made the boy's life miserable. "Duke was uncomfortable talking about his childhood," said Pilar. "He revealed the story in bits and pieces during our years together. He told of feeling unloved by his mother and victimized by his parents' many fights and their poverty." But dealing with the name Marion and being called a sissy perhaps hurt most of all.

Faced with continued ridicule from his wife, Clyde began to see himself as a failure. He realized that Mary no longer loved him, grew despondent, and began having health problems. He developed a cough that grew steadily worse. During the summer months the hack would almost disappear, but with the dampness of autumn it would start again. Through the midwestern winters his cough was relentless. Clyde often came home from the drugstore too fatigued to do more than eat and go to bed. Eventually his illness was diagnosed as tuberculosis, although depression was part of the malady. A physician told Clyde that if he hoped to recover, he must seek a hot, dry climate; another harsh Iowa winter might kill him.

In 1914 Clyde sold the drugstore and sent Mary and his two sons to

Des Moines to stay with her family, while he went to the West Coast to look over prospects. Clyde's father had moved to California a few years earlier and had homesteaded eighty acres near the village of Lancaster, on the edge of the Mojave Desert. Grandpa Morrison had built a small house on the property and had then moved to Los Angeles, where he retired on his veteran's pension. After weeks of checking other possibilities, Clyde decided to accept his father's offer to take over the forsaken farm, which was located in an area dry enough to help his congestion. Although Clyde knew nothing about farming, he hoped to turn the land into a source of livelihood, and he sent for his family.

Mary was reluctant to leave Iowa and her parents. She felt trapped by her husband's illness, but to abandon a sick man would be unforgiveable. She had no choice but to join Clyde and try to make the best of a life she knew she would hate. She and the boys took the Rock Island Railroad to Chicago, then the Southern Pacific to California. Clyde met them at the station with a horse and buggy.

Lancaster, California, in the Antelope Valley, had been initially settled by Mexican railroad workers. The town's first telephone was installed in 1902, and electric power was introduced into the valley the year the Morrisons arrived. By 1916 Lancaster would boast two paved streets and an annual rabbit hunt that brought people by train from all over southern California. The life Mary Morrison found there in 1914 was far worse than she'd imagined. The house on the family property was little more than a shack, and insects and rattlesnakes infested the land. Clyde and his sons killed rattlers by the dozens. There was no running water, and Mary found the outdoor privy demeaning. She cooked on a wood-burning stove and spent evenings reading by a kerosene lamp. Her nearest neighbors were a mile away. Seasonal dust storms proved ferocious, for the land was parched. "We were homesteaders in the real sense of the word," Duke remembered. "Those were the toughest times we had." In later years he often spoke of growing up in poverty and liked to say that if his father had one bullet, he'd better shoot two rabbits if the family was going to eat that night.

Yet young Marion felt exhilarated by the outdoor life in California and enjoyed working side by side with his father. "Imagine a seven-year-old from the flat plains being plunked down in a land that had huge mountains looming over its western rim and more mountains that stretched for hundreds of miles eastward to the Mojave Desert," said Duke. "My horizons widened; so did my love and awe of my country."

With Marion's help, Clyde cleared the homestead of sagebrush and planted corn and peas. Other farmers in the valley grew alfalfa and raised cattle, but Clyde decided that corn was the best bet, since he could not afford to buy machinery. Jackrabbits were their biggest enemy. "I remember my dad once planted five acres of black-eyed peas," Duke said, "and we went out one morning and they were showing up nice and green, about half an inch high. We went out again the following day and there wasn't a piece of goddamn green left. The rabbits had cleared the lot in one night."

It was a tough life. Clyde worked from sunrise to sunset, but his health improved and his strength returned. The corn crop their first year in California was good, even though the market wasn't. Clyde didn't make enough money to support his family for another year, and they existed on credit. Meals were scanty, mainly potatoes and beans; meat was a rarity. "There were days when I was so hungry, I thought my stomach was glued to my backbone," Duke recalled. As a boy he spent hours looking through mail-order catalogs, circling the items he wished he could buy. "I used to dream," he said, "that someday I'd have enough dollars to order everything in that damn catalogue."

Mary regretted leaving Iowa, complained bitterly, and talked about going home. To quiet her, Clyde agreed to invite her parents for a visit. Duke's grandfather Brown liked the taste of liquor, which was a point of embarrassment. Yet it was from him that the boy inherited his large physique. Mary's father stood all of six-foot-three, and Marion was growing into a tall, husky lad who thrived on physical activity. Working beside his dad made the boy feel like a man and got him out of earshot of the cold, irritable Mary.

Clyde taught his son how to handle a rifle, and Duke claimed that he learned to swim in an irrigation ditch. Twice a week Marion rode over the desert roads into town on Jenny, the Morrisons' horse, to pick up mail and groceries at the general store. "I never recall being taught to ride," said Duke. "I was riding as soon as I could walk. But I don't particularly love riding horses the way some people do."

He also rode Jenny to school, tethering her outside while he attended classes. When Jenny caught a disease and grew thin, a veterinarian ordered the horse shot. Though Marion loved the animal, he found himself blamed for her death. "The nosey biddies of the town," Duke said, "called the humane society and accused me, a seven-year-old, of not feeding my horse and watering her. This was proven in time to be a lie. I think it was occasioned by the fact that I had allowed a boy even younger than myself to get on the horse and ride the full length of the town—from one telephone pole to the next—and he fell off the horse, which did not upset him but it upset the dear ladies of Lancaster."

Since there was no money for another horse, Marion thereafter either walked to school or caught a ride on a wagon. This meant getting up at five o'clock in the morning to do his chores, then trudging to school over dusty roads that periodically became caked with mud. Marion was a shy, anxious boy, self-conscious about his height and family. He found making friends difficult, in part because of the isolation of his family's homestead. Because he talked with a midwestern accent, his classmates laughed at him, and he still had to contend with his name. "Defending that first name taught me to fight at an early age," Duke claimed.

He often came home from school dirty and bloody and with torn clothes. In Mary's mind only hoodlums engaged in street brawls, and she was determined to make Marion a gentleman. She lectured him on his need to learn better manners, but after Mary's tirades, Clyde would take the boy aside and praise him for his courage, assuring him that a man must stand up for himself and not run from a fight. "I think one of the reasons my father frequently acted so macho in later life," Duke's daughter Aissa said, "was to compensate for his boyhood torment; I believe it scarred him deeply."

Marion remained a sensitive youth, intelligent and docile in school. He possessed a natural curiosity and an interest in learning. He entered the Lancaster grammar school in the second grade but was promoted to the third grade three months later, despite his frequent absences.

The conflict between his parents grew worse as Clyde's health improved. Mary hated the farm and longed for the comforts and social life of a city. The howl of coyotes and the barren expanse of desert terrified her. At night Marion tossed in bed, sometimes pulling a pillow over his head to muffle Mary and Clyde's arguments. He felt apprehensive and feared that his parents might abandon him. Jealous of his mother's attention to Bobby, he found small solace in his younger brother, who in turn never recovered from Mary's smothering adoration. Annoyed by his mother, Marion all the while ached for her love. His only reliable companion was his father. "Duke loved his father with a quiet, steady affection," Pilar Wayne said. "He absorbed his teachings and made them part of his own character."

After two years of hell, Clyde admitted that he was no farmer and accepted defeat. His second crop was a failure, and the family's financial condition was desperate. Clyde had little choice but to return to pharmacy. He sold his father's homestead and bought a secondhand Model T Ford. The Morrisons left Lancaster when school was out in June 1916 and moved to Glendale, then a small town a few miles outside Los Angeles. Fortunately, Clyde's cough had diminished and his congestion had cleared. He found work as a clerk at the Glendale Pharmacy on Broadway and rented a house just around the corner on South Isabel Street.

Glendale in 1916 was a pleasant suburban community where everybody knew everybody and more news traveled over back fences than was communicated in the local press. Since Grandfather Morrison had died shortly before the family left Lancaster, leaving Clyde a small inheritance, the newcomers were initially viewed as prosperous additions to the community. Clyde quickly established himself as more than a dispenser of medicine; he became the town philosopher, again called Doc. "He was well-loved by all the young people," Duke recalled. "They'd go to him with their problems rather than to their own folks."

Marion was nine years old when his family moved to Glendale. He was enrolled at Doran Elementary School, and the family joined the Presbyterian Church. Clyde's inheritance was soon spent, and he drifted from one job to another. Warmhearted and personable though he was, Clyde remained an inept breadwinner. Townspeople felt the reason he lost so many jobs was that he drank too much. The Morrisons moved every year or two, usually because they were behind in their rent. Clyde again grew discouraged and began to act like the failure Mary vowed he was. As a result, the family's standard of living deteriorated still more. "Pop was a non-prosperous druggist," Duke admitted. "He was lucky if he cleared $100 a month."

Neighbors considered Mary the backbone of the family, although she did little to supplement the income of her ineffectual husband. She was a sickly woman who appeared to enjoy the attention poor health brought.

To her older son she seemed hard and unforgiving, demanding more than was reasonable. Clyde seldom argued with his wife in public and appeared to be cowed by her. As the years went by, Mary grew more active and assertive, at one point serving as the campaign manager for a local politician.

Marion was developing into a tall, gangling boy, still insecure and troubled, yearning for an escape. He made frequent trips to the Glendale library and became a voracious reader of Zane Grey novels and American history. He proved a good student and was admired by his teachers, although he always claimed that he learned his most valuable lessons from his father. Clyde told him to keep his word and never insult anybody unintentionally. "If I insult you," Duke would later assert, "you can be goddamn sure I intend to." Clyde also urged his son not to go around looking for trouble, and the adult Duke tried to heed that advice.

Despite his mother's criticism of her husband, young Marion wanted to be like his father, only more successful. "My father was a better looking man than I am," Duke said after achieving stardom. "He was a quiet, shy individual, who talked very little and had a poor head for business. He must have gone broke in the pharmacy business about ten times." If Mary was the practical Morrison, Clyde was the dreamer, full of fanciful notions that few besides Marion and the pharmacist's adolescent customers took seriously.

Duke spent his youth trying to meet his parents' conflicting demands and expectations. He had little trouble expressing himself to his father, yet was wary of his mother, though he was unable to admit his hostility toward her. Robert meanwhile either hid behind Mary's skirts or tried to stand in Marion's shadow, which the older boy tolerated only because his mother pressured him to do so.

While Duke enjoyed the company of other children in Glendale, he found little time for play. He joined the Boy Scouts, but by age eleven he was forced to take jobs after school, either delivering newspapers or delivering prescriptions for the pharmacy where Clyde worked, sometimes both. Most of the money he made went for clothes, since the looks he received from teachers and classmates when he came to school in patched pants and frayed shirts humilated him.

Trotting alongside Marion on his paper route and deliveries was the family's Airedale, a dog named Duke. Volunteer firefighters at a local station, seeing the lad and his dog together day after day, started calling the dog "Big Duke" and Marion "Little Duke." The name stuck; everybody except Mary started calling the boy Duke. "You can't image what that meant to me," the future star declared. "I really looked up to those guys. They were heroes in my book. When they began calling me 'Duke,' I made up my mind to use the name from then on."

Young Marion showed up at the firehouse one evening with a gashed lip and a black eye from a fistfight. Among the firefighters was a former professional boxer who offered to give Duke lessons in the art of self-defense. The youth accepted the challenge and soon became handy with his fists. That ended the teasing he had suffered from neighborhood bullies and classmates.

Duke graduated from Wilson Intermediate School in 1921, having won the class competition for best essay, which dealt with German atrocities in the recent war. He was to recite the essay from memory at the commencement exercises, but in the middle of his speech Duke forgot his lines and had to sit down in disgrace.

The Morrisons lived near the Palace Grand movie theater, and during his early adolescence Duke spent Saturday afternoons distributing handbills around town announcing the next week's features. In exchange he got to see the pictures free, and he became an inveterate moviegoer. He liked the swashbuckling Douglas Fairbanks, but his real heroes were Western stars William S. Hart, Hoot Gibson, and particularly Harry Carey, who seemed the most real.

During the silent era, movies were made in Glendale, in an area called Edendale, and Duke and his friends often watched films being shot. "All the kids in Glendale," he remembered, "were very movie conscious because the Triangle Studios were located in our town." Such stars as Tom Mix could be seen in the area working with a director, cameraman, and crew to make two-reel Westerns. Usually they brought along a leading lady and a band of cowboys they had hired for the day, and the stories were generally made up as they went along.

Marion and some other neighborhood youngsters played at making movies themselves. "We had actors, a director, and a cameraman," said Duke. "The cameraman used a cigar box with holes punched in it for a camera. Once, when my chance came to be a leading man, I tried jumping out of a second-story window and grabbing some vines and swinging. I ruined a beautiful grape arbor." Among Duke's closest friends in Glendale was Bob Bradbury, son of movie director Robert N. Bradbury. Bob later went to college with Marion and eventually changed his name to Bob Steele, becoming a famous Western star during the 1930s.

Emotionally, Marion had been on his own throughout most of his childhood, but by the time he entered high school the ruggedly handsome, convivial boy was surrounded by friends. "The teenage years were the happiest days of my life," Duke said. "I think the high-school age is the greatest because you have just about all the rights of an adult and none of the responsibilities." Gone were any hints of the sissy; the adolescent Duke was rambunctious, bold, and decisively masculine. The biggest trial of his Glendale years was having to shepherd his younger brother around. Wherever Duke went, Mary insisted he take Robert along.

In the fall of 1921, at the beginning of his freshman year at Glendale High, Marion stood over six feet tall, yet weighed only 140 pounds. Despite this lack of bulk, Duke became a star football player, a left guard who could be relied on to batter holes in the opponent's line. He found in his coaches the role models he needed, while his macho demeanor won him respect from teammates. He quickly established himself as a regular fellow, although he was an honor roll student, a member of the Latin Club, and a participant on the varsity debate team.

During the summer of 1922 Duke became one of seventy-two boys from Glendale who attended a YMCA camp on Catalina Island, where they slept in tents for two weeks at Camp Shaw. The next spring the boys spent Easter weekend on one of the Santa Cruz Islands, where they boated, fished, and hunted the wild boar that roamed the island where they camped.

"Duke never showed much fear of anything," a boyhood friend recalled. "I'll never forget one wild stunt he used to do. We would chase a fruit truck down the highway in my car, and when we got close to it, Duke would climb up to the very front of my car—while we were going forty miles an hour. Then while clinging to the car with one hand, he would reach into the bouncing truck in front of him and grab apples and oranges out of it."

Buried inside Duke was a hostility that surfaced on occasions. Once, when he got into a fight with another boy at a birthday party, his hostess's mother ordered him to leave. Furious, Marion went home for his air rifle, climbed onto the roof of a garage near the scene of the party, and shot down all the balloons that had been strung up in the backyard for the celebration.

Duke's classmate Ralf Eckles, later an oil company executive, remembered Marion's coming to Glendale High one morning with two bottles of asafetida, which made people nauseated. Duke and Ralf spread the foul-smelling resin around the halls and classrooms, making so many students sick that the principal had to close the school for the day.

Eckles also claimed that a favorite Saturday night pastime of Duke's gang during the summer months was to drive around town in Ralf's father's car with a case of rotten eggs or ripe tomatoes and pepper people standing on the rear of streetcars with eggs and tomatoes from the car's rumble seat. Another of their pranks was to grease the tracks of the Eagle Rock-Glendale trolley and watch it slide back down the hill. "We were just ordinary kids," said Eckles. "Glendale was a very conventional town, and nobody had much money. We were all raised very strict."

Clyde's failure in business had given Marion the incentive to succeed. Determined to avoid his father's mistakes, Duke not only did well in high school but planned to go to college, perhaps, he hoped, to the Naval Academy at Annapolis. "He was a good scholar," recalled classmate Helen Pierce Latta. "He worked next to me in the chemistry lab. It was very frustrating because he was good and I wasn't." Park Turrell, the chemistry teacher, remembered Duke as an A student.

During his junior year at Glendale High, Marion was vice president of his class, worked on the student newspaper, and was a propboy for school plays. But it was on the football field that he earned his greatest celebrity. Coached by Normal C. Hayhurst, the Glendale Dynamiters became a high school power. In November 1923 the team won its first play-off game, beating San Bernardino 15–10. The boys received much favorable notice, but lost the championship to Long Beach a few weeks later in the last six minutes of play. "Morrison was supposed to be opposite the best prep guard in Southern California," the local press reported. "If he was, Morrison has established his right to that title for he made the opposition look like a fuzzy bunny."

Teammates called him either Duke or Morrison, never Marion, and there was no question that the scrappy lad cut an imposing figure around Glendale High. He was far more at ease in a masculine world than with teenage girls, who puzzled him. He never went steady during his high school years nor became involved in a romance of any duration. He developed a crush on Helen Holmes, who lived a few blocks from the Morrisons, but was too bashful to ask her out. Girls found Duke attractive, although he seemed too busy with work and school activities to return their attention.

Part of the time he was in high school, Marion worked as a soda jerk in the drugstore where his father was employed. "My girlfriend and I used to go into the drugstore," Ruth Conrad remembered. "I had a crush on Duke, but I don't know whether he ever realized I did. He was a nice-looking boy. I enjoyed his smile. He had a funny little way of twisting his mouth up in one corner." Dorothy Hacker, another local girl, agreed that Duke was "absolutely stunningly handsome" but confirmed that he was shy around girls. "His looks alone would stop the traffic," Dorothy recalled. "He was about the handsomest young man that ever walked on two legs. He was very popular, but as far as I know he didn't date in those days."

Duke still preferred to run with the boys, whom some townspeople considered a fast crowd. His gang bought bootleg whiskey and drank rather heavily. "I would drink almost every weekend," Duke later admitted, "and didn't like dating girls who were against my drinking. I just kept my drinking companions separated from my refined Glendale friends." Already young Morrison was dividing himself into different personae. One was a serious student, an avid reader, polite and byronic. The other was a daredevil, hard-drinking, and rough. Yet in Ralf Eckles's view, "He was just a good clean-cut guy." Most of Duke's teammates would have said the same.

Marion hid his anxieties and the matters that disturbed him behind a pleasant, outgoing facade. School friends saw only the hard-driving, determined competitor. Glendale girls admired his looks and solid build and regretted his reticence in asking them out. Duke's popularity won him the presidency of his senior class, while the undefeated Glendale High football team of 1924 proved the most victorious in the school's history and won the regional championship that fall.

But young Duke Morrison was more than a well-liked high school athlete. He was a sportswriter for the student newspaper, played Mr. Forbes in a school production of *Dulcy*, won the Southern California Shakespeare Oratory Contest, was a member of the National Honor Society, and was on the reception committee for the seniors' farewell dance. He was bold

27

enough to appear in drag with some teammates in the Football Fashion Show; a photograph of the group that appeared in the 1925 Glendale High yearbook shows Duke obviously enjoying the spoof, although he has his hands in his pockets. On June 18, 1925, the young man, identified beside his yearbook picture as Marion Mitchell Morrison, graduated from Glendale High School.

Duke's boyhood ambition had been to become an officer in the United States Navy. "Ever since we moved to California," he said, "I loved the sea. More than anything else, I wanted to go to Annapolis." He applied to the Naval Academy but did not receive an appointment, being named an alternate instead. The disappointment was painful for Duke. "In a way," he said, "I guess I never really got over it."

With Annapolis no longer an option, he accepted a football scholarship to the University of Southern California, planning to go to law school. A career in law was Mary's goal for her elder son, whom she had come to recognize as a young man with ambition. Duke's success in high school became one of the few areas where she and Clyde shared a common pride. Otherwise they continued their hassles, with Mary deriding her husband for his growing limitations. She confided to Duke that she only stayed with his father for Bobby's sake.

By then Duke had learned that he had to rely on his own resources for economic security as well as emotional support. He couldn't depend on his mother for love nor on his father for much financial assistance. Still, he was grateful for the valuable lessons he had learned from Clyde. "Don't give your word easily," his father had told him, "but don't break it once you have. Don't start a fight, but if you get in one, make damn sure you finish it." Those were rules Duke was to live by.

The summer after he graduated from high school Duke stowed away on a ship bound for Honolulu. A boat's officer discovered him the third day out, and he spent the rest of the voyage shoveling coal to pay for his passage. He returned home in time to join Ralf Eckles and some other former Glendale High football stars on the University of Southern California's freshman squad that fall.

Long after he left Glendale, townspeople remembered Duke Morrison's drive and adolescent charm. "He was just an all-round likable guy," said Paul Cizek, who worked with him on the stage crew during their high school years. "He was a swell guy—very witty when he spoke and smart as a whip." Bob Hatch, who was vice president of the senior class the year Duke was president, recalled: "He was mature and conservative. He had confidence and maturity that most of us didn't have. He was a good leader."

In Winterset, Iowa, after John Wayne had become an established movie star, old-timers used to sit around the North Side Restaurant in the mornings and talk over coffee about their local success story. "Well, he's sure come a long way," they agreed. "He sure has," one area farmer might declare. "I'll bet he isn't grubbin' out stumps like I am today."

Reared in the American West just after the nation's frontier had passed, Duke Morrison prepared to take his place in the urban world during the autumn of 1925. Thanks in part to his father's tutelage, he would carry much of the rural heritage into adult life with him. Although painful remnants of an unhappy childhood continued to haunt him, he clung to the heartland values he had internalized as a boy, and through persistence and hard work he triumphed. As John Wayne he emerged as the nation's hero, yet success changed only the externals. Inside he remained the boy from Iowa who had survived hardships and flourished in small-town California. In him, the void and the glory would always remain uneasily balanced.

College Student
to Trailblazer

College football had become a rage on the West Coast by the mid-1920s, and the University of Southern California Trojans were the talk of Los Angeles. The team's soft-spoken coach, Howard Jones, counseled his players to approach the game with intellect as well as brawn, and the USC running attack won renown as the Thundering Herd. Marion Morrison and his Glendale High teammates had followed the Trojans' success with pride. Although the Naval Academy's rejection hurt Duke deeply, he entered the University of Southern California in September of 1925 eager to prove his athletic skills in the big league and pursue studies that would lead to a career in law.

His football scholarship covered tuition and fees, but Duke had to work to pay expenses. During his freshman year he washed dishes at the Sigma Chi fraternity house for his meals and worked part-time for Pacific Telephone and, during Christmas vacation, at the Glendale post office. USC, an expensive private institution, drew an exclusive student body, yet the discrepancy between Duke's social status and that of his wealthy peers seemed not to bother him. He pledged Sigma Chi and was well liked by his fraternity brothers. He wore the traditional freshman beanie, had his behind paddled when he forgot to address upperclassmen as "sir," and walked around with his trouser legs rolled up as part of the fraternity's initiation. Duke loved college life and, in part because of his football success, felt accepted.

Along with four other members of his former Glendale team, Duke earned a place on the first-string freshman squad. He stood six feet four inches tall now and was well built, handsome, and amusing, more than enough to make him a big man on campus. "We used to call him Michael or Mike," said Eugene Clarke, a college chum, "I suppose because we thought the name Marion was a girl's name." But most preferred the nickname Duke, which had followed him from Glendale.

Duke was a good student during his freshman year, held his liquor well, and proved a champion at the card table. His fraternity brothers taught him how to dress and helped polish his manners; gradually young Morrison attained a semblance of finesse. Fraternity life to him seemed like an extension of the sports field, and Duke loved the parties and horseplay of an all-male world.

Soon he discovered that college girls found him attractive. Although he was still naive about women and unsure of himself in their presence, he began dating regularly. Duke treated his girlfriends with the old-fashioned gallantry his mother had taught him, hiding from dates the hellion who frequently created mischief in the Sigma Chi house. For a time he went with Polly Ann Young, sister of actress Loretta Young, and the two remained friends long after their college years.

Duke was packing to go home at the end of his freshman year when he learned that his parents had separated. He had known since childhood that they were mismatched, yet he was enough of a small-town boy to feel shame over their plans to divorce. Suddenly he felt more alone than ever. When Mary initiated court proceedings, charging Clyde with desertion, Duke was shocked and embarrassed. He resolved the problem by distancing himself from his parents, withdrawing into the world where he felt accepted.

During the summer of 1926 he lived at his fraternity house. The Morrisons' marriage did not end legally until 1929, but Marion no longer felt that he had a home. A year after the divorce Clyde married Florence Buck, a saleswoman at Webb's Department Store in Glendale. Mary soon moved with Bobby to Long Beach, where she lived for the rest of her life. But Duke spent little time with either parent once they had separated.

To earn his keep between his freshman and sophomore years, Duke needed a job. Coach Howard Jones sent him to see Tom Mix, the cowboy star then working at the William Fox Studios on Western Avenue in Hollywood. Jones had arranged for Mix to get choice seats for some of the Trojan football games, and the star had promised the coach that he would arrange summer jobs for any of his players who needed work. Thus, Duke and his teammate Don Williams visited Mix at the old Fox lot. The actor took the boys over to his favorite speakeasy and proceeded to pump them for information about the Trojans' prospects for the coming year. After numerous drinks Mix promised to put Duke on the payroll as his personal trainer. Western stars needed to keep in physical condition, and Mix announced that the young athlete was the inspiration he needed to run two or three miles every morning.

When Duke reported for work a few days later, the studio guard told him to see George Marshall, later a famous director but then in charge of personnel at Fox. Marshall arranged for Duke and Don Williams to meet the head of the property department. The boys were given summer jobs on the "swing gang," moving furniture and set decorations and earning thirty-five dollars a week. "Motion pictures meant [only] bread and butter to me," Duke said later, "I had no feeling for the business whatever."

He returned to his studies at USC in the fall of 1926, still living across the street from the campus in the Sigma Chi house. He made the varsity football team during his sophomore year and played left guard in the season opener, although he was mainly a substitute. The Trojans received a lot of newspaper coverage that fall, and Clyde Morrison, bursting with pride, was present for every home game.

Already Duke was a smoker, though during the season he and the other players chewed tobacco rather than risk Coach Jones's ire. Duke played in the game against Oregon State, but in November his dreams of football glory came to an end when his right shoulder muscle was ripped while he was bodysurfing off Balboa beach, near Newport. Duke continued attending football practice, but his injury knocked him out of heavy contact, and hence games, for the rest of the season. In December he received his varsity letter, but his athletic scholarship was in jeopardy.

Duke never played football again; the injury proved too severe. Much of his adolescent ego had been tied up in the game, and he again felt deserted, cut off from the teammates he loved. Marion Morrison "was never a great football player," said UCLA pass catcher Woody Strode, who later played for the Los Angeles Rams and acted in films with John Wayne, "but somehow he got into [the University of Southern California's] hall of fame." That was a distinction the teenaged Marion could not have anticipated.

Duke began to sulk around the fraternity house and drink too much. He lost interest in his studies, and his grades dropped. He admitted later that he became a socialist during his sophomore year in college but said that he had abandoned that point of view by the time he dropped out of school. "The average college kid idealistically wishes everybody could have ice cream and cake for every meal," said Duke. "But as he gets older and gives more thought to his and his fellow man's responsibilities, he finds that it can't work out that way—that some people just won't carry their load."

In the spring of 1927 Duke was notified that his scholarship would not be renewed. If he stayed in college, he would have to pay his own way. Already he had borrowed funds to see him through the first two years. He decided to drop out a semester or two and save some money, but in effect his college days were over. "I got so interested in pictures that I never went back," he said.

During a weekend gathering of his fraternity brothers at Balboa the autumn prior, Duke had met Josephine Saenz, daughter of a wealthy Hispanic businessman and consul general in Los Angeles. Josephine was a great beauty, with enormous black eyes and long, thick lashes. Duke had met her on a blind date that weekend. He had been paired with her sister, Carmen, at a dance but met Josephine when Carmen invited him into her family's summer cottage when Duke walked her home. He was immediately taken with Josephine's ladylike demeanor and aristocratic bearing. For him she represented ideal womanhood—regal, cultured, chaste.

Josephine's father had been born in Spain, while her mother was of French descent. She herself had been raised in Texas, but her family fit comfortably into the Hispanic establishment of southern California. Educated by nuns, Josephine was devoutly Catholic. The Saenz family lived in the fashionable Hancock Park section of Los Angeles, and the daughters had grown up in a socialite atmosphere. Yet Josephine was impressed by Duke's earnestness and his lack of pretense. He wasn't the phony so many of the rich idlers she knew were; he was refreshing and bold.

During his last year at the University of Southern California, Duke and Josephine dated whenever he had enough money. "I was getting much confidence in myself," Duke said, "though [I was] still shy with girls, but whiskey was good in that department." Josephine's parents did not approve of the attention this young athlete paid their daughter. Duke wasn't a Catholic, and they were horrified when they learned that his parents were seeking a divorce. In their minds Duke had no breeding, no money, and slim prospects for a career. Besides, he was a high-spirited college boy, given to heavy drinking and brawling, and their daughter was still in high school. Eventually Dr. Saenz informed Duke that he was not welcome in their home, with the result that the couple found ways to meet in secret.

Their romance was problematic from the beginning, but Duke was used to that in male-female relationships. Josephine tended to be jealous, whereas Duke had just recently discovered his potential with the opposite sex. Although not experienced in sexual matters, he was hot-blooded and eager to learn. Duke was a backsliding Protestant, while Josephine was a staunch churchgoer and moralist, even though Duke claimed that she had a way of making "no" sound like an invitation. Against her parents' objections, she started going steady with Duke and they soon became engaged, with the firm understanding that marriage must wait until young Morrison could support a wife in the manner to which Josephine Saenz was accustomed.

Duke returned to the Fox studio in the summer of 1927, planning to work there for a year and save enough money to finish his studies at USC. "I hadn't gone to the studio thinking of a future in that line," he declared. Again Duke was employed in the property department, where he toted furniture and whatever else was needed to dress sets. "If the property department was a little slow," he said, "I worked in the electric department." He enjoyed being at the studio and eagerly performed the duties assigned to him. "At this time," he said, "I had no ambition beyond becoming the best property man on the Fox lot." A chief propman earned $150 a week, and that was the goal Duke aspired to, still confident that he would resume his studies the following fall.

"I was very good friends with John Wayne at the Fox studio on Western Avenue," said R. G. Springsteen, later a director at Republic. "I was working in wardrobe, and he came over; we used to go to lunch almost every day, which was just around the corner." Studio employees found Duke pleasant and a reliable worker. He lit up when they discussed football, sometimes talked about his girlfriend, but seldom mentioned his parents. As time went on, he began to learn the rudiments of picture making, came to realize that films were shot on tight schedules, and noted that even stars were laborers in an industry oriented toward product.

Duke watched the way Tom Mix mounted his horse, always keeping his back straight, and noted how effective it was. He doubled in some football scenes in a picture, appeared as a face in the crowd in a few others, and served as a part-time stuntman for extra pay. Duke later claimed that his acting owed much to his training as a propboy, and he was always close to the stuntmen and wranglers on his pictures after he became a star, frequently preferring their company over that of his illustrious peers. Yet after a year on the Fox lot he still had no intention of becoming an actor. "Hell, no," he said, "I was embarrassed seeing my face on the screen."

One day Duke was instructed to report to an assistant director on a John Ford picture. Ford needed an extra propman on *Mother Machree* (1928), a film he was making about Ireland. The first day on the set Duke was put in charge of a gaggle of geese that Ford planned to use as atmosphere in a scene depicting an Irish village. Young Morrison was told to release the geese from their pens when Ford gave the signal and herd them into camera range with a large pole. On the first few attempts, the unruly flock waddled in unexpected directions, providing more confusion than local color, much to Duke's frustration. The director lost his temper. "He was the most awkward propman we ever had," Ford said of Duke later. "He'd drop lights and knot up cables and ruin takes, but he was a nice big kid, and he tried hard to please."

When Ford, who had been a fullback in high school, learned that young Morrison was a football player, he asked him what position he played. Discovering that Duke played running guard, Ford ordered the boy to take his position. The novice propman crouched down and placed his hands on the ground; the director lunged, knocking Duke's arms out from under him, and causing him to fall on his face in the mud. Ford found that hilarious, and his cast and crew joined in a hearty laugh. Duke suggested that they try the play again. This time the young man caught Ford's legs and dumped him on the ground with a decisive thud. The set remained silent until the director smiled. Then Duke reached down to pull Ford to his feet, and the filmmaker invited the youth to lunch.

"I liked Duke's style from the very first time I met him," the legendary director declared. "I could see that here was a boy who was working for something—not like most of the other guys, just hanging around to pick up a few fast bucks. Duke was really ambitious and willing to work." Ford soon became a father figure to the eager propboy, at a time when Duke was uncertain about his own family and feeling particularly insecure. "Ford knew a little about football," the future star said, "and that created an admiration in me. Finally I realized that this was the first artist I'd known."

Duke began to observe the way Ford worked, watched how he handled people and met challenges, and gradually became intrigued with the whole business of making motion pictures. "I studied him like a hawk," Duke said. "I'd never seen a genius at work before, but I knew I was seeing one now. The man was a perfectionist, and I wanted to be like him."

Ford asked that Duke be assigned to the crew of his next picture, *Four Sons* (also 1928). In the movie, actress Margaret Mann played a mother who loses three sons in World War I. It was supposedly autumn when she received the news of her third boy's death, and Duke's job was to toss up maple leaves so that a fan could blow them out onto the set while the mother cried as she read the letter telling of her son's death. "I'd go out and sweep the leaves away and get ready to do another take," Duke remembered. "We kept doing this over and over, and it got to be fairly monotonous." During one take the still-inexperienced propboy threw the leaves into the air and watched them waft across the set. "I figured the scene was over," said Duke, "and I picked up the broom, went in, and started to sweep. I looked up, and I'm looking right into two cameras—and they're turning! I just threw down my goddamn broom and started to walk off." Ford shook his head and broke up laughing. "They took me back to Ford," said Duke, "and he bent me over and kicked me in the ass."

Disappointed in his own son, Ford needed a strong, hell-raising, hardworking substitute like Marion Morrison in his life. He taunted the handsome lad constantly—the only way Ford knew of showing masculine love—and called him "a big oaf." The two began to spend leisure time together at the Hollywood Athletic Club and in drinking bouts in Ford's home. They discovered that they'd both wanted to attend the Naval Academy and shared a love for the sea. "I just looked up to this man Ford," said Duke, "he was a big hero to me. He was intelligent and quick-thinking, had great initiative. It was just wonderful to be around him. He kept you alive and on your toes."

The director gave the boy a bit part in *Hangman's House* (again 1928), the role of an Irish peasant found guilty of a murder he didn't commit. The scene lasted only a few seconds, but Duke reappeared later in the film as an excited spectator at a horse race. This screen debut was inauspicious, but the lad was photogenic and possessed the face of innocence.

"I took a liking to him and began throwing him bit parts," Ford remembered. Duke insisted that he still wasn't interested in an acting career. "I wanted to be a director," he said. "I wanted to be on the production end of the business." The more he thought about spending ten years in the back room of a law office, writing briefs for other attorneys, the less that idea appealed to him. Moviemaking appeared to hold a brighter future, especially with all the talk about adding sound. Besides, the business fascinated him. "I wanted to be like Jack Ford," said Duke, "he was my mentor and my ideal."

Without realizing it, Duke was learning his future craft. There were no unions at the time, and workdays were long, including Saturday and sometimes part of Sunday. "In those days you could operate in every department of pictures," Duke recalled. "You didn't need a union card. So I got to know the nuts and bolts of making pictures." When not working as a propboy for Ford, he was assigned to actor George O'Brien's movies, where he sometimes functioned as a second assistant director. But he considered Ford his true teacher. "I went back to propping with him," said Duke, "so I could get more experience." From Ford he learned the importance of detail and that motion pictures should rely more on visuals than on words. "I know what a scene is going to look like on film," Duke said as a mature star. "I don't have to look at the daily rushes." From Ford he learned the grammar of the business and developed good instincts for picture making. The director saw that Duke was paying more attention to scenes than the average propman and took the boy into his confidence.

Myrna Loy starred in an early sound film directed by Ford called *The Black Watch* (1929), playing opposite Victor McLaglen, a perennial member of the director's stock company. When the movie was completed, Ford paid Loy the compliment of inviting her to a stag party at his house on Odin Street in Hollywood. "John Wayne was there," the actress recalled in her autobiography, "young and handsome and just out of college, as shy as I was. He was a property man on the picture; at least, he'd been around on the set all the time. Jack was grooming him."

By then Duke already knew the basics of filmmaking, enough to recognize the harm studio executives did in editing *The Black Watch* after Ford had turned the project over to them. "Talky" love scenes were added without the director's permission. "They were really horrible," Ford said. "I wanted to vomit when I saw them." Wayne remarked later, "I saw them ruin a picture that Jack had done with McLaglen when sound first came in." The incident demonstrated to him how films could be shaped in the cutting room. (In 1953 *The Black Watch* was remade by 20th Century–Fox as *King of the Khyber Rifles* under Darryl Zanuck's supervision.

Next on the director's agenda was a football picture to be shot on location at the Naval Academy in Annapolis. Ford not only invited Duke to go along but asked him to recruit ballplayers from USC for the action sequences in the movie, which was called *Salute* (also 1929). Duke talked with Coach Howard Jones, who arranged for twenty members of the Trojan football team to leave school two weeks early that spring so they could travel with Ford and his crew to Annapolis.

On the day the ballplayers assembled at the railroad station to leave for the East, an interloper appeared at the last minute and pushed his way onto the train. His name was Wardell Bond, a 220-pound tackle whom Duke considered a loudmouth. But Ford decided to let Bond go along after taking a look at his bulldog face. The loutish Bond had brought with him a bottle of gin, which he quickly consumed, and over Duke's protest the two were assigned to the same room when they reached Annapolis. Their quarters were over the laundry, and steam coming up made the room uncomfortably hot. Duke braced himself for a miserable experience, but by the time they returned to California, he and Bond had become best friends.

Ford used both of them in small roles in *Salute*, which dealt with the rivalry between the Army and Navy football teams. "They were both perfectly natural," said Ford, "so when I needed a couple of fellows to speak some lines, I picked them out and they ended up with parts." The three men became drinking partners and established a fellowship that lasted a lifetime. "I think my granddad liked John Wayne and Ward Bond because they stood up to him from the start," Dan Ford maintained. The younger men also made the filmmaker feel like one of the boys, which flattered Ford, since his private life left much to be desired.

A few months after *Salute* was finished, the director began making a submarine picture off Catalina Island called *Men without Women* (1930). Duke again was working props, and for a scene in which the submarine is damaged, he operated a huge pipeline that blew bubbles of air up from the deep to simulate an explosion in the ship's engine room. Men supposedly trapped in the submarine were to come up through the air bubbles as if they had been shot out of the sub's torpedo tubes. On the day for filming the scene, the sky was full of storm clouds, and the water was choppy. The actors looked at the turbulent sea and refused to dive in, complaining to Ford that to do so was dangerous. Duke volunteered to double for them in exchange for a stuntman's pay. He put on different clothes and dove overboard six times. "I had to hang onto a heavy weight which dragged me below the sea level," he remembered, "then come up into camera range." But Ford rewarded him with a small role in the picture; he gave him a few lines of dialogue and even a close-up. "I don't think Jack really started appreciating me until *Men without Women*," the neophyte said. "That was the time I started looking at pictures with a different view. I was beginning to enjoy this work."

Ford recognized that there was something special about Duke. "Sure he was callow and untutored," the director later said, "but he had something that jumped right off the screen at me. I guess you could call it star power. I wanted to keep an eye on him." The filmmaker also kept an eye on Ward Bond, who was preparing to graduate from the University of Southern California. Ford gave Bond a bit part in *Born Reckless* (1930) and later cast him in character roles in many of his finest films. But their personal relationship was also important, as Bond and Duke became permanent members of the Ford gang.

Duke propped for director James Tingling on *Words and Music* (1929), a collegiate musical, and was cast in a minor role as a student. He danced with Lois Moran in the picture, for which he received his first screen credit, being billed as Duke Morrison. He grew friendly with George O'Brien, who played romantic leads on the Fox lot and, with O'Brien's help, received a small part as a lumberjack in *Rough Romance* (1930). "Through my friendship with George O'Brien," said Duke, "I was made to feel I belonged on the lot. I loved going to work at the studio. I felt this was my life, my future."

He played another college boy in *Cheer Up and Smile* (again 1930), joining a cast headed by Arthur Lake (who later played Dagwood in the *Blondie* series) and Dixie Lee (Bing Crosby's first wife). Duke proved to have a rich baritone speaking voice, which he inherited from his father, but he relied on actor Paul Fix to coach him when dialogue was required, a practice he continued during his early years in the business.

Director Raoul Walsh noticed husky Marion Morrison unloading furniture one day at the Fox warehouse and watched him strolling around the lot. Walsh was struck by the way the youth moved and went to talk to John Ford about him. The studio was planning an epic Western about the Oregon Trail, which would be a major gamble since the recent addition of sound made filming outdoor action difficult. But Walsh, an experienced silent director, had handled sound microphones effectively while making *In Old Arizona* (1929), and Fox executives were willing to let him try again with the help of a dialogue coach recruited from the stage. Walsh had wanted Gary Cooper for the lead of his new Western, to be called *The Big Trail*, but after Cooper's success in *The Virginian* (also 1929) Paramount refused to loan the star to a rival company. Tom Mix, Fox's major Western star, was busy making a picture in Texas, and the New York stage actors the studio tested were out of their element playing a frontier scout. That's when Duke Morrison caught Walsh's attention.

Jack Ford recommended his propboy highly and assured Walsh that Morrison could handle the job. "I like the way that kid walks," Walsh told Ford; "he is a real pioneer type." Later Walsh said, "Dammit, the son of a bitch looked like a man. To be a cowboy star, you gotta be six feet three or over. You gotta have no hips and a face that looks right under a sombrero." Ford agreed that Duke had those essentials and more—broad shoulders, big hands, and a commanding carriage.

Walsh decided to test the young man and had the Fox wardrobe department fit him into a buckskin outfit. Duke was nervous when he went before the camera and fell into the trap common to most newcomers by overacting. "Speak softly but with authority," Walsh told him, "and look whoever you're talking to right in the eye." The lad caught on quickly, and Walsh liked the timber of his voice. "This one looks like a natural," the director told studio production head Winfield Sheehan.

"Let's see how much you want to be an actor," Walsh said to Morrison. "Let your hair grow. Come and see me in two weeks." By then the filmmaker had convinced Sheehan and the studio hierarchy to give twenty-three-year-old Duke the part. The newcomer would save the company money, and since the frontier spectacle was slated to cost over a million dollars, cutting corners on Duke's salary was a consideration. Yet *The Big Trail* was to be Fox's major release in 1930, and casting an unknown in the lead was risky business.

The picture was slated to be shot in standard 35mm and in a process called Grandeur, which used a 70mm negative for greater depth and scope. Making the movie would involve weeks of location work, especially difficult for inexperienced actors. "*The Big Trail*," Raoul Walsh told trade papers, "means that everyone who goes over it while the cameras record will go through just as many hardships as the pioneers of 100 years ago encountered." The director recognized problems with the script and tried to hide its limitations by adding more action. "I thought the story rambled and would have been better suited as a travelogue," Walsh reflected.

While Sheehan agreed to casting Duke in the lead, he insisted that the name Marion Morrison be changed. Marion, he said, made Duke sound like a fairy. Walsh liked the Revolutionary War hero "Mad" Anthony Wayne, but they decided that Anthony Wayne seemed too Italian. Someone suggested plain John, and everyone agreed that John Wayne had an American ring that would be easily remembered. "I never have become accustomed to the John," Duke later confessed. "Nobody even really calls me John. It's [just] a name that goes well together and it's like one word—John Wayne." But his friends persisted in calling him Duke.

"My protégé looked fine on a horse," Raoul Walsh said. "From somewhere he had picked up the natural slouch of a trail rider." Jack Padjan, an ex-cowboy in charge of livestock for Fox Film Corporation, helped make a rider out of Duke, and stuntman Steve Clemente taught the newcomer how to throw a knife and handle a gun. But Fox executives decided that the lad, who still harbored traces of a midwestern accent, needed speech lessons, so they sent him to Lumsden Hare, a British Shakespearean actor and stage director. "I had a dim view of him before I went to any of his private lessons," Duke recalled. "He was all very dramatic in his talk, all pseudo-Shakespearean." Hare insisted on nice round vowels and sweeping gestures with the arms. "I took about two weeks of that," Duke said, "then I just quit going to him."

During the initial tests the novice thought he was being considered for a minor part in the movie. Then he learned that he was to play the lead, Breck Coleman, a trapper hired to scout for a wagon train crossing the plains and mountains, bound for Oregon. Duke's salary was $75 a week, which in the months right after the stock market crash seemed to him like a princely sum. Tyrone Power, Sr., Marguerite Churchill, Tully Marshall, and Ian Keith—all from the stage, hired for their ability to deliver dialogue—were also cast in the picture. Walsh told Duke to let them guide his performance; his job was to react to the other actors convincingly.

John Wayne entered the film business at a crucial time, just as the transition from silent pictures to talkies was taking place. Outdoor movies had been generally avoided with the move to the talkies, since they caused endless problems for sound technicians. Microphones had to be concealed in trees or behind bushes and props, while cameras were encased in heavy, soundproof boxes to keep their noise from being recorded. Mobility was therefore sharply reduced and action was restricted.

But *The Big Trail* seemed worth the trouble of moving outside. President Herbert Hoover had asked for a day of national observance for the band of pioneers that had left Independence, Missouri, on April 10, 1830, and Fox had decided to commemorate the event with the movie. A line of prairie schooners was constructed for the picture, which William Fox intended to surpass the spectacle achieved by Paramount's *The Covered Wagon* in 1923. Even before shooting began, Walsh's movie received much attention from the press, yet trade papers expressed doubts about the casting of John Wayne. "Just how [Walsh] can expect a youth to carry such a picture is beyond my conception," a reporter for *Hollywood Filmograph* wrote. "If he brings in a winner with Mr. Wayne, he will be entitled to a Carnegie medal."

Location filming commenced on *The Big Trail* in Yuma, Arizona, during April 1930 and lasted for more than ten weeks. Major Hollywood studios like Fox owned huge backlots, and most Westerns at that time were shot either there or on nearby ranches. But *The Big Trail* was to be an important picture, made big in part by its lavish views of the western landscape. Ward Bond went on location with the company, at Duke's request, and played a bearded driver of one of the wagons. A replica of a frontier settlement had been built outside Yuma, but the script was still weak as Walsh began filming. Duke improvised much of his dialogue. Actor Ian Keith fired questions at him in an opening scene, and Walsh told his inexperienced lead to answer with whatever came into his mind. Duke handled the situation well, and the director concluded that he had selected his frontier scout wisely. "His acting was instinctive, so that he became whatever or whoever he was playing," Walsh recalled. "There is a lot of pride in the knowledge that I discovered a winner."

Many of the New York actors in the film were heavy drinkers, although Duke and Bond were no strangers to the bottle either. Nights in Yuma turned into alcoholic orgies, causing Walsh to claim that the name of the movie should have been "The Big Drunk." Rumor had it that Duke showed up for work some mornings in such bad shape that he had to be wired to his horse to keep his body erect.

While in Yuma, Wayne developed a bad case of diarrhea, spent a week in bed, lost eighteen pounds, and was not up to par for another two weeks. Walsh threatened to replace him unless he pulled himself together and returned to work. Still weak, Duke reported to the set for a scene with Tully

Marshall, another heavy boozer. Marshall came into the scene with a big jug in his hand, and he, Wayne, and another actor sat down and had a drink while the camera cranked. "They passed the jug to me first," Duke remembered, "and I dug back into it; it was straight rotgut bootleg whiskey. I'd been puking and crapping blood for a week, and now I just poured that raw stuff right down my throat. After the scene, you can bet I called him every kind of an old bastard."

Marguerite Churchill, *The Big Trail*'s beauteous leading lady, who later married George O'Brien, remembered Duke as "nothing but a drunk." Yet during their weeks together in wilderness locations, she played classical music for him on a windup Victrola. "I think she had a crush on him and they had an affair, which he broke off," said Churchill's son, Darcy O'Brien, "though she won't admit that. My mother was very literary; she started out in the theater in New York and didn't want to go to Hollywood. She always thought of herself as a classical actress. But she ended up going to Hollywood and marrying a cowboy."

When shooting around Yuma had finished, the company packed up and moved to Sacramento for river scenes, although a unit lingered in Arizona long enough to get shots of Wayne at the Grand Canyon. Then the crew traveled to St. George, Utah, where Walsh filmed more canyon scenes. The director continued to feel that the story needed to be bolstered with action. "We had plenty of footage of the wagon train fording rivers and toiling through rugged canyon country and crawling over the mountains in the supposedly westward trek," Walsh said. "But I needed a clincher, something to bring home to viewers how the pioneers actually put their lives on the line during such migrations."

The company came to a deep precipice with a white curl of water at the bottom. "I wanted the train to cross that canyon," said Walsh. He remembered that he had brought along some coils of stout rope and suddenly got an idea. "I would lower enough of the wagons and horses and other livestock to make a convincing sequence," he said. "There were enough trees and rocks along the canyon rim to anchor the ropes." Walsh and his head wrangler explained to Wayne and Bond what they wanted, and the two former teammates pitched in and helped supervise.

The first wagon was lowered slowly to the canyon floor, with one camera down below and another shooting the scene from above. A couple of slung steers were taken down next; then the cameras recorded a number of pioneers lowering themselves on a free-hanging rope hand over hand. "Wayne took over as soon as the cameras started to roll," Walsh said. "I had scribbled some lines for him, but he ad-libbed most of the descent. I stood and watched him waving his arms and shouting orders and wondered where the youthful linebacker had gone. Instead of a football player, I had a star."

The last wagon sent down the canyon wall provided more reality than the director had intended. As it started down the decline, a rope slipped, and the wagon hung lopsided long enough to heighten suspense. Then it fell crashing to the canyon floor, making a pile of rubble in the water below. "I held my breath until I was sure that both cameras had caught the action," said Walsh. "Now I had my clincher."

From Utah the cast and crew moved to Jackson Hole, Wyoming, where a tent city was constructed on the shores of Jackson Lake in the Grand Tetons. The site, which consisted of no more than five or six shacks when the company arrived, was called Moran Camp. "We came out with 350 people," Duke recalled, "and by the time we were through, we had about 500 people working there, with 150 wagons and horses. So we had to have a pretty big setup. We enlarged the place, built cabins and sets, and they ended up with an establishment that is now called Moran, Wyoming."

The company doubled back into California to shoot footage in Sequoia National Park, then ended location work in Moiese, Montana, where Walsh photographed a buffalo stampede. On the way to Montana, the director stopped to film sequences of Duke leading the wagon train across the mountains. "The trails that existed were primitive enough to be realistic," said Walsh, "and the toppled wagons and broken wheels that showed on the film were not fakes or purposely contrived. They actually happened."

In 1930 Moiese was a small western town with only one hotel, but nearby was the largest buffalo herd in the country. The studio rented log cabins to house the overflow crowd and procured eight hundred buffalo from the government for a convincing stampede. "The script called for the buffalo to hold up the wagon train," Walsh recalled, "and we got a realistic sequence complete with the animals' thundering feet and the whooping of the Indian 'hunters.'" Fox representatives hired forty Blackfeet and Crow for an Indian attack on the circled wagons. The Native

American extras set up their camp outside Moiese but left the area before their work was finished. When an assistant director failed to locate them for the finals shots, war paint was applied to local cowboys who agreed to substitute in the remaining scenes.

Duke took direction easily and did most of his own stunts, and his voice assumed the twang that would soon become familiar to millions of fans. "In the jargon of the trade," Walsh said, "he was a natural." Ward Bond proved almost as helpful as Wayne when it came to supervising logistics. As location work drew to a close, Walsh told Duke, "I guess I should congratulate you and your friend Bond, if only for staying sober." Wayne gave the director the lopsided grin that would become his trademark. "You hired me to act," he said. "Ward feels the same way."

The company returned to the Fox studio for final shooting. For Raoul Walsh, *The Big Trail* had been "a nightmare from start to finish." The New York actors disliked movies, complained about retakes, and drank to ease their boredom. "They hated desert sun," said Walsh, and "couldn't get used to sitting around waiting for the next camera setup." On the screen they appear stilted and melodramatic.

But Duke performed well, a youth playing a man among men. His acting was competent, and he looked good in buckskin. His physical beauty was astonishing, and he created a believable profile of an experienced frontiersman. He proved a capable horseman, and his winsome personality came through on film. Gangling and awkward though he may have been, he depicted moral authority with enough conviction to satisfy audiences ready to believe that righteousness was part of the frontier heritage. In moments of crisis Duke evoked the westering spirit, and his stalwart character avenged wrongs in the heroic manner audiences equated with justice.

When released, *The Big Trail* ran two hours and five minutes in length. The movie premiered at Grauman's Chinese Theater on October 24, 1930, and became Hollywood's event of the season. Raoul Walsh was invited to sign his name in a cement block in the forecourt of the famous movie palace, making him the first director awarded an honor heretofore reserved for stars. One of the covered wagons used in the picture was placed in front of the theater, and bleachers were set up along the sidewalk so that fans could ogle celebrities as they arrived for the festivities in tuxedos and fancy gowns.

The film opened in New York at the Roxy Theater, and reviewers compared it favorably with John Ford's *The Iron Horse* (1924). Shown in the 70mm Grandeur process, the movie drew critical raves for its effective use of the western landscape. "The scenes in this picture," the *New York Times* reported, "are a testimonial to the progress of motion picture work." The film was judged starkly realistic, despite its broad humor and stereotyped villains, although the story was found less important than the movie's impressive visuals. "Mr. Wayne acquits himself with no little distinction," Mordaunt Hall wrote in the *New York Times*. "His performance is pleasingly natural."

But *The Big Trail* was not a financial success, mainly because of the expensive technology involved. Most theater owners, having just converted to sound, could not afford to install the costly equipment necessary to accommodate Fox's new wide-screen technique. In movie palaces where the Grandeur process was employed, admission fees had to be increased, and depression audiences were reluctant to pay the higher price. Since the film was also released in a conventional 35mm print, theater owners outside the big cities opted to show the less striking version. Duke made personal appearances to promote *The Big Trail*, but the picture did not recoup its high cost, even though it proved a big success in Europe, particularly in Germany.

While John Wayne received favorable notices for his first starring role, it did not catapult him into lasting fame. Fox failed to follow up on his success, and the studio, on the verge of bankruptcy, soon canceled his contract. Since Duke and Josephine were waiting for his financial status to improve in order to marry, the disappointment affected Wayne deeply. "I sure thought I'd set the world on fire," Duke later said about *The Big Trail*. "I realize now that . . . I was totally unprepared to handle the consequences if the picture *had* launched me as a big star." Yet he had gained respect for the making of motion pictures and was determined to make acting his career. "All of a sudden I realized that this business is a damn fine business," Duke said, "and I got proud of it."

The Hollywood Gristmill

After the publicity campaign Fox gave Duke for *The Big Trail*, the name John Wayne carried enough marquee value for the studio to cast him as the lead in another picture, although one of lesser importance. From Western hero Duke went back to playing a college boy in the inexpensive *Girls Demand Excitement* (1931). Wayne later claimed that the studio threw the movie together to give work to a group of young actresses the company had under contract but didn't know how to use. Marguerite Churchill was again cast opposite Duke, while Seymour Felix, a choreographer, directed. Wayne played the captain of a men's basketball team faced with competing on the court with the women's team to decide whether the college would remain coeducational. "I was the fellow who was sour grapes, who played basketball to try to get the girls out of school," Duke said.

He hated making the picture and was embarrassed by it. Walking across the Fox lot with his head low one day, he ran into Will Rogers, the studio's superstar. "Hey, Duke, what's the matter?" the folksy Rogers asked. The youth explained to the veteran performer that he was making a movie that he knew was terrible. "You're working, aren't you?" Rogers said. "Just keep it up." Duke never forgot the advice, for work became his life's focus.

Most of Duke's friends were students he had known at USC. "I tell you," he said, "when that picture came out, I took a razzing from the college kids." Wayne's acting came from instinct, and he still looked clumsy on the screen, especially in love scenes. He knew that his performance in *Girls Demand Excitement* was no better than the picture, and his ineptness distressed him.

Wayne next played a struggling young architect in *Three Girls Lost* (also 1931), another Fox potboiler. The only bright spot in the picture for Duke was his costar, Loretta Young, a devout Catholic and a close friend of Josephine Saenz. Since Duke had dated Loretta's sister Polly Ann during his first year in college, the two knew each other and got along well. At seventeen the actress had eloped with character actor Grant Withers, a long-standing member of Wayne's drinking crowd. Later Loretta Young would be the godmother of Duke's oldest son.

Three Girls Lost was a notch above *Girls Demand Excitement* but did little to convince Fox executives that John Wayne had much of a future as a screen actor. Early in 1931 the studio failed to pick up his option, sending the work-oriented Duke into a depression. His despondency lifted when Columbia Pictures, one of Hollywood's most successful minor studios, offered him a contract. Columbia financed its better pictures with a stream of budget Westerns calculated to appeal to rural and small-town audiences. Fox's publicity blitz for *The Big Trail* had made Wayne an attractive addition to the Columbia roster, and the studio's action films seemed well suited to his talents.

At Columbia, Duke's first assignment was a leading role in *Men Are Like That* (still 1931), a military picture written by Robert Riskin, one of the studio's top writers. Production on the picture had no sooner wrapped than its recently acquired star fell out of favor with the company's crass, dictatorial boss, Harry Cohn. Immediately Wayne was reduced to supporting roles.

Duke realized that something had gone wrong when he was asked to play a corpse in a cheap thriller called *Deceiver* (again 1931). In the picture's plot the male lead, performed by Ian Keith, whom Wayne had worked with at Fox, is murdered, but the actor had to leave for New York before his character's body was filmed with a knife in his back. Rather than hire an extra for the job, the director instructed Duke to put on Keith's clothes and lie down on the set in his place. It was a humiliating experience for the young actor, who after all had starred in a major big-budget film.

A propman on the lot eventually discovered why Cohn was angry. During the making of *Men Are Like That*, the impetuous Duke had flirted with a young actress who turned out to be the studio head's current girlfriend. Cohn thought that Wayne had made a play for the starlet and that she had responded. When he was called into Harry Cohn's office, which was of a length calculated to intimidate subordinates, Duke denied the charge, but the Columbia boss refused to believe him. "Keep your goddamn fly buttoned at my studio," Cohn shouted across his desk. The meeting grew hostile as Duke maintained his innocence. "I'd been brought up to respect older people," Wayne later said, "and Cohn talked to me like I was a sewer rat. There was no communication at all."

For the next six months John Wayne was reduced to second billing in cheap, assembly-line pictures, beginning with *Range Feud* (late 1931), which starred cowboy actor Buck Jones. Duke played a young rancher falsely accused of murder. He then appeared as a football player in *Maker of Men* (1931), in a bit part as the story's heavy. Next came *Texas Cyclone* and *Two-Fisted Law* (both 1932), two Tim McCoy vehicles that benefited from the presence of supporting player Walter Brennan. Duke was cast as likable naifs in both McCoy movies, typical of the low-budget "oaters" Columbia turned out to fill the double bill of side-street theaters. In *Two-Fisted Law* his role was insignificant, although he seemed to be growing more comfortable in delivering dialogue.

At option time Duke was not surprised when Columbia dropped him. What hurt even more was that Cohn tried to sabotage him with other studios, claiming that Wayne was a drunk and a rebel. During the early months of 1932, with the depression in full swing, Duke pounded the pavement looking for a job with no success. "Harry Cohn had taken a dislike to me and was trying to keep me out of pictures," Wayne said. "For a year I couldn't get work, and I was thinking of going into the fight racket, which I was too old for." Later, when John Wayne became an established star, he refused to make movies for Columbia, since Harry Cohn continued to rule there.

Duke thought of going back to the University of Southern California to finish his degree, but that would have meant a longer wait before he and Josephine could marry. The Saenz family had grown increasingly suspect of their daughter's fiancé, particularly as persistent rumors reached them of his carousing and philandering. Josephine dwelt amid the propriety and elegance of the Hispanic establishment in Los Angeles, and Duke was the antithesis of the society she knew. She disapproved of much of Duke's lifestyle—particularly his hard-drinking friends—but loved him anyway. For Duke, Josephine represented an ideal. She was beautiful and cultured, and her exotic background made her seem the opposite of Mary Morrison. Instinctively, Duke had chosen a girlfriend outside his mother's orbit, one unlikely to kindle the repressed animosity he had harbored since childhood. Josephine, he felt, was a Madonna he could respect, yet at the same time she held a physical attraction for him. The challenge would come with turning a romantic image into a sustained reality.

Wayne was finally offered a job by Mascot Pictures, near the bottom of the Poverty Row studios. Headed by Nat Levine, Mascot made cheap action features and serials (long adventure films that played in weekly installments in secondary theaters). Nat Levine was a coarse, plump man of enormous energy and drive, who wore thick glasses and talked with a cigar in his mouth. Impressed that Wayne had been under contract to Fox and Columbia, Levine saw a chance to pick up a young actor with a familiar name for little money. Notoriously tight with the dollar, the Mascot head informed Duke's agent, Al Kingston, that he would be willing to pay Wayne $100 a week, less than half what Duke had earned at Columbia. Desperate for work and feeling like a failure, Wayne accepted the terms, knowing that the work ahead would be of marginal quality.

Levine assigned him to the lead in three successive serials of twelve episodes each. *The Shadow of the Eagle* (1932) came first, a pedestrian script shot in the Antelope Valley, near where Duke had once lived. Wayne played Craig McCoy, a stunt flier for a carnival. Airplane pictures were in demand after Charles Lindbergh's solo flight across the Atlantic in 1927 and the enormous success that same year of the movie *Wings*, one of the late silent classics.

Levine's schedule called for fast-moving action, tightly budgeted, with all twelve chapters to be completed within twenty-one working days. His crews put in a six-day week, and two directors were assigned to each serial. Cameras and sound equipment were usually rented. "Nat Levine would drive thirty miles out to a location," Mascot's chief stuntman, Yakima Canutt, recalled, "and get there before sunrise and start shooting with the headlights of the cars. And I've seen him finish up with the lights from the cars at night." The producer knew how to handle people and had a way of making them enjoy working for him. "Levine was the greatest organizer," said Canutt. "He was one of the shrewdest operators I ever knew."

On Duke's first day of shooting for Mascot, Levine picked up his star for work in his chauffeur-driven Packard at four o'clock in the morning and escorted him out to a desert location. As they drank coffee and ate Danish pastry in the car, Levine outlined the hackneyed plot of *The Shadow of the Eagle* but explained that he planned to augment the story with stunts and thrills. Yakima Canutt worked closely with the writers on action sequences. "Levine rented a house on the Palisades and put the writers there and wouldn't let them leave," the stuntman recalled. "He hired a cook to take care of them. I'd sit with the group as the story was being worked out, and we all contributed ideas."

Duke realized that turning out twenty-five reels of film in three weeks constituted slave labor, but he had no better prospects. His attitude improved once he met Canutt; the two were kindred spirits. Wayne knew Yak's reputation as a stunt coordinator, had heard about his rodeo achievements, and delighted in his kidding and practical jokes. The two cemented their friendship one night when director Ford Beebe kept them working until midnight and wanted them back on the set the next morning at six o'clock. Most of the company decided to spend the night on location rather than drive back to Los Angeles for only a few hours sleep. Some of the crew built a fire, and Wayne sat down in front of it and pulled out a bottle of whiskey. Canutt sauntered over and knelt down beside him. Without saying anything, Duke handed Yak the bottle, and the stuntman uncorked it and took a long swig. From that moment on they were lifelong friends as well as professional colleagues. "Wayne," the stuntman declared, "[was] a regular kind of a guy."

Canutt and his friend Bud Osborne played the villain's henchmen in *The Shadow of the Eagle*, but Yak also doubled Wayne in dangerous sequences, including a motorcycle chase. Each episode of a serial ended with the hero or heroine, sometimes both, trapped in a perilous situation. The work was hard and required more athletic ability than acting. "They'd change directors every day," said Duke, "but the leading man had to be there all the time. We never worked less than eighteen hours a day. . . . We'd do 101, 102 setups a day." There was no time for a formal lunch break; around noon any personnel not needed for the scene being shot were free to wander over to the caterer's rig and wolf down a quick bite. Duke and Canutt often left for home after a day's shooting with their bodies aching.

Wayne's contract with Nat Levine was nonexclusive, which meant that he could make pictures for other companies when Mascot did not require his services. Paramount hired Duke on a freelance basis for a supporting role in *Lady and Gent* (1932), which also featured future cowboy star Charles Starrett. Wayne played a young professional prizefighter, but his screen time was less than six minutes. *Lady and Gent* was superior to the movies Duke had made at Columbia, and Paramount represented a step back into the major leagues for an actor making serials for Mascot.

Levine assigned him next to *The Hurricane Express* (also 1932), a railroad melodrama combined with airplane and automobile stunts. Wayne again played a pilot in the serial, while character actors Tully Marshall and J. Farrell MacDonald appeared in the cast. Yakima Canutt performed most of the stunts and doubled various players. "I did fights and falls all over that train," Canutt said. "And transfers onto it." When the company was filming at a railroad station in Saugus, a town just north of Los Angeles, a hobo happened to be cooking stew near the tracks. "Wayne went over and had breakfast with him," Canutt remembered. "We got the biggest kick out of it."

Duke ended his tenure at Mascot with *The Three Musketeers* (1933), portraying yet another pilot, interestingly named Tom Wayne. The serial was shot in the Mojave Desert, near Yuma, where temperatures climbed to 120 degrees during the day. Ruth Hall, soon afterward married to cinematographer Lee Garmes, was Duke's leading lady, while Francis X. Bushman, Jr., and Noah Beery, Jr., were supporting players. Armand Schaefer and Colbert Clark alternated as director, and the jail in Yuma substituted for a fort in the story, which was about the French foreign legion on patrol in the Arabian desert.

"John Wayne was always on the set for *The Three Musketeers*," Ruth Hall declared, "and he was a great man to be with." Work again was difficult, lasting from sunup until dark, with the cast and crew dead-tired when they quit. The script called for more action than dialogue, but technicians still had trouble obtaining an acceptable sound.

Yakima Canutt remembered a scene in which an airplane has to make a forced landing in the desert, with Arabs closing in to capture Wayne. "As the plane is rolling along the ground," the stuntman recalled, "I walked out on the wing and an Arab on horseback rode up alongside. I leaped from the wing right onto him and threw him off his horse." For Yak to perform the stunt, dummy wings had been mounted on a camera car; as the camera crew drove along, he walked from the car out onto the wings and leaped to the Arab on horseback. Just before he jumped, the audience would be shown a close-up of Wayne. "Then wham," Canutt said, they saw "me go into my jump."

Duke looked back on his three Mascot serials as a valuable training ground where he began to develop his unique style. Physicality remained his major asset, but the rudiments of a natural, easygoing screen persona began to crystallize during the making of the three serials. "We didn't have a hell of a lot of dialogue," Duke said of the experience. "And we didn't fool around with retakes. The first take was usually the one we printed." He learned how to memorize lines quickly and how to handle himself in vivid action scenes. By the time his contract with Levine ended, Duke had taken strides toward becoming a professional movie actor.

Warner Bros. next hired Wayne to star in six Westerns, mainly remakes of silent pictures that had featured Ken Maynard. In each case Duke played a character named John, but was dressed to look like Maynard so that original footage could be inserted into the sound version. Westerns were returning to popularity in the small towns of the South and Midwest, and Warner Bros. intended to compete with those Paramount was turning out with Randolph Scott and Fox was making with George O'Brien. Sid Rogell and Leon Schlesinger produced the series with John Wayne. The pictures were action-packed and contained interesting camera work, yet were shot on a limited budget. In each case Wayne's mount was a white horse called Duke the Wonder Horse, but scenes with cattle herds and distant riders were extracted from the old Maynard films. "I had to wear those phony rodeo clothes to match the shots," Wayne explained. He earned $1,500 a picture yet each one, he claimed, "was lousier than the last."

Haunted Gold (1932), a remake of Maynard's 1929 film *The Phantom City*, launched the series; it opened at the Strand Theater in New York. "Action Gallops across the Screen," advertisements read. One sequence found Wayne escaping from a crumbling mine shaft, and another had him and the villain battling in an ore bucket suspended over a chasm.

For *Ride Him, Cowboy*, which followed later in 1932, Wayne was billed as "the screen's new star of the saddle." Ruth Hall was again his leading lady. Reviews were kind, especially to Duke; the critics agreed that he was a dashing figure of a man. The consensus was that John Wayne made a splendid hero, even with such threadbare plots. *The Big Stampede* (still 1932), with Noah Beery playing the villain, was advertised as a movie to "Bring Back the Old-Time Matinee Business." But reviewers commented more on the five thousand head of stampeding cattle that added thrills to the final reel than on the performances of actors.

When *The Telegraph Trail* (1933) opened in New York at the Strand, it was advertised as being "Crammed with Action" and containing "Thrills You'll Never Forget." In the picture Wayne plays an army scout who volunteers to finish stringing a telegraph wire across the plains after Indians have killed a friend of his. The script was fashioned to include an Indian attack from Maynard's silent movie *The Red Raiders* (1927), and Yakima Canutt performed most of the stunts.

Somewhere in Sonora (also 1933), which featured Duke's friend and acting coach Paul Fix, was based on a *Saturday Evening Post* story. *The Man from Monterey* (still 1933) brought the series to a close. Set in California during the Spanish period, *The Man from Monterey* is a costume picture rather than a traditional Western, since it takes place in the era of the sword rather than the six-shooter. Still, the picture again puts Wayne astride Duke the Wonder Horse, playing a character named John and cast opposite Ruth Hall.

While under contract to Warner Bros., Duke appeared in a minor role in First National's *Central Airport* (1933), another airplane movie, directed by William Wellman and starring Richard Barthelmess and Glenda Farrell. Wayne is seen helping passengers onto the wing of a crippled plane, but his character drowns during a rescue attempt. Duke starred in *His Private Secretary*, a romantic comedy released in June 1933 by Showmen's Pictures, a small New York production company. His costar was actress Evalyn Knapp. Duke, who never made the impact in modern-dress comedy that he did in action pictures, looks uncomfortable in the role of a wealthy playboy.

Wayne completed his agreement with Warner Bros. with two non-Westerns, *The Life of Jimmy Dolan* and *Baby Face* (both 1933), in each case playing small parts. In *Jimmy Dolan* Duke spoke only a few lines as the fight trainer for Douglas Fairbanks, Jr. "He came in while my gloves were being tied on," Fairbanks remembered, "slapped me on the back, and said, 'You okay, boss?' I nodded and he exited." *The Life of Jimmy Dolan* was one of six pictures that cast young Fairbanks opposite Loretta Young. This one was directed by Archie Mayo, a tough, overweight filmmaker known to finish assignments on time, which won him the respect of the Warner's hierarchy.

Alfred E. Green directed *Baby Face*, which starred Barbara Stanwyck and George Brent. Wayne had only brief scenes amounting to less than two minutes of screen time in the picture. He played an assistant to a department store manager but his role lacked authority. In comparison with the budget Westerns he had been making, *Baby Face* was an important production and offered the advantage of casting Duke opposite major stars. The picture aroused the ire of the censorship office, however, since it dealt with such unsavory subjects as seduction, suicide, and murder.

In the spring of 1933 John Wayne returned to Poverty Row when he signed a contract with Lone Star Productions to play the lead in a series of Westerns under the supervision of Paul Malvern. Monogram, which distributed the pictures, was considered a step up from Mascot, although the company rented most of its sets and aimed its product at unsophisticated audiences paying admission prices of twenty-five cents or less. At the time Duke went to work for Lone Star, 40 percent of the nation's theaters were showing double features, and low-budget studios such as Monogram secured playing time on screens that earlier would have been unavailable to them. "Working at Monogram or Mascot was like having a tooth pulled by a frontier dentist," Diana Cary said, "the work was painful, but it was over fast."

Between 1933 and 1935 Wayne made sixteen "oaters" for Lone Star, working grueling hours with hackneyed scripts. He knew that making the pictures for Malvern was not a good career move, but he needed to keep working. Since he didn't fit into Hollywood's current concept of a leading man, cowboy roles seemed his best venue. "Contract stars at the major studios were the movies' carriage trade," said Diana Cary. "The rest of us had to go from one picture to another and really hustle. Monogram for us was a safety net. Studios like that were welfare, but they were our salvation."

Producer Paul Malvern came from an acrobatic family and entered the motion picture business shortly after World War I. He began his screen career as a stuntman, but Trem Carr, who headed production at Monogram, elevated him to producer. Like Samuel Goldwyn, Malvern became known for his malapropisms. For example, writer Ed Hartmann walked into his office one day while Malvern was talking on the telephone. "The next time you send me an actor," Hartmann heard the producer bark into the receiver, "make sure his voice is legible!"

The unsophisticated filmmaker had grown up reading dime novels and pulp fiction. "I had those stories all in the back of my memory as a kid," Malvern said. Later he incorporated many of the same plots into his movies. "Nobody knew where the hell I got my stories," he said. "But generally they were from these old twenty-five-cent books they used to put out. I had about 75 to 100 of those stories in the back of my brain."

Like the dime novels he had read, Malvern's pictures were labeled "penny dreadfuls" by critics, who never gave them serious consideration, while audiences referred to them as "Cowboy Deco."

"All of my Westerns were action because I had a flare for that," the producer said. Budgets were tight and shooting schedules seldom ran more than six days. "You couldn't let anything get in your way," Malvern said. Since wind conditions couldn't be controlled, recording dialogue outdoors still posed problems. "So we'd duck it," the producer explained, "by changing a lot of that exterior dialogue to the inside. We kept outside dialogue to a bare minimum in case it was windy." Pace and derring-do offset some of the blemishes, and stock music was added later.

Malvern felt that locations were important. "As the producer I ran around all over the country," he said. "I would spot these various places throughout my travels in California, Nevada, and Utah. We'd write a picture and then figure out how to use those locations, if the money would permit." Most of his budgets ran between $30,000 to $40,000 per movie, low enough that Monogram was assured a profit.

Although Malvern made close to 150 pictures, they were not shot under his own banner until the series with Wayne. The producer recognized when he met Duke that the young actor was a personable man, eager to learn. "He's a hell of a good-looking guy," Malvern thought, "a big guy. I certainly can't hire any midgets to play the heavies opposite him." Wayne was contracted to work for $500 a week, which in 1933 seemed like big money.

At last Duke and Josephine Saenz could marry. Wayne later claimed that after a six-year engagement their relationship had become more habit than romance, but his sense of honor prevented his calling the wedding off. The couple became husband and wife on June 24, 1933, in a garden ceremony at Loretta Young's home in Bel-Air. Since Duke was a non-Catholic, the wedding could not take place in a Catholic Church, which created conflict for Josephine. Reluctantly, Dr. Saenz gave his daughter in marriage, while Duke's brother, Robert, served as best man.

The newlyweds began life together in a small furnished apartment on Orange Grove Avenue, between Hancock Park and Hollywood proper. While Wayne returned to the grind of making movies, Josephine busied herself with charity work. Duke often left their apartment at five o'clock in the morning and didn't return home until seven-thirty at night. Exhausted from long hours of physical labor, he wanted to take a shower, eat, relax with a few drinks, and go to bed. Josephine, on the other hand, was accustomed to a more exalted social life, and she accepted dinner invitations from Loretta Young or other close friends without consulting her husband. When Duke was away on location, which was frequent, she attended these functions alone. When he was home, he usually escorted her out of a sense of duty but felt uncomfortable in such formal settings. Frequently they quarreled. Duke would storm out of the apartment, only to feel guilty and return.

Meanwhile his career offered its own share of frustrations. His first assignment for Lone Star was *Riders of Destiny* (1933), in which the company tried to turn him into a singing cowboy, since Western musicals were popular at the time. Duke played Singin' Sandy Saunders, "the most notorious gunman since Billy the Kid." Because Wayne couldn't sing, he simply held a guitar and mouthed the words, while a heavyset cowboy who worked in pictures and had a beautiful baritone voice did the actual singing. It was a poor match for Wayne's speaking voice, and Duke later said he felt like "a goddamn pansy." He was even more embarrassed when fans asked him to sing on personal appearance tours and he had to decline.

Riders of Destiny, like most of the other Westerns Wayne made for Lone Star, was written and directed by Robert N. Bradbury, the father of Duke's boyhood friend Bob Bradbury, who by then had become cowboy star Bob Steele. George "Gabby" Hayes appeared in the picture in a supporting role, as he often did in the Monogram series. Singin' Sandy worked as an undercover agent who came to the aid of farmers in their battle with a rancher over water rights. The plot was pedestrian, but the formula appealed to an unsophisticated audience.

Next came *Sagebrush Trail* (again 1933), directed by Armand Schaefer, an experienced budget filmmaker whom Duke had worked with at Mascot. Paul Malvern, however, selected all the locations and supervised the production. "I was with every shot from the beginning to the end," the producer said. He hired Yakima Canutt to work with Wayne on stunts, and the two friends jointly developed an on-camera fighting technique that revolutionized screen fisticuffs.

Malvern realized that action was what working-class audiences wanted to see and knew that Canutt was the man with the know-how. Creating believable action scenes took time and cost money unless planned by an expert, and Canutt was the best in the business. "When I started doing stunt work as a full-time job," Yak said, "I began to figure out fight routines." He wanted them to look realistic and discovered that Wayne felt the same way. "If the heavies can throw furniture at me," said Duke, "why can't I throw it back? Why does a cowboy star have to be so stupidly noble he can't give as good as he gets?"

Duke felt that most of the Western stars of the 1920s and early 1930s had been too perfect in their behavior. They didn't drink or smoke and were gentlemen in the presence of ladies. Taking his cue from Harry Carey, who had made a series of realistic Westerns with John Ford in the early silent era, Wayne decided on a less idealized approach. "I made up my mind that I was going to play a real man to the best of my ability," Duke said. Most screen cowboys had been too pure to fight dirty, but Wayne was determined to fight back honestly. "So if a guy in a movie I was making hit me with a rose, I'd hit him with a chair," he said. "Before that, every leading man always wore white and held his fists up and waited for the heavy to get back on his feet. I knocked the stuffing out of the goody-goody Boy Scout cowboy hero and made him a believable guy. My dad told me that if I got into a fight to win it."

Canutt and Wayne began choreographing fight routines, planning their punches and making use of fake bottles and breakaway balsa wood tables and chairs. "We discovered a way to pass blows where you didn't have to hit each other on the shoulder to make it look like you were having a real free-for-all," said Wayne. "A film fight is the opposite of a real fight because the camera has to see everything. You have to reach way back and sock out and make a big show. In a real fight you hit short and close." Duke's early stunt work had given him experience in fooling the camera, but director Robert Bradbury discovered that, by placing the camera at a certain angle, an actor's fist would look as if it made contact with his opponent's face, even though it didn't even graze it. "We tried it out one day," Duke recalled, "and when we saw the rushes, we saw how good it looked. Bradbury invented this trick, which he called the pass system." The method soon became standard procedure in filming fights.

Whenever barroom brawls were called for, Canutt was charged with selecting stuntmen for the scene. Those involved in the fight would walk through what they planned to do and discuss where the camera would be. "We'd work it out so it'd be set up right," said Canutt. "We'd break it up.

We'd go as far as we could to keep it looking good, then we'd cut. We'd pick it up there and go on through." Once they had photographed the whole routine, the director would make close-ups for the film editor to insert later. "Wayne got to be terrific," said Yak. "I used to think he'd put up a better picture fight than most of the stuntmen."

Since doubles were frequently used, they were more easily disguised if they wore hats. Canutt became noted for never losing his hat, no matter how intense the brawl might get. "I had a silver band that I used to put around the crown," Yak explained." I could tighten that down where it would fit solid. A lot of times I had an extra strap that tightened behind my head."

West of the Divide (still 1933) was again directed by Robert N. Bradbury and featured Gabby Hayes in a supporting role. Hayes came from the New York stage but won lasting fame as a character actor in budget Westerns. "I had him playing old men, heavies, fathers, gangsters, and everything else," Paul Malvern said. "He was priceless." Hayes possessed a photographic memory and became a master at film acting. "He would read that script once and he not only knew his own part, but he knew everybody else's," said Malvern. Hayes would take newcomers off to one side and rehearse them while the set was being prepared for the next take. He understood that the core of an effective screen performance came from the eyes. "If you don't believe it in the eyes," Hayes said, "you don't get the point across."

Archie Stout served as the cinematographer on *West of the Divide*, as he did on most of John Wayne's Westerns for Lone Star. "He was the finest exterior cameraman ever born," Malvern declared. "These films are beautiful to look at." Later Stout worked for director John Ford, who assigned him to second-unit work on such classics as *Wagonmaster* and *Rio Grande* (both 1950).

Wayne went from one Malvern production to another. Seven were released in 1934 alone: *The Lucky Texan, Blue Steel, The Man from Utah, Randy Rides Alone, 'Neath Arizona Skies, The Star Packer,* and *The Trail Beyond.* "We put emphasis on action," Duke said. "We had no time to develop character or some long story." In pursuit of claim jumpers in *The Lucky Texan,* Wayne enters a sluice, stands on a piece of wood, is whisked along by the current, and catches up with the villains, whom he proceeds to capture. Toward the end of the movie Gabby Hayes has some riotous scenes dressed as an old woman. *The Man from Utah* found Wayne costarring with Polly Ann Young and again singing in the opening scene. Gabby Hayes plays the villain in *Randy Rides Alone,* which was directed by Harry Fraser, an experienced action director who tried to set records for making movies cheaply. "Wayne never worked harder in his life than he did in those little shoot-'em-ups," Fraser said.

One day on location Wayne was to ride over a steep hill on horseback, gallop down onto some flats, make a sharp turn, and then ride his horse out of the scene. Duke waved his hat to signal that he was ready, and Fraser started the camera rolling as the actor started down the hill. "But when he hit the bottom of the pit," the director recalled, "the horse went down, and the Duke left the saddle, sailed through the air, and missed a tree by inches." Wayne picked himself up, looked around for his hat, brushed the dirt off of it, and clamped the hat back on his head as he walked over to his horse. "I hollered at the top of my voice for him to get on the horse and ride out," said Canutt, who was watching from behind the camera. Duke jumped on the horse and rode out by the camera. The shot was used in the picture; "it really looked wild," Canutt said.

In *'Neath Arizona Skies* Yak played the villain who was supposed to make a getaway on a railroad handcar. Duke was to race over a hill on horseback and intercept the handcar in a canyon, then gallop alongside it and leap onto the car from his horse. "Pauley Malvern, who was handling production, knew that I always doubled Wayne and did my own part as well," Canutt declared. "However, he overlooked bringing out another stuntman. We were getting set up to do the stunt when it dawned on the director that if I doubled Wayne, someone would have to double me." None of the cowboys working that day was the right size to fill in for either Yak or Duke. While director Harry Fraser tried to figure out what to do, Wayne and Canutt looked at each other and nodded. "Give me your wardrobe," Duke told Yak. They exchanged clothes, and Yak doubled Wayne and Wayne doubled Canutt. For the closer shots they switched back to their own clothes.

The Lone Star pictures were made so fast that they became a blur in Duke's mind. Often they did not even have a title while the movie was being shot. But each location was a new adventure, and Wayne liked the camaraderie of the cowboys who worked on Westerns. Many of them had been driven off the range by the hard times of the depression and had migrated to Hollywood looking for work. There they could emulate the life they knew and loved. "They were losing a world," said Diana Serra Cary, whose father was a wrangler for movies, "they were the last of the last." The cowboys found solace in each other and together sustained the myth of a frontier that no longer existed.

Duke picked up on their memories, respected the cowboys, and absorbed much of their culture. He was malleable, willing to learn, and fit comfortably into their masculine world, never pulling star rank. He liked being accepted by the men, and they enjoyed having him play as if he were one of them. Duke never claimed to be a cowboy, and they admired him for that, but by osmosis he picked up a certain authenticity. He internalized the Western myth in an almost subliminal way by a close association with men who had glimpsed the dying cattle kingdom and still clung to its remnants.

Despite the hard work and long hours, Duke thrived on working with the cowboys and spent most of his evenings playing poker with them. "There was a lot of good fellowship and camaraderie in those days between the cast and the crew," Harry Fraser said. Poker games often lasted into the night, even though the company had a 4:30 A.M. call the next morning. If Duke was sleepy on the job that day, he seldom showed it. Sometimes a cowboy might bring a banjo or a guitar to the location with him, and the evening's entertainment would take a different turn. "Everyone would break forth into a songfest," said Fraser, "and before you knew it, we'd be putting a show on for ourselves, out there beneath the stars, crouched around a campfire."

Many of the wranglers working in movies preferred the outdoor life and were out of their element with home and family. Wives they considered a worry and a responsibility; women often didn't understand that a man needed to roam and bond with his own kind. "They were mavericks who did not domesticate well," Diana Cary said of the cowboys. Duke sympathized with their reservations about marriage. Like them, he was inclined to place women on a pedestal and had trouble relating to them in intimate terms. He had discovered that Josephine was gentle and submissive only on the surface; she was more than capable of ragging him aggressively about his choice of professions and lifestyle.

Wayne buried himself in work and found emotional support in a homosocial world, even turning to his comrades between pictures. He enjoyed the hazards of stunt work and the friendly rivalry that existed among performers. But he also wanted to learn their business, develop into a versatile professional, and establish himself at the top of a blossoming industry. While Josephine grew impatient, Duke became more determined to become a star of importance, as his plethora of budget Westerns continued.

The Lone Star Westerns were frequently shot in the hills behind Northridge, just outside Los Angeles, but some of the filming was done around Vasquez Rocks in the high desert, near Palmdale, or on nearby ranches. Monogram had a Western street out in the San Fernando Valley, near Newhall, which Lone Star used, but some of the scenes were inserted from stock footage. "I went in and out of those Westerns so fast that half the time I didn't know their titles," said Duke. "To play a cowboy you need a good hat and a good pair of boots; what you have on in between doesn't matter."

In *The Star Packer* Wayne organizes the ranchers against an outlaw gang, while Yakima Canutt plays a friendly Indian. "I couldn't stand to look at myself on the screen," Canutt said. The stuntman hated the sound of his own voice; his vocal cords had been damaged when he was in the navy, so that he had to force the sound out and he spoke in a monotone. "I was always sensitive to stage fright," he said. "In doing action I was perfectly at ease. But to get up and talk frightened me. That's what took me from acting into the stunt game."

The Trail Beyond, one of Lone Star's better efforts, was based on the novel *The Wolf Hunters* by popular writer James Oliver Curwood and featured Noah Beery and Noah Beery, Jr. Canutt did a stunt in the picture where he leaped from a horse onto a wagon. During the take he missed the wagon, got up, remounted his horse, and did the leap again. Malvern decided to use both shots in the film.

After the first eight Westerns for Lone Star, Wayne had renegotiated his contract and had begun earning more money. His first child, Michael, was born in 1934, so the extra income was needed. Josephine still spent much of her time in church-related activities, while Duke showed a growing aversion to organized religion. He respected his wife's background yet felt excluded from the Hispanic society in which she thrived. "Because my father was John Wayne," Michael Wayne said later, "people don't know that I'm half Latin. My grandfather is buried in Mexico." Despite Duke's desire for family, he felt isolated, shut out of his wife's Catholic world and suspect within her refined circle. Josephine in turn disapproved of his hard-drinking crowd and insisted that he not bring them home.

For two years after Wayne's success in *The Big Trail*, he and John Ford had not spoken, a breach Duke never understood. Perhaps Ford resented that his young friend had gained recognition as Raoul Walsh's protégé. A sensitive Irishman, Ford may have felt abandoned, which he was prone to do. Wayne knew that Ford was mad at him, yet did not know why. Eventually the two were reunited, and their friendship deepened. "Whenever I had vacations or he had vacations," Wayne said, "we usually took them together." Ford, Duke, and Ward Bond spent weekends together off Catalina Island on the director's yacht, the *Araner*. At other times they would drive down to San Pedro for a few drinks and a poker session when the boat was docked there. One New Year's Eve, the *Araner* was anchored off the coast of Mazatlán, and the three friends went ashore and got so drunk that Mexican officials asked them to leave. During such trips they spent their days fishing and their nights drinking, often in the Belmar Hotel in Mazatlan or one of the local whorehouses. The Belmar bar overlooked the ocean, and the three friends sat there for hours, drinking and listening to mariachis. The first one to pass out might awaken to find the bartender's pet python coiled on his lap.

"I never expected anything from Jack," Duke said. "He knew mine was a friendship. Very few people realized what a private man he was, but I was private, too." Ford considered Duke "bright and energetic," "a big handsome lad" with a future in movies. Whenever Wayne got discouraged and complained that he was tired of making assembly-line Westerns, Ford would listen patiently and say, "Get all the experience you can, in anything you can get."

So Duke continued to crank out Westerns for Lone Star: *Lawless Frontier, Texas Terror, Rainbow Valley, Paradise Canyon, The Dawn Rider, Desert Trail* (all 1935). In *Lawless Frontier* he again sang and played the guitar, with Robert Bradbury directing his own script. Buffalo Bill, Jr., who had grown up in Wyoming and was an expert at riding bucking horses, appeared in *Texas Terror* and *Rainbow Valley*. Young Bill had a knack for doing a crouper mount, where he vaulted over the horse's rear, turned, and rode backwards in the saddle. "That was a good gag when you're supposed to be making a getaway out of town," Yakima Canutt said.

Yak had a bald spot that his hair didn't always cover. In *Paradise Canyon* he doubled Wayne in a fight where Duke's character was to be thrown over the villain's head right into the camera. Canutt was playing the villain in the picture, so another stuntman had to double him while he doubled Duke. The stuntman recruited threw Canutt over, and Yak hit the floor with his back to the camera. Since he wasn't wearing a hat in this particular scene, his bald spot showed for a fraction of a second. At the preview the audience howled when they saw what was supposed to be the movie's hero with a visible bald place, and they kept on laughing until Wayne, who was in the theater, grew embarrassed. A month or so later, Yak had a girlfriend write him a fan letter and mail it from New York. "Dear Mr. Canutt," she wrote. "I saw you in John Wayne's new picture. Your work is terrific. Why don't the producers get smart and give you a break, because Wayne must be getting old. He's getting bald." Yak took the letter to the set where Duke was working and handed it to his friend. From then on, whenever they did a fight scene, Wayne grabbed some makeup and darkened Canutt's bald spot before they commenced shooting.

"John and I were both so competitive," Yak said, "both so eager to top whatever previous bit we had worked out, that this might have been dangerous if we hadn't become such close friends." Once, doing a fight in a saloon, Yak took a swing at Wayne, who stepped to one side and knocked Canutt through the glass in the big front window. "The camera outside caught me as I tumbled out end over end," the stuntman remembered, "stopping under a hitch pole at the edge of the sidewalk." When Yak stood up and started to run for his horse, Duke leaped through the window, dove over the hitch rail, and tackled him. "I have never been turned over so many times so fast," Canutt said.

Paul Fix, Duke's friend and acting coach, had a supporting role in *Desert Trail.* A former stage director and playwright turned actor, Fix would stand behind the camera while Wayne was working and offer suggestions between takes. Duke learned how to deliver lines from Fix and under his guidance developed the halting cadence that became a trademark. "Paul was the man who gave Duke his first insight into his screen persona," said Harry Carey, Jr., who married Fix's daughter. "He was the first man to put the John Wayne image into John Wayne's head. And he literally taught John Wayne what he knew about acting."

Duke told Fix that he felt awkward in front of a camera, that he didn't know what to do with his hands. Since Fix was active in little theaters around Hollywood, the veteran actor urged Wayne to acquire some stage experience. He cast Duke in a production of *Red Sky at Evening*, but Wayne was so frightened at appearing before a live audience that he drank too much before the performance and made a fool of himself. Josephine saw the play and went backstage afterwards in a fury. "You're a bum," she shouted at her husband, "a drunken bum!"

John Wayne would remain a screen actor, acquiring his skills in front of a camera. He learned to look other actors straight in the eye and respond to what they said. Initially Duke was heavy-footed and trudged when he walked. Paul Fix suggested that he point his toes when he moved, and Yakima Canutt helped him develop the rolling swagger that became one of Wayne's most distinctive features. "We used to call it his date-seed fanny walk," actress Maureen O'Hara said, "because of the way a date seed is folded in. Duke would squeeze his buttocks in like that." Wayne himself claimed, "I just imagine that I have a pea between the cheeks of my ass and I don't want to drop it." Duke worked at his unique walk until it became part of him and always considered physical presence basic to his roles. "Learn to handle your body easily and smoothly," he advised young outdoor actors.

"I relish action," Duke said, "which is an essential part of motion pictures." Yakima Canutt was Wayne's idea of a real man, and he came to revere the versatile stuntman. From Canutt he learned to slouch on a horse and ride like a cowboy. "Yak was a great horseman," said Paul Malvern, "the finest we had." Canutt had worked with horses since childhood and had grown up in the saddle. "I rode my first bucking horse when I was eleven years old," Yak recalled. Later he broke horses, entered bucking contests at county fairs, and then went into major competition. He began doing stunts in movies during the silent era and quickly learned to leap over a horse's backside into the saddle, run along the ground and jump onto a horse at a gallop, and do a "Running W" (in which cables, secured to an anchored stake, were strapped to a horse's front legs; when the cables were stretched full length, the animal came to a tumbling halt). The running W was outlawed in the United States in 1940 because so many horses were maimed or killed, but until then it was a standard practice in the making of Western movies. "I did some three hundred Running W's," Canutt said, "and never crippled a horse."

Duke was impressed by Yak's courage and daring. They spent hours talking about ways to make stunts look realistic, and Canutt showed the

65

novice how to do horse falls, how to transfer from one moving object to another, and how to capture a fleeing villain without getting hurt. "I'd ride faster than the fellow I was chasing so I could make a good jump from my horse clear over the back end of his," Canutt explained. "I'd catch him and take him right off and into a roll. That way you'd get out into the clear of the two horses as they galloped away."

On one of the Lone Star productions, Canutt had to get off a horse at the top of a bluff and jump into the Kern River. He could see a big granite rock under the surface just before the water deepened, but Yak thought he could jump clear of it. He leaped into the air too fast, however, and didn't get enough lift to carry him over the rock. "The minute I left the ledge I knew I was never going to make it," he said. "I just shoved my head back and started winding my arms to get my body at an angle to hit the water as flat as possible." When he hit, his head never went under the water, and his fall was broken before he struck the granite. "I no more than hit the rock," Yak remembered, than "Wayne was right in the water and had me." Canutt had a black and blue hip and suffered soreness, but he kept on working.

Yak was also an adept marksman and taught Wayne fancy gun tricks that looked impressive on the screen. They practiced and practiced until Duke developed a flashy draw. "It looked good," said Canutt. "But it wouldn't have been worth a damn if you were in a shooting scrap."

Yak made more money than Duke when they worked on the Lone Star pictures, for Malvern knew that believable action was what audiences wanted to see in budget Westerns. Wayne accepted the difference in pay, aware of how much he was learning from Canutt. He became fascinated with the meticulous way Yak planned his stunts. By the time the Lone Star series was finished, Duke had gained tremendous knowledge about the physical side of working in action pictures. Later, he talked the language of stuntmen, understood their humor, knew the hazards they faced, and respected their skills. "Wayne always thought of himself as a stuntman," said veteran stunt performer Gil Perkins.

The Westerns that Duke made for Lone Star ran about fifty-five minutes each and were targeted as the second half of a double bill in secondary theaters, aimed mainly at rural and working-class audiences. Monogram released the pictures to independent distributors with whom the company had agreements and accepted the best play dates they could negotiate. While the movies did not earn big money, neither did they lose any, since costs were kept low and they had an assured market. The pictures varied in quality, but they established John Wayne as a cowboy star with depression audiences who welcomed confirmation of rural ideals. Although critics dismissed the Monogram Westerns as mindless and the industry itself held them in low esteem, Malvern's budget oaters fit the mood of the times, when farmers again became folk heroes. For middle America during the 1930s Monogram's Westerns pitted moneyed interests against ordinary people. John Wayne's West, as Randy Roberts and James Olson pointed out, was "besieged by evil—ruthless merchants, monopolistic land and water agents, greedy bankers, and even dangerous friends and relatives."

Wayne felt ambivalent about his volume of bargain basement "horse operas." On the one hand he grew discouraged, fearing that he was in a rut and would be stuck there. "I'll bet I've survived more bad pictures than any other actor on the screen," he later said. "I was so disgusted with the lot of them that I would have gone back to being a prop man if it hadn't been for Jack Ford." He knew that he was filming pulp adventure tales with cardboard heroes and stock villains and claimed that some of his movies were made in four days on a budget of $11,000. "I'd change my clothes, read the lines, change my clothes, read some more lines," he said. "We'd start before dawn, using flares to light close-ups. When the sun came up, we'd do some medium-range shots. In full daylight we'd do the distance shots, following the sun up one side of the hill and down the other side." The process seemed endless, his roles monotonous. "I did a lot of thinking about the quickie Westerns I'd been making," said Duke, "and began to realize that they were a one-way street. You could last in them only as long as your brawn held up, but they certainly wouldn't take you anyplace except into the next one."

Yet he also realized that he was honing his skill and came to respect the Hollywood craftsmen who did the best they could with whatever they had to work with. "Monogram couldn't afford the really top-flight writers and directors," said Walter Mirisch, who became an executive with the company. Productions there depended on skilled technicians, inventive enough to cut corners and still make a respectable product. "Hell, I couldn't have made those pictures for that kind of money otherwise," Paul Malvern declared.

Despite similar plots, canned music, crude sound, and routine direction, the Lone Star productions were nicely photographed, well paced, and captured some of the gritty look of the old West. Companionable crews pitched in to do whatever task needed doing, whether it was moving props, helping to apply makeup, or handling stock. Duke found it all valuable experience. He learned discipline, grew in professional confidence, and came to love making pictures. He was also earning a living.

"When I started, I knew I was no actor," Duke confessed, "and I went to work on this Wayne thing. It was as deliberate and studied a projection as you'll ever see. I figured I needed a gimmick, so I dreamed up the drawl, the squint, and a way of moving meant to suggest that I wasn't looking for trouble but would just as soon throw a bottle at your head as not. It was a hit-or-miss project for a while, but it began to develop."

Although in his early movies Wayne played likable heroes, naive but genuine, he gradually developed a tougher, more complex character as his Westerns progressed. "I have tried never to play the pure hero," Duke said. He disliked the rodeo clothes that Tom Mix and other screen cowboys wore and substituted Levis, boots, and a Western hat. Rather than looking immaculate, he often had dirt on his clothes—much as Harry Carey, Wayne's screen idol, had earlier. Duke's characters were charming, yet bumbling enough to endear their portrayer to the average moviegoer. "I even had to practice saying *ain't*," said Duke.

Almost from the beginning Wayne sought to blur the distinction between himself and his screen image. During his years of making budget Westerns he established an identifiable personality and evolved from handsome stud into American folk hero. "In all my films I try never to forget that people are seeing me for enjoyment," he said, "and if there is a message to a movie, it should be a positive simple one. I believe the good guys should win and that when they don't win personally, the principle of goodness should win out."

Wayne's acting in the Lone Star series shows a marked improvement over his acting in the Westerns he had made earlier at Warner Bros. His delivery of lines, even those not well written, sounds less awkward and callow. "I began to recognize dialogue as something besides a nuisance to get out of the way before the action could start," Duke said. He developed a mastery of exposition, became a fast study, and convinced himself that acting was a respectable profession. He took his work seriously, observed what was going on around him, and absorbed the ethos that would make him a Hollywood legend. "I'd spot him off going over his lines and practicing how to play things," Paul Malvern recalled. Even in his apprenticeship, Duke was a demon for work.

"I was a happy-go-lucky fellow in those days," said Wayne of his Monogram years, but "I realized I was in a rut." He grew tired of the physical beating his body was taking and resented having so little time off between pictures. Later he claimed to have no regrets, saying that if he were starting over again, he would want his training to be the same. But that was hindsight; he never forgot how tough his early work had been. "I used to pride myself on being able to do anything on horseback that my directors had the nerve to ask me to do," Duke said. "I'm sure if I hadn't been kind of a halfway athlete that they wouldn't have used me." But all through the grind he remembered what Will Rogers and John Ford had told him: "The most important thing in this business," Wayne reminded himself, "is to work steadily."

Long Trail
to Major Stardom

In the fall of 1935, Monogram, Lone Star Productions, Mascot, and Consolidated Film Laboratories merged into Republic Pictures. The new company included the holdings of producers Nat Levine, Trem Carr, and Paul Malvern and assumed contracts held by their units. Mascot had leased the old Mack Sennett lot on Ventura Boulevard in the San Fernando Valley, and that property now became the Republic studio. The company would specialize in budget Westerns, inexpensive adventure movies, country musicals, and serials. Tobacco-chomping Herbert J. Yates, owner of Consolidated Film Laboratories, which had done business with Monogram and Mascot, headed the new company, and Trem Carr became its initial vice president. For the first year Nat Levine served as Republic's production head, but his relationship with Yates was uneasy from the start. Utilizing Levine's filmmaking experience and Monogram's distribution exchanges, the company's executives intended to develop a market outside the orbit of Hollywood's major studios.

Herbert Yates knew little about movies but a great deal about making money. Initially he had been in the tobacco business, then began lending money to Poverty Row film companies, and later decided to enter motion picture production. "Herb Yates was a tough businessman," said Republic star Gene Autry. "Socially you couldn't ask for a better guy to be around. You'd go out with him, and you couldn't spend a quarter. But once he was behind the desk and you were on the other side, he drove a hard bargain."

Between 1935 and 1952 John Wayne made thirty-three movies for Republic. "Duke and I were the first two players under contract when Republic was formed," said Autry, who had been a radio singer before going under contract to Mascot. "At the same time that I was shooting *Tumbling Tumbleweeds* near Barstow and Bakersfield, Wayne was up in Lone Pine shooting a picture called *Westward Ho!* That was in 1935; we made the first two pictures under the Republic banner. Wayne and I became close friends; Republic was always a close-knit group."

Other contract players described the atmosphere at the Republic studio as a family or a big country picnic. "It was like Texas, very down-home," said Dale Evans, later queen of the studio's Westerns. Located on what were then the northern outskirts of Los Angeles, with only a few farmhouses scattered about, the studio included stables and a Western street and looked something like a Spanish hacienda. "If you were shooting over on Stage One," actress Peggy Stewart recalled, "you could see straight down the street, and you knew exactly who was working there. You'd yell down to some prop man and visit friends between scenes. There was so much kidding on that lot, because you were with those people six days a week."

Republic had no commissary, but a good restaurant opened just a block away. "The Valley was a quiet place in those days," said actress Adele Mara. "There was one bar on Ventura, but no big markets. It was pretty much a wilderness. Everybody at Republic worked fast, and we worked overtime." Twelve-hour days were common, and Yates cut corners wherever possible. "They would paint the wall of a set to the height of the leading man," said screenwriter Ed Hartmann. "The top remained unpainted because they would only photograph to the height of the leading man. They didn't waste a thing!"

Yet in comparison with Mascot and Monogram, budgets at Republic were bigger and the production crews better, even though most of the company's product had an assembly-line look. Yates believed in a sure thing and was more interested in profitable movies than in artistic ones. Cheap Westerns had proved to be a reliable source of income during the depression decade, and in 1935 Yates agreed to pay John Wayne an annual salary of $24,000 to star in four Westerns a year over the next two years.

Wayne began his career at Republic with *Westward Ho!*, produced by Paul Malvern and directed by Robert N. Bradbury, the same team he had worked with at Lone Star. The picture was of a higher quality than those Malvern had produced for Monogram, but its appeal still relied heavily on the action and stunts devised by Yakima Canutt. Filmed in the high Sierras, *Westward Ho!* cost nearly $85,000 and used a herd of five hundred cattle in several scenes. "That was a class picture," Malvern said, "and it was my story."

Malvern had concocted a plot about two brothers who came west in covered wagons as small boys. An Indian attack separated them, and one went bad while the other remained good. "No Western before this had a story where brother was fighting brother and didn't know until the last scene, when the bad one got killed, that they were related," Malvern maintained. "Hell, that's got heart to it!" He repeated the idea in *Ali Baba and the Forty Thieves* (1944), which he produced as a big-budget picture at Universal, changing the relationship to two sweethearts. "You'd never know it was the same story," said Malvern.

Duke played the good brother in *Westward Ho!* He becomes a vigilante searching for a notorious bandit without knowing that the outlaw is his missing brother. "I had seventy-five white horses in that movie," Malvern remembered, "which were all ridden by vigilantes with white hats and black kerchiefs around their necks so they could identify one another, and the same amount of boys in browns as the heavies when they clashed. In the background we had Mount Whitney with snow on it, and the photography was beautiful. We made that picture in eight days."

Wayne again sings in the movie, although the voice this time belonged to one of director Robert Bradbury's twin sons, a physician by profession. The dub is still not good and the song seems ludicrous coming from Duke's mouth. Yet *Westward Ho!* was the most expensive picture Wayne had made since *The Big Trail*, and he was pleased with the results. "I regard it as one of the finest things I have ever appeared in," he wrote the Iowa Theater in Winterset.

Westward Ho! played for two weeks at the Pantages Theater in Hollywood during the late summer of 1935, a prestigious booking for a budget Western; it had reputedly grossed $500,000 by the end of the year. John Wayne had risen to the top rank of Poverty Row's cowboy heroes, but his movies since *The Big Trail* had made little or no impact on the major studios and film critics. His audience was centered largely in rural areas and small towns, yet Duke made few apologies for his work. "The cowboy is the folklore of America," he said. But as a serious actor he knew that he hung on the edge of respectability.

Although Wayne understood little about politics in the 1930s and had no time for direct involvement, his basic philosophy was taking shape. A Roosevelt supporter at the time, he thought of himself as a liberal Democrat. As he studied his Western roles, he became captivated by how men have faced the dangers of their time. He grew convinced that "the finer and more manly qualities" are enhanced under stress. During the years Duke served his apprenticeship, he formed an outlook on life that would remain with him thereafter; it was drawn from both the frontier heritage and the populist values of the 1930s. The budget Westerns he made for Monogram and Republic were formulaic offshoots of the nation's creation myth, which Wayne accepted as basic to the American way. His was a simplistic viewpoint, founded on an unswerving belief in rugged individualism, self-reliance, laissez-faire economics, bold masculine virility, and warranted violence. The persona that Wayne invented for himself, onscreen and off, incorporated values that would soon be at odds with a collective society. Unrealistic though they might be in a modern world, Duke accepted these anachronisms as fundamental truths.

The link between the American past and her husband's screen cowboys was lost on Josephine Wayne, who viewed Duke's livelihood with disdain. "I was part of the movie group," said Duke; "she was part of the society group." Elegant and vibrant, Josephine was much loved within the Catholic enclave of Los Angeles, who knew her as a woman of great dignity, warmth, and humor. But she and her husband lived in incompatible worlds. "Josie didn't like my friends and I didn't like hers," Duke said. Although the couple drifted apart, they maintained a common belief in marriage and family. Their daughter Antonia Maria, called Toni, was born in 1935, and while Duke was a loving, tender father, he spent little time at home. He was either on location making a film or out carousing with John Ford, Ward Bond, and their gang.

Duke later admitted to feeling frustrated, unhappy, and guilt-ridden during his first marriage. He wanted to love Josie but sought to be accepted on his own terms. She tried to make him into a gentleman, encouraged him to assume more formal dress and behavior, and pressured him to become a Catholic. To Duke, Josephine's world spelled pretense; he resented coming home to a house full of socialites and clerics. He was too earthy and high-spirited to conform to the conventions of her refined friends, and his quick temper often embarrassed his wife.

Like his frontier heroes, John Wayne reveled in masculine companionship. He had grown up at his father's side, suspicious of feminine restraints. Among men, he was gregarious, comical, sometimes boisterous, full of the joy of living. "Wayne is a man without pretense," Gene Autry said. "He could be tough and rowdy." Aboard the *Araner*, at the Emerald Bay Yacht Club, or at the Hollywood Athletic Club, Duke enjoyed the spirited horseplay of a clique that called themselves the Young Men's Purity, Total Abstinence, and Yachting Association. The name could not have been less appropriate, since the organization's charter defined their purpose as the "promulgation of the cause of alcoholism." The group revolved around John Ford and prided itself on a capacity to consume large quantities of liquor without appearing drunk. Weekdays its members spent hours in the steam room sweating out booze they had devoured the weekend before. Duke loved this all-male group and gave them his best, sharing himself with them in ways he never could with women.

How much of a womanizer young Wayne was is unclear. Probably he was more of a flirt than a philanderer, although the opportunities for casual sex were abundant in Hollywood and on most locations, where movie people were lionized. Duke possessed the looks, the virility, and a personality that appealed to women, and he claimed that Josephine was not the most responsive partner in bed. Growing up in Iowa and rural California had instilled in Duke a puritanical attitude toward sex, but alcohol may have mollified his restraint. The movie business abounded in beautiful women, and bed-hopping was part of the fraternal code. Yet the cowboys that Wayne worked with tended to disapprove of unbridled hanky-panky. Like Duke, most of them came from a straight-laced background. Wayne made frequent jokes about sex, but that was mainly to amuse his cronies. The extent of his extracurricular bedroom activities remains conjecture.

Duke loved his children and needed the security of marriage. "I didn't want to break up," he said. "I had grown up in a home of bickering, and I know how children suffer when their parents fight." For Josephine, stalwart Catholic that she was, divorce was never an option. Yet the couple came to accept that theirs would be a limited relationship. Their arguments were too bitter to forget, and resentment replaced their love for one another. While Duke demanded his freedom to wander, he felt like a failure as a father and husband. Guilt accompanied his resistance to Josephine's efforts to domesticate him, resulting in a no-win predicament. He found his escape in work and devoted himself to building a career that would pay the bills and strengthen his self-esteem.

John Wayne quickly emerged as one of Republic Pictures' top money-making stars. The studio released *The New Frontier* and *Lawless Range* in the fall of 1935, both produced by Paul Malvern, with Duke the featured attraction. *The New Frontier* was more violent than most of Wayne's oaters and climaxed with the burning of a town. *Lawless Range* found Duke singing and strumming a guitar, again playing a hero named John, and helping a valley of ranchers get their cattle to market. Robert Bradbury directed the picture, and Archie Stout's outdoor photography enhanced its production value.

The Lawless Nineties, King of the Pecos, The Oregon Trail, Winds of the Wasteland, and *The Lonely Trail* were all released by Republic in 1936. Joseph Kane, a former film editor at Paramount, directed three of the five, emphasizing action over story. Like most of Wayne's early directors, Kane shot his pictures in six days. "Before you start out in the morning, you have to plan out what you're going to do," the director said, "so you don't waste any time. . . .We had to come up with fifty-four minutes of picture." Ann Rutherford, Duke's leading lady in *The Lawless Nineties* and *The Lonely Trail,* served as a pleasant foil to Duke's manliness, yet even an actress of Rutherford's charm proved a secondary interest. "The cast is kept so busy that it can find very little time for such luxuries as romance and convention," the *New York Times* reported when *The Lawless Nineties* opened at the Rialto in Manhattan.

Rutherford was again Wayne's love object in *The Oregon Trail,* which Paul Malvern produced. Nat Levine took over as producer of *Winds of the Wasteland* and *The Lonely Trail,* but he left Republic the following year. The studio's oaters continued to depend on Yakima Canutt for stunts, although stock footage was often inserted. Republic took pride in the look of its films and the quality of its sound and wisely hired skilled technicians. Where the company faltered was in its lack of attention to scripts and a disregard for dramatic nuances. "Most directors at Republic tended to have things played pretty broadly," Dale Evans recalled.

But Wayne aspired to more. He deepened the timbre of his voice and continued to improve his delivery of dialogue. He carried his share of the action, but listened to his directors, paid attention to the character actors he worked with, and watched the way crews worked. Slowly he found his way, learned to handle light comedy, responded to fellow thespians, and sharpened his craft. If he was not yet an actor of great dimension, Duke had grown during his decade in the business. Yet the grind was relentless, particularly in the summer months when days were long and the work was concentrated.

Most of his movies seemed like the last one; the horses never changed, though the leading ladies did. From April to September crews at Republic "would work like hell," Wayne remembered, "making our quota of pictures, which were already sold in advance in a package to the exhibitors." Then Duke would have several weeks off, during which he could hunt and fish or spend time aboard the *Araner* with John Ford, Ward Bond, and maybe Grant Withers or Henry Fonda.

When Trem Carr left Republic in 1936 to produce a series of action pictures at Universal, Wayne temporarily went with him, signing for a six-picture deal. The films Duke made at Universal would have bigger budgets and stronger casts than those he had been making at Republic and would be shown in better theaters. They also gave him a respite from Westerns. Wayne welcomed the change, even though the action melodramas Carr produced using the Universal facilities still fell into the budget category.

In *The Sea Spoilers* (1936), the first of the series, Duke played a coast guard commander, and Fuzzy Knight headed the supporting cast. *Conflict* (also 1936), based on the Jack London story "The Abysmal Brute," came next, with Wayne and Ward Bond playing prizefighters. Set in the lumber country of northern California, *Conflict* made no pretense at epic proportions, although its logging sequences were authentic and its fight scenes were believable. "The picture has enough two-fisted ruggedness to stand on its own feet," said a reviewer for the *New York Times*.

The last four of Wayne's films for Trem Carr were directed by Arthur Lubin, who had become a house director at Universal and would later turn out Abbott and Costello movies, the *Francis* pictures, and dozens more. *California Straight Ahead* (1937), Lubin's initial assignment with Wayne, misled some of Duke's fans, since it wasn't a Western. Instead, the movie dealt with a race between a fleet of trucks and a freight train to transport aviation parts to the West Coast before the outbreak of a labor strike. Lubin found his star "a charming man" and encountered no problems with Duke at all. The director remembered Wayne's telling him, "I'm not a very good actor; I enjoy my work, and I enjoy working with you, Lubin. I love my producer, Trem Carr, whom I'm very indebted to." Arthur Lubin concluded, "[John Wayne] was a joy to work with."

Like Duke's earlier pictures for Carr, *California Straight Ahead* was shot in six days. In the middle of production the company received a phone call announcing that snow had fallen around Newhall, just north of Los Angeles. The crew decided to bundle up its equipment and photograph the picture's caravan of trucks moving through the snow, convinced that the film's atmosphere would be enhanced without adding to the cost.

I Cover the War (also 1937), Lubin's second movie with Wayne, cast Duke as a news photographer sent to cover an Arab revolt. "We have checked with the Trem Carr office," a studio memo reported, "and are informed that they intend to actually photograph all of the scenes as written in this script and not resort to the use of stock shots. If this is so and they fulfill their promise to use 400 mounted men as the Arab band and 150 mounted men as the British cavalry, we believe their budget of $70,000 for this production is a very conservative one." California doubled for the Khyber zone in the picture, and critic Frank S. Nugent judged the results "an ingeniously romantic fable which never stoops to logic and is content to tell a good lie." John Wayne, the critic said, was "pleasant enough," but Duke feared that he might be losing his Western fans and grew eager to return to familiar ground.

Cast as a hockey player in Carr's *Idol of the Crowds* (again 1937), he refused bribery and won the big game. *Adventure's End* (still 1937), the last of the series at Universal, was intended "to be very extravagant," according to Lubin. A sea yarn, based on a story by Ben Ames Williams, *Adventure's End* had a ten-day shooting schedule and cost $90,000, which was extravagant by budget-movie standards. "It was going to be a big picture," Lubin insisted. "I think the reason they selected that [script] was that there was a boat on the Universal lot, and they could use that." Duke played a pearl diver working on a whaler in the film. Studio executives expected that the movie would be difficult to make and considered the project a gamble. "We will watch with great interest the final results," a memo stated. Upon its release, critics dismissed *Adventure's End* as a pale rehash of earlier Hollywood sea epics.

While the action tales that Trem Carr produced were entertaining, they were cheaply made and proved disappointing at the box office. Carr "was cutting costs and production values as if he were still making Republic cheapies," said Wayne. "This time we were not competing with other Poverty Row operators and their programmers. We were competing with quality pictures that cost $500,000 and up."

Duke next made *Born to the West* (1938) for Paramount. The movie, based on a novel by Zane Grey, cast him opposite Marsha Hunt, James

Craig, and Johnny Mack Brown. "The John Wayne I acted with over half a century ago," said Hunt, "was a winningly unassuming, gentlemanly, easygoing, while quite professional, young man. I heard somewhere that when John Ford saw him in our Western, he cried out, 'That's the man I want for *Stagecoach*'!"

But starring in a Ford picture would come later. After making the movie at Paramount, Duke returned to Republic, where Herbert Yates welcomed him back with less than open arms. Rather than the $24,000 a year Wayne had been paid by the studio earlier, he now received $16,000. "Yates put the screws to me," said Duke. "And I would have to go into those terrible series they had."

Republic assigned him to replace Bob Livingston as Stony Brooke in "The Three Mesquiteers" series, which also featured Ray Corrigan as Tucson Smith and ventriloquist Max Terhune as Lullaby Joslin. Based loosely on characters created by William Colt MacDonald, the series emphasized action yet contradicted itself by mixing the nineteenth century and the present, a frequent practice in budget Westerns. While Wayne's provincial fans loved "The Three Mesquiteers," the series was inexpensively produced and represented an embarrassing comedown for Duke.

Wayne starred in eight Mesquiteer movies, all under the direction of George Sherman. They were among the dreariest assignments he undertook. Four were released in 1938: *Pals of the Saddle*, *Overland Stage Raiders*, *Santa Fe Stampede*, and *Red River Range*. Set in contemporary times, *Pals of the Saddle* borrowed from recent headlines that had heightened America's concern over subversion and possible sabotage by Nazi perpetrators. The plot revolved around enemy agents striving to gain control of a valuable chemical, which they intended to smuggle into Mexico for villainous purposes.

Overland Stage Raiders, another modern story, marked the last screen appearance of the legendary silent star Louise Brooks. Aware that she was reaching the end of her career, Brooks was nonetheless insulted to be working in a budget Western, the unreality and the two-week schedule of which disgusted her. But Brooks needed the money, even though her salary was a measly $300.

Early one morning in August 1938 she was driven in a studio car to the ranch where Republic shot its Westerns. "Up the road a bunch of cowboys were talking and laughing with two men who stood slightly apart from them," the actress recalled. "When the company car honked for them to get off the road, the two men looked around, saw me, and came to greet me. One was a cherub, five feet tall, carrying a bound script; the other was a cowboy, six feet four inches tall, wearing a lovely smile." The cherub was the director George Sherman, who introduced Brooks to the cowboy, who was John Wayne. "Looking up at him I thought, this is no actor but the hero of all mythology miraculously brought to life," the actress said.

Despite untold setbacks, the John Wayne mystique was taking shape—at least among Hollywood workers and limited audiences. Louise Brooks later claimed that Wayne was what Henry James defined as the greatest of all works of art—"a purely beautiful being." Poorly written though most of his characters were, Duke had established the screen persona of a capable, no-nonsense, nonintellectual activist who took control of a situation and got the job done. "His screen self drawled his sparse lines almost hesitantly, seeming to grope for what he wanted to say," said Marsha Hunt, his costar in *Born to the West*. "He was big, he moved and rode well and handled guns with great ease." Yet far more men than women admired him.

Although his popularity would remain strongest in rural areas and with laboring classes until the end of the decade, John Wayne had entered the America consciousness. He had received little assistance from film critics, and Republic's publicity office was no match for the champions of bally-hoo at Metro-Goldwyn-Mayer, Paramount, or any of the larger studios. Wayne's impact was restricted, since it came from Hollywood's bargain basement, but an image was building. All Wayne needed was the proper vehicle—a well-written part, a saga in need of a hero, and a director of genius.

He had all but given up hope for that as the drudgery at Republic continued. *Santa Fe Stampede*, which featured film veteran William Farnum in a supporting role, opened in Manhattan at the Rialto Theater. Duke was nearly hanged by a lynch mob in the movie, a mob the *New York Times* judged to be typical of Republic Pictures—"filmed in close-up, for economy's sake." The reviewer facetiously remarked that the success of the Three Mesquiteers "is probably due to the fact that nobody has thought of ambushing them with a Flit gun."

Red River Range came next and did nothing to relieve Wayne's depressed state of mind. At thirty-one years of age he felt burned out. He had been performing in movies for ten years, had made over sixty motion pictures, and seemed to have gotten nowhere. He considered himself more of a stuntman than an actor. His wife had no respect for his profession and therefore understood few of his frustrations. Gracious, witty woman though Josephine was, Duke had trouble communicating with her about things that mattered to him. Their third child, Patrick, was born in 1938, but the barriers between husband and wife had solidified. They maintained their marriage for appearances and for the sake of their children.

Duke felt his youth passing. His father, Clyde Morrison, died of a heart attack shortly before Patrick was born. While Clyde always had a difficult time financially, he basked in his son's glory and never questioned Duke's success. Toward the end of his life, one of Clyde's arms went numb from an electric shock. He was standing on a ladder trying to locate a flaw in an electric cable when he suffered the shock. "We found him after he'd fallen to the floor," said Duke. "He just wasn't right after that."

Wayne always described Clyde as "a fine man and a wonderful father." He clung to the memory of his dad's kindness and never forgave his mother for berating the man for his failures. "I owe him a great deal," Duke said of his father in later life, "and only hope I can live up to his example." Wayne supported Clyde's widow until her death, although he and his stepmother were never close.

After Clyde Morrison's death, John Ford became even more of a surrogate father to Duke, although Ford preferred to see himself as an older brother. "In Ford's presence," Gene Autry observed, Wayne "could be as obedient and innocent as an altar boy." In professional matters Ford's word was law, and Duke was eager to absorb all he could from a man he considered a master of his craft.

During the summer of 1938 Ford and Wayne spent a weekend together aboard the *Araner* off Catalina Island. During the outing Ford handed Duke a script that Dudley Nichols had just finished for the director's next picture. Based on a story called "Stage to Lordsburg" by Ernest Haycox, which *Collier's* magazine had published the year before, the script depicted a set of Bret Harte-like characters on their way by stagecoach across New Mexico Territory during an Apache uprising. Among the travelers was a drunken doctor, a prostitute, a whiskey drummer, a gambler, a dishonest banker, and the pregnant wife of a Southern cavalry officer, but the hero was a lonely gunfighter called the Ringo Kid. Producer Walter Wanger had Gary Cooper in mind for the male lead, but Cooper's price proved too high for the picture's limited budget. "Read this for me," Ford said, as he threw Wayne the script. "I'm having a hell of a time deciding whom to cast as the Ringo Kid. You know a lot of young actors, Duke. See what you think."

Bruce Cabot, who had earned success in *King Kong* (1933), had tested for the part, but Wayne had recently seen *The Texas Rangers* (1936) and been impressed by the performance of Lloyd Nolan. "Why don't you get Nolan?" Duke asked. Ford didn't say anything more about the part until they docked at San Pedro that evening. "You idiot," the director then said to his friend, "couldn't you play it?" Wayne was stunned. "It was like somebody had hit me in the face with a baseball bat," Duke said. "Our relationship had reached a point where I didn't think of it in terms of work."

Ford later admitted that he had Wayne in mind for the Ringo Kid from the start, but he had trouble talking Walter Wanger into gambling on a cowboy star from Monogram and Republic. Wanger wanted a recognizable name in the part and insisted that Wayne make a test with actress Claire Trevor, cast in the role of the prostitute. The test centered on the two characters' most intimate scene together, the tender moment after the birth of Mrs. Mallory's baby. Ford did everything he could to encourage Duke, and the results were impressive enough to persuade Wanger to give Wayne the part.

Without Ford's knowledge, Duke asked Paul Fix to coach him for his role in *Stagecoach*. "He was so tense and wooden," Fix recalled. "I told him he had to be like a prizefighter and be on his toes all the time. He'd come to my house at night . . . and we'd go over things for him to do, natural things." At last Wayne's moment had come, and he was clearly nervous to be working with such experienced character actors as Thomas Mitchell, John Carradine, and Donald Meek.

Although the Ringo Kid has broken out of jail, he is innocent of the crime that put him behind bars. He has escaped from prison to pursue the Plummer brothers, who murdered his father and brother and sent him to jail. The kid is good-humored, polite, chivalrous, sensitive, and vulnerable, yet in time of crisis he becomes a tower of strength and a man in motion. The Ringo Kid stands high among John Ford's consummate outsiders, at odds with a society he rescues then abandons.

Stagecoach would be Ford's first Western in twelve years. Once sound recording became practical outdoors, budget oaters had flooded second-rate movie houses in such numbers that Westerns were no longer taken seriously. Movie audiences, not to mention critics, considered them shabby and mindless, a diversion for children. Ford had something more important in mind. With *Stagecoach* he wanted to create an American epic, with sweeping action, indelible characters, and awesome landscapes.

Rather than film his Western on a backlot or at one of the studio's ranches, the director decided to take his company (the technicians and those actors working outside the stagecoach) to Monument Valley on the Utah-Arizona state line, on the Navajo reservation. Filming on location that far from Hollywood was rare in those days, and Monument Valley in 1938 was remote. Roads leading into the area were no more than two wheel tracks, which washed out during heavy rains. But Ford intended to make Monument Valley emblematic of the frontier West. Its towering monoliths and rugged terrain projected a sense of the eternal; the valley seemed a world unto itself. As John Wayne would remember it twenty years later, "Monument Valley in 1938 was heaven."

The only accommodations in the area consisted of a few cabins at Goulding's Trading Post, hotels in Kayenta and Tuba City, and a camp built for the Civilian Conservation Corps. Wayne stayed in one of Harry Goulding's guest cabins, which Duke shared with Yakima Canutt. The company arrived there in October, just before the first snowfall. "Most of the Monument Valley work was done by a second unit," Wayne recalled, "and then we did a lot of process stuff on the stage, which was the best way to handle the interior of that stagecoach. It would have been useless to try to shoot those scenes with the grinding and rattling of the wheels of the stagecoach and the clippity-clop of six horses."

Ford patterned the Ringo Kid after a Western hero he had devised with Harry Carey during the silent era. Carey had played a saddle tramp called Cheyenne Harry in a series of movies he and the young director had made for Universal, shot mainly on Carey's ranch near Saugus, California. Now Ford costumed Wayne not in the flashy attire of the standard Hollywood cowboy but simply, much as Cheyenne Harry had dressed, wearing suspenders instead of a belt. Wayne had seen the Carey pictures as a boy and had chosen him as a role model when he first became an actor in Westerns. Duke patterned his manner of speaking and his way of telegraphing dialogue after the veteran actor, whose career extended into the sound era. "Harry Carey projected a quality that we like to think of in men of the West," said Duke. "Ford and the great Western directors built on his authenticity."

Wayne's first scene in *Stagecoach* is unforgettable, for it immediately commands the audience's attention. Ford wisely delayed introducing the Ringo Kid until the drama had begun to unfold. Suddenly Ringo appears out of nowhere, alone on the valley floor—180 pounds of solid hero, his legs apart, a Winchester in his right hand, his saddle on his other arm, facing the oncoming stagecoach. He is young, handsome, and sexually appealing, and he emits an aura of bedrock strength. Already Wayne's imposing image suggests mythic proportions. The Ringo Kid's horse has gone lame, and he joins the passengers on board the stagecoach. He is basic, raw as a frontier hero should be, tender and resilient at the same time. He looks at the prostitute Dallas (played by Claire Trevor), and their sexual attraction leaps off the screen, despite his outward gallantry. A Hollywood superstar was about to be born; Duke was on his way to becoming an immortal Western hero.

The victory was not easily won, however. Ford pulled the performance out of Wayne. "Nobody could handle actors and crew like Jack," Duke said. "He was probably the finest artist I've ever known." Wayne admitted later that his first three weeks in Monument Valley were the most difficult of his career. Ford realized that Duke's approach to acting was instinctive, that to some degree he would always play himself. But the director sought to elicit a performance that rose above mechanical reactions. To achieve that goal, he berated and bullied Duke unmercifully, treating him like a half-witted child. "Stop slurring your dialogue and show some expression," the director yelled. He called Wayne "a big oaf" and "a dumb bastard" in front of the actors and crew. "I really should get Gary Cooper for this part," Ford muttered in disgust. "Can't you even walk, instead of skipping like a goddamn fairy?" the director shouted at Duke. Claire Trevor remembered Ford's grabbing Wayne by the chin and shaking his head: "Why are you moving your mouth so much?" the director demanded. "Don't you know that you don't act with your mouth in pictures? You act with your eyes!"

Wayne took the abuse Ford hurled at him, but the pressure mounted until he felt like quitting. "He got me angry," Duke admitted. "He would turn me inside out. I would want to murder him. But Ford knew what he was doing. . . . He knew I was ashamed of being a B Western cowboy in the company of these big stars." The director reasoned that if he pushed his friend to the limit and roused his ire, Wayne would shake loose from the bad habits he had acquired making cheap Westerns and give a creditable performance. He also counted on his abuse to provoke the veteran actors to the point that they would rally to Wayne's support. The ploy worked, for the cast felt sorry for Wayne and did everything they could to help. "I had the whole cast on my side," Duke said.

"It's true that working with Jack Ford could be pure hell," said Native American actor Iron Eyes Cody, who was in the *Stagecoach* company. "He was a sadistic man if there ever was one, but there was also a reason behind most everything he seemingly did for the sheer hell of it. . . . He would simply do anything to bring out the best performance an actor had to deliver. He was ruthless in the pursuit of excellence. In Duke's case, Ford knew perfectly well that behind all that swagger was an insecure man, completely ill-at-ease amid these stars."

The role of the Ringo Kid was tailored to Duke's strengths and showcased him to the best advantage. "I had a great deal of time in the picture when other people were talking, and all my stuff was just reactions," said Wayne. "They became very important throughout the picture; they built my part. . . . Ford treated me with great care."

Action came easily for Duke, but under Ford's direction he also handled romantic dialogue with conviction. "Ford was the finest editor I've ever seen," Wayne declared. "When Dudley Nichols was writing *Stagecoach*, he made Nichols write a scene five or six times till Nichols was just about drenched. Then he'd find three lines out of what Dudley had written and use them for that particular speech. He knew how to draw lines out that established character and progressed the story at the same time."

Not only is Wayne's performance as the Ringo Kid fresh and honest, but he began to understand the difference between A productions and the budget variety. "In an A picture," Duke said, "you're given the chance to walk into a situation and react rather than tell the audience what's going to happen, tell them where you're going to go, then tell them that you're there, and then tell them what you're going to do in scene after scene. . . . It was great experience."

Yakima Canutt was on hand to plan exciting stunts during the location work on *Stagecoach*, repeating some of the ones he'd perfected at Mascot,

Monogram, and Republic. As always, Canutt's work looked dangerous yet had a balletic quality to it. Yak's most famous trick, which he had first performed doubling Jack Randall in *Riders of the Dawn* (1937), had him as an Indian jumping from his pony onto one of the horses pulling the stagecoach. When the Ringo Kid shoots the Indian, Canutt drops to the tongue of the stagecoach, drags for a few seconds, then lets go, as the horses and coach pound over him. "When you do that gag," Canutt said, "you have to run the horses fast so they'll run straight. If they run slow, they move around a lot. When you turn loose to go under the coach, you've got to bring your arms over your chest and stomach. You've got to hold your elbows close to your body, or that front axle will knock them off. I always got on hard ground, so those wheels wouldn't sink down. . . . I never used any pads for that gag."

Yak and Duke had worked together for so long that they functioned in tandem. At night in Monument Valley they complained to one other about John Ford's treatment, yet as filming progressed, their respect for the filmmaker grew. "Mr. Ford was indeed a great director," said Canutt. "He was, you might say, a psychologist. He understood people and how to bring out the best in them. . . . [Wayne] was new to the big leagues, and Ford treated him like the greenest tenderfoot."

Producer Walter Wanger visited the location and was horrified to see Wayne climbing out of the moving stagecoach and up onto its roof. Fearful that his star might injure himself and not be able to finish the picture, Wanger voiced objections. Duke retorted that he had had years of experience as a stuntman and knew what he was doing. Yakima Canutt and the Hollywood cowboys had schooled him well.

From Monument Valley the company moved to a dry lake outside Victorville, California. Winter had set in, and the temperature plummeted. "In my life I've never been any colder than those two or three days that we were up there on that dry lake," said Duke. "The wind was blowing, and there was a fine silt dust. My lungs became raw, and my vocal pipes were shot." Andy Devine, who played the stagecoach driver, shared Duke's discomfort. "I was so cold," Devine remembered, "that sitting on top of the stagecoach I couldn't hold the reins so that I could slide them the way I should; my hands were so cold that they actually locked on them. I don't know how those poor guys just in breech clouts stood it, because the wind was blowing down."

After Christmas the company went up to the Kern River to shoot scenes where the stagecoach is ferried across a stream. The rest of the movie was filmed in Hollywood. Ford used the Western street at Republic and shot interiors at the Samuel Goldwyn studio. The director continued to demand more of Wayne than Duke felt he had in him, but Ford would accept no compromise, even on small details. "I had a scene where I was supposed to splash my face with water," Duke said. "I turned around and wiped my face with a towel, but I didn't seem to satisfy Ford. He made me do it over and over again, until my face was almost raw from rubbing it with the towel."

Claire Trevor remembered the movie as a complete delight; she didn't want the production to end. She considered Ford among the three greatest directors of her career, along with William Wyler and John Huston, who guided her to an Academy Award as best supporting actress in *Key Largo* (1948). During the filming of *Stagecoach*, she and Wayne developed a friendship that lasted a lifetime. "He adored Claire," Trevor's friend Mary Anita Loos said, "as she did him."

In the final reel of *Stagecoach*, the Ringo Kid brings about law and order by taking the law into his own hands. With his trusty Winchester he brings down the Plummer boys, after diving to the ground to dodge the last of their bullets. Ringo emerges as the quintessential Western hero— the loner, the rugged individualist, the self-reliant frontiersman who employs violence to civilize the wilderness, then rides off to begin life anew. And the picture marked a fresh start for John Wayne as well. "He was just a stick of wood when he came away from USC," veteran director Allan Dwan said. "Jack Ford was a hypnotist and could do anything with actors, if he liked them. Jack gave Wayne character."

Stagecoach previewed at the Fox Westwood Theater, near the UCLA campus, on February 2, 1939, to an audience of mainly college students. Watching it for the first time, Claire Trevor became so caught up in the movie that she forgot she was in it. "Westwood was the toughest place in the world to show a Western," said Trevor. "But the college kids stomped and screamed and were quiet at the right time. Ford just had them mesmerized with this picture." Duke was present at the showing and began to beam when he realized how sincerely the college kids liked his performance. He had given two tickets to the preview to Republic executives, who attended but did not bother to congratulate him on their way out of the theater. Nor did he hear from them for another two days. "On the third day," Duke said, "I went into the production office and said to my boss, 'I saw you fellows at the film the other night, but I've heard nothing from you.'" Even then their response was unenthusiastic. "Everybody who saw that film, except the people at Republic Studios, knew that my father was a major star after *Stagecoach*," Michael Wayne remarked years later.

Pilar Wayne once asked John Ford why he had waited so long to use Duke in a major role. "Duke wasn't ready," the director answered. "He had to develop his skills as an actor. . . .I wanted some pain written on his face to offset the innocence." In *Stagecoach* Ford elevated the screen persona that Wayne had developed over the past decade to the level of popular art, giving Duke deserving dialogue, an able cast, and a classic story in the Western genre. "*Stagecoach* was a wonderful piece of movement," said Wayne. "Ford put in motion the moods of Remington and Russell."

The picture opened in New York on March 2, 1939, at Radio City Music Hall. "Here, in a sentence, is a movie of the grand old school, a genuine rib-thumper, and a beautiful sight to see," wrote critic Frank Nugent. "The Ringo Kid is impatiently awaiting his cue to stalk down the frontier-town street and blast it out with the three Plummer boys." The actors, the *New York Times* reviewer said, have "all done nobly by a noble horse opera, but none so nobly as its director."

Stagecoach was nominated for an Oscar for best picture of the year, but it lost to *Gone With the Wind*. Polls showed a consensus among the moviegoing public: John Wayne was a sensation in the film. Hollywood began showing Duke more respect, while colleagues seemed freer in voicing what they had witnessed for years. "Duke is a perfectionist," Andy Devine said. "You wouldn't know it, but he works very hard at his trade and expects others to do the same. Duke is of the old school, which insists on discipline." If nothing else, making scores of budget movies had taught him professionalism.

Shortly after his rise to fame, Wayne was talking with Olive Carey, Harry Carey's wife. "Well, Duke," Olive asked, "now that you're a big star after *Stagecoach*, what are you going to do?" Duke replied, "Well, now that I can have a little more to say about the roles that I take, I might do something like *The White Company*," an English novel about knighthood and chivalry. Ollie Carey, never one to mince words, shot him a stern look and growled, "You are a big, dumb son of a bitch. The people have told you how they like you. They're your audience. You give them what they want, not what you want." Suddenly a light went on in Duke's head, and he never forgot what Ollie told him. "My father always followed her advice," Michael Wayne maintained. "He didn't care about producers, he didn't care about heads of studios, he cared about his fans."

Wayne returned to work at Republic, where he was still under contract, to find that executives there treated him no differently than they had in the past. Charles Feldman, one of Hollywood's most powerful agents, had signed Duke as a client and negotiated the loan to United Artists for the role in *Stagecoach*. Feldman got Herbert Yates to accept that Wayne could make movies for other studios—so long as Republic continued to enjoy his services at the same low salary agreed upon earlier. Yates was eager to cash in on Wayne's success in the major leagues, but less eager to bestow star treatment on him at Republic, fearing that to do so would end up costing the studio money.

Four additional Mesquiteer movies were made quickly and released in 1939: *The Night Riders, Three Texas Steers, Wyoming Outlaw*, and *Frontier Horizon*. Duke was back on the white horse as Stony Brooke, under the direction of George Sherman. For *The Night Riders* the Mesquiteers stepped back into the 1880s, put on capes and hoods, and defeated a fraudulent Spanish don with a phony deed. In the film Ray Corrigan says, "You know, there used to be a time when being an American meant something." Wayne replies, "It still does. It stands for freedom and fair play." Duke's political philosophy was beginning to surface, and it was closely linked to his screen image.

The Night Riders was released in April 1939, a month after *Stagecoach* opened in New York. *Three Texas Steers*, which introduced Carole Landis to the screen, reached the theaters in June, followed the next month by *Wyoming Outlaw*. Having experienced adroit direction and a distinguished script, Wayne grew discouraged with such inadequate material. But then he remembered what Ford had told him years before: "Duke, you're going to get a lot of scenes during your life. They're going to seem corny to you. Play them. Play them to the hilt. If it's *East Lynne* [an old melodrama], play it. You'll get by with it, but if you start trying to play it with your tongue in your cheek and getting cute, you'll lose sight of yourself . . . and the scene will be lost." Even bad scripts Duke tried to play as honestly as possible.

Frontier Horizon (also called *New Frontier*), the last of Wayne's Three Mesquiteers movies, was ready for distribution in September. The picture was also among the more interesting of the Mesquiteer series, since its plot dealt with the competing needs of rural and city people for water. Wayne's leading lady in *Frontier Horizon* was Phylis Isley, who was making her first screen appearance. The Western and her other Republic roles later became an embarrassment to the actress when David O. Selznick put her under personal contract, changed her name to Jennifer Jones, and maneuvered her to an Academy Award for *The Song of Bernadette* (1943).

Wayne's rapport with Claire Trevor in *Stagecoach* was so unmistakable that both RKO and Republic reunited the stars before the year was out, hoping to entice return audiences. RKO's entry was *Allegheny Uprising* (released in October 1939), a rather ponderous, unexciting saga set in pre-Revolutionary America. Based on a story by Neil H. Swanson, the picture was directed by William Seiter and produced under the supervision of Pandro S. Berman. Besides Wayne and Trevor, the cast included George Sanders, Brian Donlevy, and Chill Wills.

The company spent six weeks on location making *Allegheny Uprising*, during which time the actors lived in tents and ate lunch and dinner together. George Sanders, a difficult man, looked down on the other performers and stayed to himself except for meals. Duke fiercely disliked him and happily kept his distance. One day at lunch Sanders remarked that the colonial Yankees had been a bunch of fairies. Wayne lunged across the table at him, and it took four men to hold him back.

Duke never drank during the working day, a lesson he'd learned from John Ford. But he enjoyed having drinks before dinner and, when not working on a picture for Ford, usually continued his tippling until bedtime. He seldom seemed drunk, simply gregarious, although Claire Trevor admitted that she had seen Duke drink "till he fell on his face."

Republic paired the two stars again in *Dark Command* (1940), billing Trevor above Wayne. The picture was the studio's most expensive production to date, budgeted at $700,000; it also reunited Duke with Raoul Walsh for the first time since they'd made *The Big Trail* together. Republic borrowed Walter Pidgeon from Metro-Goldwyn-Mayer to give *Dark Command* additional prestige, and the film's supporting cast featured Roy Rogers in a dramatic role, Marjorie Main, and George "Gabby" Hayes. A fictionalized treatment of Quantrill's Raiders, with Pidgeon playing the villain, *Dark Command* was received far better than *Allegheny Uprising* by reviewers. When the Republic epic opened at the Roxy Theater in New York, Bosley Crowther called it "the most rousing and colorful horse-opera that has gone thundering past this way since *Stagecoach*." The critic went on to say that "the most pleasant surprise of the picture is the solid performance of John Wayne as the marshal. . . . Given a character to build, he does it with vigor, cool confidence, and a casual wit."

Republic's hierarchy felt vindicated. "If they want Westerns made," film distributor Maurice Goldstein said, "they ought to let Republic do it." Yates, aware that John Wayne was becoming a major box-office draw, decided to expand in the direction of bigger-budget features. Duke continued to view Yates with a jaundiced eye, even though the two got along well enough personally. "Herb wasn't cheap," said Wayne, "he just didn't understand things. He had no taste."

Three Faces West (also 1940), Republic's next assignment for Wayne, cost over $100,000 and had a superior script, at least in the opening scenes, by a team of top screenwriters. Among them were F. Hugh Herbert and Samuel Ornitz, the latter eventually one of the Hollywood Ten called to Washington to testify before the House Un-American Activities Committee. *Three Faces West* begins as an honest story about a group of Dust Bowl farmers who migrate to Oregon during the Great Depression, but the film becomes melodramatic and stilted before the final reel. Its cast included the distinguished character actor Charles Coburn and Norwegian actress Sigrid Gurie. Gurie was a sultry, aggressive woman, whom Duke found irresistible. The two enjoyed a brief flirtation, although Duke was not, by Hollywood standards, promiscuous.

Life with Josephine had not improved, and the couple resigned themselves to a marriage in name only. After the success of *Stagecoach,* the Waynes bought a Spanish-style house on Highland Avenue, but Duke rarely slept there. He either stayed with friends, at the Knickerbocker Hotel, or at the Hollywood Athletic Club and went his own way. Despite the couple's growing disaffection, their fourth child, Melinda, was born in December 1940. Nonetheless, Duke felt free to see other women, even though guilt always accompanied his extramarital liaisons.

Most of Wayne's leisure hours were spent drinking, playing cards, or boating with John Ford and Ford's circle of macho friends. Maureen O'Hara first knew Duke from parties at the director's house. "I always had to sing," the actress said, "whether I liked it or not. And Duke had to sing, which he could do. But Ford wanted him to sing 'Mary' to his wife, Mary Ford, off-key, and Duke would do it. Everybody would scream with laughter and fall on the floor."

One night Wayne had had a great deal to drink, and Ford insisted that O'Hara drive his rambunctious friend home. The young actress protested that she wasn't sure she could handle Duke in his condition, but Ford insisted that she could. So the two drove off together. Somewhere en route Duke ordered her to stop the car. "I need a drink," he announced and started up a walk to a home of total strangers. When the homeowners opened the door, Wayne signaled for O'Hara to join him. The surprised hosts offered Duke the drink he asked for, and the four of them sat and talked a while. Then Duke and O'Hara got back in the car and left. At Lakeside Country Club he ordered her to stop again. Inside Wayne ran into some friends and began talking to them, at which point O'Hara decided to leave Duke in their care.

Ford arranged to borrow Wayne for another film produced by Walter Wanger, an important picture called *The Long Voyage Home* (again 1940), based on four one-act plays by Eugene O'Neill. Duke played a Swede, Ole Olsen, an innocent youth not obsessed with destruction and death, as the script's other characters are. A dark, expressionistic film about a crew of seamen in search of inner peace, *The Long Voyage Home* is a major departure for Wayne. His Ole stands as a ray of optimism in an otherwise bleak drama. The sailors aboard the freighter hope to redeem themselves by getting Ole off the ship and home to his farm before he becomes as contaminated as they are.

Duke accepted the challenge at Ford's urging. Danish actress Osa Massen, under contract to Wanger, coached Wayne in his Swedish accent. The two spent several hours a day together for weeks going over lines, until Duke's accent became convincing. "The night before I went to work for the first day's shooting on that picture," Wayne said, "I worked until probably midnight on a picture that we'd made in six days for Republic." In *The Long Voyage Home*, he recalled, "I had to play a straight part as a Swede, and my accent couldn't clash with John Qualen's, who was playing a comic Swede. I wanna tell you, that was quite a switch from the night before, [when I was] knocking people around and jumping on a horse."

But Duke gave a commendable performance in the film inspired by O'Neill's plays, one of the few times he did not play John Wayne. He felt he really acted in the picture and proudly listed Ole among his favorite roles. The picture's cast was a powerhouse that included Thomas Mitchell, Barry Fitzgerald, Mildred Natwick, John Qualen, Arthur Shields, and Ward Bond. "I thought John Wayne was awfully good in *The Long Voyage Home*," said Natwick, a Broadway actress who played a prostitute in the movie. "I liked him terribly much; he was helpful and good and easy to work with."

Duke remembered *The Long Voyage Home* as a forceful picture, in part because of the photography achieved by Gregg Toland, a quiet, patient man who earned high admiration from his peers. "Gregg was probably the best cameraman in the world when it came to composition," said Wayne. "He was very helpful to Pappy Ford and Pappy was helpful to him. Between the two of them, they got about as beautiful a photographed picture as I've ever seen."

Dudley Nichols wrote the script, which won universal acclaim from film critics and praise from Eugene O'Neill. "Gene and I love the job you did," Carlotta Monterey, O'Neill's wife, wrote Ford. "The casting was marvelous and the photography very fine. We were deeply moved and proud that *you* had directed it." Wanger's staff feared that the film might be too highbrow for general audiences, but the preview in October 1940 went well. "I don't believe I have ever read so many good things about one picture as I have about *Long Voyage*," Wanger's secretary wrote her boss. "Newspaper people seem to go out of their way to drag it in and heap praise." When the movie opened in New York, Bosley Crowther judged it "one of the most honest pictures ever placed upon the screen."

John Wayne's Ole Olsen, gentle yet powerful, came as a surprise to many. Guided by Ford, Wayne played a character of psychological dimension, far from his normal screen personality. Impressed by Duke's portrayals in *Stagecoach* and *The Long Voyage Home*, film editor Robert Parrish asked Ford how he managed to draw such superb performances from Wayne when other directors could not. "Count the times Wayne talks," Ford replied. "That's the answer. Don't let him talk unless you have something that needs to be said."

The Long Voyage Home was hailed as one of the best films released in 1940. Critical success though it was, the picture disappointed at the box office and was ignored by Duke's rural fans. As an actor, he needed to broaden his appeal, and he felt he would benefit from a popular success that cast him as a romantic lead opposite an established femme fatale. Universal offered Wayne the right opportunity by pairing him with Marlene Dietrich in *Seven Sinners* (still 1940), a robust tale with passion and plenty of excitement. Dietrich had just scored a spectacular comeback in *Destry Rides Again* (1939), which reclaimed her standing as a Hollywood superstar. *Seven Sinners* was conceived as a vehicle for her along the lines established by *Morocco* (1930), with the actress again surrendering to the man she loved. The mood tends to be light in *Seven Sinners*, but Dietrich plays a shady lady skilled at handling her admirers. Duke, as an American naval officer, appears embarrassed in the clutches of such a seductive star.

Behind the scenes he apparently behaved more adeptly. Dietrich had spotted Wayne in the Universal commissary one noon and thought him attractive. After Duke had signed as her leading man, a meeting was arranged with him in her dressing room. Wayne claimed that Dietrich invited him inside, closed the door, and locked it, while he stood gaping at the lavish decor. "I wonder what time it is?" she said, and before Duke could check his watch, the star lifted her skirt, revealing a black garter on her upper thigh with a timepiece attached. Dietrich looked at it, dropped her skirt, and sashayed over to Wayne. "It's very early, darling," she said in her husky voice. "We have plenty of time." Duke later told Pilar that he did "what any other red-blooded American male would have done under the circumstances."

For a time Dietrich and Wayne were intimate and appeared together at the Mocambo, the Trocadero, and other Hollywood night spots, all of which was good publicity for Duke. Dietrich attended football games and prizefights with him, and they spent weekends together hunting and fishing. She brought him home-cooked meals on the set, and they played chess while the crew prepared the next scene. She introduced Wayne to her business manager, Bo Roos, whom Duke hired to take charge of his finances. Dietrich pressured Roos, who in turn pressured Duke's agent, Charles Feldman, to renegotiate Wayne's contract with Republic. Eventually Herbert Yates agreed to give Wayne a percentage of the profits on the pictures he made for the studio.

Duke later described Dietrich as "the most intriguing woman I've ever known." His friends were divided in their reaction to their relationship.

Some maintained that it was purely sexual; others claimed that Duke would have married Marlene had he been free. "She was great," Wayne said of Dietrich in later years, "just a German hausfrau."

The exotic star herself evidently found the affair disappointing, for she remembered Duke as an "ungifted amateur," both on-screen and off. "Wayne was not a bright or exciting type," she wrote in her memoirs. "Unknown, penniless, he begged me to help him. . . . I can't really say he was my 'partner,' since his performance was kept within very strict bounds—he spoke his lines and that was all. I helped as best I could."

Yet Dietrich showered Duke with affection during the filming of *Seven Sinners*. While he responded, Wayne was, after all, a married man and couldn't devote himself to her exclusively. Not used to reticence, Dietrich later enjoyed telling stories about his inadequacies. "John Wayne must have made Dietrich really mad about something to get her that riled," the German star's daughter, Maria Riva, declared.

Pilar Wayne said that she never learned from Duke why his affair with Dietrich ended; she only knew that he liked Marlene enormously. In London, many years later, Wayne and Maria Riva dined together with mutual friends. Maria eventually asked Duke how he managed to break away from her mother's spell. Wayne laughed, took a slug from his drink, and grunted, "Never liked being part of a stable—never did!"

Seven Sinners, although nowhere near the quality of *Destry Rides Again*, became a box-office hit and earned a great deal of money for Universal. Wayne's acting had come a long way; he seems relaxed and natural in this film, except in the scenes where Dietrich presses him too hard. Director Tay Garnett remembered *Seven Sinners* as "a fun picture" to make, even though he had to ask producer Joseph Pasternak for two extra days to stage a brawl in the cafe where Dietrich sings. "That was the best fight ever made in a picture," Pasternak said. "I walked over to the set when they were shooting it. I remember that the stars [Wayne, Broderick Crawford, and Oscar Homolka] did their own stunts."

The production ran over budget, finished six days behind schedule, and cost $760,000. Universal previewed *Seven Sinners* at the Pantages Theater in Hollywood and held its world premiere on October 31, 1940, at the Orpheum Theater in New Orleans. Dietrich raved to the press about the marvelous time she had had making the movie. "I don't believe any future picture will ever mean to me what that one did," she told reporters.

While John Wayne was billed below the title, he was emerging as one of Hollywood's most sought after leading men. Duke's association with Marlene Dietrich did much to enhance his reputation, and they soon made two more pictures together.

Shooting on *Seven Sinners* finished late on a Saturday night, and Duke reported to Paramount the following Monday to begin work on *The Shepherd of the Hills* (released in 1941). Duke's affair with Dietrich had not run its course yet, and Marlene stayed at a hotel by the lake while Wayne was on location at Big Bear filming *The Shepherd of the Hills*, sometimes making it difficult for him to reach the set on time. "One morning Wayne was late coming to work," director Henry Hathaway remembered. "He was rushing in and hit a corner and turned over in his station wagon." Mainly Duke suffered embarrassment.

Based on Harold Bell Wright's best-selling novel of 1907, *The Shepherd of the Hills* was Wayne's first movie in Technicolor. Duke worked well with Henry Hathaway, a fine technician but so difficult on the set that cast members referred to the director as Howling Hank. "Wayne never was an actor," said Hathaway, who would guide Duke to an Academy Award for *True Grit* (1969). "And because he wasn't an actor, he had to do everything real. There wasn't anything in Duke that would allow him to pretend he was something. He couldn't be French, he couldn't have an accent, he couldn't be Olivier. Whatever the actor was called to do in the script, he *did* it. It wasn't a question of acting, it was a question of reality."

Wayne felt that *The Shepherd of the Hills*, the way Hathaway shot it, was "one of the finest pictures I've ever seen." But studio heads took over the editing of the film and ruined it. "They took all the suspense out of the picture by having me told that Harry Carey was my father," Wayne said. Duke was thrilled to be working with Carey, his screen idol, as well as actress Betty Field and a strong list of character players. But when the movie was released, critics found the story dated, too sentimental and sweet for contemporary tastes, and full of platitudes. Still, *The Shepherd of the Hills* was a big production from a major studio. It opened at the Paramount Theater in New York and served as another boost to Wayne's career.

Then came three routine assignments from Republic, all released in 1941. *A Man Betrayed* (also called *Wheel of Fortune*) paired Duke with actress Frances Dee, but the picture was more talk than action. Although Wayne gave a good performance, *A Man Betrayed* was a comedown from the movies he had just completed for Universal and Paramount. *Lady from Louisiana*, while full of clichés, was an expensive production—at least for Republic—and the studio wanted its money to show. Amid extravagant costumes and sumptuous delta mansions, Duke played a faultless hero dispatched to clean up political graft in the state's lottery, while Ona Munson (best remembered for her performance as Belle Watling in *Gone With the Wind*) was his love interest. *Lady for a Night* found Wayne cast opposite Joan Blondell and making an attempt at light comedy. While Duke liked playing comedy, *Lady for a Night* is a dreary, old-fashioned "woman's picture." None of the three movies for Republic gave Wayne much satisfaction and revived doubts about his capabilities as an actor. "I just can't act, that's all," he told reporters in June 1941. "I never learned and I never will." That belief was to haunt him throughout his career.

Lady for a Night was Wayne's last completed movie before the United States entered World War II. While he was rapidly ascending as king of the Republic lot and commanded more expensive pictures at the studio, Yates still considered him a cowboy star who could handle action and adventure yarns. Critics rarely took Wayne's casual performances seriously, unless he was directed by John Ford. Yet by 1941, on the eve of the bombing of Pearl Harbor, the John Wayne persona was in place, lightweight to be sure, but polished and amply publicized when he worked for major studios. All Duke needed was the proper climate, and a sustained sequence of hits, for his image to crystallize into legend.

Fighting the War on Film

World War II gave John Wayne the chance he needed to become a superstar. With Charles Feldman as his agent and Bo Roos his business manager, the mechanism for an important Hollywood career was in place. While Wayne's contract with Republic did not carry the prestige that Clark Gable enjoyed at Metro-Goldwyn-Mayer or Errol Flynn had at Warner Bros., Duke's films for the smaller studio provided him with continuity and a broad exposure. By 1942 Herbert Yates had under contract an expanded circle of actors, directors, producers, and technicians, but he agreed to pay Wayne 10 percent of the gross on movies Duke made for him, an almost unprecedented arrangement at that time. But Wayne was also free to work for better studios. During the war Duke would make expensive pictures at Paramount, Universal, RKO, and MGM, as many as five films in a single year.

Imbued with the work ethic, Wayne approached acting as a tradesman. If he had marked time during his apprentice years, he was ready to soar during the years his country was at war. Not only had he mastered the fundamentals of naturalistic acting, he understood what was involved in filming action and knew about lights, props, camera, and editing. Wayne possessed unfailing instincts for performing effectively without calling attention to technique. That plus an enchanting persona would remain his overriding strengths. His fans could identify with the image he projected; he seemed one of them—just an ordinary guy who did extraordinary deeds while speaking the commoner's language.

"I'm lucky to have survived the dozens of B pictures I made," said Duke. "They killed off many fine actors." But in Wayne's case, they taught him the trade. Never the well-read man that John Ford was, Duke demonstrated intelligence and a keen ability at analyzing screenplays and understanding the relationship of characters. When director Cecil B. De-Mille sent him a draft of *Reap the Wild Wind* in April 1941, Duke read the script between midnight and dawn and dictated his reaction to it before leaving on a trip the next morning. "I was disappointed in the lack of color and character in Jack Martin," Wayne said of the character DeMille had in mind for him. "However, I recalled the picture of Martin that Mr. DeMille painted for us in his office, so I disregarded the play of the character as painted by the writers. . . . At the entrance of Steve into the story Jack becomes negative in all scenes that include the three principals. I think there is a possibility of developing him into a great character without distracting from Steve or Loxi and will add color to the script as a whole and will make Loxi's part more believable. This can be done simply by making him an individualist played boldly and impulsively instead of being played as a plodding dullard."

Wayne by then clearly had insight into his profession and showed little hesitation in speaking his mind, even to a giant the size of C. B. DeMille. "Steve is the suave, eloquent, and mental type written with care," Duke advised the director. "Jack should be brusque and sure of himself in all physical situations because of the station of life that he has reached at a youthful age. He doesn't need to be a mental giant—maybe a little short on logic, but must not be dull—must possess a definite sense of humor to help him through two or three melodramatic situations that arise." Far from a Poverty Row hack, Wayne had developed a sense of what made his screen characters work and had sufficient assurance to state his case with confidence.

Reap the Wild Wind, a $2 million Technicolor opus, would be Paramount's biggest picture of 1941. A DeMille unit began shooting in Charleston, South Carolina, during late April, and the picture remained in production for four months. Wayne worked on the film for eleven weeks, earning $25,000 for his services. His leading lady, Paulette Goddard, received $35,000 for the role of Loxi, while Ray Milland played Steve and Susan Hayward played Goddard's cousin, who dies at sea. Duke was aware that Paramount would tend to favor Milland, a contract player at the studio, and feared that he might wind up with a supporting role. "The only reason you're calling me over here is to make Ray Milland look like a man," Wayne told DeMille. The director asked Duke to trust him, telling him that he had considered Errol Flynn, Fred MacMurray, and George Brent for Wayne's part but had decided on Duke after seeing *Dark Command*.

Set in 1840, when America's lifeline was the sea, *Reap the Wild Wind* focuses on sailing vessels lured to reefs off the Florida Keys so that their cargoes can be plundered. "DeMille practically took over the city of

Charleston," screenwriter Charles Bennett remembered. "The street lamps were all pulled down while he was shooting, so that the streets would look genuine, which they did. DeMille was thorough." The studio's research department checked every minute detail related to the picture: dress, schooners, sea slang, storms, specific locations of slave dances, even when the first patent on matches was issued in the United States.

DeMille could be dictatorial and rough with actors. "I heard him take Paulette Goddard apart," supporting player Milburn Stone recalled. "He said things to her that I just could not believe." Duke resented DeMille's treatment of Goddard and the director's tendency to yell at performers, most of whom cowered in his presence. But the veteran director liked Wayne, invited him to sit at his table during lunch, and enjoyed Duke's company. He not only protected Wayne, he treated him with deference and respect.

Wayne's performance in *Reap the Wild Wind* is excellent and did much to establish the actor's appeal with urban audiences. Duke was grateful for the opportunity to work in a picture of such prominence and with such a distinguished cast. "My appearance in *Reap the Wild Wind* was the highlight of my career," he wrote DeMille after the movie was released in March 1942.

When the studio tested *Reap the Wild Wind* at the Paramount Theater in Hollywood, many of the preview cards stated that John Wayne had given the strongest performance. The picture premiered in Charleston in a manner reminiscent of the gala MGM had arranged for *Gone With the Wind* in Atlanta two years earlier. The DeMille epic opened in New York City as the Easter show at Radio City Music Hall. While Wayne was said to make a rugged shipmaster, critics dismissed the story as just another bold adventure tale. Still, with the nation at war, quintessential make-believe was in demand, and *Reap the Wild Wind* filled the need masterfully.

The movie's most memorable sequence has Wayne and Milland fighting a giant squid at the bottom of the sea. Dozens of letters from sailors, biology classes, and curious housewives poured into DeMille's office after the picture was released, requesting information on the squid and on how those scenes were filmed. Since romance was central to Hollywood's output, a battery of publicists worked overtime to sustain the image of glamour and fantasy. "It is the policy of the studio," Paramount's minions responded to inquiries about the giant squid, "to release no information on technical details of any motion picture because it would detract from the dramatic illusion."

In actuality, *Reap the Wild Wind*'s squid was born out of necessity. Neither DeMille nor his writers could devise a satisfactory ending for the movie. They explored a number of ideas in story conferences, all of which DeMille rejected. Charles Bennett, who wrote the script with Alan LeMay and Jesse Lasky, Jr., remembered leaving the studio one evening after an exhausting session, baffled by how to meet DeMille's demands for an exciting climax.

The next morning Bennett was taking a bath when all of a sudden he thought, "Giant squid!" At a story conference with DeMille and his colleagues later that morning, Bennett broke in with his idea: "Giant squid," he blurted and then proceeded to act out what he had conceived in the bathtub. "I was John Wayne, I was Ray Milland, I was the squid," Bennett remembered. "I acted the whole scene out in front of DeMille." When the writer finished, the great filmmaker leaned back in his chair with an ecstatic look. "Yes, Charles," said DeMile. "In Technicolor."

The sequence with the squid took about ten days to shoot and cost a quarter of a million dollars. It was staged in a huge tank at Paramount studios. "The tank was almost the size of a football field and about twenty-five feet deep at the deepest part," Ray Milland recalled. "Down there they had built a marine wonderland: the hull of a wrecked ship, strange and jagged rocks, a slowly moving aqueous forest. And caves, dark and frightening." The squid itself was the creation of the Paramount property department. "It was truly a marvelous piece of work," said DeMille, "with its heavy red tentacles fourteen feet long weaving realistically and menacingly through the water to grip and crush John Wayne, until Ray Milland drove a cargo hook between the monster's malevolent eyes."

The director had used scenic effects brilliantly and had built his tempo to a thrilling climax. *Reap the Wild Wind* had mystery and drama, power and romance, but above all it was entertainment in the grand escapist tradition. The picture was Wayne's most expensive film since *The Big Trail* and proved that Duke could hold his own with an ensemble from the big leagues.

The shadow of war had fallen across America even before the Japanese bombed Pearl Harbor, and Hollywood felt its effects. "In casting young men for *Reap the Wild Wind* for sailors, etc.," a Paramount interoffice memorandum of April 24, 1941, stated, "it would be wise to determine their status on being called in the draft." John Wayne was still draft age at the outset of World War II, but he had a wife and four children to support and therefore was exempt from serving in the armed forces. Despite his macho image Duke was also not in the best physical condition. He suffered a chronic inner-ear problem from working underwater in *Reap the Wild Wind* and had the old shoulder injury and a bad back from years of fight scenes and horse falls. When he tried to enlist in the military shortly after the United States declared war, he was rejected.

Wayne had valid excuses for staying out of the war, but his exempt status troubled him, particularly when so many of Hollywood's leading men either volunteered for the service or were drafted. Initially he appeased his conscience by serving as an air-raid warden in Los Angeles, alongside his friend Ward Bond and some of the over-age cowboys he had worked with in films. "How does Uncle Ward look with a tin hat and a pair of binoculars?" John Ford wrote Duke from Washington, D.C., in January 1942.

Ford by then was serving in a special Field Photographic Unit attached to the Office of Strategic Services; the unit included a number of Duke's friends. Yakima Canutt had offered his services to Ford in October 1941: "If you decide to put a running W on either Hitler or Mussolini or some of the Japs," Canutt wrote, "I will do the job for a very reasonable adjustment." Seven months later Wayne made an effort to join Ford's unit. "Have you any suggestions on how I should get in?" he wrote Ford. "Can I get assigned to your outfit, and if I could, would you want me? How about the Marines? You have Army and Navy men under you. Have you any Marines or how about a Seabee or what would you suggest or would you? No, I'm not drunk. I just hate to ask favors, but for Christ sake you can suggest, can't you? . . . No kidding, coach, who'll I see?"

How serious Duke was about joining the service is another matter. Ford did not follow up on his request, and others encouraged Wayne to stay in Hollywood and serve the war effort by making morale-boosting pictures. Yet he found it embarrassing not to be in uniform, and not fighting in the war left Duke with permanent guilt. On film he soon became the embodiment of the warrior ideal, yet he himself had avoided the definitive male experience of his generation. The dilemma posed lasting problems for him and probably explains much of his superpatriotism and later hawkish attitudes.

But in 1942 Duke knew that his moment in Hollywood had come. With so many of the industry's established male stars in the military, Wayne became one of the few screen heroes available to filmmakers. The time to solidify his career was ripe. After a decade of thankless toil in Poverty Row programmers, he suddenly had a choice of major productions. If he had gone into the service, he might have been too old later to take advantage of the opportunities thrust upon him by the war. In 1942 Duke was in demand, and the action movies popular during the war were what he did best. "It must have weighed heavily on him which way to go," said John Ford's grandson Dan. "But here was his chance and he knew it. He was an action leading man, and there were a lot of roles for him to play. There was a lot of work in A movies, and this was a guy who had made eighty B movies. He had finally moved up to the first rank. He was in the right spot at the right time with the right qualities and willing to work hard. Would I have done any different? The answer is hell no."

Six movies starring John Wayne were released in 1942. After *Reap the Wild Wind* came *The Spoilers*, which again cast Duke opposite Marlene Dietrich. Set in the Klondike gold rush, *The Spoilers* was shot around Lake Arrowhead and featured Randolph Scott, Margaret Lindsay, and Harry Carey. Wayne and Scott tore up the set in a brawl of he-man proportions, and the bedlam pleased critics and audiences alike. One reviewer called the fight "a minor masterpiece of stunt action." Dietrich found Wayne more sure of himself than he had been when they teamed for *Seven Sinners*, although she later remarked that he was less concerned with the quality of his acting than Randolph Scott was. Duke's growing fame, Dietrich contended, "had not increased his talent."

Her affair with Duke had not yet burned itself out, and the two were seen together frequently. Wayne spent evenings at Dietrich's house, confiding his marital problems to the sympathetic actress. He was restless and bored with Josephine and spent as little time at home as possible. He confessed to Marlene that his sex life with Josie was minimal. "Four times in ten years," Duke snorted, explaining his four children. Dietrich had introduced him to more erotic sex; she made him feel like a man in bed and admired him physically. Although the dignified Josephine seemed cold by comparison, Duke continued to praise his wife as "a wonderful, religious woman" and an ideal mother. "She's responsible, in breeding and behavior, for what [our children] turned out to be," he said.

About the time *The Spoilers* appeared in the theaters, Wayne moved out of the house at 312 north Highland Avenue and announced that he and Josephine had separated. "I didn't really ever do anything wrong," he told reporters, "except stay away from home too long maybe. I was working so damn hard, and I thought I was doing the right thing then. Jo and I just drifted apart." Josephine still wouldn't speak of divorce, which put Duke under great stress. He missed his children, felt guilty about not being available for them, and grew despondent. "The part of Duke's personality that was like his father rejoiced in his new freedom," Pilar Wayne wrote, "the part that was like his mother punished him with remorse."

"I think he was under a lot of tension," Duke's friend Budd Boetticher said. "When he separated from the mother of his kids, it really hurt him. I think it nearly killed him." Yet every studio in Hollywood was scratching at his door, waving contracts. Despite the pain of his personal life, Wayne had become an authentic star. His handprints were soon placed in cement in the courtyard of Grauman's Chinese Theater, and fan magazines covered his every move. What he had spent his entire adult life working toward suddenly was his.

Professionally the thorn in his side was the contract with Republic. Detrimental though it was, Wayne was locked into his agreement with Herbert Yates and could not get free. But Duke took his work at the studio seriously, even when he hated the picture he was making. He had become Republic's biggest attraction, which meant that he was awarded preferential treatment and to some extent could dictate terms.

Shortly after the war began, Wayne reported to Republic to film *In Old California*, a high-budget production for the company, although the story was routine horse opera. Duke played a pharmacist in the picture, a role he patterned after his father, but audiences objected to such a subdued hero. Photographed upstate near Kernville, *In Old California* benefited from a supporting cast headed by Binnie Barnes, Albert Dekker, and Patsy Kelly, while its director was William McGann. Duke recognized that the movie added up to fairly dreary entertainment, even though the studio had spent generous sums on costumes for him and his leading lady.

Yates next assigned him to *Flying Tigers*, Duke's first war movie. If he could not take part in the action overseas, he could placate his conscience by making patriotic pictures that teemed with fighting men, propaganda, and unabashed flag waving. *Flying Tigers* was Republic's tribute to the

American flyers who had volunteered to fight for the Chinese against the assault from Japan. The movie was full of aerial acrobatics and exciting dogfights but proved more an adventure film than an accurate record of the famous American airmen.

Wayne played a serious, loftily motivated squadron leader in *Flying Tigers*, tough as nails yet a force who inspired confidence in his men. "I'd always been madly in love with John Wayne," said Anna Lee, Duke's romantic interest in the picture. "I first saw him in *Stagecoach* in England when I was very young, and the idea of playing opposite him was just lovely. But he was a man's man, he wasn't a woman's man, and I certainly wasn't his type. He liked dark, Latin women." The blonde actress remembered Duke's asking her, "Are you a Republican?" while they were dancing together in a scene. Lee, freshly arrived from England, didn't know what a Republican was and thought he had said "publican," which in Great Britain refers to the operator of a pub. "No," Anna Lee replied, "but I'm very fond of beer." Duke laughed uproariously, and they became friends. Later they worked together as members of the John Ford stock company.

Flying Tigers opened at theaters in September 1942 and fared well at the box office. John Wayne's image proved an effective boost to American morale, and he looked good in uniform. With Duke's celebrity in bloom Metro-Goldwyn-Mayer, Hollywood's top studio, signed him for *Reunion in France* (still 1942), a Joan Crawford vehicle with a wartime theme. Studio executives hoped that pairing Crawford with a virile romantic partner might rejuvenate the star's fading reputation, but the effort failed.

Although *Reunion in France* is Crawford's picture, Wayne plays a wounded American flyer in the Royal Air Force who parachutes into France during the Nazi occupation to work with the French underground. His is a thankless role, and the plot is shallow melodrama. Crawford, elegantly gowned by MGM's Irene, is cast as a wealthy, spoiled American living in Paris, who discovers compassion after the defeat of France. Critics found Duke unconvincing as Crawford's love interest and objected to the film's glib attitude toward serious matters.

When *Reunion in France* was shipped to Argentina for exhibition, film editors in that country, where sympathy for the Nazi cause ran strong, worked it over with a heavy hand. In one scene in the original version, a German officer enters a room and asks Wayne who he is. The American explains that he is in France fighting for the British, whereupon the German spits at him. Wayne then strikes a blow to the officer's chin, knocks him unconscious, and escapes. In the Argentinian version, the German's spitting was eliminated: the officer comes in and merely looks at Wayne, whereupon the American knocks him unconscious. It cast Wayne in a less-than-heroic light, and MGM pulled the movie, refusing to allow the picture to be shown in Argentina.

Duke later maintained that Joan Crawford became infatuated with him during the making of *Reunion in France* but claimed that he had not responded to her overtures. Crawford often trifled with her leading men, although Duke said that in this case her fixation on him lasted several years. Crawford was entirely too aggressive a woman to suit Wayne's tastes.

Wayne's third picture with Marlene Dietrich was a lusty yarn called *Pittsburgh*, again made at Universal. The picture reflected current attitudes on businesses flooded with war orders. Duke plays a selfish coal mine operator who changes his attitude after Pearl Harbor is bombed. Randolph Scott is also in the film, and he and Wayne throw punches at each other in a brawl meant to duplicate their fight in *The Spoilers*. This time audiences were disappointed with such routine entertainment; critics called *Pittsburgh* synthetic and labeled its message glossy propaganda.

Paul Fix played a part in the movie and continued to coach Duke in his acting. Since directors resented outside tutoring on the set, Fix and Wayne devised a set of signals. "Duke had a wonderful natural expression where he'd furrow his brow," Fix said. "It was very effective on the screen, but he tended to work it to death." Fix would indicate when Wayne was going overboard, and he continued to urge Duke to get experience in local stage productions.

Except at Republic, studio executives were not certain that Wayne could carry a picture by himself. Major producers wisely cast him opposite established stars the caliber of Dietrich, Crawford, and Goddard, aware that the actresses' fans would see their movies and that would give Wayne a lift. In 1943 RKO paired Duke with Jean Arthur in *A Lady Takes a Chance*, produced by Arthur's husband, Frank Ross. Wayne plays a cowpuncher in the film, originally entitled *The Cowboy and the Girl*. Arthur had developed into one of Hollywood's most delightful comediennes, and while Duke makes a sturdy accessory, the movie belongs to her. *A Lady Takes a Chance* provided wartime audiences with welcome fun, and

Robert Ardrey's script proved bright enough to make an old formula seem almost new.

Then it was back to Republic for Duke and another routine Western. This one was originally called *In Old Oklahoma* (1943), part of a series produced by that studio, but in 1950 the picture was reissued as *War of the Wildcats*. Republic hired Yakima Canutt to devise stunts for the movie and oversee filming the action. Canutt went to Kanab, Utah, with a crew three weeks before the rest of the company arrived. He bought wagons from local farmers, and Hollywood craftsmen built twenty-five horse-drawn oil tanks to be used in the picture.

In Old Oklahoma has a strong supporting cast, which includes Martha Scott, Albert Dekker, George "Gabby" Hayes, Marjorie Rambeau, Dale Evans, Grant Withers, Sidney Blackmer, and Paul Fix. Martha Scott, recently of the New York stage, remembered how uncomfortably hot it was in Utah, which made work particularly miserable for her since she wore velvet costumes in the picture. To relieve their discomfort, she and Duke played double solitaire in her trailer. During the games they got playfully angry at one another and spent a lot of time laughing. "John Wayne was so helpful," said Scott, "he did his best to lessen my anguish."

Most of the movie was shot on an isolated location in Utah. "It's fifty miles of dust from Kanab," Wayne wrote John Ford. To make matters worse, the production ran a week over schedule—"for the first time in the history of Republic," Duke claimed. The delay posed problems since Wayne was scheduled to begin *The Fighting Seabees* immediately upon finishing the assignment in Utah.

Although *In Old Oklahoma* was a Western cut along familiar lines, Republic gave it expensive trappings. "The producers have blown the budget on some fancy sets loaded with all the gewgaws the prop department could find," the *New York Times* reported, "and in the finale they have turned out a really bang-up climax, with dozens of oil-laden wagons racing toward the refineries despite brush fires and all the other dastardly obstacles the villain has put in their path." Wayne, the reviewer said, "is as convincing as a knockout punch."

When not working on a movie, Duke devoted most of his time to drinking and carousing with friends. While imbibing he could be coarse and belligerent, and his temper could erupt violently. According to Selden West, Spencer Tracy's authorized biographer, John Wayne is the only actor

Tracy ever spoke unkindly about. "I think it might be traced to a double date," said West, "in which Spencer was so loaded and pugnacious that Wayne removed him from the affair, bought him a hotel room, and tried to put him to bed." When Tracy, drunk and mad, tried to object, Duke hauled off and knocked him out.

Wayne and Ward Bond spent many evenings and weekends together, during which they engaged in their share of horseplay and badgering. "Tales of Wayne's hard drinking, frequent party brawls, and ultra right-wing political views seemed to enhance his image among his followers," said actress Marsha Hunt. "They often blended the man and his roles into a mix impossible to separate." Duke did seem to believe that an occasional fracas was part of manhood, and the crowd he ran with did little to dispel such notions.

Occasionally during the war Duke and Bond dropped by John Ford's house to visit the director's wife. Wayne visited his children regularly and from time to time socialized with Josephine, despite their estrangement. To celebrate Henry Fonda's birthday in May 1943, Fonda's wife, Frances, gave a party while her husband was home on leave from the navy. "I went with Duke and Josie," Mary Ford wrote her husband. "The usual gang was there and the usual line of chatter." Duke also wrote Ford about the gathering at Fonda's house: "Toward the wee hours we arose and in full voice sang the Ford stock company anthem . . . and there wasn't a dry glass in the house."

Wayne was never a fixture in the Hollywood social whirl; he tended to be somewhat of a loner, except for his immediate crowd. Duke still enjoyed mixing with the wranglers and stuntmen who had mentored him and was delighted to be accepted into their ranks. If one of the cowboys was broke, he could always count on Duke Wayne for a few hundred dollars with no strings attached. "Everybody said of him that he was the easiest touch in Hollywood if you needed cash," Native American actor Iron Eyes Cody wrote. "He was without a doubt the most generous man I ever knew."

Male bonding still seemed more important to Duke than relationships with women; he appeared almost preadolescent in that respect. Like the cowboys he had met at Monogram and Mascot, he tended to view women with suspicion, while engaging in excessive displays of machismo. Wayne's penchant for Hispanic women remained unswerving. He was attracted to them physically, but he also liked their sweetness and what seemed to be a pacificity and submission to their men. "I don't think Wayne was ever a womanizer," director Budd Boetticher said. "I think he was a one-woman man." After he and Josie separated, Duke enjoyed an occasional dalliance, but he made rare appearances on the Hollywood nightclub circuit, even though he was an excellent ballroom dancer. Not only did Duke not relish bad publicity, he simply preferred relaxing with his own crowd in private.

At least that was his pattern until he met Chata. Wayne first encountered Esperanza Bauer, nicknamed Chata, in Mexico a few months before the United States entered World War II. He and some other clients of his business manager, Bo Roos, had flown to Mexico City to look into buying a motion picture studio there. Ward Bond was part of the group; so were actors Ray Milland and Fred MacMurray. Milland introduced Duke to Esperanza, who claimed to be an actress. "In fact, she was a high-class callgirl who'd had a bit part in a Mexican film," Pilar Wayne later maintained. "Milland was one of her clients."

Voluptuous and vivacious, Chata exuded sex appeal, in sharp contrast to the ladylike Josephine. For the somewhat repressed Duke, she seemed like an exciting liaison. The two became inseparable during Wayne's visit to Mexico, much to his friends' alarm. Milland cautioned Duke about Chata, but Wayne paid no attention. Others pointed out that she had been born in the slums of Mexico, had grown up in poverty, and had a background of dubious morals. But Duke was infatuated with her and turned a deaf ear to all warnings.

Esperanza claimed that she and Duke met in Mexico City at a luncheon given in his honor. "The very first time I saw John, I fell in love," she supposedly told a writer for *Screen Guide*. "I think it was his eyes, so full of expression, that first attracted me. Then it was his wonderful, honest smile, his personality, and his sense of humor that completely disarmed me." But this was fan magazine fabrication.

If Duke was unsophisticated in the ways of love, Chata was an expert. Fiery by nature, sensual and experienced, she demonstrated an eagerness to match his liquor consumption drink for drink. After marriage to the virtuous Josephine, Duke found Chata enticing. He enjoyed romping with her in bed and found her uninhibited and amusing. Esperanza had been married before, strangely enough to a young man named Eugene Morrison, a student in Mexico City. But Duke soon convinced himself that he was in love with Chata and that they had much in common. From the outset it was apparent that sex would be the crux of their relationship. Sally Blane, sister of Loretta Young and an actress Wayne had known at Mascot, remembered overhearing Duke tell a priest Josephine had summoned to their house in an effort to resolve their marital difficulties, "Father, you just don't know what it means to really *screw* a woman!"

Wayne returned from Mexico and spent most of 1942 pressuring Herbert Yates into giving Esperanza Bauer a screen test. Chata arrived in Hollywood shortly after Duke and Josie separated. Wayne was seen escorting her around town, and he occasionally took her by John Ford's house. Duke had been staying with Paul Fix and his wife, but when Chata arrived, the lovers moved into a penthouse apartment at the Chateau Marmont on Sunset Boulevard. Esperanza enjoyed shopping and partying, but the couple spent most of their evenings together drinking. When Chata drank, she became nasty and inclined to fight. Duke at first found their battles stimulating, but his friends recognized trouble ahead.

Pushed to the limit by Duke's open affair with Chata, Josephine Wayne appeared in the Superior Court of Los Angeles County on June 4, 1943, and asked for a legal separation, which the judge granted. Josephine was angry and mortally wounded by Duke's indiscretion, although she remained civil for the sake of their children. The Saenz family, however, proved less generous in their attitude. "Things don't seem to have improved in that direction," Duke wrote Ford early in August 1943. "Anyway I don't give a four letter word, [so long as] I can see my kids. . . . My warrior's fling before going to battle is working like Hell and staying sober to fool the local board of busy bodies."

With his private life bordering on scandal, Wayne began filming *The Fighting Seabees* for Republic in September. It was his second war movie, a salute to the construction battalion of the navy. Part of the film was shot at a camp near San Diego. Away from Chata, Duke spent evenings at the Carlsbad Inn with off-duty marines, singing verses of "Dirty Gertie from Bizerte," a war song recently imported from North Africa. From time to time a serviceman would try to pick a fight with Wayne, demanding to know why he wasn't in uniform. "Wayne would lose more fights than he won," director Edward Ludwig said, "and I had to forbid him going there if I expected to get him through the picture in one piece."

Ludwig himself stood only five feet five inches tall. On the first day of shooting *The Fighting Seabees*, Duke came up to him on the set, picked the director up by the collar, and said, "Okay, coach, what is it you want me to do in this picture?" Actress Adele Mara remembered Wayne's being casual and friendly during the making of the movie. "I wasn't in awe of John Wayne," said Mara, "because I didn't know too much about him. I didn't even know he was doing the lead. All I knew was that he was supposed to do some kind of a dance with me." Since Mara had originally been a dancer, she told him, "All you have to do is just hold me, and I'll do the dancing." Duke indicated that he understood, and at one point in their jitterbug, he adeptly moved her from one of his knees to the other. "I think he had fun doing it," said Mara, "and I enjoyed myself. In those days I had fun doing anything. I wasn't under contract to Republic; I just needed a job."

Susan Hayward played the female lead in the picture, while Dennis O'Keefe, Paul Fix, Grant Withers, and William Frawley (later Fred on the *I Love Lucy* television series) rounded out the supporting cast. *The Fighting Seabees* begins slowly, but the film eventually turns into an action-packed melodrama with plenty of bravura. "It's nice to see our side dispatching the Japs to their ancestors," the reviewer for the *New York Times* commented upon the movie's release, "even though the tactics seem to smack more of Rover Boy than Navy tradition." Wayne is killed in the movie, his second death on the screen—his character dies at the end of *Reap the Wild Wind* too—but he plays a sensible leader who learns to accept military discipline.

On October 30, 1943, Josephine Wayne sued her husband for divorce, charging him with extreme cruelty. Josie continued to live in their house in the fashionable Hancock Park section of Los Angeles, and Wayne's four children by her would grow up there amid the French furniture and antiques their mother had collected. Once the divorce was granted, Josephine devoted herself to her children and church events, having no intention of remarrying so long as Duke was alive. Along with actresses Loretta Young and Irene Dunne, Josephine Wayne emerged as a leading figure within Hollywood's Catholic enclave.

Outwardly Duke was relieved to be free of a marriage in which he felt so little understanding and acceptance; inside he was plagued by remorse and a sense of failure. "Duke told me he walked away from the marriage with his clothes, his car, and an overwhelming feeling of guilt he never completely put behind him," Pilar Wayne recalled. Mainly he regretted that he would not be present on a daily basis to watch his children grow up.

To compensate, he buried himself in work. Early in 1944 Duke reported to RKO for a rousing Western entitled *Tall in the Saddle*, written by his friend Paul Fix and produced by Robert Fellows, later Wayne's business partner. Duke is a woman-hating ranch foreman in the picture, but falls in love with a peppery cattle owner played by Ella Raines. He had used his influence to get the film produced, mainly as a courtesy to Fix, and insisted that the cast include his friend Ward Bond.

Raines remembered meeting Wayne, Bond, and Fix and having lunch with them at Lucey's, across the street from the RKO lot. The actress walked to the restaurant with Paul Fix; crossing the street, she heard Duke ask Bond, "Shall I use four-letter words?" Raines came to realize that her costar was prolific at swearing, although he didn't mean to be offensive. "We had lunch, and I liked them all so much," Raines said. "I adored Duke—big old lunk of a thing, never mind his four-letter words. They just seemed to be like black pearls cast on hay—you overlooked them." On the way back from Lucey's, the actress overheard Duke say to Bond, "I'll be goddamned if she doesn't even walk like Arly." Raines didn't know then what he meant; only later did she discover that Arly was to be her role in the picture.

Raines found *Tall in the Saddle* a difficult movie to make. "It was the first time where I felt I was not well liked by the director, Edwin Marin," she said. Also, the actress was costumed in an uncomfortable outfit— long, gray woolen trousers with chaps over them, a shirt, a gunbelt, a vest, and riding boots. "Everything was made for me," Raines said, "but it was difficult to maneuver in all of that. I went from 118 pounds down to 107 shooting the film. For me to go to the ladies room involved my stand-in and my wardrobe mistress. Then the director would be upset because I took so long."

Duke informed his costar that Marin was unhappy because he had wanted a girlfriend of his in the part of Arly. "I don't know how true that is," Raines said, "but I just grew to be enchanted with Duke. We would go over to his dressing room after work and have a drink. I would sit around with Ward Bond and Paul Fix and Duke and laugh about the events of the day. We'd talk about the next day and rewrite a few lines, then I'd go home."

Leaving the studio one evening the actress noticed two very large women waiting for her in a car. For the next two or three nights the women followed her convertible as she left the lot. "I started taking different routes so they wouldn't find out where I lived," said Raines. Finally she told Duke about the incidents. "Oh, my God," he said, "don't you know that they're lesbians?" Raines didn't know what he was talking about. "Imagine having gone to a big university, living in a dormitory, working in New York, and not knowing what a lesbian was!" she later exclaimed.

Duke told her to drive through the RKO gate slowly that evening; he and Ward Bond would be walking right behind her. Raines did as she was told. "I looked in the rear view mirror of my car," she said, "and I could see these two great big hulks lumbering toward the car with these two women in it. I saw Duke and Ward lean in through the window of their car as I drove away." The lesbians never waited for her again.

On location near Lake Sherwood, Wayne and Raines had a scene on horseback where they were to ride a few feet behind the camera . They had about two minutes of dialogue, and in order for the sound boom over their heads to pick up their words, they slowed to a canter and rode exactly the same speed as the camera truck. Ed Marin had them rehearse the scene, and everything went well. Then the director announced that they were ready for a take. Wayne and Raines got their horses up to speed, and the camera bell rang to signal that the operator had started rolling the film.

When the bell rang, Blackie, Ella Raines's horse, took off, dashing around the camera truck. "I was so embarrassed," the actress said. "I had gone out to the trainer's ranch and had ridden Blackie. We'd become good friends." Nevertheless, when the bell sounded, Raines lost control of the horse. Duke, by then a skilled rider, smiled at her as she rode back to his flank, and the crew prepared to do the scene again. "They had to back up all the camera gear," Raines recalled, "which was about three-quarters of a mile, scrape the road to wipe out the tire tracks, and get ready to start the scene over." When the camera bell sounded on the second attempt, the same thing happened; Blackie darted around the camera truck with Ella Raines struggling to bring him to a stop. "I thought I was going to die," the actress declared. "And Duke was getting a little bit irritated." As they prepared to try again, Wayne said to her, "I thought you told me you could ride."

On the third take it happened again. Duke got mad this time and really blew. "I'll ride that damn horse, and you take mine," he barked at his embarrassed costar. They exchanged horses, prepared to start over, and got their mounts up to speed. The bell rang, and Blackie off took around the camera truck with John Wayne astride. Duke was furious. As the crew gathered to determine what to do next, the horse's trainer arrived. "Oh, I meant to tell you," the trainer said, "Blackie is a former race horse." On the next take the bell was eliminated.

RKO released *Tall in the Saddle* in September 1944. Two months later, on November 29, Wayne's divorce became final. "Because of my religion," Josephine announced to the press, "I regard divorce as a purely civil action, in no way affecting the moral status of my marriage." She continued to regard herself as Mrs. John Wayne, and in her mind she was the only legal wife Duke ever had. That was what she taught her children, and Michael particularly had trouble accepting his father's later marriages and second family. Wayne never stopped sending money to Josie and always credited her with raising their children along the lines he respected. But he felt that his first family blamed him for the divorce and, because of their religious training, still considered him married to their mother.

In the divorce settlement Josephine received the house, a car, 25 percent of the first $100,000 Duke earned each year, plus 10 percent of the rest. While Wayne lived up to his financial obligations, loved his children, and devoted time to them, he regretted not being able to give them the support his father had shown him. Duke praised Josie as their four children matured with so few of the emotional traumas common among Hollywood children. He voiced pride in them as adults, yet the guilt of divorce and abandonment tormented him for the rest of his life.

In the months after the divorce, Duke continued to live with Esperanza Bauer. He was more visible on the Hollywood nightclub scene than at any other period of his life. Chata enjoyed the high life; she liked being seen and photographed. For a time Chata represented passionate lovemaking beyond anything Duke had experienced. He overcame much of his mother's insistence that sex was an expression of masculine lust and therefore depraved. But his abandon soon gave way to a sense of depletion, and his relationship with Chata grew stormy as the sexual thrills paled. They drank too much and usually ended up shouting at one another. Duke was emotionally at loose ends; he needed an anchor, and only his male cohorts seemed constant and lasting.

During the years that John Ford was in the navy, Wayne spent a great deal of time at Ford's home visiting with the director's wife, Mary. "I think Duke was particularly fond of my grandmother," Dan Ford said, "and looked upon her as a civilizing influence, almost as a parental figure." Wayne knew that Mary Ford was alone and he wanted to be supportive of her, but he also needed a stabilizing force in his own life. Duke's world at the time was spinning so fast that there were times when he felt out of control.

His work in pictures slowed down in 1944. In January, Wayne left on a three-month tour of the southwest Pacific, where he entertained troops for the USO. Lynn Cowan, who had a band that played at the Egyptian Theater in Hollywood and had operated a nightclub in Singapore before the war, traveled in the unit with Duke. "We have developed a show that the men like," Wayne wrote Charles Feldman, his agent, on January 26. "Someone should explain to our industry that these men deserve the best shows possible." Duke was moved by his reception overseas and felt that he was contributing to the war effort. "When you look out and up into a natural bowl that only recently was jungle and see 5,000 and 6,000 men sitting in the rain and mud, you wish you had the best show on earth," he wrote Feldman. "They are wonderful guys when the going gets tough. They get back to fundamentals out here. It's the greatest thrill and privilege anyone can ever have to see them yell and relax in front of a show."

Wayne said that he came to realize during his visit to the South Pacific that he could accomplish more by entertaining troops and boosting their morale than he would have had he joined the armed forces. "I was America to them," he said of the servicemen he met. "They'd taken their sweetheart to the Saturday matinee as teenagers and held hands through a John Wayne Western." Duke decided that he had done right by staying out of the military. "It was better that I go into the war zones on tour," he said.

Dan Ford later became convinced that his grandfather had been instrumental in sending Wayne to the South Pacific. John Ford's grandson contended that William Donovan, head of the OSS, wanted to learn more about Gen. Douglas MacArthur's objectives in the war and sent Wayne to Australia to find out what official channels could not. President Roosevelt was wary of MacArthur, and MacArthur in turn was suspicious of the OSS. But Duke always denied that he had been sent into the war zone as a spy, although he admitted that he had gotten to go places where others could not and did meet MacArthur in New Guinea. "I just made a report," said Wayne.

Duke returned from the South Pacific toward the end of March with his allegiance to conservative American beliefs intensified. Actor Thomas Mitchell had recently made a trip for the American Federation of Labor. "He seems to be a little befuddled as to the value of the capitalistic form of government that we have been experimenting with for the last 140 years," Wayne wrote Ford. That attitude would solidify over the years ahead, as Duke became more outspoken about the preservation of traditional American ideals.

Republic Pictures celebrated its tenth anniversary in 1945 by releasing a John Wayne feature called *Flame of the Barbary Coast*. Herbert Yates approved a budget for the film of $600,000, a huge sum for the studio, and secured Ann Dvorak, Joseph Schildkraut, Virginia Grey, Paul Fix, and Butterfly McQueen as supporting players. Joseph Kane directed a script by Borden Chase, which is set in San Francisco during the 1906 earthquake. Reviewers found the movie lavish, if a tale too often told. "John Wayne is perfectly cast," the *New York Times* declared. "That is, he gambles, fights, woos, and rides with consummate ease if not histrionic aplomb."

Duke had become sensitive to the snobbish attitude of critics and concluded that the eastern intellectual establishment was against him. He admitted that he had made more than his share of bad movies but knew that he had developed strengths as a performer. Wayne approached picture making as a business, one that should entertain and turn a profit. But he also believed in craftsmanship, which for an actor meant honesty in characterization and an ability to retain a level of emotion through a hard day's work, no matter how many interruptions might occur.

Back to Bataan (1945), another war movie, was next on Duke's agenda, part of a one-picture-a-year deal with RKO. Wayne plays a singled-minded guerrilla leader in the Philippines bent on winning the war. *Back to Bataan* proved a difficult project to finish, requiring 130 days to shoot. "We were rewriting every day to keep up with the news," director Edward Dmytryk said. "We were about two-thirds of the way through, when all of a sudden MacArthur returned to the Philippines. Every day prisoners were being released. I had the writer with me constantly; new pages of script were coming out every day. I hated to work that way."

Dmytryk and Wayne got along well together, despite the fact that the director, later one of the Hollywood Ten, was a Communist. Dmytryk thought Duke was "an amazing man," who "lived life with gusto" and proved "a good worker." The director remembered Wayne and Anthony Quinn's playing "Chinese poker" to kill time when the winter weather in California turned too damp for filming. On sunny days Wayne, Dmytryk, and some Filipino extras played kickball during lunch breaks, and the director recalled Duke's throwing his 245-pound body around "like a lightweight gymnast."

"I think Wayne knew through channels that I was a Communist," Dmytryk said later, "but I didn't know that he knew. We got along well during the shooting and even attended a number of the same affairs thrown by our mutual business manager." Duke claimed that Dmytryk was "the only guy that ever fooled me about politics." It wasn't until the director started talking about "the masses" that Wayne detected Dmytryk's leftist sympathies. "As soon as he started using that word," said Duke, "I knew he was a Commie." Wayne later claimed that Dmytryk and a group of "pro-Red" actors even sang the "Internationale" at lunchtime when they worked together.

Eastern critics dismissed *Back to Bataan* as heroic fiction cut from the "gun and glory" pattern. Bosley Crowther in the *New York Times* called the picture "a juvenile dramatization of significant history." But the film scored well at the box office and was a huge success in the Philippines.

As a special favor to Herbert Yates, Wayne agreed to star in *Dakota* (again 1945) opposite Yates's girlfriend, Vera Hruba Ralston, a Czechoslovakian ice-skater whom the producer was determined to make queen of the Republic lot. "I don't think John Wayne wanted to work in a picture with Vera," Adele Mara said, "and I don't blame him. She didn't really have a chance as an actress, because everybody thought she was a big laugh. She was no beauty, she had no figure, and she wasn't an actress." But Wayne was eager to produce his own movies, and working with Vera Ralston was one means of earning the right, since Yates had reason to be grateful. "Anytime Wayne did something with Vera," Mara said, "he got something out of it."

Dakota, based on a story by left-wing screenwriter Carl Foreman, was directed by Joseph Kane and aided by a supporting cast headed by Walter Brennan, Ward Bond, Ona Munson, Paul Fix, Grant Withers, and Mike Mazurki. The picture proved no more than an entertaining action drama but offered a spectacular prairie fire as a climax. Despite all the absurdities and claptrap, Westerns still remained popular with mass audiences.

In the waning months of World War II, John Ford took a leave from the navy to make *They Were Expendable* (still 1945) for MGM. Taken from William L. White's stirring best-seller, with a script by Ford's friend Frank "Spig" Wead, the picture focuses on a squadron of PT boats that held out against heroic odds during MacArthur's evacuation from the Philippines. The director selected John Wayne for the lead, and *They Were Expendable* became the actor's first outstanding war film. Duke was joined by a strong cast that included Donna Reed and Lt. Robert Montgomery, also on leave from the armed forces. The movie was shot around Key Biscayne, Florida, a location still undeveloped at that time. "It took us a week to get there," character actor Donald Curtis remembered. "We went by train from Hollywood to Chicago, then down to Florida."

"Duke was easygoing, but very serious about his acting," recalled Metro contract player Marshall Thompson, who played a young enlisted man in the picture. "He just worshipped Ford." Cast members on a John Ford picture learned early that the director was the boss; to offer creative suggestions or raise a question meant incurring Ford's wrath. The director reigned over his sets like a tyrant, sucking on a dirty handkerchief and wearing tinted glasses and an eye patch that he lifted to read. "He'd bully John Wayne and make a quivering pulp out of him," said Curtis. "Ford had an honest affection for Duke, but Wayne was scared to death of him."

After the company returned to the studio, Ford fell and broke his leg, and Robert Montgomery took over the direction of the picture for about a week. Montgomery detested Ward Bond, who played a part in the movie although he too had been in a recent accident. When Montgomery proved unnecessarily rough with Bond, Wayne became irritated. "Duke kept telling me how he wished Jack Ford was there," said Thompson. When Ford returned, he had a cast on his leg but barked louder than ever. The director had insisted on real glass in the windshields of the PT boats, and when an explosion shattered some of them, Ford flew into a rage. "You clumsy bastard!" he shouted at one of his crew members.

They Were Expendable opened in New York in December 1945, three months after the Japanese surrender had brought World War II to a close. By then audiences were tired of war stories, and the Ford film seemed like a postscript to the tensions of the past four years. Had the movie been released a few months earlier, its success would probably have been far greater. Later *They Were Expendable* became recognized as a stunning motion picture, honest and real, at its best when it approximated a documentary. The scenes of MacArthur and his wife leaving the Philippines for Australia—detailed, yet distant enough to suggest an accurate recreation—still tug at the heartstrings. "*They Were Expendable* is the only picture I ever felt that Jack put a message into," Duke said. "But the message to stay ready is there."

By the end of the war John Wayne had become a superpatriot and would remain such the rest of his life. Part of his ardent nationalism may have been an atonement for having prospered during his country's time of need. Nothing could fully convince Duke that he hadn't shirked his duty by not serving in the military. In 1951, at an American Legion convention in Florida, General MacArthur told Duke, "You represent the American serviceman better than the American serviceman himself." Even so, Wayne was haunted by the knowledge that he had stayed at home and won fame while others gave their lives.

Wayne felt that he owed his country a debt, and his love for America ran deep. Having voted for Franklin Roosevelt, Duke considered himself a liberal, but above all he saw himself as an independent thinker and a valiant supporter of Jeffersonian democracy. The American system had given him the opportunity to rise to the top. Duke never doubted that others could do the same, and he had no tolerance for the excuses of those less fortunate. "I'd like to know why well-educated idiots keep apologizing for lazy and complaining people who think the world owes them a living," he said.

Duke's father had taught him that courageous men have a duty to speak out on their beliefs. By the end of World War II, Wayne saw Communism as the major threat to the American way of life, a menace that could weaken the country from within. In February 1944 several hundred members of the film industry met to organize the Motion Picture Alliance for the Preservation of American Ideals, a group that was fervently anti-Communist. Wayne was among the alliance's early members. Other leaders of the organization included Ward Bond, Cecil B. DeMille, Robert Montgomery, gossip columnist Hedda Hopper, actor Adolphe Menjou, and director Sam Wood, all of whom feared that the picture business might be taken over by individuals who secretly belonged to the Communist Party.

For staunch conservatives, the Motion Picture Alliance for the Preservation of American Ideals represented a champion of good over evil. As a right-wing spokesman, John Wayne, the quintessential movie hero, seemed to hordes of his fans to be spearheading another fight for right. In the common vision he stood for moral authority, much as the warriors he played on the screen did. During the postwar years his heroic screen image made a quick transfer to reality. Millions saw John Wayne's conservative politics as a brave defense of fundamental Americanism. He and the Motion Picture Alliance were to them an avenging posse bent on rescuing the values outlined by the country's founders.

It was a simplistic view to be sure. If Wayne himself was trying to amend for not sacrificing more during the war, his public preferred to see him as the supreme war hero, the symbolic equal of Alvin York and Audie Murphy. Soon after World War II, screenwriter Edmund Hartmann was talking to a nun at a party. Somehow the subject of the U.S. Army came up in their conversation. "You know," the nun said with total assurance, "our most decorated soldier is John Wayne." Hartmann tried to respond as tactfully as possible: "I think you're wrong," he said. "Wayne was never in the army. He never fired a gun in earnest in his life. John Wayne never shot anybody who didn't get up and go for coffee afterwards!" The nun refused to believe him. Nor would countless fans who envisioned John Wayne as the ultimate military hero. For them the illusion had become real.

Screen Favorite

In 1945 Hollywood's studios were a beehive of activity. The Golden Age of moviemaking had reached its zenith; every soundstage in town was bustling with famous stars and craft workers who would later become legendary. John Wayne finished *They Were Expendable* at MGM and two days later went to RKO to begin *Without Reservations.* American films grossed $1.7 billion in 1946, as average weekly attendance at movie theaters soared to 90 million; it was the most profitable year in motion pictures' half-century of existence. By the end of the decade John Wayne would head the list of the screen's most popular entertainers and would go on to outlast most of his touted contemporaries.

"It took me a long time to find out that I was a star," Duke said in his later years. Through dedication and conscientious work, he had risen to the top despite years of discouragement. Many actors returned from the war and complained that Hollywood no longer seemed real; some even felt fraudulent appearing in front of a camera after facing a world of terror and death. But John Wayne continued to view movie acting as a legitimate business and considered himself "damned lucky" to have developed a popular following. He felt that he owed his fans something and responded to them with humility. Celebrity poses were not for Duke; he was an artisan who fretted and stewed when he thought a production was not going well.

"To be a successful film star as opposed to a successful film actor," British thespian James Mason once said, "you should settle for an image and polish it forever." John Wayne instinctively understood that and settled on a screen persona he would hone to precision. During World War II he had emerged as a model leader—adaptable, pragmatic, brave, and compassionate. Duke believed in those virtues and tried to incorporate them into his professional approach. On film he fought valiantly for what he respected; yet he was willing to circumvent the rules to achieve necessary goals. His military heroes enjoyed an easy camaraderie with the men serving under them but retained their respect. On screen Wayne took full responsibility for his actions and seldom compromised. Duke's strength as a performer was an ability to project feelings shared by the average American, voice them in a common language, and expand them to heroic proportions.

While Wayne was always the virile Hollywood male, he was seldom considered one of the screen's great sex symbols. Barrel-chested and handsome in his youth, Duke nonetheless became identified as a man of courage and action rather than a bedroom virtuoso. Yet women claimed to find a sensuality in the way he walked and the wiggle of his posterior. "God, I get hot when they say I wiggle my rear," said Duke. "I must walk different from other people. . . . God knows, if I don't do anything else, I move well."

Few considered Wayne an actor in the strictest sense. "He's John Wayne, a big hulk of a man who has learned how to walk in a very masculine sort of way with high boots," said motion picture star Dana Andrews. Duke's impact was greatest in Westerns and war movies where action counted. "I'm immediately acceptable in an outdoor adventure picture," said Duke. But when he put on contemporary civilian clothes, his impact diminished. He was incapable of assuming a restrained pose with conviction, in part because audiences refused to accept him as anything short of a hell-for-leather man of brawn. Wayne later admitted that it was sometimes hard to maintain the image he had worked so hard to create.

Without Reservations (released in 1946), a frothy little comedy, does not rank among Duke's better efforts. Wayne's talent for comedy at that point was modest at best, and the chemistry between Duke and Claudette Colbert, his costar, did not produce the gaiety intended. Wayne lacks the proper timing in his delivery of lines and seems stiff. Although Colbert was an adept comedienne, neither she nor Duke was eager to make the picture. "They wouldn't commit themselves until I promised them an outstanding director," producer Jesse L. Lasky said. Lasky chose his cousin, Mervyn LeRoy, for the job.

"*Without Reservations* began my friendship with Duke Wayne," LeRoy contended. "I'd known him before, but this was the first time we worked together. We became very close." Yet LeRoy was not able to infuse the romantic comedy with the needed warmth and merriment, and *Without Reservations* comes across as a heavy-handed imitation of *It Happened One Night*, Colbert's monumental success of 1934, for which she had won an Oscar.

Wayne earned over $68,000 for *Without Reservations* and was treated like a superstar at RKO. Writer-director Richard Fleischer was working at the studio during the time the picture was made and remembered how Mervyn LeRoy and his company waited interminably while Duke had his morning bowel movement. "Then the door opened and out he stepped," Fleischer recalled. "Big as life. Big as all outdoors. Big as the wheat fields of Kansas, the oil fields of Texas. America's hero. He strode toward the set, greeting his friends on the crew. Soon he was lost to view, surrounded by the director, the camera, and its crew, electricians, wardrobe people, and anyone else who was trying to look busy. What I had witnessed was a display of unadulterated, raw power. Who else could halt production for hours, at great cost to the studio, by peristalsis alone? It was too awesome to think about."

Duke might enjoy regal handling at the bigger studios, but he felt more at home on the smaller Republic lot, where a John Wayne picture had become a prestigious event. Work at Republic involved little folderol, and Duke was surrounded by old friends there. Herbert Yates rarely even tested his performers; he simply put them in a Western and assessed the results. Although the movies Wayne made for Yates earned him less money than those produced by the majors, Duke took pride in the work he did for Republic and approached it as a professional. He could relax at Republic, where he was the undisputed king of the lot.

By 1946 Duke's position with Yates had elevated to the point that Wayne could demand to produce a picture himself. He wanted more control over his movies and the roles he played, but he also needed a means for converting some of his income into capital gains to reduce the tremendous tax bite. Yates, on the other hand, saw how bigger studios were courting Duke and feared that Republic might lose its hottest property. It was therefore to the mogul's advantage to provide Wayne with opportunities not readily available to him elsewhere.

Duke chose *Angel and the Badman*, a modest Western, for his first John Wayne production. He cast himself as a gunman torn between a life of violence and the Quaker girl he comes to love. Duke selected his favorite screenwriter, James Edward Grant, to write and direct the picture and borrowed dark-haired Gail Russell from Paramount to play his leading lady.

Angel and the Badman (released in 1947) was the only movie James Grant ever directed. The author had come to Hollywood in 1939, after gaining success as a short story writer, and scored well with his first picture, *Boom Town* (1940), which teamed Clark Gable and Spencer Tracy. Wayne soon became convinced that nobody could write dialogue for him as suitably as Jimmy Grant. The two became close friends and collaborated on projects until Grant's death in 1966. The writer kowtowed to Duke and tended to tell the star what he wanted to hear. One longtime observer maintained that Grant played chess with Wayne for over twenty years and managed never to win a game. But the screenwriter understood the kind of roles that Duke played best and tailored his scripts to the actor's strengths, giving him dialogue that was simple and direct. "Grant never wrote strong parts for women," Adele Mara maintained, "his stories were for men."

He was an effective screenwriter and, more important, he knew how Wayne thought. But Grant was an alcoholic, and his judgment was not always the best. *Angel and the Badman* proved a leisurely Western with a dearth of action, more concerned with romance and pacifism than bad men and gunplay. While critics liked it, Duke's fans found the movie slow.

Chata hated Jimmy Grant. She also became convinced that Duke and his costar, Gail Russell, were having an affair. Russell was only twenty-three years old at the time, but she had a past of emotional instability. As her career gained momentum, so did her dependence on alcohol. Wayne sensed her insecurity and went out of his way to show the fragile actress consideration. Possibly Russell developed a crush on Duke during the making of *Angel and the Badman*, and they did spend time together in her dressing room. But Wayne vehemently denied that there was any wrongdoing. He simply knew the problems Russell was having and sympathized with her.

By the time *Angel and the Badman* was made, Duke and Esperanza Bauer were married. A simple wedding ceremony had taken place in his mother's church in Long Beach on January 17, 1946. Ward Bond, still using a cane after his recent accident, was best man, while Harry Carey's wife, Olive, whom Duke adored, served as matron of honor. Herbert Yates gave the bride away, and Duke's mother, by then married to Sidney Preen, a sewer inspector in Long Beach, arranged a reception at the California Country Club.

Duke and Chata rented a modest ranch house on Tyrone Street in Van Nuys, near the Republic studio, where they continued their tempestuous relationship. Duke would come home from the studio exhausted from the combined strain of playing a part in *Angel and the Badman* and attending to countless production details. He wanted to have a few drinks, eat a big steak, and go to bed. Instead, he was often greeted by an outraged Chata, in a jealous furor over what she imagined was going on with Gail Russell.

Yates had arranged a screen test for the twenty-four-year-old Esperanza and had even signed her to a contract, but Chata never made a movie for Republic. Duke dissuaded her from acting, yet his sultry wife was no homebody. Unable to bear children, she quickly grew bored with suburban Los Angeles and drank more heavily. When drunk, Chata swore at Duke and the fireworks would begin. He took her to nightclubs and parties, only to be humiliated when she caused a disturbance. Chata in turn discovered that living with John Wayne was less exciting than she had supposed. "My husband is one of the few persons who is always interested in his business," she complained. "He talks of it constantly. When he reads, it's scripts. Our dinner guests always talk business, and he spends all of his time working, discussing work, or planning work."

Esperanza understood Duke even less than Josephine had. She preyed on his insecurities, knew that personal security was a weak point in his disguise, and found infuriating him a way to arouse his passion. While there were moments of tenderness between them, their drinking bouts got out of control, and they fought savagely. "Our marriage was like shaking two volatile chemicals in a jar," Wayne said. "It wasn't all bad. We had a lot of fun at first."

During the fall of 1946 Duke was in Arizona, near Elgin, shooting *Red River* (not released until 1948). The picture, directed by Howard Hawks, would become a Western classic and mark a major shift in Wayne's career, foreshadowing parts he would play as a mature actor. Tom Dunson, the aging, tyrannical, socially isolated cattle baron he played in the picture, is a man obsessed, wrong more often than he's right. Duke was only thirty-nine years old at the time and wasn't sure that he should accept the older part. Dunson is a romantic lead only in the opening minutes of the picture. Then the story jumps ahead and finds him a fanatical, late-middle-aged man who ruthlessly drives his men and his herd of cattle up the Chisholm Trail.

Duke accepted the role of Tom Dunson largely because his agent, Charles Feldman, was the picture's executive producer. Yet Wayne's characterization is so finely honed that critics took notice. "I was young, and this was a challenge," said Duke. "It was the first time I felt like a real actor." Wayne later remarked that *Stagecoach* had established him as a star, whereas *Red River* ten years later established him as an actor. He also credited Howard Hawks, who would direct him in five pictures, with being the second great influence in his professional life.

Veteran character actor Walter Brennan played a crusty cook in *Red River*, and Hawks asked him to teach Wayne how to walk like an old man. Brennan demonstrated the moves of a tottering patriarch, but Duke decided that Tom Dunson should stand erect and be assertive. Hawks maintained that the aging rancher should turn coward in the final confrontation with his adopted son, assuring Duke that the reversal would win him an Academy Award. But Wayne disagreed and insisted that the cattleman should remain powerful throughout. "If I had played the part the way Hawks originally had in mind," Duke said, "it would have hurt the picture."

Tom Dunson emerges as a stubborn and ruthless figure without losing the sympathy of the audience. The director gave Wayne sufficient latitude to frame the character as he saw fit. *Red River* is regarded as the big screen's ultimate cattle drive, a Western masterpiece in which John Wayne found a dimension only hinted at earlier. Even John Ford voiced surprise at the depth of Wayne's performance. "I never knew that big son of a bitch could act," Ford told his friend Howard Hawks.

Red River cost nearly $2 million and took about three and a half months to film. The company worked in Arizona from September 1946 until Thanksgiving, then finished the picture shortly after Christmas at the Goldwyn studio in Hollywood. During the weeks on location, work was delayed because of rain. "We were living in tents," actress Coleen Gray remembered, "and the rain beat down and we were surrounded by mud." Duke caught a cold, actress Joanne Dru suffered from influenza, and most of the cast sneezed and coughed. Hawks's company ate meals served from a cook wagon, but they had no place to sit except out in the open somewhere. "Then it would start to rain," the director recalled, "and we'd be sitting there with the rain falling in our food."

Hawks and Feldman had chartered a private plane to scout locations south of Tucson, and they hired fifteen hundred head of cattle for the crew to drive. "It was a physically hard picture to do," said Hawks. "We had to get up and get started early in the morning, sometimes with ice on the ground, because the light is more interesting early and late. So we made our scenic shots early or late in the day to get the use of shadows and clouds. Then we could make the close-ups almost any time."

Wayne had a scene in the picture where he reads some Scripture at a burial. Hawks noticed a black cloud coming across the mountains behind him. "Duke," the director said, "start talking and if you forget your lines, just keep on talking until I yell at you." The actor did as he was told, and the camera caught the cloud moving across the mountain range in the background. "It made a fine scene," said Hawks. "Russell Harlan was a great cameraman; the worse the weather was the better scenes he could get."

Although Hawks was an austere, dignified man, he worked well with actors. "He gave actors the feeling that they were part of creating a scene," Wayne recalled. "He let them come up with ideas, then went over and wrote them down." Hawks wanted spontaneity and sometimes gave his performers lines without informing others in the scene of the changes he had made, intending for them to respond naturally. The director told Wayne, "Duke, if you can make three good scenes in this picture and don't annoy the audience the rest of the time, you'll be okay." Wayne trusted the filmmaker. "Hey, is this one of those scenes?" Duke would occasionally ask. Hawks usually replied, "This is the one where you get it over as quickly as you can and don't annoy the audience."

The chemistry between the two men was undeniable, and Wayne did some of his best work for the director. "I was just the paint for the palettes of Ford and Hawks," Duke said. Yet Hawks gave the star more credit. "What you get from Wayne is authority," the seasoned filmmaker said. "He looks like he belongs in Western clothes. You also get a personality. . . . He's got so much power that he just blows anybody else with him off the screen. Duke told me that he enjoys working with Ford and me because we take care of all the worrying."

In *Red River* Hawks wanted to tell the story of the King Ranch, but the problems of getting releases from the people involved proved insurmountable. He settled for a *Saturday Evening Post* story by Borden Chase and added to its scope. "It's not always easy to find a story like *Red River* that has movement," the director said. But the picture also has hardy characters and intense relationships, particularly between Tom Dunson and his son, Matthew Garth. "I remember Hawks talked about the strong bond that exists between a father and a son," said Coleen Gray, who played young Tom Dunson's sweetheart, "and *Red River* is a father-son duel. The film is so wonderful at the end when the two men are reconciled. It's like the resolution in Bach, when the tension and dissonance of the piece are resolved."

For the part of Matthew Garth, the filmmakers selected Montgomery Clift, a slim, aesthetic-looking method actor recently arrived in Hollywood from Broadway. When Duke met Clift for the first time, he asked Hawks, "Howard, do you think we can get anything going between that kid and myself? I don't think we can make a fight. That kid isn't going to be able to stand up to me." Clift worked hard on his riding, got up at five o'clock in the morning, and practiced with wranglers for an hour before the day's shooting began. Duke was impressed by the young actor's determination and began to coach him on how to handle a gun and throw punches that looked impressive on film. Clift responded to Wayne's power, and their different approaches blended brilliantly. Since Clift was so much smaller than Wayne, Hawks decided to have Tom Dunson get shot in the leg before his final confrontation with Matt, so that their fight would seem more realistic.

"Montgomery Clift was the most magnetic guy I'd ever met in person," said Harry Carey, Jr., who played a role in *Red River*, "and on the screen he was double that. I'd watch him, and he didn't seem to be acting at all. He'd talk in a soft-spoken way and sort of touch his nose and do the little mannerisms he had. It was a whole new style of acting that he brought to the screen. He was a terrific guy, but I found him a little mysterious."

While the company was on location, Clift shared a tent with Walter Brennan. Since the newcomer to films had to roll a cigarette in the picture, light it, and hand it to Duke, Brennan taught him how to make a smoke using Bull Durham tobacco. But Clift spent most of his leisure hours in Arizona palling around with actor John Ireland, whom he had known in New York. "We were working near Nogales, Mexico," Ireland remembered, "so we'd go there every other night and have great Mexican food. We'd go into town on the weekend and rent a suite in the hotel, fill the bathtub up with ice and beer, and invite the wranglers in." Hawks eventually complained that his actors were drinking too much, and he held Ireland responsible. As a disciplinary measure, the director began cutting lines from Ireland's dialogue.

Coleen Gray recalled that the long shots of her scene with Wayne were filmed on location, but the close-ups were done in the Goldwyn studio against a backdrop. Care had to be taken to match the two. Since Gray was short and Duke so tall, Hawks had her stand on an apple box during their farewell embrace, after which Tom Dunson leaves his sweetheart with a wagon train, while he himself strikes off for Texas. "Wayne was enormously polite and considerate," said Gray, "not particularly convivial, but smiling and gentle. I would see him after the day's shooting, and I'd always come up and kick him in the shins and say, 'Dummy, you should have taken me with you,'" referring to Dunson's decision to leave her character behind, where she's killed by hostile Indians. Duke would laugh and then go his own way, apparently not wanting to be accused of intimacy with another leading lady, although Gray was not his type. "I was a Minnesota farm girl," she said. The actress also was married and had a new baby. "I still had a little poochy tummy," she remembered. "I was concerned about that, particularly since Joanne Dru, who played Monty Clift's girlfriend in the movie, was so slender."

The release of *Red River* was held up by a lawsuit that Wayne filed against Monterey Productions, the company that produced the picture. Duke claimed that the backers of Monterey had promised him $75,000 plus a percentage of the film's earnings, yet nothing had been paid. He asked that the defendants be restrained from distributing the movie until a settlement could be reached. Charles Feldman argued that "a fraud has been perpetrated."

When *Red River* finally premiered in August 1948, critics not only found the picture authentic and gripping, but some called it the first adult Western, since it deals with the complexity of men's lives rather than their fondness for violence. The original cut ran too long, so Howard Hawks asked John Ford to take a look at it. Ford suggested having Walter Brennan narrate the story, which tightened the action. "When I see a good Western," said Brennan, "I just sit there. I was thrilled with *Red River*, because I believed in it. Wayne was so good; I believed in him."

With Tom Dunson, Duke played his first tragic hero. Critic Pauline Kael described Wayne's cattle baron as "mulishly magnetic" and said that the actor had pushed his character "past the point of breakdown." Duke's character is multilayered, driven by interior demons, forced to search his soul despite a determination to have things his way. It was a time in America when maturity was being redefined in terms of adjustment to corporate living and the team player was replacing the self-made individual as a national ideal. Tom Dunson was a throwback to an earlier era, when men decided their own destiny and resisted compromise.

To celebrate the completion of *Angel and the Badman* and *Red River*, Duke and Esperanza took a belated honeymoon to Honolulu in December 1946 with James Edward Grant and his wife. The trip was unpleasant for everyone. Disliking Grant and viewing him as an accomplice in Duke's supposed dalliance with Gail Russell, Chata turned surly and aggressive. "Pushy dames really scare Duke," said Grant. "He's really old-fashioned about women; no off-color stories in their presence, for instance." But Chata became loud and vulgar when drunk and peppered her broken English with obscenities. Duke tried to drown his annoyance with her in whiskey, but his exasperation boiled with invectives. "I still don't understand women," he said; "I don't think there is any man who does."

He returned to California emotionally shattered, yet unwilling to admit that his second marriage was a far bigger mistake than his first. Duke gave in to Esperanza's plea and brought her mother up from Mexico to live with them. An only child, Chata had always been close to her mother, although Mrs. Ceballos, an attractive woman, looked more like her daughter's older sister. After their reunion the two women spent most of their time drinking together, and the strain on the Wayne marriage became greater. Mrs. Ceballos fanned the flames of Chata's jealousy, yet mother and daughter engaged in their own battles, which sometimes degenerated into physical abuse. Duke reacted, as he had in his first marriage, by staying away from home as much as possible and burying himself in work.

Despondent over the lukewarm reception of *Angel and the Badman*, Wayne reported to RKO to satisfy his yearly commitment there. The studio had planned to make *Duel in the Sun* (released in December 1946) with Duke in the role of the roguish Lewt. But when the RKO management experienced repeated problems in selecting a female lead for the Niven Busch story, David O. Selznick bought the property and turned the Western into a mammoth spectacle, with Jennifer Jones as a miscast half-breed and Gregory Peck in the part intended for Duke. "I don't think Wayne would have been as good as Peck," Busch said, "but he might have. He was a better actor than a lot of people thought."

Instead, RKO cast Duke in *Tycoon* (1947) opposite Laraine Day. "*Ty-*

coon was pure soap opera," said Day, "it was so corny. Picture me as a South American girl living in the Andes with black hair and a clipped accent." Yet the actress enjoyed the northern California location and the gorgeous clothes designed for her to wear in the Technicolor production. She also liked the association with John Wayne. "I worked a great deal with him on *Tycoon*," Day said. "He wasn't trying to give a performance; he was just John Wayne. But he was a good man and very likable."

Judith Anderson played a stuffy duenna in the movie, and Sir Cedric Hardwicke was Laraine Day's English father. Duke seemed relaxed during the making of the film, in part because his friends Paul Fix, Grant Withers, and Anthony Quinn were in the cast. "Anthony Quinn was playing a secondary part," Day recalled, "and at that time I thought he had very little talent." Critics dismissed *Tycoon* as overlong and wordy, unworthy of its expensive trappings and memorable mainly for its beautiful color.

In the picture Wayne played an engineer who overcomes his marital problems. In private Duke was not so fortunate. Turbulence at home combined with an escalating work schedule kept him in turmoil, and he developed an ulcer soon after *Tycoon* wrapped. He arrived at his office at Republic one day with red welts on his face. Chata had gotten drunk at a party and clouted him when he picked her up. Duke even noticed that some of his friends were avoiding them. John Ford wanted no part of Chata, and the director and Wayne exchanged angry words on the subject. Their confrontation ended with Ford's shouting, "Did you have to marry that whore?"

Adele Mara remembered being on a train when she, Duke, Chata, and Forrest Tucker were sent on a tour to publicize one of Republic's Westerns. "Chata didn't seem very vivacious to me," Mara said, "she was kind of ordinary. She wasn't extremely beautiful, and she didn't talk to many people. All she did was follow Wayne around and go back to their room and drink."

Esperanza had acquired her nickname Chata because of her nose, "Chata" being a diminutive of the Spanish term for "pug nose." She had a skin problem, which her compulsive drinking did nothing to remedy. Already it was evident that the years would hang heavy on her. "Duke really loved Chata," director Budd Boetticher maintained, "but their marriage wasn't ever going to work. They'd go to the airport for an international flight, check in, and head for the bar. When their plane left, only one of them would be on board. They'd have a big fight, and either Duke would go home or Chata would. Duke spent a lot of time alone."

In July 1947 Wayne returned to Monument Valley to film *Fort Apache*, the opening segment of John Ford's cavalry trilogy. Duke looked forward to the picture, was eager to work again with Ford, and welcomed the serenity of living for a month without Chata in the seclusion of the Navajo reservation. He took along his teenage son Michael, and he enjoyed the camaraderie of old friends during the filming. Despite the presence of actresses Shirley Temple, Anna Lee, and Irene Rich, Ford's company was male-dominated. The director surrounded himself with physical types—his actors, his stuntmen, his wranglers, the Navajo extras he hired in Monument Valley to play Apache warriors—and social life revolved around masculine pastimes.

Wayne trusted Ford's judgment and put himself completely in the director's hands. Since *Fort Apache* was made by Argosy, Ford's production unit formed in partnership with Merian C. Cooper, Duke had none of the worries he had experienced with *Angel and the Badman*. Wayne simply did what Ford instructed. Despite his casual exterior, Duke was a worrier. But when he worked for Ford or Hawks, he could ease up. *Fort Apache* was Wayne's fourth picture for Ford, and by then he and the director had worked out a set of signals that required little conversation.

"Jack was always so far ahead of everybody else," Wayne said. "He was very sure of what he was doing, but let actors bring to their role whatever was unique in their personality. Ford melded the spoken word to his actors and allowed them time to relax. Nobody could handle actors and crew like Jack. He would have been a success at anything he'd undertaken—except public relations."

Duke knew how tough Ford could be on the set and sometimes cringed at the director's cruel side. From time to time the old man made a buffoon of him, but Wayne accepted the abuse like an errant schoolboy. "Sorry, Coach," Duke would murmur, confident that the performance Ford drew from him would be worth the humiliation. He realized that part of Ford's method was to keep his actors on edge, uncertain about what would happen next. Yet the director could also be sympathetic and paternal, shaping the performance he wanted with patience and kindness.

Wayne recognized during the filming of *Fort Apache* that Ford's experiences in World War II had given the filmmaker a deep feeling for the military. Duke understood that underneath the director's brusqueness beat the heart of a sensitive man, more obvious now than earlier. Making films for John Ford was like painting a picture, in which mood, characterization, story, and action were all brought together on a single canvas.

Duke never doubted that Ford was the greatest influence on his professional life. "I hero-worshipped Jack and loved him," Wayne said time and again. Many of the Ford regulars maintained that the director created in Duke's screen persona an alter ego for himself. One of those regulars was Harry Carey, Jr., or Dobe, as he was known. "Somehow Wayne exemplified physically what Ford wanted to be," Dobe said. "Ford wanted to be a two-fisted, brawling, heavy-drinking Irishman and clean up a barroom all by himself. He couldn't do that, but part of Ford's genius was that he created that image in John Wayne on the screen."

With *Fort Apache* Wayne continued his development as a serious screen actor. Having shown his talent in *Red River*, Duke wanted to make movies he could take pride in and play roles worthy of his expanded reputation. His salary had jumped to $100,000 a picture, the same as his *Fort Apache* costars Henry Fonda and Shirley Temple. Again Ford succeeded in lifting Wayne's basic personality to epic proportions, coloring it with hues from the director's unique palate. Kirby York—a knowledgeable frontiersman, forceful yet human—stands among John Wayne's most memorable screen portrayals. Ford imbues his cavalrymen and their women with strength and dignity, while their Native American counterparts are honorable and justified in their grievances. Based on James Warner Bellah's story "Massacre," *Fort Apache* became Ford's version of the George A. Custer legend. Wayne's character is the voice of reason. York sympathizes with the Indians, tries to circumvent disaster, but in the end sanctions the legend that has grown up after the death of a martinet who in truth was arrogant and foolish. Ford draws strong performances from both Wayne and Henry Fonda (who played Col. Owen Thursday, the fictionalized Custer character). Yet he also captured a mythic vision of the frontier cavalry worthy of Frederic Remington, balancing visual splendor with moments of social insight.

Michael Wayne loved being in Monument Valley with his father and remembered the dinners at Goulding's Trading Post and evenings when the company gathered for amusement. A tent city had been constructed to house the crew on the flat below the lodge, and at night Ford, Duke, and some others would play cards. Young Michael's relationship with Ford was never a good one; the director harassed the boy without mercy. Initially Ford had thought that Michael was his godson but later found out he was the godfather of Wayne's second son, *Patrick*. From then on the crusty director gave Michael a hard time. "I think Ford resented me because I was more aggressive than his son, Pat Ford, who was kind of laid back," Michael said. Duke assured the distraught boy that Ford was toughest on those he loved best. "Your Uncle Jack loves you," Wayne told his son. "Look at the way he treats Ward Bond."

Bond was Ford's favorite whipping boy, and Duke joined in the amiable abuse. Both men loved Ward but delighted in making him look foolish. Bond harbored a monumental ego, was forever boasting, thought he was irresistible to women, and repeatedly claimed that he should be playing Wayne's part. "Ward had all the gall in the world and spoke before he thought," said Duke. "He was so thick-skinned that ridicule bounced right off him." The actor left himself open to practical jokes, and poking fun at Ward Bond became a favorite sport on a John Ford set. "Our picking on Ward let him feel important," Duke said, "it made him the center of attention." Wayne and Bond would hurl sarcastic remarks at one another until newcomers became convinced they were ready to tear each other apart. "We had great times together," Wayne recalled.

Such horseplay was part of the fun Duke enjoyed on a John Ford picture. Since the director used many of the same people over and over, Wayne knew beforehand that he would be surrounded by friends. Character actor Hank Worden, who was a veteran on Ford's pictures, remembered Duke's coming up to him, putting an arm around his shoulder, and saying, "Hank, you old son of a bitch." Worden accepted the greeting as a sign of friendship: "If Duke called you a son of a bitch, you knew you were in," Worden said.

"Having Wayne put his arm on your shoulder is like having somebody dump a telephone pole on you," declared Frank Nugent, who wrote the script for *Fort Apache*. But Wayne was well liked by crew members, and he fraternized easily with them. Workmen admired Duke's willingness to do his share of the dirty work and respected his honesty. Hank Worden remembered Duke's saying to him, "I always tell it like it is, so tomorrow I won't have to be wondering what I was lying about yesterday."

One of the few people who did not like John Wayne was Ford's brother,

Eddie O'Fearna, Jack's perennial second assistant. For some reason O'Fearna had it in for Duke and was inordinately rough on him. The actor retaliated by playing tricks on O'Fearna and trying to fluster him. Since Ford often quarreled with his brother, Duke's antics were sometimes encouraged. But O'Fearna felt vindicated when Ford began hurling invectives at Wayne, which he did with regularity. "We all had our turn in the barrel," Ford's actors agreed.

Since *Fort Apache* was John Agar's first picture, he was the company's outsider. Agar had recently married teenaged Shirley Temple, and for some reason Temple's young husband became the director's patsy during the weeks in Monument Valley. Ford complained about Agar's faulty delivery of lines, his awkwardness on a horse, and almost everything else the newcomer did. "I was petrified," Agar recalled, "knowing as little as I did about movies and working with all those superstars." Wayne took the lad aside and told him how badly Ford had treated him when they made *Stagecoach*. "He's just trying to get a performance out of you," Duke explained.

Ford admired women who spoke their minds and held up under trying circumstances. Filming a scene in *Fort Apache,* the director kept Anna Lee, Irene Rich, and Shirley Temple standing in the broiling sun so long, wearing tight corsets, that Lee fainted. "I woke up in John Wayne's arms," the actress said. "He carried me down from the deck we were standing on." Lee discovered how much Ford liked her when he started kidding her about her poor head for sun. The filmmaker simply ignored people he did not respect.

The *Fort Apache* company left Monument Valley in August 1947 and finished shooting at the Selznick studio in Culver City. The film would be a commercial success and fare well with critics. It had no sooner wrapped than Ford sailed for Mazatlán aboard the *Araner.* Duke, Ward Bond, and Henry Fonda met him there, and the three men toured the Mexican bars and whorehouses together, until Ford's alcoholism temporarily incapacitated him.

Chata was irate at not being allowed to accompany Duke to Monument Valley, but Ford never encouraged the presence of wives on location. She became absolutely furious when her husband took off for Mexico without her. She resented Duke's allegiance to Ford and was jealous of the time her husband spent with his children. Duke in turn came to dislike Chata's possessive mother and grew disgusted with the constant bickering between the two women.

As Wayne's second marriage deteriorated, his relationship with Josephine improved. He often stopped by her house to talk. After their divorce Josie's patrician ways and prudish attitudes seemed to bother him less, since they no longer threatened him. From a distance he could appreciate his former wife's dignity. "She never made the children hate me," Duke said with gratitude, and he never stopped blaming himself for leaving a good woman who was the mother of his children. "I destroyed my first marriage," he later said. "I was a different man back then. I was much more selfish."

Wayne genuinely wanted to be a strong, loving father, and from all accounts he succeeded in the quality, if not in the amount, of time he had to give. "I believe I got along better with my children and saw more of them *after* Josie and I were divorced," he said. Above all he wanted to be a pillar of support for his sons. Michael and Patrick were different in looks, build, and temperament, but Duke made a lasting impact on them both. Michael was stocky and gregarious and got along better with Chata than his brother and sisters did. Patrick grew into a tall, handsome lad; he was shy, sensitive, thoughtful, and introspective. Duke instilled in his boys an appreciation for hard work and other values his own father had imparted to him as a youth.

"We were young when our parents were divorced," Wayne's daughter Toni said, "but we went to see [my dad] all the time, because we were crazy about him. We knew we could never get away with anything bad, because he had a stern look and the master's voice. He was also old-fashioned." Toni's younger sister, Melinda, recalled, "If any of us did something he didn't approve of, he'd give us the Silent Treatment. He just avoided us and wouldn't talk to us."

Yet their father was busy and absent much of the time. At forty years of age Duke's had reached the height of his career, although he was still not the legend he would become later. In March 1948 Wayne, Ford, Bond, and Merian Cooper went to Mexico City to scout locations for *Three God-fathers*, Argosy's remake of Ford's silent classic, *Marked Men* (1919). Eventually the director changed his mind and decided to shoot the sound version in Death Valley, but not until he and his friends had enjoyed a Mexican holiday.

Filming on *Three Godfathers* began during the latter part of May, and working on the sand dunes of Death Valley proved miserably hot. The company began shooting around 7:30 in the morning, worked until 11:00, then went back to their quarters until 3:30 or 4:00. Often they wouldn't finish filming until sunset. "Duke, Pedro Armendariz, and I drank Poland Springs mineral water which came from Maine," remembered Dobe Carey, who played the youngest of the movie's three outlaws. "Duke sent for cases of it. If it hadn't been for him, I probably would have quit a couple of times, because Ford rode me hard on that picture."

The company was housed at the Furnace Creek Ranch, which wasn't air-conditioned but had a swimming pool that became the crew's oasis. Wayne and Armendariz shared a cabin, while Bond roomed with Dobe Carey. At night, after a shower and dinner, Ford, Wayne, Armendariz, and Bond played dominoes, while Carey served as errand boy. The game was friendly so long as the director won. "The rest of us stood around and listened to them," Hank Worden recalled. "Ford couldn't stand to be topped, so he cheated." Pedro Armendariz, a major star in Mexico, was a delightful man, but he had a bad temper. Ford enjoyed goading him, and the others took pleasure in watching the sparks fly.

The sand and blinding heat on location made *Three Godfathers* a difficult picture to make. The company worked for a month in Death Valley under tremendous stress. Dobe Carey noticed that Duke lit one cigarette after another all day long. Carey studied all of the star's ways and admired his technique. "Duke was only fourteen years older than me," Dobe said, "but when I was in high school, he was making movies. I loved his early Westerns. No one had a presence on the screen like John Wayne. Physically he was overpowering."

Dobe first worked with Wayne on *Red River* and had seen Duke only a few times at social functions since then. "He was always sort of distant and hard to talk to," said Carey. "No matter how many times you worked with Duke, unless you were totally alone with him and therefore had his complete attention, you never felt quite sure he heard a word you were saying."

In *Three Godfathers* Wayne played the part that Harry Carey, Dobe's father, had played in Ford's silent film. The senior Carey had died the year before, not long after making *Red River*, his last picture. Wayne not only had grown up watching Carey's movies, but had developed a deep respect for him as a professional, taking the veteran actor as his model. "God, I love that old man!" Duke told Carey's son. Ford loved the actor, too, and dedicated *Three Godfathers* to "the memory of Harry Carey—bright star of the early western sky."

The Technicolor film is an allegory. Three outlaws come upon a dying mother in the desert and become the caretakers of her newborn child. In Ford's hands the story suggests the journey of the three wise men to Bethlehem. Much of the emphasis is on the trio's walking, then plodding, and finally staggering across endless sand and salt flats. While there are scenes of visual grandeur and moments of tenderness, critics did not treat the picture kindly, finding it labored and sentimental. Yet Howard Barnes of the *New York Herald Tribune* said, "Wayne is better than ever as the leader of the badmen."

With Duke spending so much time on location, Chata felt neglected, and there was an angry display of fireworks when Gail Russell was selected to costar in Wayne's next picture for Republic, *Wake of the Red Witch* (released early in 1949). Duke would receive 10 percent of the gross from the film and therefore had a say in casting. Herbert Yates had suggested contract player Catherine McLeod for the female lead, but Wayne turned her down. McLeod remembered going to Duke's office, where he was visiting with Ward Bond, Paul Fix, and some other pals, and being rudely treated. "Not knowing what else to do," the actress said, "I gently laid the script on his desk and backed out the door." It was clear to McLeod that she would not get the part.

Wayne felt sorry for the alcoholic Gail Russell, knew she was having disastrous personal problems, and insisted on her again playing opposite him. Russell was a painfully shy young woman, and her celebrity terrified her. "She was a loner," said Adele Mara, who was featured in *Wake of the Red Witch*. "Gail Russell certainly was a pretty girl, but she stuck to herself. I think the only person she ever really talked to was Wayne, and probably just because she had scenes with him. People in makeup and hairdressing would talk about her drinking. The rumor at Republic was that they had to take a lot of bottles out of her dressing room every day." Russell died of alcoholism in 1961, at the age of thirty-six.

But Esperanza remained convinced that Duke and Gail Russell were having a prolonged affair. Nothing her husband said could persuade her that the relationship was innocent. During the making of *Red Witch* Chata flew into a rage when she heard that Wayne had given Russell a car, although in truth he had only loaned her money for a down payment. That fury, however, was nothing compared with the bedlam Chata created the night Duke stopped by his leading lady's house for a nightcap. "Her mother was there," Wayne insisted, "and we all had a couple of drinks. That's all there was to it." But Chata chose to believe the worst.

Wake of the Red Witch, a lusty sea adventure based on a popular novel by Garland Roark, was a big picture for Republic. Wayne played a swaggering ship's captain, who is agreeable enough sober but who becomes a beast when drunk. (The name of the powerful trading company in the film is Batjac, a name Duke would appropriate later for his own production company.) *Red Witch* involved extensive underwater sequences for Wayne in a studio tank, and in shooting those scenes, he picked up a fungus infection in his ears from saltwater fish that had been placed in the tank to enhance the ambience. Filming on the movie lasted thirty-nine days, plus several more days' work for the studio's special effects department. The budget ran over a million dollars.

Running parallel with John Wayne's rise in stature as a Hollywood superstar was mounting tension in his private life. Duke drank too much, as most of his cohorts did. "He never drank at the studio—ever," Adele Mara insisted. But after work he and his pals spent most evenings in haunts near the Republic lot, and Mara saw him occasionally staggering to the men's room. "You just waited to see him coming back," the actress said. "First of all, he had that wonderful walk, and when he was a little tipsy, it became exaggerated. It was really fun to watch."

But Duke stayed with his own crowd. "I don't think anybody saw him socially except for the men he drank with," said Mara. "He kept very much to himself. He was one of those people who liked to drink with the boys; it was a macho thing for him. At the studio he was strictly business—very nice and easygoing, but I never saw him hit anybody on the back or tell a joke. Nor did I ever hear him yell or scream at anyone. Nobody ever said mean things about John Wayne. Actually people didn't speak too much about him at Republic."

One of Mara's few personal conversations with Duke came while they were making *Wake of the Red Witch*. Since the supporting actress knew that Gail Russell was going to wear her hair down in the picture, Mara decided to pull hers back in braids above her head, feeling that the hairdo would make her look exotic and be more appropriate for her role. Wayne came up to the actress on the set one day and said, "Why do you wear your hair so severe, instead of letting it flow?" Mara interpreted his remark to mean that Duke preferred women who looked softer. "I don't know whether it mattered to him whether my hair was in character or not," she said.

The turmoil in Duke's home life seemed beyond repair, and that contributed to his drinking binges. Not only did he have Chata to contend with, he also had her mother. Like her daughter, Mrs. Ceballos had a nasty tongue, and both of them relished off-color jokes. From time to time the two women packed up and flew to Mexico City, staying gone for a month or two. Duke came to realize that Esperanza had married him for what he could do for her, and he felt used and degraded. In his frustration he often became insulting to her, which usually led to physical outbursts. Then he would feel guilty and try to make amends by taking his wife dancing, since Chata loved to dance and to be seen at the better nightspots. Soon they would get into another squabble, and the insults would start all over again.

Finally Duke insisted that Chata's mother return to Mexico, although she continued to spend holidays with them. A loan from billionaire Howard Hughes, who had recently bought RKO, enabled Wayne to purchase a $125,000, twenty-two-room farmhouse in Encino, set on a small hill in a five-acre estate. The grounds, at the corner of Rancho Street and Louise Avenue, included a swimming pool, a pool house with guest room, and stables for several horses. Encino at that time was still an undeveloped area within the San Fernando Valley, and Duke's property was surrounded by small ranches and similar estates. Wayne built a high brick wall around his domain and added an electric gate for security. But living in luxury did nothing to improve his marriage.

Duke welcomed the opportunity to return to Monument Valley in late October 1948, this time to make *She Wore a Yellow Ribbon* for John Ford. The company went by train to Flagstaff, then by car over dirt roads to Goulding's Trading Post. Wayne and Ford each had a cabin to themselves at Harry Goulding's lodge, but the rest of the cast doubled up. Even those assigned to individual cabins had to share a toilet and a shower, since none of the units came equipped with a bathroom. "The shower," Dobe Carey remembered, "was an old five-gallon oil tin with holes in the bottom. It hung from a wooden beam." There was no hot water, so bathing became an adventure on cold mornings.

She Wore a Yellow Ribbon, the second movie in Ford's cavalry trilogy, provided Duke with one of his favorite roles, Capt. Nathan Brittles. Brittles, his hair streaked with silver, is a man more than two decades Duke's senior, on the verge of retirement. The officer has spent forty years in the cavalry; he understands Indians and is sensitive to the welfare and needs of the men serving under him. Brittles was a role that required authority but also tenderness and emotional depth. Wayne had a graveyard scene in the picture, where the widowed officer visits the burial site of his deceased wife. The intensely personal moment could have become overly sentimental. But Ford knew how to relax his actors, just as he knew how to unnerve them. "He gave me plenty of leeway," said Wayne, and the graveyard sequence comes across magnificently.

As Brittles's hour of retirement approaches, his men give him an engraved silver watch, which brings tears to the old man's eyes. "I imagined I couldn't cope with that scene any more than Brittles did," said Duke. "Pappy Ford had me take out a pair of spectacles and make quite a thing out of reading the inscription. He was conscious of each actor's sensitivity; he knew that my reaction would be simplistic and moving. He knew that I'd give an emotional reaction rather than a studied response to lines." Ford judged correctly, for Wayne handled the scene with aplomb.

Duke felt that the part demonstrated a soldier's finer qualities. "There are no nuances because Nathan Brittles, like Tom Dunson, is folklore and legend," Wayne said. "They're men working against strong handicaps. But *Yellow Ribbon* may be the part I'm most proud of." More than an actor, John Wayne had become a creative influence in the films he made. "His presence is so magnetic that it conquers a screen," critic Maurice Zolotow wrote. "His entrance changes a movie."

Ben Johnson, who played Sergeant Tyree in *She Wore a Yellow Ribbon*, claimed that he and Wayne shared a similar approach to acting. "Duke's idea was always, 'How would John Wayne do it?'" said Johnson, who began his own career as a rodeo rider. "And that's the same theory I've got. I don't consider myself an actor; I consider myself a character, Ben Johnson. Everybody in town is a better actor than I am, but I can play the hell out of Ben Johnson. Duke more or less played himself."

Yet with Brittles the image is lifted to greater heights. Wayne maintained that the director cast him in the part because Ford wanted to be responsible for Duke's topping his performance in *Red River*. Both succeeded, for there was talk of an Oscar nomination for Wayne. But Ford presented Duke with a more personal award. When *She Wore a Yellow Ribbon* was finished, the director sent Wayne a cake bearing a single candle and the message: "You're an actor now."

Although Cliff Lyons doubled Wayne on the picture, Duke did most of his own riding and some of his stunt work. Joanne Dru, who played the female lead in *Yellow Ribbon*, was best friends with Barbara Ford, the director's daughter, and insisted that Barbara accompany her to Monument Valley. The two young women spent a great deal of their time together laughing. "I really didn't like Duke very much," said Dru, "and I was terrified of horses." But one day the actress and Barbara Ford were watching Wayne shoot a scene on horseback. Suddenly Barbara said, "Joanne, why are we out here watching him ride a horse?" Dru replied, "Because he turns us on, Barbara." The director's daughter thought a moment. "Yeah," she agreed, "but once he dismounts—nothing. John Wayne on a horse is the sexiest thing in the world. But once he gets off, he's just Uncle Duke again."

As important as characterization was to Ford, the landscape often emerged as the real star of his movies. With *She Wore a Yellow Ribbon,* the director photographed Monument Valley in color for his first time. "You take that kind of background," Ben Johnson said, "and the actors don't have to be too good. The background sells the picture." In *Yellow Ribbon* Ford tried to capture the West of Frederic Remington, even using some of the artist's colors and composition. The atmosphere of frontier army life has never been more beautifully evoked on film. The scene of the cavalrymen leading their mounts through a storm, with lightning flashes in an awesome sky, became a classic moment in cinema history and helped win cameraman Winton Hoch an Academy Award.

Although working in the desert location was arduous, the nights in Monument Valley were extraordinary. Ford and his cronies played pitch or poker, and occasionally the company assembled for a sing-along. Just behind Goulding's lodge is a gigantic rock wall, and the trading post overlooks the valley's magnitude. "Right down below us, like a quarter of a mile," Ben Johnson recalled, "a fire would start up, and the Indians would start singing and dancing. The sound bounced off this rock wall and out into the valley; it was the eeriest sound."

Location shooting on *She Wore a Yellow Ribbon* finished before Thanksgiving, and the picture was completed at the old Pathé studio. Ford and his Argosy partner differed on how the movie should end. The director wanted to close with Brittles's reaching into his pocket and saying, "Let's see what time it is by my brand new silver watch. Three minutes after twelve. I've been a civilian for three minutes. Hard to believe." Then he would ride off. But Merian Cooper insisted that Tyree should chase after the retired officer and bring him back to the post for another assignment.

In 1949 John Wayne became the first winner of the Silver Spur award, sponsored by the Chamber of Commerce of Reno, Nevada. But Duke had become more than the leading cowboy star. After working in Hollywood for two decades, he had become a member of the film industry's establishment, and he was determined to purge it of left-wing influences.

In March 1949 Wayne was installed as president of the Motion Picture Alliance for the Preservation of American Ideals, a position he held for three consecutive terms. Duke was relieved that Congress had undertaken an investigation of alleged Communists within the entertainment business and gave Sen. Joseph McCarthy his full support. Although Wayne was never called to testify before the House Committee on Un-American Activities, he endorsed the industry's blacklisting of workers who were deemed politically subversive or found to be members of left-wing organizations. "The only thing our side did," Wayne later said, "was just run a lot of [Communist sympathizers] out of the business."

Duke never apologized for his unabashed conservatism, and he refused to make movies that were critical of the United States or its governmental process. He denounced the film version of *All the King's Men*, which won the Academy Award for best picture of 1949, maintaining that it smeared the machinery of the country's government. Wayne claimed that the film would "tear down people's faith in everything that they have been brought up to believe is important in the American way of life." Later he called *High Noon* (1952) "the most un-American thing I've ever seen in my whole life." Duke incorrectly remembered the Western's final scene as one in which the United States marshal played by Gary Cooper throws his badge to the ground and steps on it. "I'll never regret having helped run Carl Foreman [*High Noon*'s screenwriter] out of the country," Wayne said.

Duke was severely criticized for his extreme right-wing politics, and some alleged that he had become the tool of studio heads. "It was a terrible, terrible period," said liberal agent Sam Jaffe. "It was just shocking. I remember sitting with Jack Warner in the dining room at Warner Bros., and John Wayne was there. Wayne said, 'We oughta get these guys outta here and let them go over to Russia if they're so pinko.' This man had no substance. He was a great American hero actor, but he was crude. He was uneducated. He had no idea what democracy stood for."

In Duke's view he became the victim of a mudslinging campaign instigated by his political opponents. "I was called a drunk, a pervert, a woman-chaser, a lousy B picture Western bit player, an unfaithful husband, and an uneducated jerk," he said. But as Wayne gained wealth and power, he cared less what people thought. He spoke his mind and acted on his principles with the force of his screen heroes.

Coworkers vowed that they knew exactly where they stood with Duke. "There wasn't any subterfuge with him," said John Agar, who worked in several of Wayne's pictures, "he was right out front. If he didn't agree with you, he'd let you know quick." Most of Duke's friends agreed with his conservative political views. Ward Bond was perhaps even more reactionary; so were James Edward Grant, Cliff Lyons, and *Red River*'s scriptwriter, Borden Chase. John Ford tried to encourage moderation during the anti-Communist hysteria, but he came to lean increasingly to the right. Wayne claimed that his group were merely good Americans who demanded the right to speak out. Like Thomas Jefferson, Duke believed that the best government is that which governs least. He also argued that one should fight to win, and during the early years of the Cold War he insisted that his country's fundamental values were in jeopardy.

Yet he wasn't without forgiveness. When actor Larry Parks confessed that he had once been a Communist Party member, reporters raced to John Wayne for a statement. Duke thought a moment, said it was unfortunate that Parks had been a Communist, but added that it was damn courageous of him to admit his mistake. "When any member of the Party breaks with them," said Wayne, "we must welcome him back into American society. We should give him friendship and help him find work again in our industry." At the next meeting of the Motion Picture Alliance for the Preservation of American Ideals, second vice president Hedda Hopper scolded Wayne for his lenient attitude toward Parks. "She berated me for an hour!" Duke claimed. Hopper contended that Wayne deserved the chastisement. "Duke is a little dumb about these things," she told a friend.

More and more now, Wayne wanted to produce his own motion pictures. He earned that right at Republic for a second time by agreeing to star again opposite Herbert Yates's paramour, Vera Hruba Ralston. *The Fighting Kentuckian* (1949) ranks among his lesser efforts, distinguished mainly by Lee Garmes's photography. Ralston still had trouble with English, she hadn't improved noticeably as an actress, and Wayne blamed her for the picture's limited appeal. The Czech skater would make twelve films at Republic, and only the two with Duke showed a profit. "Yates made me use Vera Hruba," said Wayne. "I've always been mad at Yates about this because we lost the chance to have one damn fine movie."

On any Ralston picture Yates was a frequent visitor to the set, an inconvenience that irritated Duke. Sometimes the actress required fifteen or more takes before the director found one good enough to print. Ralston was a pleasant, genuine person, yet everyone on the lot knew that she was the boss's girlfriend and kept a distance. Yates and Ralston made a curious couple—he was a testy little Yankee in his sixties at the time, a man who chewed tobacco and often missed the spittoon, while Ralston was a tall woman and rather regal. But workers at Republic respected Yates and accepted Ralston as part of the package when they went under contract to the studio.

Wayne avoided both of them so far as possible and continued to surround himself with his own people. A journalist who visited the set of *The Fighting Kentuckian* wrote that the assemblage gathered there looked like an overgrown Western family: "In one corner, the Duke in coonskin cap, suede jacket, and dirty horsehide pants was playing chess with his stand-in. Grant Withers, Paul Fix, Bob Morrison—the Duke's brother, who is assistant director—and other compadres straddled around shooting the breeze."

Now in his forties, Wayne had to rely more heavily on a double for stunts, but he had difficulty finding one to measure up to Yakima Canutt, who by then had graduated to second-unit director. Duke used stuntman Chuck Roberson as his double for the first time on *The Fighting Kentuckian*. Roberson, about the same size as Duke, would work with Wayne throughout the remainder of his career. Occasionally he was rewarded with a bit part and a line or two of dialogue, and he fit comfortably into Duke's professional stable.

Wayne was unhappy about the mediocrity of *The Fighting Kentuckian*, but he already had in mind a film about the siege at the Alamo and hoped that Yates would feel indebted enough to allow him to produce the project. Duke's next assignment at Republic, however, stands among his most memorable performances—the role of Sergeant Stryker in *Sands of Iwo Jima* (again 1949). The picture would be Duke's quintessential war movie; it earned him an Academy Award nomination, increased his power as a Hollywood star, and helped make him a national legend. "Sergeant Stryker was right down Duke's alley," said costar John Agar. "It showed the tough part about him, the soft part about him, and it was really very much like him in my opinion."

Sands of Iwo Jima profited from a solid script, plausible character development, and insight into human relationships under the stresses of war. "It wasn't just plot and action," said the film's director, Allan Dwan. "These were guys that altered as time went along." The idea originated with producer Edmund Grainger, who took the finished script to Republic. Herbert Yates agreed to make the film so long as it could be produced for less than $200,000, which Grainger insisted was impossible. In desperation the producer talked his father, Jim Grainger, head of sales at Republic, into putting pressure on Yates. Eventually the studio head consented to a budget of $1 million with the conditions that John Wayne star in the picture and a seasoned director be hired. "Yates had heart failure when he had that much money tied up in one picture," said Dwan.

The director wasn't sure that Wayne would accept the assignment until the day before the picture went before the cameras. In fact, Dwan made final preparations at Camp Pendleton, near San Diego, with no actor signed to play Stryker. As a safeguard, the director had asked a general at the camp to be ready to step into the part should no one else be available. "Finally Wayne came down," Dwan recalled, "and brought James Edward Grant along to rewrite his scenes for him. The script was perfect for Wayne, except that he wanted to say things in a certain way, and a writer sometimes writes a phrase a little differently. Wayne was very simple and very plain, and he seemed to think that Grant was the only man who could put the words the way he ought to say them."

Duke and the veteran director worked well together. Dwan was impressed with Wayne's preparation for the role; he spent hours talking with marines at Camp Pendleton in an effort to give his impersonation authenticity. Once filming got underway, the director noted that Wayne was particularly good at faking punches in fights. "I let him and Forrest

Tucker slug it out," said Dwan. "They took over their fight scenes and worked them out." On the second day of shooting Duke told Dwan, "You're my kind of director."

Esperanza went down to San Diego with Duke, but spent much of her time there alone. When the couple were together, they generally fought. Most evenings Wayne drank at a bar near the marine base at Oceanside, staying out until quite late. One Saturday night he and John Agar remained at the bar until closing time. "There were some people we met in there who suggested we go over to their place," Agar recalled, "and we were there till four, maybe five o'clock in the morning. Duke had an appointment that morning with a bunch of Marine Corps officers at eight o'clock in the morning, and by gosh he was there."

Wayne seemed to have a limitless capacity for handling liquor, although even Ward Bond had begun urging him to cut back on his drinking. Duke delighted in being able to outdrink men much younger than himself; to him it meant he need not worry about age. Some of the actors in the cast tried to keep up with him and were a pathetic sight when they reported to work the next morning. To teach them a lesson, Allan Dwan turned some hungover performers over to a drill sergeant with instructions for him to put them through their paces. "Not one of them ever stayed up late again," the director said. "They crawled into that hay at 10 o'clock, and they avoided Wayne like a plague. Even Agar got straightened out, and he was a tough one, because he liked the bottle."

Duke could identify with Sergeant Stryker, a professional soldier with a disastrous home life. In one sequence Stryker picks up a woman who has hustled him in a club and goes home with her, only to discover that she has a baby and needs money for food. He picks up the child and, to the woman's surprise, handles the infant with loving care. "I know about babies," Stryker says. The line could have come from Duke himself and the poignancy required little acting. Wayne's performance, honest and convincing throughout, holds the picture together.

At the end of the movie Stryker is shot by a Japanese sniper. It is a disturbing moment, harsh and unexpected. The shot happens abruptly, just after Stryker has told his men how good he feels. The impact on audiences was devastating. "The story would be nothing with a so-called happy ending," said Allan Dwan. The filmmaker's goal was to treat war in a thoughtful manner, stressing the price a military victory costs in human lives. "I don't think anyone could have been any better than Wayne," the director said.

The famous flag raising on Suribachi was recreated with the marines who had actually lifted the colors on Iwo Jima. "We dug them up from all over the place," Dwan said. Ira Hayes, a Native American, had returned to his reservation after the war. "He loved the bottle and was a sad sight," said Dwan. "He would get himself lit, so we had to put a guard over him."

Wayne was paid $180,000 for *Sands of Iwo Jima*, plus 10 percent of the profits. The picture opened in Los Angeles at Grauman's Chinese Theater, then moved to four Fox theaters in the city, including the prestigious Fox Wilshire. Duke received an award from *Photoplay* magazine for his performance and for the first time appeared on the list of Hollywood's ten most popular stars. While he lost the Oscar for best actor to Broderick Crawford (for *All the King's Men*), the nomination added to Wayne's professional standing. And the movie became one of the ten most popular films of 1950, grossing $5 million in domestic rentals alone.

Critics now began taking John Wayne more seriously, while his public exalted him as a symbol of Americanism. Even the marine corps sanctioned his reputation as a war hero by dubbing a flat instrument used to open C rations, and worn attached to dog tags, a "John Wayne"; the can opener was used by servicemen for the next forty years.

Duke accepted his new status without losing perspective. He was grateful for the reputation, yet he could joke about his image. He was aware of his importance but was never one to lord it over anyone. His humility was genuine. "I think that he acted the way he did instinctively," his son Michael said. "He had courage, he was self-sufficient, and he was fiercely independent."

Obligated to make three pictures at RKO for Howard Hughes, Wayne agreed to star in *Jet Pilot* (not released until 1957). Hughes, an aviation enthusiast, had been planning the movie for four years, hoping to make another *Hell's Angels*, a film he had directed in 1930 about flyers in World War I. With *Jet Pilot* the multimillionaire aimed to simulate for audiences the experience of flying at supersonic speeds. Hughes knew about some of the air force's newest jet planes before they had been seen by the general public. But eccentric personality that he was, the new RKO head played with the film for seven years; by the time *Jet Pilot* was released, the planes he had expected to be so astonishing were obsolete.

147

Hughes had induced Josef von Sternberg out of retirement to direct his picture, but the project was not a happy experience for the celebrated filmmaker. To begin with, the aging Sternberg had to make a test to prove to Hughes that he could still handle the job. Once production started, it became evident that Hughes himself intended to retain full control. "My labors lasted some seven weeks, not counting the many weeks of preparing the film and editing it," Sternberg said. "I was told step by step, day by day, movement for movement, word for word, precisely what I was to direct." But on the set, when Hughes was not around, Sternberg assumed command. "His approach was brilliant," said Janet Leigh, who starred in the film opposite Wayne. "Duke and I both knew that the minute he started directing. His choice of camera angles and presentation were unique and startling. Unfortunately he was a dictatorial man and caused a great deal of trouble on the set. I hadn't been exposed to that kind of arrogance."

Leigh found Wayne a "very sincere actor," but "always John Wayne." Duke was far more patient with Sternberg than his young costar was, although he mumbled under his breath at some of the ridiculous suggestions the director made. "Honey," Duke told Leigh, "if I ever let loose, if I ever started on him, I'd kill the son of a bitch." Over the next two years, as retakes were needed, producer Jules Furthman took over as director.

The air force cooperated with Hughes on the production; fourteen air bases scattered between Alaska and Florida participated in the filming. A photographic unit traveled more than 40,000 miles and spent over 250 hours in the air during the sixteen months required to shoot the flying sequences alone. Furthman supervised the second unit and all of the work with miniatures. Then he and Hughes went to work cutting and recutting the movie, running up the cost to over $4 million. "They played with that footage like kids playing with toy trains," Janet Leigh said.

When *Jet Pilot* was finally released, its reviews were devastating. Critics claimed they blushed at how silly and outrageous the film was, and audiences saw why. Not only were the aircraft outmoded, the movie's situations and propaganda were dated as well. Wayne played a pilot, while Leigh, looking fresh and voluptuous, was a Russian flyer who deliberately strays into an American zone to spy. When Wayne is assigned to watch the intruder, the two have a playful affair, and he in time wins her over to the American side. Leigh remembered *Jet Pilot* as "a giant dud," and fortunately for everyone, the picture was quickly withdrawn.

When principal photography on Hughes's movie finished early in 1950, Wayne decided to take Chata on a trip to Central America. Afterwards he returned to Republic, where he was still trying to talk Herbert Yates into letting him produce his film about the Alamo. Duke had scored points with Yates by persuading John Ford to move Argosy, Ford's own production unit, to Republic. The director had a pet project in mind, too, an Irish story called *The Quiet Man*, which Ford wanted to shoot in color in Ireland. Yates was flattered to have Hollywood's most celebrated filmmaker working at his lot, but he insisted that Ford make a commercial Western for the studio before he would agree to finance the Irish picture. Almost every studio head in Hollywood had turned *The Quiet Man* down, and Yates did not expect the movie to earn a profit unless costs were held to a minimum.

To satisfy Yates, Ford turned to the third segment of his cavalry trilogy. Ultimately called *Rio Grande*, the Western teamed John Wayne with Maureen O'Hara for the first time, a combination that would prove the most successful of Wayne's career. If Duke was the macho man, O'Hara was the macho woman, and they harmonized with compatible vigor over the five pictures in which they worked together. Their rapport is more sexual than Wayne projected with any other actress, for O'Hara's spunky, self-confident personality made their attraction plausible. "There was a chemistry between us that you don't get very often in the picture business," the actress said. "It was there with Spencer Tracy and Katharine Hepburn, and it was there with William Powell and Myrna Loy. But I was tall and strong, and Duke was tall and strong." When the two quarreled on the screen, it was a battle between equals. Both were stubborn and determined, yet each brought out a vulnerability in the other. "I think the audience enjoyed imagining what it was like when we made up," O'Hara said.

In private Duke treated O'Hara almost like another man, although the actress was feminine and undeniably beautiful. When asked once his opinion of O'Hara, Wayne replied, "The greatest guy I ever knew." The rapport between the two off screen was as strong as it was on. They teased each other, played pranks on one another, and respected each other enormously. O'Hara stood up to Duke, paid him back shot for shot, and endeared herself to him in a nonromantic way. He respected her natural attitude—no coquettish airs or false allure. With her he could be honest, reveal his sentimental side, and let his flaws show. O'Hara was an original.

"She was all woman," her brother, Charles FitzSimons said, "but she was in control. She fulfilled every woman's desire to match up to her man."

Ford decided to film *Rio Grande* near Moab, Utah, then a small Mormon town with limited facilities. Eager as always to work for Ford, Wayne agreed to cut his fee nearly in half, since Yates insisted that the Western be made in black and white on a limited budget. The picture's cast included a number of regulars from the John Ford stock company—Victor McLaglen, Harry Carey, Jr., Ben Johnson, Grant Withers, along with the director's customary wranglers and stuntmen, two of whom died in a river accident while making the movie.

Duke's twelve-year-old son Patrick went to Utah with his father, arriving there on June 14, 1950, and the handsome lad was rewarded with a small part in the movie and a couple of lines of dialogue. "That work was special for me at that age, because I was on location with my dad," Patrick Wayne declared. "Of my four brothers and sisters I was the only one who was working with Dad; I had my father to myself. I wasn't having to compete with my brothers and sisters for his attention. And I was the apple of my godfather's eye. As far as John Ford was concerned, I could do no wrong."

The company filmed around Moab for three weeks and lived under primitive conditions. It was so hot that a huge pit, the size of a room, was dug in the ground, and a wet tarpaulin was put over it. Some metal cots were placed in the pit, and whenever the actors weren't working, they went down there and stretched out on the cots. "On our way home every night," Maureen O'Hara remembered, "there was a place where a spring came out of a rock wall. We always stopped there and filled our bottles with spring water. We said it was to recharge our batteries."

Duke, as customary, did his share of whatever needed to be done. "I've seen him put his shoulder to a location truck that was stuck," cinematographer Bert Glennon said, "or hold a pair of shears and a comb for a hairdresser when she had to make a hurried change on one of the characters." But Chuck Roberson, who doubled Wayne, was most impressed with Duke's ability to handle demanding action. "John Wayne throws the best punch of anyone in the motion picture business," said Roberson.

Duke, cast as a taciturn military man (the same character he portrayed in *Fort Apache*) estranged from his wife and son, yet filled with a love for both that he cannot fully express, gives an excellent performance in *Rio*

Grande. A recurring theme in later John Wayne movies first surfaced here; it has Duke, the resolute older man, initiating young males into adulthood. On the surface he is tough, willing to accept no compromises, yet he shows his sensitive side when a challenge presents itself that allows the youth to prove his mettle. It was a page drawn from Duke's own boyhood and mirrored his relationship with his own father. He played those scenes with remarkable conviction. By assuming the role of a nurturing mentor on the screen, he seemed to be attempting to ease the guilt he felt over being a sporadic presence for his own children.

Time and again Wayne said, "I don't act; I react. Whatever part I'm playing, whether it be a cowboy, pilot, or sea captain, I always have to be John Wayne, just living through the experience." His approach appeared so natural that for years critics disregarded the talent involved. "I know that the hardest thing to do in a scene is to do nothing, or seem to do nothing," Wayne said, "because doing nothing requires extreme work and discipline. . . . Nobody can be natural; you'll drop a scene if you're natural." Duke possessed the discipline required and gradually mastered small movements to communicate what words could not. "I figure one look that works is better than twenty lines of dialogue," he said. Motion picture acting, Wayne claimed, is "like sitting in a room with someone and talking across a table. If you overact, they're quite aware of it; if there's too much falseness, you lose them." Like James Stewart and Gary Cooper, Wayne came to understand that realistic film acting meant experiencing the part—thinking it more than physically expressing what a character feels or does, and letting those thoughts register in the eyes.

"Nobody seems to like my acting but the people," Duke often remarked. He was wrong, of course; within the business many champions recognized Wayne's genius, perhaps even before he did. "Duke is the best actor in Hollywood," John Ford had said after they had completed *She Wore a Yellow Ribbon*. The director admired Wayne's total involvement as an actor and his passion for his work; he advised Duke to ignore his critics, as Ford himself did. Both accepted that film drama differs from live theater, which without benefit of closeups actually results in a less intimate encounter between actors and audience. Ford directed only one play on the stage, a production of *What Price Glory*, which opened at Grauman's Chinese Theater in March 1949, as a benefit for the Military Order of the Purple Heart. The all-star cast, which included Maureen O'Hara,

Gregory Peck, George O'Brien, Oliver Hardy, and Ward Bond, then traveled by bus to San Francisco and San Diego. Wayne played one of the extras, his only attempt at professional theater. "That's completely out for me," he said. "It's a different racket altogether."

Duke did not like to talk much about acting, and when he did, it was always in down-to-earth terms. "A good actor," he said, "can play all kinds of parts." That was never his strength, and he accepted his limitations. "My roles have to be tailored to fit me," said Duke. "All I do is sell sincerity, and I've been selling the hell out of that ever since I started. But I'm an investment, and I gotta protect that investment." Ever the pragmatist, Wayne accepted his status as a movie personality who simply found himself in various situations on the screen.

Wayne claimed that he worked as hard as he did to earn a living. "I don't have a capital gains setup like some of these guys," he said, "and I've got two families to feed." The truth was that he had become a fanatic about work. He remembered his poverty and feared that his good fortune might someday reverse. He invested in such things as apartment buildings, a motel, a country club, a yachting marina, a beach club, a frozen food company, oil wells, and common stocks. Still, he was a driven man where work was concerned and approached the picture business as if it were any other commercial venture, determined to leave his family comfortably well off.

At one point in 1949 eight John Wayne movies were playing simultaneously across the country, some of them reissues. The next year he was Hollywood's number one star in box-office popularity, and he stayed in the top ten for another twenty-four years. He was a particular favorite with men but ranked high with women and children as well. Friends warned Duke that if he continued to represent the militant, right-wing Motion Picture Alliance for the Preservation of American Ideals, his career would suffer. When just the reverse happened, Wayne grinned with delight. "I guess the Reds ruined me," he said facetiously.

But Duke had the backing of a smart agent, Charles Feldman, and he was astute in selecting appropriate roles. "There were certain guidelines that my father used," Michael Wayne said. "The biggest thing was, would his fans accept him in this role. Would they be disappointed? Because he said, 'They're the ones that pay my salary.' So everything he did was based on giving audiences what they wanted."

Duke genuinely liked people and needed to be accepted. "I like the idea of being popular with a great number of people and having an identification with them," he said. Long before the video bonanza, John Wayne's films had grossed over $700 million at the box office, more than the films of any other star in history. "The great thing about John Wayne," Duke's son Michael said, "is that he guaranteed a bottom," that is, the lowest possible profit a picture could be expected to earn. "He wouldn't guarantee a top, although some of his pictures went through the roof. But they never lost any money. That's what was great about him. The theater owners and the producers loved him for that. Movie stars carry films for producers, and that's what my father did more than anybody else."

His Own Company

On May 2, 1949, Wayne signed a contract with Warner Bros. to make seven pictures for the studio over the next seven years, for which he would be paid a salary plus 10 percent of the gross on each film. Part of the agreement was that Wayne's own production unit would be allowed to make films at the studio, which Warner would distribute. Duke was still free to make pictures elsewhere, and he hoped that he would ultimately be given a chance to try his hand at directing. "My films will be Westerns most likely," Wayne predicted, "since that's the type of picture I feel most at home with."

Duke liked and respected Jack Warner, the studio's boss, and Warner welcomed Wayne back into his fold, aware that the actor's movies meant certain profit. But by 1956 Duke's arrangement with Warner would turn sour, and when their agreement ended, the two were barely speaking. Wayne was convinced that Jack Warner had been guilty of skullduggery. "Nobody came out with a sizable profit from doing any deal with Warners," screenwriter Niven Busch said. "They had the most foolproof, plate-steel accounting system in the world. . . . Wayne went to Warners, and he *never* made failures, but [there] he was in red ink! It was kind of a putdown [for] him."

Duke returned to the Warner Bros. lot in the fall of 1950, after an absence of seventeen years, to make his first film under the new agreement. The movie was *Operation Pacific*, and his costar was contract player Patricia Neal, then in love with Gary Cooper, who became a frequent visitor to the set. "John Wayne had enormous appeal for the public," Neal said, "but I did not find him appealing in the least. I think my charms were lost on him, too. He was going through marital problems, which kept him in a bad humor all the time. Duke was at odds with the director and could be a bully, particularly with a gay publicity man who seemed to draw his wrath at every turn."

Written and directed by George Waggner, *Operation Pacific* proved only a modest success when it opened at theaters in January 1951. Wayne played a navy man, more in love with his submarine than with his ex-wife, whom he is courting. Critics labeled the picture a waste of time, but John Wayne's name on the marquee guaranteed a respectable return.

Faced with competition from television and dwindling audiences, Hollywood's major studios had begun cutting costs and easing expensive stars out of long-term contracts. Within the next ten years movie houses across the country would close, as the nation's population shifted to the suburbs, where they concentrated on buying homes and rearing children. "Duke's one of the few sure-fire box-office things left in Hollywood," Howard Hughes declared in the early 1950s.

Wayne had high regard for Hughes, admired the billionaire's courage, and respected his sovereignty over RKO, capricious though his control might be. In 1950 Hughes paid Duke $300,000 to star in *Flying Leathernecks*, then the highest salary ever awarded an actor for a single picture. Wayne returned to the marine base at Camp Pendleton to shoot the film, which Nicholas Ray directed. James Edward Grant wrote the script, and Robert Ryan shared star billing with Wayne. As long as the story unfolds in the air, *Flying Leathernecks* is an exciting movie; on the ground its characters seem cliché and Grant's dialogue borders on the absurd.

Duke was becoming increasingly serious about producing his own pictures, as well as projects that featured other stars. In 1950 he grew interested in *The Bullfighter and the Lady*, a film based on the early career of director Budd Boetticher. Wayne agreed to meet with Boetticher at the Hotel Reforma in Mexico City, and after many drinks and several hours of talk he agreed to produce Boetticher's film. The two returned to Hollywood with the hope of convincing Herbert Yates to put up the money. Yates was reluctant, since a reader in Republic's story department had told him that the plot was merely a rehash of Tom Lea's *The Brave Bulls*. When Wayne became insistent, Yates agreed to assign the production a limited budget.

Robert Stack was cast as the young American bullfighter, and the company left for Mexico. Much of the movie was shot in Xayai, a small village built around a bullring. Wayne was there on the first day of filming and showed signs of taking over as director. "Six times Duke walked in front of me," Boetticher recalled. "The first shot of the picture, in the middle of a scene, he walked in front of me and grabbed Stack by the shirt and said, 'Jesus Christ, Bob, if you're gonna say the line, say it with some balls.' He scared Stack to death." Finally Boetticher called Wayne aside and asked, "Duke, do you think you could direct this picture better than

I can?" They returned to the set, and Duke confessed to the assemblage that he'd been scolded by their director. "He told me that one of us has to go home," Wayne said. "I'm leaving tonight and won't see you until the end of the picture."

True to his word, Duke left Boetticher and his crew alone. The problems the director faced thereafter on the picture stemmed not from Wayne's interference but from James Edward Grant's script, which was based on Boetticher's thirty-seven-page treatment. "Jimmy Grant, who could be absolutely charming, was a real drunk," said Boetticher. "He disappeared for a week and was living in a whorehouse in Mexico City, writing my script. The screenplay that he delivered to me looked like he had been living in a whorehouse. It was just awful. We never rewrote the screenplay; we simply shot my treatment." When Grant saw the rough cut of the movie, he threw a fit, and that ended Boetticher's friendship with the writer. "Jimmy Grant could be a son of a bitch when he wanted to be," said Boetticher, "and he had a lot of control over what Wayne thought and did."

The director also experienced problems with Stack's costar, Gilbert Roland, whom Boetticher found arrogant to the point of exasperation. "I think the big reason that Roland was so damned good in the picture was because I hated him so much," the director said. Stack gave a solid performance and later looked back on *The Bullfighter and the Lady* with pride. "It has a good premise," said the actor. "As the American going into the bullfight field learns the game, the audience learns it with him. There wasn't one phony thing in that picture. The whole story was shot in the bullrings. It was a difficult movie. One man was killed and another was grievously wounded."

Wayne returned to Mexico in time to celebrate the end of shooting and to give a party for the company in Queretaro. The festivities included three mariachi bands and lasted until sunrise. "All hell broke loose," said Robert Stack. "Many local characters had been recruited as extras. They were casually invited to join our company, but we later discovered that the guns they wore on and off camera were full of live ammunition." Budd Boetticher remembered Duke's coming up to him at the party and handing him a half-empty quart of tequila. "I could tell by his eyes who had consumed the other half," said Boetticher. "He produced another full quart. . . . So I locked arms with him, and we began swallowing." As the evening progressed, Duke fell over a verandah railing into some bushes.

Chata had accompanied her husband to Mexico for the wrap party, and before the company dispersed, they attended a bullfight. "It was a big bullfight," said Boetticher, "and there were twelve empty seats in the first row. All of a sudden, just before the opening parade, we heard a rumbling and looked around. Here came Jimmy Grant with eleven hookers. I remember Chata turning to Duke and saying, 'If you even smile at those girls, I'm going to hit you.'"

Back in Los Angeles, Boetticher and Wayne ran into difficulties editing their film, so they called in John Ford. In Duke's office at Republic the master filmmaker got a look at his protégé in an executive capacity; he hadn't anticipated what he saw. Wayne paced the floor amid the constant ringing of telephones, his agitation starting to boil. When they settled down to discuss *The Bullfighter and the Lady*, Duke seemed full of ideas. Feeling the need to seize control, Ford said, "Well, Jesus, Duke, if you're going to start to think, I'm in the wrong office." Boetticher maintained that Ford's suggestions actually damaged the picture.

Still, Wayne and Boetticher worked hard and put together an impressive film. They often ended their week by getting drunk together at the Tail-of-the-Cock, a restaurant and bar near the Republic lot. "We would actually call each other about one o'clock the next day and try to reconstruct where the hell we'd been," the director said. "I don't think Wayne was an alcoholic; he was a Saturday night drunk. Duke worked his ass off, but every Saturday night we all got drunk."

"Duke and I really had a romance," said Boetticher; "I mean he was so damn great with me. But little by little Jimmy Grant would come in behind. He finally sabotaged John Wayne and me, and eventually Wayne and I did not end up great friends." But in the course of making *The Bullfighter and the Lady* (released in 1951) and *Seven Men from Now* (1956), which Wayne's brother produced, Boetticher got to know Duke well. "He was a bastard on one side and a wonderful guy on the other," the director said, "according to what his attitude was that day. Because of his power, there was no middle road. You were either the greatest guy in the world or a bastard. He could be really cruel, although I don't think Duke had a mean streak in his body. When he did something that hurt somebody, which he had to do on occasion, it hurt him. He would fret and stew when he did those things."

Despite Wayne's immense power, Boetticher sensed that Duke was an insecure man. "I think he was very aware of what he had to live up to," the director said, "and he was brilliant as far as his career was concerned. But I don't know that Duke was ever happy. Obviously he was happier on the set or carousing than he was at home. He worked hard not to be lonely, which tells me that he must have been. Anybody who keeps that busy has got to be lonely. But he is the only star I ever knew well that didn't have a lot of affairs. You can't be that discreet. Somebody had to catch him, and nobody ever did. As naughty as I was during that period, I thought John Wayne was kind of square."

Boetticher sensed that most of the people who knew Wayne never let themselves get too close to him, and nobody ever seemed to argue with him. During postproduction on *The Bullfighter and the Lady*, Duke and the director frequently disagreed. "He would walk away," Boetticher remembered, "and his group would walk with him, while I waited. He would turn around to say something to me and I would still be where I'd been, and he would get furious. If there were ten people in the room besides Duke, nine of those people would agree with everything he said; I would tell him he was full of crap. Duke and I fought a lot, particularly about politics, but I got to know him intimately."

Boetticher knew that Duke needed to be John Wayne and knew that he played the macho star better than anybody. "I think he knew everything about John Wayne," the director said; "he knew every move, everything he was going to say, every reaction. If you do something really well, you want to keep on doing it. It's your ego. If you play tennis, you want to play tennis in front of a lot of people. If you're John Wayne, you want to act. He had that kind of ego and needed to keep up his reputation."

"What you saw was what you got with John Wayne," said Robert Stack, who was under contract to Wayne's company for one picture a year after *The Bullfighter and the Lady*. "He was what he was in a very innocent way. He carried his stardom well and did what he was supposed to do. But he was a guy who made up his own mind and lived by his concept of protocol and right. He would cut through a fairly complex question in a very simplistic manner. He believed in God and the flag and America and apple pie and home and mother, and he was what he was. In this complex, hypocritical profession of ours, where everybody pretends to be something they're not, I found there was a basic charm to him. And that came across on film. He had the firm belief that if somebody portrayed something on film, he had to be that. In many ways he and Budd Boetticher were alike."

With *The Bullfighter and the Lady* finished and his yearly commitment to Howard Hughes out of the way, Duke flew to Ireland on June 4, 1951, to costar with Maureen O'Hara in John Ford's long-postponed *The Quiet Man*. Filming began on the Technicolor movie three days later around the village of Cong in County Mayo. The company was housed there in Ashford Castle. Ford arranged for a big dinner party to launch the project so dear to his heart; he wanted to express his happiness at making this picture with so many of his closest friends. O'Hara loved and respected Ford as much as Duke did, and the cast included several of the director's regulars: Ward Bond, Victor McLaglen, Mildred Natwick, Barry Fitzgerald, Arthur Shields, Ford's brother Francis, and the director's son-in-law, Ken Curtis. In addition, several members of the famed Abbey Players were in the cast, which pleased Wayne as much as it did Ford. The filmmaker was thrilled to be in Ireland for six weeks, while Duke enjoyed getting out and mixing with the local folk.

Ford had bought the rights to Maurice Walsh's story "The Quiet Man," published in the *Saturday Evening Post*, in 1933. He made a handshake agreement with John Wayne and Maureen O'Hara in 1944 that they would play the leads. "Every summer I went out on Ford's boat, the *Araner*, to Catalina with Pappy and his family," O'Hara said. "Mary Ford would take the kids to the beach in the afternoon, and I would sit there with Ford and take down notes for the script in shorthand. Then I'd go into the Yacht Club and type up the pages he had dictated." The initial script for the picture was done by Richard Llewellyn, who wrote *How Green Was My Valley*. But Llewellyn was quite political, and his draft was full of political overtones. "Ford wanted *The Quiet Man* to be more of a love story," O'Hara said, so Frank Nugent wrote the final script.

The story is a heartwarming romantic comedy that reflected much of the director's nostalgia for his ancestral homeland. Ford packed the picture with marvelous characters, stereotypical Irishmen more theatrical than real. He also achieved superb visuals from meadows, fields, and streams around the vicinity of Cong. *The Quiet Man* would earn Ford his fourth Academy Award for best direction of a feature film. (He won two more for documentaries.) For John Wayne *The Quiet Man* was a different kind of picture, yet it remains among his most popular.

"That was a goddamn hard script," said Duke. "For nine reels I was just playing a straight man to those wonderful characters, and that's really hard." Primarily a love story, *The Quiet Man* was a challenge for Wayne. Its plot is simple and has less action than mood and atmosphere. Even Ford worried that the ingredients might not jell once the project got underway. Duke wasn't comfortable with intense love scenes, yet pitted against the spunky Maureen O'Hara, he came across with an intensity not seen before. "I think that Maureen was as much woman as my father was man," Michael Wayne said. "She was very feminine and just illegally beautiful, but Maureen could be a steamroller. She was just as strong as any guy, although still a lady. But, boy, she'd throw the overhand right if things weren't going right, just like a guy would."

The electricity between Wayne and O'Hara proved to be high voltage in *The Quiet Man*. Mary Kate, O'Hara's character, hits her suitor when Wayne first kisses her. "I got so mad at Duke I was ready to kill him," O'Hara recalled. "I hauled off with every bit of strength I had and socked him in the jaw. He saw it coming and put his hand up, and my hand snapped off the tip of his fingers. I cracked a bone in my wrist, but I didn't open my mouth. I hid my hand in that red skirt I had on. The pain went up under my armpit until I thought I was going to die. But I was determined not to let Duke know." Finally Wayne came over to her and said, "Let me see your hand. You nearly broke my jaw!" O'Hara replied that that's what she had intended to do. Eventually she was sent to a hospital, where doctors found a tiny crack in her wrist.

On their wedding night Mary Kate angrily locks her husband out of their bedroom. As originally written, Sean Thornton, Duke's character, a former boxer, was to pick up his boxing gloves and feel sorry for himself. Wayne argued that Sean should stand up to his wife and kick in the door. After much discussion Frank Nugent agreed with Duke. Ford balked at first but finally yielded. The scene became one of the film's highlights, focusing the tension between the American husband and his spirited Irish bride.

Later Wayne drags O'Hara across the Irish countryside in a classic battle of the sexes and wins Mary Kate's respect in the process. Most of the sequence where Duke drags O'Hara was filmed on the golf course of Ashford Castle. Since it was cheaper to have the golf course sheared by grazing sheep than by mechanical mowers, the ground was covered with sheep manure, which stunk beyond belief. "Duke's gang, Ford, and Bond kept kicking more and more of the manure in," O'Hara said, "and my gang kept kicking it out. They won, and I was dragged on my stomach down through that sheep manure." Afterwards she tried to get a towel or some water to get the stuff off, but instructions had been given that she was to have no water and no towels. That night Neva Burn, the wardrobe woman, had to clean and iron the skirt the actress had been wearing. "She hit that skirt with the steam iron," O'Hara recalled, "and the smell came up with the steam. She took the skirt off the ironing board, opened the window, and dropped the skirt out into the bushes." Fortunately, there was an identical replacement for the actress to wear the next day.

Wayne and O'Hara had rehearsed every bit of the dragging scene without Ford's knowledge. They planned the action meticulously—how they would come onto a bush and O'Hara would lose her shoe, how she would be down on her behind and put the shoe on, how she would get up and take a swing at him, how she would turn and he would kick her in the rear end. They waited until just the right moment. Then Duke said, "Now!" and they went into their act. When the scene was over, Ford announced proudly, "You see. When things aren't rehearsed and they're spontaneous how wonderful they are!"

By present standards *The Quiet Man* is blatantly sexist, yet audiences still respond to the film's magic. Maureen O'Hara insisted that Mary Kate had triumphed over both her brother and her husband. "Just look at the twinkle in her eye at the end," the actress said. "She was stuck between two men, and she won. She'd conquered her brother and gotten her husband to do the conquering for her. If she really thought that her husband had dragged her all that way out of cruelty, Mary Kate would have chopped his head off. It was all a big act. Besides, Wayne could never abuse O'Hara because she was big enough to sock him on the jaw!"

During the weeks on location each day's footage of *The Quiet Man* was packaged up in the evening, driven from Ashford Castle to the airport at Shannon, and flown to the Republic studio. Herbert Yates hated what he saw, complained that the countryside looked too green, objected to Ford's Irish humor, and ordered the director to hold down the costs, still convinced that he was financing a dud. While Ford claimed to be impervious to such demands, in truth he was nervous about the picture's box-office potential.

The situation grew worse when the director developed a stomach problem and was confined to his bed for a day. "Pappy didn't know whether or not he had a picture," Wayne said, "and everything seemed to hang heavy." Ford had quarreled with his son Pat, a second-unit director on the movie, and asked Duke to film enough footage to keep Yates happy. Wayne supervised O'Hara's walking up from the beach, but Ford was back on the job the following morning.

Duke drank only once during the making of the picture. He had an afternoon off and went to a local pub, where he proceeded to overindulge. After work that evening Ford and his assistant director, Andrew McLaglen, went looking for Wayne, fearing the worst. "Jack Ford and I walked in that pub," McLaglen recalled, "and Duke was as drunk as I've ever seen him. He was falling-down drunk." The director told Wayne that they were just checking to see that he was all right and let the actor have his spree. "That night about twelve o'clock, I took some milk and a sandwich up to Wayne," said McLaglen. "He had the worst hangover, but by the next morning he was okay." Ford liked to tell the story of Duke's getting drunk in Ireland, but Wayne insisted that the episode had gotten exaggerated. "That's how legends are born," Duke said.

Most evenings after work Wayne and Ward Bond went fishing, while Barry Fitzgerald played golf. After dinner Ford walked the women up the river to a waterfall, then played gin rummy with Duke, while Victor McLaglen napped in a high-back chair in front of a fireplace in Ashford Castle. Chata visited her husband in Ireland, bringing Michael and Toni with her. Eventually all four of Wayne's children spent time in Cong with their father, and Ford used them in a brief scene, sitting or standing around a cart with Maureen O'Hara. While the children enjoyed their stay, Chata did not. As usual she was resentful of Duke's devotion to his sons and daughters and did not respond well to John Ford. It was evident that Duke's second marriage was doomed.

But for *The Quiet Man* company the time spent in Ireland was glorious. Ford stayed in a good mood, and the weather that summer was excellent. "I used to lie out in the long grass along with my makeup man and hairdresser," O'Hara recalled. "When Chata was there and I had a day off, I would take her to see the different sights—monuments, castles, and old monasteries in the area. We got on well together." The Wayne children had fun, and it became Mike's job, since he was the oldest, to keep the rest in line. He became known as "the hatchet man," much to the amusement of his brother and sisters. Whenever Mike came looking for her, Melinda, the youngest, would say, "Hide me." Maureen O'Hara and some others would hide her so that she didn't get sent off to bed too early. "Duke had a great relationship with his kids," O'Hara said. "He was wonderful with his boys."

As usual, the pranks and razzing on a Ford set were endless. Bombastic Ward Bond took much of the teasing. "Ward should have been in grand opera," said Charles FitzSimons, "but underneath it all was a caring person." Bond, Wayne, and Victor McLaglen were all big men, and each tried to be taller than the other. At one point Ford yelled, "Okay, guys, take off the high heels before we shoot one more scene!" At dinner Ford sat at the head of the table, and the jokes never ceased. Herbert Yates, who kept fussing about costs on the production, became the brunt of much abuse. One morning Wayne and Bond climbed up on top of a tower and with a piece of slate scratched, "Fuck Herb Yates," in a large stone, knowing that the production manager would be up there later in the day.

At the end of *The Quiet Man*, when O'Hara takes the stick from Wayne and throws it away, Duke registers a look of terrific shock. "It was genuine shock," the actress said. "Nobody but Duke and Ford know what I whispered up close to his ear. And nobody ever will." Ford told O'Hara what to say to get the reaction he wanted. "Oh, I can't say that!" the actress protested. "I'm sorry," Ford said, "you can and you will." The three of them ended up laughing so hard after the scene was shot that everyone else on the set got curious about what O'Hara had whispered in Duke's ear, and fans later hired a lip reader to try to unravel the mystery—to no avail. "There was a deal between Ford and Duke and myself that what I said would never, never be divulged," O'Hara maintained. "Not even Michael Wayne nor my daughter know." Then with a chuckle she added, "Those were great days!"

Duke returned home from Ireland on August 4, 1951, in an expansive mood, certain that he had done some of his best work there. But no sooner had he arrived in Los Angeles than he had a showdown with Yates over the film he and his partner, Robert Fellows, wanted to make about the battle of the Alamo. In disgust Wayne ended his association with Republic. *The Quiet Man* would be Duke's last picture for the studio. He had spent more than fifteen years working on the Republic lot and had made thirty-three movies for the company. "We grew up together," Wayne said. But he had become convinced that Yates had learned nothing about the picture business in all the years he had headed the studio. The Republic boss had grumbled about *The Bullfighter and the Lady* and even argued that *The Quiet Man* was not a good title for a John Wayne movie, since it suggested no action. Yates suggested either *The Prizefighter and the Colleen* or *The Fabulous Yankee* as alternatives with more box-office appeal. "The man has the soul of an accountant," said Duke. Wayne had stayed at Republic mainly because Ford was there and because Yates had pledged to finance Duke's film about the Alamo. Yet the situation at the studio had become as insufferable as his marriage.

In 1952 Wayne formed an independent production unit with veteran producer and former Paramount executive Robert M. Fellows. "Sink or swim," Duke said, "it had to be better than working with men like Yates and Cohn." John Wayne would be one of the first Hollywood stars to launch his own production company, a farsighted venture that soon became a trend. The details of incorporation seemed endless: "Still fighting lawyers," Duke wrote John Ford in March 1952.

Big Jim McLain, financed and distributed by Warner Bros., would be the first Wayne-Fellows production. Duke starred in the picture and surrounded himself with a crew of technicians whose work he knew would be consistent with his style. Edward Ludwig, whom Wayne had worked with on *Wake of the Red Witch,* directed; James Edward Grant polished and tightened the script; and Andrew McLaglen, who would direct several of John Wayne's later pictures, served as Ludwig's assistant.

The film allowed Wayne to put forth his political beliefs without mincing words. Big Jim McLain is an investigator working to expose a Communist spy ring in Hawaii. The hearing room of the House Committee on Un-American Activities is shown, along with witnesses who take the Fifth Amendment and refuse to answer the committee's questions on grounds that their answers might incriminate them. The research department at Warner Bros. had cautioned that the congressional investigations must not be shown in an offensive manner. "While I appreciate that the writers' endeavor is to laud and not demean these activities," the studio's head of research wrote in a preproduction memorandum, "I submit that this story could backfire in its present form—even to the possible extent of placing *us* in contempt of Congress." As James Edward Grant revised the script, there was no need for worry.

Most of the picture was shot in Hawaii. Esperanza accompanied Duke to Honolulu, but the couple fought when he went to a stag party on

Waikiki Beach with friends. She returned to Los Angeles in a fury and soon engaged the services of Jerry Giesler, a lawyer noted for securing advantageous divorce settlements for clients. While Wayne was still in Hawaii, Chata entertained hotel heir Nicky Hilton, Elizabeth Taylor's first husband, as an overnight guest in their home. Hilton later claimed that nothing inappropriate took place during his stay there and branded allegations to the contrary as ridiculous. But rumors reached Duke that his wife was spending most of her evenings in bars along Ventura Boulevard in the San Fernando Valley, where she was picking up strangers and subsequently spending the night with them.

The Wayne marriage had been tenuous almost from its beginning. The couple had even separated briefly in 1951, shortly after Duke returned from Ireland, and Chata had gone back to Mexico. "She is highly nervous, and she needed medical attention," gossip columnist Louella Parsons reported. "She thinks the doctors in her home town are better." The Waynes reconciled and made a last attempt to save their marriage in February 1952. "I blame myself for our trouble," said Duke. "I devoted too much time to business and not enough to making a home for Esperanza and me."

But when Wayne flew back to Los Angeles after completing *Big Jim McLain*, he rented a house on Longridge Street in the Valley, leaving Chata in possession of their Encino estate. He felt that she had deceived him and grew despondent over a second failed marriage. "Duke was broken up when he realized his marriage with Chata was on the rocks," Ward Bond said. "He was sick about it." Mainly he felt defeated, unsure of himself where intimate relationships were concerned, and fearful that he could not trust his judgment about women.

Aware that his private life was in shambles, Duke left for Mexico City, where the second Wayne-Fellows production, *Plunder of the Sun* (1953), was to be shot at Churubusco Studios, with Glenn Ford in the lead. Wayne was emotionally destroyed by the debacle of his second marriage and the scandal he sensed was coming. He worried about the effect the gossip would have on his children, about what Josephine would think, and about the impact on his career. But the Hollywood establishment remained loyal to its own. In the summer of 1952 the dispensers of movie gossip did their best to camouflage the tawdry relationship that was about to end. "I happen to know the real reason back of the rift," Louella Parsons wrote in her column. "Mrs. Wayne is desperately jealous of John's devotion to his four children by a previous marriage." Respectful of Josephine and hesitant to reveal Duke's second marriage for what it was, the duennas of Hollywood gossip attempted to sanitize a shabby situation.

Wayne's despair deepened when *Big Jim McLain* was not well received. At the movie's preview at the Warner Theater in Huntington Park, California, the response was negative. "More action and less talk," was one comment. "Did every speech have to have a propaganda context?" Another viewer wrote, "Good in spots, except for the too, too obvious propaganda—and I am *Not* a Commie." Another stated: "One wonders about the future of his country when this sort of tripe passes for Americanism." When the film was released in September, critics found *Big Jim McLain* to be little more than crass anti-Red propaganda; some reviewers even labeled it irresponsible. While the movie was a disappointment at the box office, Wayne later claimed that it helped reelect Sen. Joseph McCarthy. "McCarthy was a friend of mine," said Duke. "Whether he went overboard or not, he was of value to my country."

Wayne had another political statement to make, one he thought to be more positive. Still eager to produce his film about the siege at the Alamo, Duke left for Peru in the late summer of 1952 to scout the possibility of making the film there. Faced with rising costs in Hollywood, motion picture companies were increasingly working abroad, lured by the cheap, nonunion labor available in foreign countries. Duke had initially thought of making his Alamo movie in Panama, then considered Peru, where he planned to invest some capital. Wanting to escape the turmoil created by Chata, Wayne decided to fly to South America on a working vacation.

He had been told to look up a young American sportsman named Richard Weldy when he arrived in Lima. Weldy worked for Pan American Grace Airways and conducted safaris up the Amazon as a sideline. Duke met Dick Weldy, liked him, and discovered that they shared similar interests. Weldy's estranged wife at the time was making a movie in Tingo Maria, a few hundred miles into the interior. Wayne's new acquaintance volunteered to fly the star's entourage into the jungle to see how a Peruvian motion picture crew operated, and Duke thought the experience would be interesting.

They arrived in the interior late one afternoon, as Weldy's wife, Pilar Palette, was filming a dance sequence. "I was dancing barefoot by firelight, wearing a low-cut gypsy costume," Pilar remembered. She was flushed and out of breath when introduced to John Wayne, and her long hair fell around her shoulders. Duke was charmed by this Latin beauty, and she thought him the handsomest, most overpowering man she had ever met. "I couldn't believe anyone's eyes could be so turquoise," Pilar said. "I'd never been so immediately and powerfully affected by a casual meeting with a man the way I was by my meeting with John Wayne. . . . Something elemental about the man, a sense of great strength, appealed to me."

The director told his cast and crew to take the rest of the day off and announced that he was giving a dinner that evening in Wayne's honor and that they were all invited. The guests were told to gather for cocktails on the patio of the Plaza Hotel. "I'd never realized what a romantic setting it was until I arrived that evening," Pilar recalled. "A great, pale jungle moon illuminated the night sky, candles glowed on the tables, and the soft murmur of a stream flowing a few feet away added to the atmosphere." As she made her entrance, Wayne stood up and motioned her to his side.

Pilar Palette had not seen her estranged husband in several months. They had separated when Dick Weldy became involved with another woman. Pilar and Weldy had met when she was a stewardess for Pan American Grace Airways and had married when she was quite young. The daughter of a Peruvian senator, Pilar's upbringing had been cultured and opulent, with limousines taking her to school and back. *Green Hell*, the film she was making when Wayne met her, was her second, but she had never really liked the movie business.

Pilar had seen American films, but in the early 1950s ten years might pass between the release of a Hollywood movie and its appearance on the screens of South America. Since she did not particularly care for Westerns, Pilar only vaguely knew who John Wayne was. At dinner that first evening, she found talking to him difficult. Finally in faltering English she said, "You were wonderful in *For Whom the Bell Tolls*." Duke gave her his lopsided grin and explained that she was thinking of his friend Gary Cooper, but her blunder seemed to put both of them at ease. "He was fun," she said, "loved a good party, and liked the lush jungle where we were. There was an electrical quality about him."

Later in the evening Pilar played the guitar and sang. Duke was struck by her dignified bearing, her classic face, her huge, dark eyes, and her slender figure. The black-haired Peruvian beauty clearly made an impression on him. Although she was twenty-two years younger than he, Wayne admired her serenity and sensed that here was a woman of strength and intelligence. Pilar thought him easygoing and natural but mistook his mask for self-confidence.

Duke left the next morning, visited Chile, Argentina, and Brazil, and stopped off in Mexico City to check on the progress of *Plunder of the Sun.* "He was killing time," Pilar said, "because he wanted to get away from Esperanza and not go back to the States for a while."

Wayne returned to Los Angeles in September to make *Trouble along the Way* for Warner Bros. The picture (released in 1953) was screenwriter Melville Shavelson's first opportunity to produce; he and his partner, Jack Rose, had written the screenplay, which was based on a story in the *Saturday Evening Post.* In the movie Wayne played an alcoholic football coach who is running away from a broken marriage and winds up at a small Catholic college, where he attempts to improve the school's football team. Duke claimed that the script needed polishing and insisted that James Edward Grant do a rewrite, explaining to the producer that Grant had a good feel for his way of talking. What Grant submitted sent chills of horror through Shavelson, so they ended up with two scripts. Wayne was given one, and on days when he wasn't working Shavelson and director Michael Curtiz shot the other. "Only one thing went wrong," Shavelson said. "Duke showed up on the set on a day he wasn't supposed to be there and found out what was going on."

"Ordinarily Wayne is one of the kindest and most levelheaded of men," the writer-producer said. "But when crossed, and particularly when double-crossed, he can make an underground nuclear explosion seem like a baby's sigh." Upon discovering the deceit, Duke grabbed Shavelson, and a serious confrontation ensued. "To be grabbed by a guy who is six feet four, who is running the goddamn picture, was a terrible moment," Shavelson recalled. They finished the film Wayne's way, but the producer and star were no longer on speaking terms.

On September 12, 1952, Duke and Esperanza filed simultaneous divorce suits. Wayne beat his wife to the courthouse by thirty minutes, charging physical and mental cruelty. She filed for separate maintenance on a similar charge. "This will be one of the hottest contested battles of anytime," Louella Parsons predicted. Chata enjoyed the limelight that the divorce proceedings engendered and courted the tabloids to create sympathy for her position. She was determined to win as strong a financial settlement as possible. Before long reporters were camped outside Duke's house on Longridge Street, awaiting the next scoop.

In the midst of the furor, Pilar Palette arrived in Hollywood to dub dialogue for an English version of *Green Hell*, the film she had just completed in Peru. Pilar maintained that she and Wayne crossed paths purely by accident at Warner Bros. while she was there making a new soundtrack for her movie, but the serendipity is questionable. Duke hated being alone and needed companionship, yet the ensuing affair with Pilar had to be kept secret since both parties were still married. Wayne soon moved Pilar from the Biltmore Hotel to an apartment in a building owned by actor Fred MacMurray, while he kept the house on Longridge.

Their complicated living arrangement had its effect on the shooting of *Trouble along the Way*. "Wayne at the time was going through his divorce troubles," Melville Shavelson remembered, "and he was having an affair with Pilar, who had come up from Peru. The wife who was divorcing him put a detective on his tail, and if she could catch him with Pilar that would change the size of the settlement tremendously. So he was going out of his mind. One day he shook the detective and didn't show up on the set for a week." Warner Bros. had to close down the picture during that time. When Duke finally returned to work, he had a fixation that whenever he did a scene with a woman, she should make a play for him. "I don't know what he was building up for himself," Shavelson said.

Trouble along the Way was finished in November, three days behind schedule, and did not fare well at the box office. "The picture never made any money," Shavelson claimed, "because people didn't want to see Wayne in something other than his normal Western. There wasn't a horse in the picture." With television cutting deeply into Hollywood's market, the movie quickly disappeared and proved one of John Wayne's lowest-grossing films.

Duke and Pilar occasionally went out together, but they had to be discreet. He took her to the Sunset Strip area, where she expected to see Lana Turner and Hedy Lamarr and all of Hollywood's glamorous people. "We got there," she said, "and there was nothing like that at all." Duke did not care much for the nightclub scene, and most of their outings were to a Spanish restaurant, where gypsy music was played. "Duke used to go crazy over that," Pilar said. She had been told by her studio that she would be in Los Angeles for a month, but she never went back to Peru to live. Duke told her about his problems with Chata, and she gave him support and understanding. "I felt sorry for Esperanza," Pilar said. "She was an illegitimate child and had been abused by her mother's husband. Duke was a one-woman man; that's all he wanted in his life. In the years we were together, I never saw him flirt with anyone, ever."

Island in the Sky (released in 1953), became the second Wayne-Fellows production to star Duke. While it did better business than *Trouble along the Way*, the picture was still not the success its producers wanted. Based on a novel by Ernest K. Gann, the movie featured a number of Wayne's friends—Paul Fix, Harry Carey, Jr., Andy Devine, James Arness (who had worked with Duke on *Big Jim McLain*)—and was directed by William Wellman. Called "Wild Bill" because of the noise he made on the set, Wellman was more bark than bite and a fine old-time filmmaker. Wayne-Fellows had contracted with him to make six pictures for the company—three with Duke and three with other stars. "I started out like a racehorse with *Island in the Sky* and *The High and the Mighty*," the veteran director said, "then fell on my skinny butt." Wellman was better with action than with character development, but at their best his pictures had muscle and were visually exciting. Wayne admired him and on *Island in the Sky* accepted the director's tough approach with little interference. "He's a wonderful old son of a bitch," Duke said of the filmmaker. "He had a metal plate in his head from some accident, and he'd go around belting all these big, tough guys and they'd be afraid to hit him back for fear they'd kill him."

Critics, however, complained that *Island in the Sky* was static and talky. The picture alternates between convincing action and Duke's pithy axioms on matters eternal. Wayne later insisted that Warner Bros. had failed to advertise the movie properly, and signs of a rift between Duke and the studio's hierarchy were already apparent.

Much of *Island in the Sky* was shot on location, so Wayne and Pilar were separated for several weeks during early 1953. When he was in town, they spent evenings together. "I'd turned my back on the life I'd known, the strict morality of my Catholic upbringing, by beginning an affair with Duke," Pilar declared. "I loved him so much that I had no thoughts of right or wrong, but only thoughts of him." Duke respected her as a lady, yet liked her feisty side. He asked her to give up future plans for work; he wanted her to devote herself to him. "I have to ask you to take a chance on me," Duke told her. "I'm not a rich man. In fact I owe half a million dollars right now, and there's no telling how much the courts will award my wife Chata."

Whenever Wayne had to deal with reporters, Pilar stayed out of sight. Often that meant that she had to wait hours for him, but she was patient and tolerant. "I'd never known a more confident man," she said, "so comfortable with his own body. He never took a false step or made an awkward move. His star quality was as potent off screen as on."

Then Pilar discovered that she was pregnant. In the Hollywood of the 1950s, for Duke to father a child out of wedlock would have been scandal enough to wreck his career. When Ingrid Bergman, still married to Dr. Peter Lindstrom, announced in 1949 that she was expecting a baby fathered by Italian film director Roberto Rossellini, fans were shocked and the media attacked the actress viciously. Bergman's reputation in the United States was destroyed for nearly a decade; she was even denounced on the floor of the Senate. Now Wayne faced a similar scandal. No less alarming was the effect a child born under such circumstances would have on his pending divorce and the shame it would bring to Josephine and his children. "Duke was an intensely romantic and passionate but very moral man," said Pilar. Yet his career was everything to him.

For a Catholic to end a pregnancy meant eternal damnation in the eyes of the church, and Pilar struggled with her decision. "When I didn't dare wait a day longer," she said, "I called the number the doctor had given me. The next day I went to an address on Sunset Boulevard where I was met by a man who turned out to be a doctor practicing without a license." Emotionally, the resolution nearly destroyed her.

Meanwhile Duke spent hours closeted with his divorce lawyer, Frank Belcher. As if all his other difficulties were not enough, Wayne's partnership with Robert Fellows showed signs of stress. Fellows and Bo Roos, Duke's business manager, had gotten at odds with one another. At a party Wayne gave at Romanoff's after the opening of *Island in the Sun*, Roos had enough drinks to say what he thought of Fellows. "In essence," an informant wrote Duke's agent, "it amounted to Fellows not being on the level, being incompetent, and definitely wanting to crush everyone who got in his way—no exceptions."

But the biggest fracas of Duke's life began in April 1953 when Esperanza

Wayne charged that her husband had threatened and struck her during their marriage. She asked that he be restrained from inflicting further violence on her. Duke denied the charge and said that his wife's statements came from her distorted imagination. When he showed up for a temporary alimony hearing, the courthouse was mobbed with female admirers, some carrying signs that read, "John Wayne, you can clobber me any time you want." Duke lost his temper when Chata called him a liar during the proceedings, at which point he smashed his fist down on the guardrail and half rose from his seat. "I have never struck my wife, but on many occasions have had to protect myself from her temper," he testified. "I have held her hands and I have held her feet, but only to protect myself."

The court awarded Esperanza a temporary settlement of $1,100 a month. She bit her lip and blanched when the judge read his decision, since she had counted on more. Duke deplored the sordid accusations and the headlines that accompanied the hearing and left for Mexico to film *Hondo* early in July 1953, aware that the worst was yet to come.

"These have been the three most hectic weeks in my forty-six years," Wayne wrote John Ford from Mexico, "what with a psychiatric opponent [Chata], and the same can be said about her lawyer. Belcher had to be on his toes. The $150,000 they asked for attorneys fees and investigation and appraisers and court costs was cut to $20,000; her $9,000 a month was cut to $1,100 a month cash, and $1,400 a month maintenance of the house. So I guess you can say I won a moral victory."

Initially, Glenn Ford had been scheduled to play the title role in *Hondo*, which would have fulfilled the actor's two-picture agreement with Wayne-Fellows Productions. But Ford had disliked working with the often callous John Farrow on *Plunder of the Sun*, and since Farrow was slated to direct *Hondo*, the star backed out. Rather than delay production, Duke stepped into the role after James Edward Grant had revised the script.

Based on Louis L'Amour's short story "The Gift of Cochise," which the author later expanded into a best-selling novel, *Hondo* was filmed in 3-D, a short-lived craze launched by the success of *Bwana Devil* (1952) and *The House of Wax* (1953). Shooting in 3-D required two cameras mounted side by side, which was a cumbersome process that taxed Duke's patience. When Warner Bros. demanded that one of their cameras on loan to Wayne-Fellows be returned to the studio, Duke lost his temper. "I am goddamned sick and tired of every time I come in from location to have my Production Department say that you want that other camera," he wrote Steve Trilling, Warner Bros.' head of production. "We're spending around $30,000 a week down here keeping this troupe running. If you don't want to cooperate in this, just call me up and tell me to bring the camera back, and I'll bring it back and cancel our relationship—I'm god-damned mad enough to."

Duke calmed down when the studio sent a new "all-media camera" for his unit to initiate, and on June 12 he wrote Jack Warner that things were progressing nicely—"if that monster got what we pointed it at." Then he added, "It's wonderful working with Farrow and this crew." The Western required Wayne to be in the saddle a great deal, and Duke was still not fond of horses. "I can hardly walk," he wrote Warner. A few days later Wayne complained that the production was moving slowly because of the all-media camera. "For instance, this morning for a two-shot, because we're being so careful of this first picture with your new camera, it took us an hour and a half," he reported to Warner. "It would probably save us three hours a day to have two cameras here. . . . At this rate our picture will take us forty-five days, at least a third longer. I feel that this is very unfair to us, particularly when this camera was not completely practical mechanically. . . . Please, Daddy, send more money or camera." Warner eventually did send a second camera, but he restricted its use to ten days.

A crew of 130 was housed at the Motel Baca in Camargo, Mexico, during the location work on *Hondo*. Wayne brought Michael and Patrick along for company but sent Pilar, still recovering from her abortion, back to Peru for a visit. "It wouldn't be smart to take you with me," he told her. "A beautiful woman like you would stick out like a sore thumb down there. I don't want your name used in my divorce." She feared that Duke might be starting to tire of her.

Every so often Wayne and John Farrow flew to El Paso to watch footage they had shot during the few days previous. Jack Warner saw the daily rushes in Burbank and complained that the director wasn't placing the camera close enough to his actors. "Everything seems to be too far away," Warner said. Duke defended the director, saying that they had been told that the 3-D lens necessitated keeping a certain distance. "Farrow has done everything but play music to try to get camera in for close shots," Wayne wired the studio boss. Although John Farrow was directing the picture, "Duke's word was law," Chuck Roberson noted. Wayne always exercised tight control over the pictures he produced and more and more showed signs of trying to dominate directors other than Ford, Hawks, or Hathaway.

Duke's production company relied heavily on actors and craftsmen Wayne had come to know from working with John Ford over the years. Archie Stout was the cinematographer on *Hondo*, while Andrew McLaglen served as production manager and Cliff Lyons headed a second unit, all of them Ford veterans. Since so many of his people were working on the picture, Ford himself decided to pay a visit to the set, showing up on the Mexican location dressed in army fatigues and a wide-brim hat cocked over one eye. Wayne arranged for him to supervise some of the second-unit work.

One afternoon when Duke wasn't working, he and Andy McLaglen met for a beer in the hotel cantina while they awaited the company's return from shooting at a nearby lake. The hour grew late, and the two men began to worry about the crew, since it had begun to rain several hours before. As night fell they borrowed a fifty-five-foot launch and went out on the lake looking for the company. Soon it was pitch-dark and pouring rain. McLaglen stood in the bow with a flashlight, while Wayne peered over his shoulder. "Finally we saw the fires in the distance," McLaglen remembered, "and lo and behold our crew had been cut off by the rain and totally isolated. The Mexicans were drinking tequila and having a great time. They'd found some goats on the mountainside, and they were grilling the goats for *cabrito*. All of the Americans were huddled up and frightened." Duke and his production manager loaded their colleagues onto the launch, with the excess weight shoving the boat down in the water, and they edged their way back to headquarters.

When it wasn't raining, the weather in Camargo was miserably hot. Since there was nothing else to do, Wayne spent evenings drinking, playing poker, and swearing. "He loved to swear," said Geraldine Page, Duke's leading lady in *Hondo*. He was also fond of jokes, and anyone who knew a good one made sure Duke heard it, since that was a way of winning his favor. "He had the warmest, most spontaneous, most wonderful laugh," said Page. "Everybody just adored him in the most hysterical way."

Duke's leading lady had recently come to Hollywood from Broadway; she was scheduled to appear in the screen version of Tennessee Williams's *Summer and Smoke*, which she had performed on the New York stage.

Page had no sooner arrived at Warner Bros. than executives there informed her that 3-D had made intimate dramas like *Summer and Smoke* impractical. Instead, the studio was assigning her to a John Wayne Western to be filmed in Mexico. "Not in my wildest dreams did I picture myself in a Western with John Wayne," she said.

"We had a monstrous camera that was shooting the film in 3-D, widescreen, and regular screen all at once, and it was a very temperamental machine," the actress remembered. "So we had lots of time to sit under the broiling Mexican summer sun. I sat and listened to Mr. Farrow and Mr. Wayne in horror. Everybody tried to be Duke's right-hand man and his favorite. It was like the stories you hear about the old court days. Everybody was trying to slice everybody else's reputation in the Duke's eyes. There was tremendous, tremendous competition."

Page thought that the original script of *Hondo* ranked among the best she had ever read, full of beautiful language. "There was one speech that Hondo had that was sheer poetry," she said. "I'd never seen a Western in which the Indians were characterized as humans, not bloodthirsty savages. What we ended up with was not the script I'd been shown, but it was still a fairly good movie."

Since *Hondo* was Page's first motion picture, she seemed a little on the peculiar side to Wayne and his cronies, especially to the wranglers and stuntmen who thought her eccentric. Duke complained about her whiny voice and inexperience before the camera. "She may have been great on Broadway," he said, "but she didn't know a damn thing about making movies." A few months later he was shocked when Andrew McLaglen telephoned to say that Geraldine Page had been nominated for an Academy Award for her performance in *Hondo*. "There was silence on the other end of the phone," McLaglen recalled. "Duke couldn't understand it."

Wayne was not in the best of spirits during the making of the picture and often grew impatient. Page agreed that Duke, more than John Farrow, directed the movie. "Every morning," she said, "when he would be hungover, he would have a screaming fit. He'd yell at somebody until he got hoarse. He would pick on some technical point, and he was always right." Wayne did one scene over and over with Lee Aaker, the child actor who played Page's young son in the movie. "Wayne got tired of it," the actress remembered, "and he kept trying to bully the child into doing what he wanted, and the boy wouldn't do it."

Working with Duke on an isolated location gave the actress an opportunity to glimpse beneath his exterior, and she gradually came to understand what made John Wayne so popular. "He hates all kinds of hypocrisy and folderol," Page said. "He's a terribly honest man, and that comes across on the screen, underlined by the kind of parts he plays. One of his first mottoes, I think, is always to be the hero to the people around you. Wayne has a leadership quality, so that people revere him."

Ward Bond was also in the movie, and Page often heard Duke and Bond talking politics. "I noticed that when they had philosophical political discussions that John Wayne would talk so sensibly," she said, "while Ward Bond was just an oversimplifying bully. John Wayne, I feel, was a reactionary for all sorts of non-reactionary reasons. He would always say such sensible human things; he was so quick about everything, mentally as well as physically."

Duke later maintained that the popularity of *Shane* (also 1953) took the edge off *Hondo*, since both films dealt with a relationship between a man and a boy, but the picture came to be one of his favorites. "You don't get that kind of story very often," he said. The movie has action, humor, and romance and depicts the Native American sympathetically. "I've done as much as any man to give human dignity to the Indian," said Wayne. "My Indian in *Hondo* was a great guy" justifiably angered by treaty violations.

When the movie opened at theaters in November, the reaction was favorable. A fan in Canton, Ohio, wrote Jack Warner, "There were only two days of publicity in our paper concerning this picture, but on the opening day there was a line one large block long. When John Wayne is mentioned, that is all people need." The movie also did well in Europe and grossed enormous profits in Japan. "*Hondo* holds up after all of these years," Michael Wayne said in 1991. "I think my father looked his best and was at his best at that time. In a way that film set some of the characters he played later. It wasn't his best film by a long shot, but it set his character."

By the time *Hondo* wrapped in August 1953, Duke was exhausted and his patience had worn thin. He asked Pilar to meet him in Mexico City, where he seemed distant to her and preoccupied. One evening they were dining in one of Wayne's favorite restaurants. Duke was drinking tequila and smoking cigarettes at a feverish rate. "He'd ordered his customary steak," Pilar said, "and the minute his plate appeared he cut a large portion of meat, jammed it on a fork which he pushed hard into my face, saying in a vicious tone, 'Here, try this.'" Humiliated, she ran from the restaurant, with Duke trailing after her to apologize.

Meanwhile back in Los Angeles, Chata was fighting off creditors that had contacted her once the Waynes' divorce suit became common knowledge. On July 30, she drove a ton-and-a-quarter pickup truck to Domestic Relations Court to ask for additional financial support. She said that her automobile had been seized to cover an unpaid grocery bill; the truck, used by the couple's gardener, was the only means of transportation she had. Reporters noted, however, that the second Mrs. Wayne was wearing a $300 blue raw-silk suit and a $90 scarlet straw picture hat.

The divorce trial in October proved even uglier than Duke had anticipated. Esperanza described her husband as a drunken, vicious, unfaithful brute. She testified that Wayne came home from a stag party at Budd Boetticher's house one night with a stripteaser's bite on his neck. She claimed that on another occasion she had almost shot her drunken husband when he couldn't find his key and broke into their home early one morning. Her mother had gone with her to investigate the noise and, fortunately, Mrs. Ceballos had recognized the intruder before her daughter pulled the trigger.

For two and a half days Chata held the witness stand, detailing the atrocities of the Wayne marriage. In discussing her husband's infidelities, she named Gail Russell as one of the other women in his life. "Why did Chata have to drag that poor kid's name into this?" Duke asked. "I never had anything to do with Miss Russell except to make a couple of pictures with her."

When Duke took the stand, he testified that his wife drank heavily and had a fishwife's temper. He claimed that the night he had come home late and had broken a glass panel to let himself in, Chata was drunk and hysterical and demanded to know if he had been at a motel with Gail Russell. The time that Nicky Hilton stayed in the Wayne home, while Duke was away on location, was introduced in court, and Wayne's lawyer produced doodles in Chata's hand where she had written "Chata Hilton" and "Chata and Nicky."

Duke was asked to describe the most trying experience he had suffered during the marriage. He described a night that he and Esperanza had gone to a party at Budd Boetticher's house. Sometime well after midnight the revelers decided to drive to the nearby Tail-of-the-Cock restaurant for something to eat. Chata was quite intoxicated and did not want to go, so Boetticher told Duke and his own wife to go ahead, since the restaurant was about to close; he and Chata would join them in a few minutes. "I went back in and argued with Chata for about ten minutes," Boetticher recalled, "then picked her up and threw her over my shoulder and got to the Tail-of-the-Cock fifteen minutes, at most twenty minutes, after they'd left us alone." But in court Wayne testified that Chata and Boetticher had probably been alone for two hours.

Boetticher was in the courtroom on the day of this testimony, sitting behind Chata. After the proceedings Duke and his director friend were walking down the street to their cars. "That was a despicable thing you did," said Boetticher, referring to the erroneous testimony. Wayne looked surprised. "It wasn't any two hours," Boetticher protested. "You know it was fifteen or twenty minutes, Duke. Look what you made it look like. That wasn't fair. Why do this to me?" Wayne replied, "You didn't want me to lose the case, did you?"

After hearing both sides, the judge allowed Duke to keep most of his estate. He awarded Chata the outright sum of $150,000, plus an additional $50,000 a year for the next six years. "To be a good wife and make him happy, that was all I wanted," Esperanza said when the trial ended. "But it was not to be. Now it is all gone. My career—that is gone, too. I feel so lost, so confused."

She did not live to collect the entire settlement. After the divorce, Chata moved back to Mexico City, where she took up residence in a small hotel following the death of her mother. She became a recluse, continued to drink heavily, and seldom ate. She died of a heart attack in the late fall of 1954, thirteen months after the divorce from Wayne was granted, her room strewn with empty liquor bottles. She was thirty-eight years old at the time.

Undoubtedly Chata wanted to humiliate Duke during their divorce hearings, and her lurid accusations mortified him. The press reported the sordid disclosures in graphic detail, and Wayne grew upset about the effect the reports would have on his children. "Certainly everybody once in his life goes through a period on a low ebb, morally and mentally," he said, "and this was it for me. This is not the way human beings want to live."

He referred to his seven years with Esperanza as "a miserable chapter" in his life. "It was an embarrassing ordeal to live through," Wayne said of their stormy divorce. "I think I tried to live in a dignified, respectable way, and twenty-five years of trying to live a decent life was almost ruined. I guess I have been a romantic all my life. A romantic about everything, not just about women."

He claimed that he was not cynical about women as a result of the bad experience, but "they are a little lower on that pedestal," he admitted. "Maybe I'm still afraid of women. I am awed by their presence. I feel there is something beautiful about a fine woman." His money situation in the fall of 1953 was precarious, and he felt that he had been used as a doormat, both by his former wife and by the press. But, Duke said, "I'm not complaining. I'm living in a good country. I'm doing work I love."

Pilar waited in Mexico City until the litigation was over, although Wayne's divorce would not be final for another twelve months. Once a settlement had been reached, Duke suggested that the two of them celebrate in Acapulco. He rented a house with red-tiled hallways, bougainvillea climbing the walls, and a view of the ocean. He and Pilar spent afternoons scuba diving, waterskiing, and sailing, and the relaxation was sorely needed.

Wayne made personal appearances in Texas to publicize *Hondo*, then he and Pilar moved into his home in Encino. "I looked forward to returning to Hollywood in a new role," Pilar wrote, "that of John Wayne's future wife. The time had come to move out of rented quarters and establish a real home." She didn't share Duke's enthusiasm for the Encino house, asserting that Chata's massive Spanish antiques overwhelmed the place. "To tell the truth," she said, "if the house had been mine, I would have sold it. But at that time I had no taste. I didn't know what I wanted." Wayne promised she could redecorate, which she did with reproductions of Early American furniture. "When we remodeled, we would open doors and there would be empty bottles that Esperanza had left there," Pilar recalled.

Duke's new love quickly came to realize that he was compulsive about work and that the driving force in his life was making pictures. When Spencer Tracy at the last minute bowed out of *The High and the Mighty*, a Wayne-Fellows production scheduled to go before the cameras on November 12, 1953, Duke stepped in to play the copilot of a distressed airliner on its way to the mainland from Hawaii. As producer, Wayne had cast Robert Cummings as the pilot because Cummings could actually fly a plane. But director William Wellman gave the part to Robert Stack. "With Duke you were what you were," Stack said. "In other words, the performance factor to him was less important than getting some guy that really knew how to fly an airplane." Wayne accepted that his casting choice had been overridden, but according to Stack, "it did make for a couple of pretty hairy first days of shooting."

Based on a best-selling novel by Ernest K. Gann, *The High and the Mighty* was shot mostly on the Goldwyn lot in Hollywood. It was Duke's first movie in CinemaScope and the last he would make under the Wayne-Fellows banner. Since an entire planeload of passengers had to spend day after day, week after week in their seats, the work became tedious for the actors. "Everybody whose ear was in camera range had to sit there," Claire Trevor remembered; "it was a dreary picture to make." Laraine Day solved the problem by doing cryptograms with John Howard. Ann Doran and Phil Harris, playing a husband and wife on their second honeymoon, stayed in character and, according to Doran, "got a little silly." To add to the cast's discomfort, the weather turned cold and the Goldwyn soundstage wasn't heated properly. "It was uncomfortable, everybody got cold," Doran remembered. "Most of us sitting in the plane were sick—fevers and runny noses and head colds."

Since Wayne's performance took place mainly in the cockpit, he did not work with the planeload of actors, only Stack. But he was on the set most of the time as producer. "I had a row with Duke," William Wellman recalled. "I made three pictures with him . . . , and in *The High and the Mighty* he suddenly wanted to become a director." In front of the entire crew Wellman said to him, "Look, you come back here behind the camera and do my job, and you're going to be just as ridiculous doing it as I would be going out there with that screwy voice of yours and that fairy walk and being Duke Wayne." Wayne respected Wellman and offered no more interference.

"With all of Bill Wellman's bad language and ripping around, he knew how to get the performances he wanted," Ann Doran said. "Sometimes it was because he yelled at people; he bawled them out, he belittled them, and they showed him by giving a superb performance. Other times he was so nice and so sweet and so understanding that you exploded all over. That's what he did with me to get me to cry. I had such a dreadful cold when we got to the close-up that I couldn't see. Somehow he knew how to approach each one of us and get the thing that he wanted. Wayne realized that no matter what he played, he must be John Wayne. That was his saleable point. The only argument he had with Wellman over his performance was when Bill would suggest something that was inconsistent with the John Wayne persona. And Bill could always see his point."

Robert Stack grew fascinated with how Duke could say lines as written and still make them sound like John Wayne. "I'd get behind a flat and listen to his reading of the dialogue," Stack said, "and I'd think, 'Man, that's really not very good.' And for radio it wasn't very good. But the minute you saw that great American face up there on the screen, it didn't matter. He could have been talking in Esperanto and nobody would give a damn."

Laraine Day remembered that Pilar sat on the set most of the time *The High and the Mighty* was shot. "She was delightful," Day recalled, "very shy, and she had none of the obvious attributes of an actress. She seemed sort of in a shell." Others found Pilar aloof and attributed her standoffish nature to her aristocratic South American background. In truth she was sensitive about her lack of formal education and limited command of English, yet found living in the big, isolated house in Encino lonely. "I always felt like I was in the way when I went to watch Duke shoot," she said. "They would put out a chair for me, and then I'd have to move because I was in the way of cables. I found it all pretty boring and not really as glamorous as I'd thought." Eventually Pilar began playing tennis at Robert Stack's house in Holmby Hills and became best friends with Duke's secretary, Mary St. John.

The High and the Mighty proved a huge commercial success. While its plot is somewhat synthetic, the special effects and performances make for an engaging film. Faced with declining box-office returns, Hollywood producers had learned that a title song could be an effective way to publicize current movies. The theme music Dimitri Tiomkin composed for *The High and the Mighty* soared to the top of the Hit Parade charts, remained there for many weeks, and contributed greatly to the movie's popularity.

Wayne was committed to make one more picture at RKO for Howard Hughes, but delay followed delay on the project Hughes had in mind. The eccentric RKO head had thought that Duke should undertake no other assignment until the one he was preparing had reached completion, but when Wayne found out through his agent how nebulous Hughes's idea was he had gone ahead with *The High and the Mighty*. The picture for RKO was still not ready to go before the cameras when the final Wayne-Fellows production ended, and Duke vented his ire. "My beefs are very simple," he wrote Hughes in February 1954. "At the other studios and for my own company, in which I have a huge stake, I seldom get involved on a picture for more than eight to ten weeks overall. I am paid top terms for this time. At RKO . . . I wind up giving six months of my time—and it's hectic, uncomfortable, and unpleasant time—for a fraction of the compensation paid me by the other studios and for only a portion of my present market value."

When delays at RKO persisted, Warner Bros. also became incensed, since Wayne was slated to make another picture there. "This is the most inequitable and unethical treatment that we have ever experienced," a Warner Bros. attorney wrote Duke in April. "In July 1953 you were a picture behind schedule under our contract. When your divorce litigation arose, there were delays that ensued. When you requested us, in order to fulfill your obligation with RKO, to permit RKO to move its starting date back to January 4, 1954, in order to cooperate, we complied and moved back the starting date for your next picture under our contract accordingly."

Early the next month Wayne again complained to Hughes: "It is your studio's responsibility to have scripts ready for me on the dates you request for my assignments." Finally in June 1954 the picture for RKO got underway. Called *The Conqueror*, the film would not be released until 1956 and proved a $5 million fiasco. Duke played Temujin, better known as Genghis Khan, and looked ludicrous made up with slit eyes and a divided mustache. *The Conqueror* was arguably the worst picture of Wayne's mature career and possibly even contributed to his death.

The film was shot in the Escalante Desert near St. George, Utah, about 140 miles from the atomic testing site in Nevada. The crew spent six weeks there, in heat hovering around 120 degrees, working in radioactive sand that may have been lethal. "We were in the direct path of the fallout of the nuclear testing range," stuntman Gil Perkins said. "A tremendous number of people in that area have contracted cancer and died." Certainly the deaths from cancer among the cast and crew of *The Conqueror* ran alarmingly high: John Wayne, actress Susan Hayward, director Dick Powell, actors Pedro Armendariz and Thomas Gomez, character actress Agnes

Moorehead, the head of special effects, and at least thirty-four others. It is true that many of them were heavy smokers; Duke, for instance, smoked no fewer than three packs of cigarettes a day at the time. Others who were there—Pilar and Gil Perkins, for example—lived long lives, but most of them were not smokers.

Whether working in the contaminated area caused the deaths or not, it was a miserable location. "Sometimes we'd be Cossacks, sometimes we'd be Mongols," Perkins said of the stunt performers, "and we'd have these hot fur jackets on, sometimes steel helmets, sometimes fur helmets, and hot flannel pants and high boots. We were working in Snow Canyon for about four or five days, and it was 128 degrees in the shade. You'd come in at night, and you weren't fit to talk to until you'd had three gin and tonics. The only two locations I was glad to leave were *Virginia City* in 1939 and *The Conqueror* in 1954."

Howard Hughes chose actor Dick Powell to direct the picture, Powell's first time in that capacity, and while he was pleasant enough, his skill as a director left much to be desired. Pilar, who was there the whole time, later claimed that Susan Hayward, playing the daughter of a Tartar chief, developed a "wild passion" for Wayne. "She was headstrong and determined," Pilar said. "My presence in St. George fed her jealousy, and her heavy drinking diminished her inhibitions."

Everyone involved was relieved when location work on *The Conqueror* ended on July 14. When the picture appeared in the theaters, it was an embarrassment. Audiences laughed at Wayne's stilted dialogue, and critics hooted at what most considered a Western set in the Gobi Desert. Some said Duke portrayed Genghis Khan as a gunfighter. The debacle spelled the end for Howard Hughes as a motion picture mogul. "Everything points to RKO getting further out of the business rather than getting into active production," the press reported early in 1957.

Duke was at last free to honor his commitment to Warner Bros. In mid-September 1954 Wayne began shooting *The Sea Chase* in Hawaii for the studio. Duke and Pilar arrived in the islands a few days before filming began on the movie so that he could show her the sights. They moved into a house Warner had rented for them. They spent time snorkeling, and by the time shooting began Wayne had developed an ear infection. "The ear festered and swelled up, and the pain was so severe he had to take codeine for it," remembered Duke's costar, Lana Turner. "The medicine didn't help his memory for his lines. Often his eyes were glazed from the pain and the codeine. His ear was so swollen that for a number of days they could shoot only one side of his face. Between takes he'd go to his bunk and lie down."

The production seemed troubled from the start. Duke and director John Farrow were still working on a script with the writers after they had arrived in Hawaii. Lana Turner, on loan to Warners from MGM, detested Farrow and developed an antagonistic attitude toward the male-dominated cast, many of whom were Wayne's pals. "Some of her hostility spilled over onto Duke," Pilar said, and "he reacted to her coldness with a deep freeze of his own." Making love to Turner on the set proved a challenge, since she complained if Duke touched her face or hair, fearing he would ruin her makeup or hairdo. "She was overly concerned about her looks," Pilar said, "and that destroyed the rapport that everybody had expected."

Most of *The Sea Chase* takes place on a German freighter. "It was actually a steel-hulled tramp steamer anchored in the harbor," said Turner, "forty-five minutes away by speedboat. We had to wake up at the break of dawn to take advantage of the light. Around two every afternoon clouds would roll over, and we'd all be drenched in rain." The picture was shot off the Kona Coast of the island of Hawaii, about an hour's flight from Honolulu. Wayne played a German, with no attempt at an accent. The movie is slow-moving and suffers from a poor script. What resulted was commonplace fare that critics panned. Wayne later blamed Farrow, saying that the director had "failed to tell the good story that was in the book," but other factors worked against the picture's success.

Wherever he went in the islands, Duke was mobbed by fans, which was one of the reasons he insisted that Warner Bros. rent a house for him. "I stayed at the Kona Inn the first night I was here," he wrote Steve Trilling in Burbank, "and of the 100 guests there I had my picture taken with at least 25 of them, and signed at least 60 to 70 autographs. I was put in a position that it would be embarrassing for me to leave them without some social chitchat. Perhaps other actors can walk away from people and not be friendly and gracious. I cannot—not only because of my own personality, but business-wise I cannot afford it."

The picture fell behind schedule because of Wayne's ear infection. "I have been the little man who wasn't there for the past three days," he wrote Trilling on October 3. "A little thing like an earache can make you awfully disinterested in story lines—or even food." By October 7, Duke was back on the job, but bad weather put the company further behind. Wayne was still taking medication for his ear trouble in November, and a physician informed him that he might need an operation.

Duke's spirits lifted late in October, when he received a telephone called from his attorney saying that his divorce had become final at last. By then Pilar's marriage to Richard Weldy had been annulled, and she and Wayne were free to marry. The couple were wed by a justice of the peace in a brief ceremony on November 1, 1954, in Kona. The nuptials took place at sunset on a lawn overlooking Keakoa Bay. The setting was high on a cliff, and the sound of the surf could be heard as the couple took their vows. The bride wore a pink organdy cocktail dress and was given in marriage by John Farrow. Wayne's secretary, Mary St. John, served as matron of honor, while Francis Brown, a wealthy friend of Duke's from Pebble Beach, was best man. Lana Turner and her husband, actor Lex Barker, were in attendance. "As we prepared to take our vows," Pilar recalled, "a crowd of Hawaiians, the women in muumuus and the men in colorful island shirts, appeared in the garden carrying gifts of flowers."

The bride was twenty-six, the groom forty-seven. Duke told the press, "I was a married man at breakfast, single at lunch, and married again by dinner!" The next day he and Pilar flew to Honolulu and then home to Los Angeles, where work on *The Sea Chase* would finish at the Warner Bros. studio in December, eleven days behind schedule. Wayne's house in Encino was still undergoing remodeling, but the newlyweds planned a party to commemorate their marriage as soon as workers left. "The carpenters are still pounding on our walls," Wayne wrote Jack Warner on December 14, "or you would have long since received an invitation to a little Wayne hospitality."

Pilar soon learned that John Wayne offscreen was not the assured man that his movie image suggested. Filled with self-doubts, Duke needed people around him at all times. "Although he talked about wanting privacy," Pilar said, "we were almost never alone." Pappy Ford dropped in at all hours. So did Ward Bond, Grant Withers, Andrew McLaglen and his father (actor Victor McLaglen), Yakima Canutt, James Edward Grant, Charles Feldman, Web Overlander (Wayne's makeup man), and an endless stream of Duke's macho friends.

Pilar discovered that her husband was not a deeply religious man, but he was far better read than she had imagined. "Duke enjoyed a good mystery, read all of Churchill, and perused most new novels looking for stories that would make good movies," she declared. "He's certainly no handyman," she said. "He can't hammer a nail or hang a painting. And he's no gardener either." But Pilar found him "the most tender man I have ever known." While he angered easily, he got over his rage quickly and seldom harbored a grudge.

When asked why he had married three Hispanic women, Duke answered, "To me they seem more warm and direct and down-to-earth." Asked the same question years later, Pilar got a glint in her eye and responded, "He was just lucky, I guess." She understood early in their marriage that Wayne was a devoted family man and she herself envisioned a big family. She saw the uninhibited display of affection Duke showered on his sons and daughters and noted the love they gave him in return. She also realized that her husband was tormented by things from his past, particularly his first divorce and the breakup of his family. "Michael's still angry at me," Duke told Pilar shortly after they met; "I'm afraid he always will be."

1922 University of Southern California freshman football team with Marion Morrison in the middle row, third from right. (Courtesy of the Academy of Motion Picture Arts and Sciences)

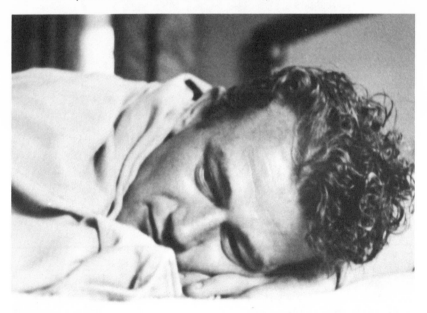

Young John Wayne in a relaxed pose. (Courtesy of the Academy of Motion Picture Arts and Sciences)

John Wayne in his first serial, *The Shadow of the Eagle*. (Courtesy of Larry Edmunds Cinema Bookshop)

John Wayne and Josephine Saenz on their wedding day, with Loretta Young in attendance. (Courtesy of The Bettmann Archive)

John Wayne during his budget Western years. (Courtesy of The Academy of Motion Picture Arts and Sciences)

John Wayne in costume for another budget Western. (Courtesy of the Academy of Motion Picture Arts and Sciences)

John Wayne and Claire Trevor in *Stagecoach*. (Courtesy of the Lilly Library, Indiana University)

John Wayne in an uncharacteristic pose, costumed for sea duty. (Courtesy of the Academy of Motion Picture Arts and Sciences)

John Wayne and Marlene Dietrich in *Seven Sinners*. (Courtesy of Larry Edmunds Cinema Bookshop)

John Wayne and Ella Raines in *Tall in the Saddle*. (Courtesy of Larry Edmunds Cinema Bookshop)

Winning World War II in *Back to Bataan*. (Courtesy of Larry Edmunds Cinema Bookshop)

John Wayne and Gail Russell in *Wake of the Red Witch*. (Courtesy of Larry Edmunds Cinema Bookshop)

John Wayne flanked by his wife Esperanza, serving coffee, and Esperanza's mother. (Courtesy of the Academy of Motion Picture Arts and Sciences)

John Agar framed by John Ford's composition. (Courtesy of the Lilly Library, Indiana University)

John Wayne in *Sands of Iwo Jima*. (Courtesy of Larry Edmunds Cinema Bookshop)

John Wayne's friend and colleague Pedro Armendariz. (Courtesy of the Lilly Library, Indiana University)

Maureen O'Hara, Duke's favorite leading lady. (Author's collection)

John Wayne in a casual pose on a Ford location. (Courtesy of the Lilly Library, Indiana University)

Duke Wayne and John Ford at a gathering late in the director's life. (Courtesy of the Lilly Library, Indiana University)

Right, Jeff Hunter and Natalie Wood in *The Searchers.* (Courtesy of the Lilly Library, Indiana University.) *Below,* John and Pilar Wayne on their return from Hawaii after their wedding. (Courtesy of Pilar Wayne.)

John Wayne and Angie Dickinson in *Rio Bravo*. (Courtesy of Warner Bros., Inc.)

Aissa Wayne (left), friend, and father at Aissa's fifth birthday party, March 1961. (Courtesy of the Academy of Motion Picture Arts and Sciences)

John Wayne in classic Western garb. (Courtesy of the Academy of Motion Picture Arts and Sciences)

John Wayne spanks Maureen O'Hara in *McLintock!* as Patrick Wayne looks on. (Courtesy of Larry Edmunds Cinema Bookshop)

John Wayne as Rooster Cogburn. (Courtesy of Larry Edmunds Cinema Bookshop)

A mature John Wayne in costume. (Courtesy of the Academy of Motion Picture Arts and Sciences)

Launching Batjac

With the completion of *The High and the Mighty*, Wayne bought out Robert Fellows's interest in their production unit and renamed the company Batjac. "Fellows was a friend of mine who came in and didn't quite do the job," said Duke. "Besides, I didn't like the idea of my name being in the name of the company." The first film produced under the Batjac emblem was *Blood Alley* (1955), and the agreement with Warner Bros. to distribute Wayne's own pictures continued. Duke intended to film simple stories, some of them with parts suited to his personality.

Wayne first offered the lead in *Blood Alley* to Humphrey Bogart, but Bogie's price was too high. Consequently, he signed Robert Mitchum for the role and cast Lauren Bacall, Bogart's wife, to play opposite him. On the third day of shooting director William Wellman telephoned Wayne and complained that Mitchum was drinking all night, raising hell, and sleeping through morning wakeup calls. A few days later Mitchum stormed off the set, claiming he could not work with Wellman.

Batjac had invested a fortune in constructing a replica of a Chinese village near San Rafael, California, for the production, and Duke realized that his company stood to lose a vast sum of money unless he moved fast and came up with a substitute leading man. So in mid-January 1955 Wayne took over Mitchum's part. Toward the end of the month the picture was delayed again when Wellman became ill with influenza; Duke temporarily had to assume the director's responsibilities as well.

Blood Alley is both an adventure story and a Communist-bashing vehicle that reflects Wayne's politics. Its plot deals with the escape of some 180 villagers from Red China to freedom in Hong Kong. They flee on a ferry down the Formosa Strait, a three-hundred mile stretch known as "Blood Alley." Duke played a merchant marine captain rescued from a Red prison by the villagers to guide their escape.

Wayne was hospitalized for a few days during the making of the movie when he suffered back pains after performing some of his own stunts. He and Bacall got along famously, despite their opposing political views.

Duke admired Bacall's backbone, her confidence in her beliefs, her humor, and her ability to express her convictions.

By the end of March, Wayne was back home, aware that *Blood Alley* would likely be a disappointment. When the movie was released seven months later, audiences found it slow-moving, and critics were even less impressed. "Mr. Wayne is not adding perceptibly to his acting range," a reviewer for the *New York Times* declared. "He is still the familiar, hard citizen of yore, who speaks laconically in a monotone, and he is a fine gent to have around when the brawl begins."

Forming his own production company not only assured Duke of a larger percentage of the profits from his movies, it also allowed him the financial security to become more selective in the work he did. When director Hall Bartlett tried to convince him to play the lead in *Unchained* (1955), Wayne turned the part down, saying he would not play anyone who had been a convicted criminal. Duke was also offered the role of Marshal Matt Dillon in the television series *Gunsmoke* before the show launched its twenty-year run on CBS in September 1955, but Wayne did not want to do television work and suggested his friend James Arness, a relatively little known actor whom he had under personal contract. "The men who own theaters have given me a pretty good life," Duke said. "I wasn't going to mess that up to start a television series." He did appear on an episode of *I Love Lucy*, first aired on October 10, 1955, and had a good time playing himself.

Batjac provided Duke with an opportunity to help a number of people he cared about, and many of his pals appeared in the casts and crews of the pictures his company produced. Hiring them was not pure generosity since Duke preferred workers who were knowledgeable in his particular style. The presence of old friends also ensured Wayne that he would not lack for companionship on distant locations.

Duke's brother, Bobby, frequently held positions in Wayne-Fellows productions and later worked for Batjac, in part because their mother insisted upon it. "What are you going to do for Bobby?" Mary Morrison Preen repeatedly asked her more successful son. So Duke created jobs for his brother and helped Bobby establish himself in the industry. Outsiders found Robert Morrison a delightful man, warm and friendly, in some respects an imitation of Duke. Over the years Wayne had grown fonder of his brother, and as adults the two developed a teasing relationship.

By 1955 Duke's mother had turned into a dignified, gray-haired lady, still living in Long Beach. Mary had mellowed considerably, and she thoroughly enjoyed her status as John Wayne's mother. After hearing Duke's description, Pilar had been nervous about meeting her mother-in-law, but Mary instantly welcomed the newcomer into the family. "I loved the woman," Pilar said, "and she fell in love with me and insisted that I call her Mom." Wayne still felt uncomfortable around his mother yet was quite fond of her husband, Sidney Preen. He was grateful to Sidney for keeping Mary out of his life except for special occasions. "I think Duke tried to do the right thing by his mother," Pilar said, "but she never was content with just the right thing." After years of trying to please her, he had given up and accepted the distance between them.

Wayne and his new wife settled into a comfortable relationship, devoid of the traumas Duke had experienced with Chata. They watched late-night television together, often curled up in bed or snacking on salami; sometimes they read aloud to one another. Duke was fond of Pilar's dog, a dachshund named Blackie, who frequently spent evenings on his lap. Weekends the couple spent with the Fords or the Bonds or some of Wayne's other friends. Insecure among the Hollywood set, Pilar soon grew frustrated with the number of her husband's acquaintances that seemed to surround him most of the time. "I liked John Ford," Pilar said, "and he respected me because I stood up to him. But Ford felt shut out. He wanted to be with Duke all the time, and that wasn't possible because Duke had a new marriage." Pilar liked Ward Bond, too, but she was bothered that Wayne's crowd all drank too much. "After a while it got tiresome being around drunks," she said.

Whenever possible Pilar went on location with her husband, which did not please Ford at all. In June 1955 Wayne returned with Ford to Monument Valley to film *The Searchers*, a classic Western that possibly gave Duke his greatest role. Pilar later joined him in Utah, although by then she was expecting their first child. "That was one of the happiest sets we ever had," Pilar remembered. "The picture was so dramatic, but around six o'clock every evening we would all gather together, and it was a happy time. We had a ball in that horrible little place where Ford housed his company."

Jack Warner had agreed to release *The Searchers*, then balked at its $3,750,000 budget. Wayne had exploded during a meeting with the studio boss in April and sent him a bitter letter threatening to terminate their relationship unless Warner agreed to Ford's terms. For several days he refused to answer Warner's calls. Ford had suffered a breakdown while filming *Mr. Roberts*, and Duke felt particularly protective toward him. When Warner finally accepted Ford's budget for *The Searchers*, Wayne expressed relief, although he would end his association with Warner Bros. the following year. On *The Searchers* he turned production details over to the director, and both arrived in Monument Valley determined to make a masterpiece,

The company again stayed at Goulding's Trading Post. Duke, Ford, Bond, and the other stars bunked in small cabins up on a hill, while the rest of the actors and crew slept in army tents with wooden floors on the flat below. "Of all the John Ford pictures I worked on," wrote Harry Carey, Jr., "the set of *The Searchers* was unlike any other. Uncle Jack was much more serious, and that was the tone that pervaded the cast and crew." Wayne knew that playing the tormented Ethan Edwards was possibly the greatest challenge of his career, and therefore he wasn't as relaxed as he had been on other sets. "When I looked up at him in rehearsal," Dobe Carey said, "it was into the meanest, coldest eyes I had ever seen. He was even Ethan at dinner time. . . . Ethan was always in his eyes." Yet alone with Pilar, Duke could relax and generate the energy he would need to face the cameras the next day.

Most cast members recognized that there was something special about *The Searchers* from the start. "Wayne was so powerful in that picture," said Carey, "he had really done his homework. Duke was at his best as an actor in that one." Dobe's mother, Olive, played a part in the film and cautioned Wayne to keep his performance under control. "If you go overboard with histrionics," the veteran actress told him, "people will get up and go for a drink." Duke respected Ollie Carey and followed her advice.

Vera Miles, another member of the company, roomed with Olive, and her admiration for John Wayne deepened during their weeks on location together. "They used to say of the old West, 'Men were men and the women were grateful,'" Miles said. "Well, that's how Duke made you feel—like a woman." Ward Bond, who shared a cabin with Dobe Carey, did his best to attract Miles's attention, but the actress paid him scant notice, much to Bond's distress. He had to content himself with exchanging barbs with Ford and Wayne for amusement.

Duke's teenage son Patrick played a role in *The Searchers* and during the weeks in Monument Valley developed a crush on young Natalie Wood, also in the picture. "I had a friend who was my age," a mature Patrick Wayne recalled, "so that I wasn't completely dependent upon my father or an adult for my entertainment. There was a pretty girl, a super gal, with us on location. So *The Searchers* was great for me in the daytime as well as the nighttime."

By 1955 Duke and Ford approached filmmaking with a similar attitude, yet to draw the performance he wanted from Wayne, the director continued to needle his friend relentlessly. "I've seen Duke Wayne blubber like a child, and Ford just sitting there, humiliating the hell out of his star player," said Frank Baker, who had known the director since silent picture days. "There was always an essence of fear in every Ford camp. You were waiting for him to jump on you." By the time *The Searchers* was made, Wayne understood Ford's idiosyncrasies and accepted them. After the weight of responsibilities Duke had shouldered while producing his own pictures, he found working for Ford a relief. "Jesus Christ, it was great," he said, "you didn't have to think." Duke knew that the director would not let him give a bad performance, but he sensed on *The Searchers* that Ford was trying to pull a multilayered portrait from him. The filmmaker understood the importance of not letting his actors drift into emotional idleness on the set and kept Danny Borzage there at all times to play the accordion between takes, a trick he had learned during the silent picture era to keep spirits up.

Although days were hot in Monument Valley and the sand often blew, evenings there were cool and pleasant. John Wayne became a real-life hero to the Navajo when a two-year-old girl on the reservation contracted double pneumonia and Duke offered his plane to transport the child to the nearest hospital, a hundred miles away. The Navajo awarded him a special name for the deed—"The Man with the Big Eagle."

Wayne's Ethan Edwards became more than the complex character demanded by the script. Obsessed to the point of fanaticism, Ethan begins a ten-year quest, searching for a niece captured by Comanches, more concerned with vengeance than with rescuing the girl. Edwards is a racist full of hate, uncomfortable with domesticity and sexually repressed. In *The Searchers* the legendary toughness of the frontier hero becomes a parody; the champion of old has been brutalized by too much violence, yet he is incapable of modifying his values. Despite Ethan's rigid nature, Wayne succeeded in communicating the man's abject loneliness and his human side. As the West had become increasingly settled, the rugged individualist had evolved into a social misfit, and Ethan's mission borders on the psychopathic. He is prepared to kill his niece rather than accept her bedding with an Indian. His certainty of rightness is plainly anachronistic. Unwilling to bend to inevitable realities, Edwards is a miserable man, a warrior trapped in a bygone world—unable to change, impatient with civilized conventions, clinging to savage ways that had once made him victorious.

Perhaps Wayne's most memorable scene as an actor comes toward the end of *The Searchers*, after he races up an embankment after Natalie Wood, who played the captured niece by then living as the wife of an Indian. Wayne seizes the girl, lifts her above his shoulders, and with his back almost to the camera, lowers her to his arms and says, "Let's go home, Debbie." The tension of the moment becomes almost unbearable. For Ethan it is as close as the character can come to a reconciliation. He brings Debbie to the house of his brother's neighbor, yet remains too much the outsider to enter. The nomad stands alone at the doorway after the other players, including Olive Carey, have passed beyond the camera. Then comes a moment of cinematic nostalgia. Wayne raises his left hand, reaches across his chest, and grabs his right arm at the elbow. It is a gesture that Harry Carey, Ollie's husband, had often used in the movies Duke had seen as a boy in Glendale. Wayne stares at Olive for a couple of seconds, then turns and walks away, as the cabin door closes.

"Ollie and I had talked about Harry in that stance on occasions," Duke remembered. "I saw her looking at me, and I just did it. Goddamn tears came to her eyes. I was playing that scene for Ollie Carey." Ford shot the sequence late in the afternoon, and the actors sensed its importance at the time it was being played. Olive Carey said she felt the impact even before Wayne assumed the Harry Carey pose. "Duke was the most graceful man I'd ever seen," she declared, and his gesture affected her deeply.

Wayne maintained that *The Searchers* was the best picture Ford ever made, and many critics and film historians came to agree with him. Most consider the ambiguous Ethan Edwards to be Wayne's finest performance. "I loved him and I loved playing him," said Wayne. "I think I've always been popular in Westerns because I've played the kind of fellow who had a little bit of bad in him as well as a little bit of good." Even the Marxist French director Jean-Luc Godard admitted that while he hated John Wayne for supporting political reactionaries like Barry Goldwater, he loved him when he abruptly takes Natalie Wood into his arms toward the end of *The Searchers.*

Ford's classic Western wrapped on August 16, 1955. Duke and Pilar returned home from Monument Valley to await the birth of their first child. Thrilled as he was over his impending fatherhood, Duke admitted to John Ford that he hoped to be a long way "from Lordsburg" (the destination of the passengers in *Stagecoach*) when the birth occurred. "I'm afraid of those Indians," he said. Not at his best in domestic matters, Wayne would gladly have avoided such tense moments. But he was at St. Joseph's Hospital in Burbank on March 31, 1956, when Aissa Maria was born. Shortly after the baby's birth, he was ushered into Pilar's room at the hospital. "Move over!" he told his wife. "I'm pooped!" And he flopped down on the bed beside her.

"At first Duke could not have cared less about a second family," Pilar said, "but that all changed when the baby was born." He considered the new baby a second chance at fatherhood, and he was determined to do things right this time. But Aissa's birth upset Duke's older children, a fact he tried to ignore. "This pattern of avoiding family confrontations continued for the rest of our life together," Pilar wrote. "Duke had always seemed so forceful, so outspoken to me. I'd never seen him back down from a fight before. Learning that he couldn't or wouldn't protect me from his own family came as a great disappointment."

Aissa was born a few weeks before Duke turned forty-nine, but his baby daughter made him feel young and virile again. "She was the most spoiled child," said Pilar, for Wayne lavished his daughter with attention. After the birth he and Pilar seemed closer than ever. The Encino house crackled with energy. Yet Aissa would realize at an early age that there was something unsettling about the way her father behaved toward her. While he showed her endless affection, Aissa, even as a child, quickly sensed that he needed constant reassurance that she loved him back.

Soon after *The Searchers* was completed, Wayne joined his son Patrick, Vera Miles, and Ward Bond for an episode of the *Screen Directors Playhouse* series on television, a segment John Ford directed. Called "Rookie of the Year," the show aired on December 7, 1955, and featured young Patrick in the title role. Duke made only a brief appearance as an umpire. He accepted the part as a courtesy to his son and his favorite director, still convinced that television work was not for him.

Hollywood was changing, and John Wayne wasn't happy about what was happening to the motion picture business. He hated what he called "the Tennessee Williams effect" on movies. When 20th Century–Fox prepared to film Ernest Hemingway's *The Sun Also Rises* (released in 1957), Duke was asked to play Jake Barnes, an American expatriate whose genitals had been shot off during World War I. Wayne refused, pointing out that no one would believe him in the part even if he were foolish enough to attempt it.

In 1956 Duke was invited to a private screening of *Lust for Life*, a film biography of painter Vincent van Gogh with Kirk Douglas in the central role. Wayne became noticeably upset as the picture unfolded. At a dinner party at actress Merle Oberon's house afterwards, the distressed actor motioned Douglas out on the terrace, where Duke berated him. "Christ, Kirk!" said Wayne. "How can you play a part like that? There's so goddamn few of us left. We got to play strong, tough characters. Not those weak queers."

But the John Wayne who rode to the rescue on the CinemaScope screen was far from the young athlete who had ambled through budget Westerns. He had begun wearing a hairpiece in films, and his leathery skin not only disclosed advancing age but became something of a trademark for him in the decades ahead. Privately Duke was reminded of the passage of time when his daughter Toni married Donald LaCava, nephew of director Gregory LaCava, in May 1956. Wayne gave his daughter in marriage at a service in Blessed Sacrament Catholic Church in Hollywood. A lavish reception followed at the Beverly Hills Hotel, given jointly by Duke and Josephine Wayne. There was one major note of discord: Pilar was expressly not invited to the wedding. "Duke was properly enraged," the third Mrs. Wayne said, "but he never expressed that anger to his children."

In the summer of 1956 Wayne joined John Ford and Maureen O'Hara to make *The Wings of Eagles*, his third and least successful pairing with O'Hara. Based on the life of Frank "Spig" Wead, a pioneer in naval air power and a tough military man, the picture honored a man Duke admired. When an accident left Wead paralyzed, he had turned to screenwriting and collaborated with Ford on *Air Mail* (1932) and *They Were Ex-*

pendable (1945). The director's penchant for rambunctious humor gets out of hand in *The Wings of Eagles*, but Wayne played the flying ace as a dedicated career man who puts his job ahead of marriage and has the determination not to let physical adversity rob him of a productive life.

The Wings of Eagles suffered because Wead's wife, played by Maureen O'Hara, was not shown as an alcoholic. "The scenes where she was drinking were all shot," O'Hara said, "and I thought I was bloody good. Then when the Wead children saw the film, they objected to their mother's being shown like that. Her drinking is implied, but the scenes aren't there." Dan Dailey provided humor for *The Wings of Eagles*, but the picture was a great disappointment to all concerned.

After Aissa was born, Pilar was not as free to travel with her husband as she had been in the early months of their marriage. Making two or three movies a year would keep Duke away from home six to nine months, and both of them realized the strain that long separations could put on a marriage. Yet Pilar intended to be a good mother. Wayne expected her to go with him in November 1956 when he left for Africa to make *Legend of the Lost*, which Batjac coproduced with an Italian film company, and he was nonplussed when she refused. Their first serious disagreement occurred when Pilar argued that she could not leave their baby in the care of a nurse for three months. In the end they compromised; Duke would go to Libya by himself, but Pilar would join him when the cast and crew moved to the Cinecitta studio in Rome to shoot interiors.

Director Henry Hathaway had written the original story for *Legend of the Lost* in an effort to extend his talent into a different field of motion picture production, then turned his material over to Ben Hecht, a distinguished screenwriter. "The script never worked," Hathaway admitted, "but I told the idea to Wayne and he was fond of it. The picture was a fiasco. Everybody tried to change it from my original concept." Wayne liked Hathaway and respected him enough to feel confident that the director would pull the film together into something workable, but the obstacles proved insurmountable.

Having ended his association with Warner Bros., Duke arranged for *Legend of the Lost* to be released through United Artists. He drove a hard bargain: "The deal is either worth it or it isn't," he told United Artists executive Bob Blumofe. "I see no room for negotiation." Wayne presented the studio with a package consisting of himself, Hathaway, Hecht, Sophia

Loren, and Rossano Brazzi and demanded its acceptance or rejection within a week. When the management of United Artists expressed reservations, Duke held firm. "It is pretty easy to look so closely at the details of a contract that you overlook the value of the deal," he replied.

Once underway, the production was difficult for everyone. "We are working at an oasis in the middle of the Sahara Desert, 400 air-miles from Tripoli," Wayne wrote from Africa early in February 1957. "This little village is completely isolated from the rest of the world: no radio, telephone; no modern facilities. We bunk in tents. In the days it's sunburn hot, at sundown the temperature drops to around thirty degrees. We have to sleep in all our clothes bundled in sleeping packs to keep warm, even with kerosene stoves burning full blast all night."

A few days into production Duke fell and tore two ligaments in his left foot. He cabled Pilar that he needed her. She left for Libya immediately; there she found Duke quartered in a mud-plastered, thatch-roofed room. "Our compound boasted a single bathroom," she wrote, "which we shared with the rest of the cast and crew." Learning that Duke had suffered a foot injury, John Ford sent condolences from Hollywood. "I hope Pilar is well," the director wrote. "I called the house, and the baby is fine. She is calling Ward 'Papa.'" Ford knew that Wayne would get a chuckle out of the hint that Bond had usurped his position as master of the house in Encino.

Pilar hated the African location and was miserable the whole time she was there. She landed at Erg on an airstrip the French had built during World War II. Each evening their quarters had to be washed down and fumigated. Pilar needed to keep busy, yet there was nothing for her to do in the desert but worry about Aissa and what was happening at home.

Sophia Loren, who played an Arab street girl in the movie, agreed that *Legend of the Lost* was a rigorous assignment. In fact, the Italian actress almost died on the Sahara location when the space heater in the room where she was sleeping exhausted the oxygen supply and left her with nothing to breathe except carbon monoxide.

Loren, however, found working with her costar a pleasure. "I was relieved to find that John Wayne was exactly as advertised," she said. "Big, authoritative, gruff, but polite, and a pro through and through. He showed up right on the minute, knew all his lines and moves, worked hard all day long without letup, and quit right on the minute. There was no doubt that he was in command, the captain on the bridge of the ship. He did not have to exert his authority overtly because everyone automatically deferred to him. Even the director, Henry Hathaway. But he never abused his powerful position. He simply assumed his stance and kept it. With me, he was polite and pleasant, but distant. He did not show affection toward anyone but neither did he show any hostility nor make outrageous demands. But everyone was in awe of him, scared of him somewhat, and a great concerted effort was made to anticipate his needs."

On March 30, Wayne notified Charles Feldman from Rome that shooting on *Legend of the Lost* was finished. Duke took a week's vacation, traveled through northern Italy and Switzerland to scout locations for John Ford, then joined Henry Hathaway in London to check on the editing of their film. "I think we have a good one, Charley," Duke told Feldman, although he did suggest two possible problems. Wayne thought the picture had so many scenes that there was no time to establish a mood for each one. "I think music will be very helpful to correct this," Duke said. The other problem he anticipated was that the Italian accents of Loren and Brazzi juxtaposed against his American inflection seemed to throw off the rhythm of their scenes together. "I could be very wrong in this judgment," he said.

His error was in thinking that they had made a good picture. *Legend of the Lost* proved a disaster and lost money. Neither the actors nor the director were able to overcome the weaknesses of a contrived script that tried to combine sex, sand, and sway, but ended up a lethargic treasure hunt. Duke seems out of place, while Loren comes across as one-dimensional. Henry Hathaway, a fine technician who had earned a reputation for rescuing troubled projects, was incapable of salvaging the one story he had originated.

When Pilar returned to Encino, she found herself resenting that Aissa had grown while she was away. She still felt awkward in Wayne's world of wealth, talent, and famous people. Yet Duke wanted her near him at all times and was eager for her to meet his friends and associates. Occasionally the couple gave intimate dinner parties in their home, where the atmosphere was casual. When actress Marsha Hunt and her husband, Robert Presnell, Jr., one of several screenwriters who had tried to improve *Legend of the Lost*, were invited to Duke's house for an informal evening, they were astonished to learn that the real Wayne was educated and articulate. "He was a thoughtful and charming host," said Hunt, "and his home handsome and tasteful. We spent a comfortable, delightful time together. As we drove home afterward, Robert and I agreed that we would have to adjust our opinion of the man."

Wayne helped his brother line up *Seven Men from Now* (1957), which Robert produced with Andrew McLaglen and Budd Boetticher directed. The picture marked Gail Russell's last screen appearance. The company had been on location in Lone Pine and returned to Hollywood in time for a wrap party at Boetticher's house. "Gail got just blind drunk," the director remembered. Andy McLaglen, who had fallen in love with the troubled actress, spent three days looking for her. "They found her in her bathroom," said Boetticher. "Andy claimed that her stomach was so swollen it looked like she'd swallowed a football."

Duke was at last finalizing plans on his movie about the Alamo; he had made arrangements for the picture to be filmed in Texas. While an old San Antonio street was being constructed near Brackettville, Wayne pursued other projects. He appeared as himself in a scene with Angie Dickinson in *I Married a Woman* (released in 1958), a comedy that starred George Gobel. In 1956 Duke had signed a contract with 20th Century–Fox that made him the highest paid actor in Hollywood to date. He would receive $2 million for three pictures, beginning with *The Barbarian and the Geisha* (also 1958).

In November 1957 Wayne left for Japan, where the initial project under his Fox contract would be filmed. Pilar declined to go along but promised to join her husband before Christmas. Originally entitled *The Townsend Harris Story*, the movie centered on an American diplomat sent to Japan in 1856 to implement a trade agreement imposed on the isolationist nation under threat of military intervention. Wayne and the picture's director, John Huston, were at odds from the beginning. Duke complained that he was never able to get a reading on Huston's personality, much less the character he was playing in the movie. "It's a little frustrating trying to arouse the . . . sleeping talent of our lead, Mr. Huston, who wears the clothes of an Irish country gentleman," Wayne wrote John Ford. "Maybe I'm prejudiced, but I'd say without the manner."

Script revisions were still being made after filming began in Kyoto; Huston was shooting during the daytime and writing future scenes at night. "I am sure [Huston] must be marking time so he can get everything set in his mind," Wayne said. "We came out here with little or no story. But I have a feeling that in the three days' work that we've done so far . . . that I am working in a narrated tapestry." Duke vowed not to worry; "no more ulcers for me," he said. The pay was good, and he claimed that was what mattered. "I'm going to live in this world of Mr. Mitty," Wayne told Ford.

But he felt lost and soon became infuriated at the director's vague approach. "I liked Huston well enough," said Wayne's double, Chuck Roberson, "but the guy drove Duke up a pagoda, the way he hemmed and hawed over directing a scene." Wayne later called Huston a liar and said that "actors were like figures on a Japanese screen to him; they were just things in the foreground. . . . I found it impossible to make any contact at all." Duke was also uneasy about his costuming. "[Huston] had me started out dressed like Abe Lincoln," the irate actor said, "and everybody knows I'm John Wayne. . . . There were all sorts of things he could have done to make us human beings, but he was only concerned with his tapestry, which he thought was more important than the human story."

The experience went from bad to worse. In early December, Duke came down with flu. "I haven't the time and I don't wish to stir my ulcers to the point of explaining how I feel about this picture," Wayne wrote his agent a few days before Christmas. "I hope and pray that for the first time in thirty years my instinct is wrong." When Pilar arrived in Japan for the holidays, Duke unloaded his feelings about Huston to her. "I can't work with the son of a bitch," he said.

Wayne failed to understand the director's artistic concept. "*The Barbarian and the Geisha* turned out to be a bad picture," said Huston, "but it was a good picture before it became a bad picture." The director felt that by casting John Wayne as Townsend Harris a nice contrast would be established—Wayne's "massive frame, bluff innocence, and rough edges," as opposed to the small, highly cultivated Japanese. "The physical comparison would help serve to emphasize their dissimilar viewpoints and culture," Huston declared. He thought that he had put together "a sensitive, well-balanced work" by the time the company left Japan. The filmmaker then took on another foreign assignment and turned the film over to 20th Century–Fox. "John Wayne apparently took over after I left," Huston wrote in his memoirs. "He pulled a lot of weight at Fox, so the studio went along with his demands for changes." When the director saw the final print, he was aghast. "By the time the studio finished hacking up the picture according to Wayne's instructions," said Huston, "it was a complete mess."

Critics pointed out that John Wayne looked bewildered in the movie, but many of them found it a lovely film to watch. Some even compared the sets and costumes used in *The Barbarian and the Geisha*, a title Huston hated, with those of the Japanese classic *Gate of Hell*. Bosley Crowther in the *New York Times* said that John Huston had achieved "single shots of exquisite composition and incredible delicacy of hues." But Duke could never accept that his picture with Huston had any merit at all. "Don't talk to me about that Japanese thing," he later remarked.

On January 14, 1958, after Pilar had returned home from Japan but while Duke was still there, she awoke around three o'clock one morning when Blackie, her dog, began barking at her bedside. Pilar opened her eyes to see smoke hovering around the ceiling. She made a rush for Aissa's room and found the hall filled with smoke. She grabbed the baby from her crib and raced downstairs to discover that the house was on fire. She carried Aissa to safety, located a fire extinguisher, and rushed back upstairs. As she approached the top of the stairs, flames burst across the carpet, and Pilar was burned slightly on one arm. Soon the entire second story was ablaze, with flames shooting skyward. Firefighters battled the inferno for over an hour. Before the fire was extinguished, the top floor of the Encino house was gutted and the downstairs was badly damaged by smoke and water.

Counting the loss of antiques and personal belongings, the destruction totaled over $500,000. Duke took the loss in his stride, saying that the fire had given them an opportunity to remodel. The couple rented a house while theirs was being repaired, and by September they were able to move back in. Workmen enlarged the floor space of the Wayne home, adding a screening room, an exercise room, and his and her dressing areas.

But around the time renovation on the house got underway, Pilar made the decision to divorce Duke. His frequent absences simply put too much stress on their marriage. She felt that their relationship had suffered from their separations, yet she could not be a dutiful wife and travel with her husband without relinquishing her responsibility as a mother. Pilar had come to feel that Duke was smothering her own personality and that she had no identity other than that of Mrs. John Wayne. Their friends were all *his* friends, and her life was expected to revolve around a superstar, no matter where he might be. After a brief separation, Duke persuaded his wife to change her mind, but the tension between them was never fully resolved.

When Wayne left for Arizona early in May 1958 to film *Rio Bravo* in Old Tucson, Pilar remained behind to oversee the details of remodeling. Duke stayed at the Santa Rita Hotel in Tucson, joined there by his costars Dean Martin, Ricky Nelson, and Angie Dickinson. Howard Hawks was to direct the picture, and Wayne had high hopes that the Western would be a big success, which he sorely needed after the mishaps of *Legend of the Lost* and *The Barbarian and the Geisha.*

Having turned fifty, Wayne no longer felt comfortable playing romantic leads, yet he had no intention of accepting anything less than starring roles. Sheriff John T. Chance, Duke's part in *Rio Bravo*, was ideal for him and established an image that he would return to in future assignments. Sheriff Chance is courageous, a man of principle, yet realistic. He doesn't ask for assistance, even stubbornly refuses it, knowing that amateurs get in the way of a job that demands professional skill. In his scenes with Angie Dickinson, she becomes the aggressor. Chance is virile but compliant, not assertive. "Wayne is better when the girl is forcing the issue," said Hawks. Chance's romance with Feathers (the Dickinson character) consists more of implication and innuendo than an attraction the seasoned lawman acts upon.

Hawks, like Ford, frequently focused his Westerns on male bonding. In *Rio Bravo* Wayne establishes a strong rapport with Dean Martin, who played a drunk who regains his self-respect under fire, and the two actors got along well privately. On the set Duke proved helpful to teenage idol Ricky Nelson, assigned the role of a young gunslinger reminiscent of Billy the Kid. Since Wayne had gotten past the age of romantic involvement in his pictures, producers felt the need to include a current heartthrob in the cast to ensure their acceptability to younger audiences.

Rio Bravo was Howard Hawks's second picture with Wayne, and the director discovered that the star's instinct for what was necessary to make an effective scene had become almost infallible since they had made *Red River* together. "He'd never learn lines before I talked to him," said Hawks, "because he said that threw him off. He could memorize two pages of lines in three or four minutes. He never squawks about anything.

He's the easiest person that I've ever worked with." Duke, on the other hand, found Hawks "the coldest character I've ever met in my life" but agreed that the director was an excellent filmmaker. Hawks preferred to print the first take, yet was patient with people and seemed imperturbable, even when actors had trouble delivering what was expected of them. Wayne admired the director's professionalism and trusted him implicitly. "You and Ford spoiled me," Duke told Hawks.

Budd Boetticher visited the set of *Rio Bravo* on a day when nearly two hundred guests were watching the company work. Wayne was supposed to enter a saloon and say to the villain, played by Claude Akins, "You're coming with me." Akins was to reply, "I don't think so. Look around." Duke was then to glance around and note that he was surrounded by guys pointing guns in his direction. Akins's next line was "So what are you going to do now?" When they reached that point in rehearsing the scene, Wayne replied, "Well, the first thing I'm gonna do is change the tone of my voice if all you assholes are going to talk just like I do." Hawks asked what he meant. Duke said, "Well, goddammit, everybody is playing John Wayne!"

Hawks's view was that a Western should start off with a good dramatic sequence to grab the audience's attention, then lighten up and include some humor. "It starts off being very serious," he said, "and then before the audience realizes it, [they're] starting to have some fun." He thought dialogue should be kept short, and, again like Ford, Hawks often pared down lines as filming progressed. "Westerns just happen to be something that I like," the director said. "I like to get out of the studio; I like to get out in the air."

Old Tucson was a frontier town built as a movie set several years before Hawks filmed *Rio Bravo* there, although his company added an upper end to the assemblage of buildings. Two-thirds of *Rio Bravo* was shot there, the rest in Hollywood. Much of the location work was done at night. "You can't have men sneak around and do some of the [action] in daytime shots," the director said. "It looks ridiculous. So you have to light up a street and make it shadowy and make it eerie and make it dangerous, and it's a job to light a big street enough to film."

Wayne returned to Los Angeles in mid-July 1958, feeling confident that the movie he was making with Hawks would put his career back on track. His fee by that time was $750,000 a picture, and he was playing a strong hero, older but wiser. Future director Peter Bogdanovich considered *Rio Bravo* Wayne's "most endearing performance." Others commented that the picture was familiar but well made and concurred that Wayne's performance ranked among the Western's more refreshing aspects.

By the late 1950s John Wayne had become an indelible symbol of the Old West to audiences around the globe. While his heroes possessed human frailties, they personified the idealized American—quiet, resourceful, self-reliant. Although his characters were guilty of what would later be considered male chauvinism, they fought for what they believed was right and tolerated no one's pushing them around. "It used to be that the Western was folklore and legend," said Wayne in 1972. "Before and right after World War II, every country in the world loved the image of the West—the music, the dress, the excitement, everything that was associated with the opening of a new territory. It took everybody out of their own little world. Now that we've become embroiled in the world's politics, the picture's not so clear."

For millions Wayne had come to represent the mythic American individualist, the man of action, the eternal cowboy who could resist society's dictates and triumph on his own terms. "The cowboy is the hero of American folklore," Duke's son Michael declared, "like knighthood and chivalry are part of the folklore in England. My father became the symbol of that cowboy. I didn't realize how great he was until I started looking at these old pictures. They're just breathtaking."

Duke and Pilar had no more than settled into their renovated house than Wayne's daughter Toni presented him with a granddaughter. A few days later the jubilant grandfather was off to southern Louisiana to film *The Horse Soldiers* with John Ford. The picture began shooting in late October 1958, with most of the company housed in Alexandria. Wayne, Ford, and leading lady Constance Towers, however, stayed in private homes in Natchitoches, while Duke's costar, William Holden, took up residence in Shreveport, where he could drink without Ford's interference.

Based on the heroics of Benjamin Grierson's raiders, a Union cavalry unit that sloshed its way through six hundred miles of Confederate territory during the Civil War, *The Horse Soldiers* was produced by the Mirisch Company at an estimated cost of $5 million. Since John Ford was an American Civil War buff, he entered the project with great enthusiasm. The director's ardor was dampened when Fred Kennedy, a Hollywood stuntman for more than twenty-five years, died of a broken neck after performing a horse fall for the picture. Ford blamed himself for Kennedy's death and lost interest in the film. The director began drinking and suddenly looked like a beaten old man, much to Wayne's alarm.

But Duke had his own crisis to deal with. Nervous and frequently unable to sleep, Pilar had developed an addiction to sleeping pills. A few days after her husband left for Louisiana, Pilar followed with Aissa and their maid. "I barely remember making the trip," she later said. Two days after arriving on the Louisiana location, Pilar began to hallucinate. "I was told that I tried to slash my wrists," she said. "Duke hired a private plane and sent me home with two nurses and a maid. I woke up in an Encino hospital." Wayne's public relations staff hushed up his wife's addiction, so the press never reported the incident, and by the time *The Horse Soldiers* wrapped, Pilar had recovered enough to rejoin the company on location.

Interiors of the Ford picture were completed on the Goldwyn lot in Hollywood, and additional exteriors were shot on Lot 3 at MGM. While *The Horse Soldiers* contains interesting moments, the film falls apart toward the end. Depressed over Fred Kennedy's death, the director improvised a hasty conclusion. The script called for the movie to close with a bloody battle at a bridge, but Ford neglected to shoot the sequence in detail. "It was awful," said screenwriter John Lee Mahin. "They charged across that damned bridge and not one guy fell off the saddle. I didn't know what the hell was the matter." Wayne was shocked by how devastated Ford looked when they said goodbye on the final day of shooting. Duke was convinced that the director would never work again.

Both Wayne and Ford were appalled by what was happening to Hollywood; they deplored the sex and violence that the screen had begun to display. Duke lashed out at *Suddenly, Last Summer* and *They Came to Cordura* (both 1959) as examples of the corruption of the industry. "Ten or fifteen years ago," he said in 1960, "audiences went to pictures to see men behaving like men. Today there are too many neurotic roles. . . . We're supposed to be in the business of illusion." He was convinced that Hollywood's current fascination with weaklings, depravity, and vulgarity stood to diminish the fiber of American society. "I happen to believe our country's going soft," he said. "We're allowing machines to run it, not men; the Federal government to run it instead of local governments."

More than ever Wayne's screen persona stood as a symbol of manly incorruptibility. While his characters often seemed ruthless in their pursuit of a mission, audiences sympathized with the impetus that drove them, aware that Duke's off-screen position was no less single-tracked when it involved fundamental principles. By the late 1950s John Wayne was consistently the highest-paid actor in Hollywood and considered the industry's most bankable star. He received an average of eighteen thousand fan letters a month. Duke was proud of the motion picture business and remained adamant in his belief that filmmakers should portray a morally balanced world in the entertainment they produced.

In the mid-1950s Jack Warner received a postcard from "a former fan" who complained that he had just seen the worst movie ever in his thirty-five years of watching motion pictures. "Another one like this and you fellows will be making doughnuts instead of pictures for a living," the writer declared. As the popularity of movies declined during the 1950s, all sorts of alibis and explanations were offered by worried executives. One veteran producer listened to his colleagues with mounting irritation and finally expounded: "There's nothing wrong with this damned industry that a dozen John Waynes couldn't cure."

Wayne, the former serial performer, had emerged as perhaps the most lasting star from Hollywood's Golden Age. Rather than quitting the business or phasing into supporting roles, Duke continued doing what he did best, while his impact appeared to broaden. Not only did he *play* archetypal American heroes, he *became* one, as merciless in private with those who stepped off an acceptable path as were the characters he played in movies. "There's only one John Wayne," Duke's son Michael said, "as there's only one John Ford and one Maureen O'Hara. They're unique; they have special qualities. They not only survived in a killer business, they thrived."

Ahead lay some of Wayne's greatest challenges and one of his biggest disappointments. After years of planning and with Batjac in full operation, Duke was ready to film his story of the Alamo. The project would tax his skill, his patience, his energy, and his financial resources, but it represented a moment in history that Duke thought a nation beset with problems needed to remember.

Metaphor for America

John Wayne had dreamed of making a film about the siege at the Alamo since 1944; it was a subject he often talked about over supper. He began working on the movie in 1946, referring to it as "my baby, my pet." He talked with Texas folklorist J. Frank Dobie, whom he discovered was a fascinating spinner of tales, and later to Texas author Lon Tinkle, who had written a book on the siege. For Duke, the battle of the Alamo was *the* great American story, a dramatic reminder that liberty had not been won cheaply. He wanted to recreate on film a moment from the past that would illustrate for successive generations the values on which the United States had been founded. Rather than an episode of rampant imperialism, the defeat at the Texas shrine was for Duke symbolic of the sacrifices brave men had been willing to make for liberty.

Wayne was an aficionado of American history, and *The Alamo* (released in 1960) reflects his personal slant on politics more than any movie he ever made. In Duke's mind the time was ripe for a saga of courage and devotion to the country's founding principles. From the outset his intent was to reawaken American patriotism. "That was something in my heart," he said of the film. He wanted to put before a cynical public "the bloody truth of what some of their forebears went through to win what they had to have or die—liberty and freedom." *The Alamo*, according to Pilar Wayne, "would be [Duke's] response to all the flag burners, draft dodgers, and the faint-hearted who didn't believe in good, old-fashioned American virtues."

"You wouldn't have to know Duke long before he set you straight about his political thinking," Wayne's friend Dobe Carey said. Wayne always stated his position forcefully, disregarding the contradictions of intellectuals and Hollywood liberals. More than other film stars of his era he succeeded in integrating his politics and his profession. In private he talked vigorously about freedom, the rights of the individual, and his hatred of dictatorships. For John Wayne the story of the Alamo said it all: brave men dying in a struggle against despotism. "Every man ought to have something he thinks is worth dying for," said Wayne. "For these men that something was a concept of liberty."

In the early 1950s, while still under contract to Republic, Duke had spent weeks scouting locations in Panama for his Alamo film. "There was a perfect area just outside Panama City," he said, "that looked like the San Antonio area in Texas of the time. Panama was having a depression right then that would have made the whole operation cheaper. Also, there was a two-mile airstrip nearby that the Americans had built, so transport would have been easy." Preparations had been made, John Ford's son Patrick had written a script, and Wayne was ready to start work when Herbert Yates became nervous about the costs involved and called a halt. "We'll talk about it again when I get back in two weeks," Yates had told Wayne. But as soon as the Republic boss left town, Duke summoned a van and moved his belongings out of the studio. "I never went back," Wayne said. Four years later Yates made his own movie about the siege at the Alamo, called *The Last Command*, a modest-priced epic that starred Sterling Hayden.

Disgusted with Yates's continual procrastination, Wayne had decided to produce his pet project himself and to find distribution for the picture elsewhere. He spent the years after leaving Republic talking about the Alamo, planning the production, and researching details. He not only wanted to make a statement, he wanted to make a classic motion picture that would be a monument to the defense of American ideals. Eventually Duke decided to direct the film himself, even though his partner, Robert Fellows, and John Ford advised against it. Fellows ultimately wanted no part of such a risky venture, while Ford argued that an inexperienced director could not possibly handle the burdens of producer and star and direct such a big picture at the same time. But Duke did not want to risk having his dream distorted by letting someone else take the helm.

Having lost his enthusiasm for shooting the movie in Panama, Wayne next considered South America, then Mexico. Finally he decided that if *The Alamo* was to be a metaphor for America, it needed to be filmed within the United States.Then, late in 1956, just before he left for Africa to make *Legend of the Lost*, Duke met James T. "Happy" Shahan, a feisty rancher and building contractor from Brackettville, Texas, who told Wayne that if he made his picture anywhere but in Texas, the Daughters of the Republic would never sanction the movie's being shown in the Lone Star State.

Since *The Last Command* had been shot around Brackettville, Shahan knew something about picture making. He began talking to Duke about filming *The Alamo* on his ranch and letting him supervise the construction of the Old San Antonio set that would be needed. "We argued until September 1957," Shahan remembered. "We argued a lot of places, but we always argued. It took me two years to convince Duke that I could do what I said I could do. Wayne's feeling that the Alamo was symbolic of the American fight for liberty was evident from the first day I talked to him, and it remained so every minute."

Convinced at last that the area around Brackettville was the place to make the movie, John Wayne launched what he hoped would be the biggest, greatest motion picture ever made. Building a replica of the Alamo and an Old San Antonio street took two years. Construction began on Happy Shahan's ranch, with Shahan serving as contractor. Duke visited Brackettville and immediately wanted to know who the construction foreman would be. Shahan had hired Chato Hernandez, an experienced Mexican builder who hadn't finished the third grade in Mexico and didn't speak much English. Wayne assailed Hernandez with questions, which the foreman answered in his broken English. After fifteen minutes or so Duke glowered at the builder and said, "Chato, do you think you can build the Alamo?" Hernandez, scarcely more than five feet tall, looked up at the towering star and said, "Mr. Wayne, you think you can make a picture?" Duke laughed uproariously and asked no more questions, convinced that his project was in good hands.

Shahan's rugged twenty thousand-acre ranch seven miles north of Brackettville was mainly brush and had a similar terrain to that around the Alamo. Hundreds of laborers were brought in from Mexico to duplicate the old mission and the town of San Antonio de Bexar as it looked in the early 1800s. More than a million adobe bricks were made for the construction of complete buildings. Rather than putting up false fronts, interiors were finished so that they could be used in photographing scenes. Wells were dug on the property, sewer lines were installed, thousands of feet of electrical cable were laid, and a dirt landing strip was bulldozed just behind the main set—all at great cost. Wayne's movie was in financial trouble even before the cameras started to turn; construction of the sets alone cost $1.5 million.

Brackettville, near the Mexican border, had a population of only twenty-two hundred people at the time. Duke voiced concern over how the fourteen hundred horses and saddles he needed for the picture could be obtained in such an isolated area. Shahan told him not to worry. The rancher acquired the mounts through a contact he had in Uvalde and built corrals to hold them. The enterprising Texan also located wagons, buckboards, and appropriate set dressings, while cannons for the battle were made on his property. "The barrels were steel and everything else was molded wood and fiberglass," Shahan recalled. Duke was in constant contact with the rancher by telephone, and once a month Shahan made a trip to Hollywood.

The preproduction activity on *The Alamo* stimulated the economy of Brackettville, but Wayne was in a whirl raising enough funds to keep the work going. "He was a ball of nerves," Happy Shahan remembered, "but he was brilliant in his business. I think Wayne would have been a hell of a car salesman; he knew how to make people like him." Duke courted Texas millionaires, such as the McCulloughs of Houston and Clint Murchison of Dallas, who invested heavily in *The Alamo*. But Wayne also put his own money into the production. Before the movie was finished he had mortgaged his Encino estate, his condominium in New York, Batjac, and even his family's automobiles. "I've gambled everything I own on this picture," he said, "all my money and my soul."

United Artists agreed to release *The Alamo* and put up part of the money, which eventually reached $12 million, more than any Hollywood movie had cost up to that time. The studio insisted that Wayne play a role in the picture, in addition to producing and directing, on the contention that audiences expected to see John Wayne in a John Wayne movie. With expenses escalating, Duke had no choice. He would have preferred to play Sam Houston, a supporting role, but executives at United Artists encouraged him to play Davy Crockett, even though Duke was too old for the part. Wayne later claimed that J. Frank Dobie gave him the key to the role when the folklorist remarked that Crockett never ate on an empty stomach nor drank on a full one. "That kind of tells his character," said Wayne, "it gives an attitude of how to make a human being out of a legendary hero."

Duke wanted *The Alamo* to be a family affair. Batjac produced the picture, employing a number of people that Wayne had worked with through the years. His son Michael served as assistant producer, Patrick Wayne played James Bonham, Duke's brother Bob functioned as a producer's aide, daughters Toni and Aissa had speaking parts, and Pilar worked as an extra. James Edward Grant, who had recently begun attending meetings of Alcoholics Anonymous, wrote the screenplay after reading dozens of books, diaries, and journals on the subject. William Clothier became the film's cinematographer, and Cliff Lyons, a former stuntman, headed the second-unit work. Ken Curtis, John Ford's son-in-law, played Captain Dickinson, and Wayne found cameo roles for numerous friends: Olive Carey, Chuck Roberson, Hank Worden, Veda Ann Borg (Andrew McLaglen's wife), among others. Meanwhile executives at United Artists were getting increasingly nervous about the studio's investment.

The cast and crew began arriving in Brackettville early in September 1959. Three hundred and fifty of them were housed and fed at Fort Clark, which had been an operating military installation until 1944, when it became a guest ranch and later a retirement center. Since the company needed more rooms than Fort Clark's two barracks could provide, thirty-eight motel rooms were added to Batjac's expense. Most of the extras were quartered in a bunkhouse in Spofford, Texas, a rail junction twenty miles south of Brackettville. Wayne and his family stayed at the Wainright House, which provided them with ten bedrooms, while Richard Widmark (who played James Bowie) became the houseguest of Happy Shahan and his wife.

"My father had looked forward to that picture for so long," said Patrick Wayne. "In fact the joke was that when he initially wanted to do *The Alamo* he was right for the part that Frankie Avalon played. That's an obvious exaggeration, but he ate, slept, and dreamed that picture." Wayne's obsession with the movie soon began to transfer to other members of the company. "This picture is America," Duke told them. "It's the first time in my life I've been able to express what I feel about people." Even Pilar was amazed at her husband's commitment to the project and claimed that she fell in love with him all over again. "John loved *The Alamo* as a man loves a woman once in a lifetime—passionately," said actress Linda Cristal, who played a featured role in the film. "He wasn't making a movie," Pilar maintained, "he was on a crusade."

Although Wayne was not a religious man, over three hundred members of the cast and crew assembled in the plaza of the completed set on Tuesday morning, September 22, 1959, to inaugurate the first day's shooting of *The Alamo* with a prayer by Father Peter Rogers of St. Mary's Church in San Antonio. Duke's dream was at last coming true. "The camaraderie and joy behind the scenes was something I'll always remember," said Chuck Roberson. "The crew had fun!"

Wayne put his heart into making *The Alamo*, but the toll on him was tremendous. "Watching my father direct was pretty revealing to me," said Pat Wayne. "I never thought of him as a person with much diplomacy and tact, but I suddenly realized that he had a lot of savoir faire." While Duke remained outgoing and friendly on the surface, the pressure frequently built until he exploded. His fury scorched many, even his closest friends; he smoked more than usual, up to a hundred cigarettes a day, and began coughing up phlegm.

Wayne proved to be best at directing action sequences, weakest in the interrelationships of characters. "Duke worked for results," Linda Cristal said. "He didn't go into any of the complicated motivations. The problem with that is that it's hard to touch someone's heart if you don't know how it ticks." Like John Ford, Wayne wasn't altogether comfortable directing women. His method followed Ford's command-and-control model: "This is the way I want it to look," he would say. If someone mentioned his improved talent, he usually replied, "That's what comes of being around Pappy Ford all these years."

Duke was up on weekday mornings at the crack of dawn, eager to begin work. "He seemed to be everywhere at once," Pilar recalled, "correcting the way an extra sat his horse or carried his gun, rearranging props, working with the actors, praising his crew." Despite the pressure and endless responsibilities, Wayne's love of filmmaking showed. He wasn't striving for reality in the picture; he wanted to capture the legend and heroics of men dying for a cause.

"We are working like hell," Duke wrote his agent in late September, "but the cast is wonderful, and the backgrounds are magnificent. [Richard] Boone did a beautiful job as Houston, and we have found an exciting manner for opening the picture to take advantage of Todd-AO [a wide-screen process]. I can't tell you how beautiful the weather is here. We haven't had one unusually hot day—beautiful mornings and evenings."

Wayne found Richard Widmark a difficult actor, one who repeatedly challenged his directorial authority. The two men argued a great deal on the set and eventually had a thunderous confrontation. "Widmark was a different sort," Happy Shahan said. "In my house he'd look at a paper or sit down and read a magazine just to get away from people."

English actor Laurence Harvey, who played William Barret Travis, entertained the company by telling hilarious stories. Despite rumors about his sexuality, Harvey was well liked and worked easily with Duke. Wayne later admitted that Travis might have been a better role for him than Crockett, but explained, "I didn't think I ought to be hogging the whole picture."

Michael Wayne, who had been working in the Batjac offices for several years and had learned much about the business, became his father's right-hand man on the production. Duke and Michael had their share of fights, and his son always called Wayne J. W., never Dad. If Duke had time on weekends, he, Michael, and Patrick enjoyed talking sports. Wayne doted on his daughter Aissa, who spent three months on the *Alamo* location. "I got pretty bored," Pilar admitted. "I looked after Aissa and got interested in photography. Duke's daughter Toni and I were the best of friends, so we used to go to San Antonio or Dallas once in a while. Brackettville was nothing, but the beauty of the setting and the horses and the pageantry were very rewarding."

Most nights Duke stayed busy with production details and was under constant stress. He routinely conferred with Jimmy Grant about the script, talked to Alfred Ybarra about details of art direction, and consulted with Happy Shahan about the logistics of upcoming scenes. "I felt that Wayne had done his homework," said Shahan, "but every time I was with him he was under pressure." One night around 11:30 Duke awakened Shahan from a sound sleep with a phone call. "I want you to come over," Wayne said, "I need your help." When Shahan arrived, Duke and Jimmy Grant were in an argument over whether Travis actually drew the line for the Alamo heroes to cross. Shahan sided with Duke, agreeing that Travis's line was probably myth. "Who in New York or Hollywood will know what the history books say?" Grant queried, intent on a dramatic climax. But Wayne vetoed the change his scriptwriter wanted, preferring to remain closer to historical facts. "That was a typical night," Shahan said.

"Duke can spot holes in a script faster than most writers and directors," James Edward Grant declared. In the case of *The Alamo* Wayne was tireless in his resolve to put on the screen an epic of bold courage. He demanded that Grant fashion dialogue that would develop character as well as advance the story. He could be stubborn and uncompromising, sometimes abrasive and callous. Duke's friends tolerated his outbursts, knowing that he would likely apologize before the day was out. "Underneath that big frame, Wayne had a big heart," Happy Shahan maintained. "He loved people, he was a family man, and he loved his country."

Many felt that Duke should have let someone else direct, that he had taken on too much, that he was sometimes out of his element. "That was the first time I worked with Wayne as a director," cinematographer William Clothier said. "He took charge even of photography. It was sometimes hard for Duke to visualize things. I'd have to call him over and say, 'See it through the lens.' He couldn't stand back and visualize how a scene would look on film."

Besides producing, directing, and starring in *The Alamo*, Wayne had the burden of promotion and publicity. At the end of each day's shooting there were rushes to watch, processed at a film lab in Dallas and flown to the airstrip on Shahan's ranch. While Duke was an excellent field general, his patience wore thin. Always there was anxiety over the escalating budget—$4 million more than had been anticipated. Duke was determined that *The Alamo* would be his masterpiece, but the magnitude of the project overwhelmed him. "I felt very frightened for Duke," Pilar said. "He had put every penny he had on the line for this film and wanted to do it so badly. But I saw him going through such anguish." Still, nobody was going to take one frame of the picture away from him.

Since Batjac shared offices in West Hollywood with John Ford Productions, the great filmmaker was fully aware of his protégé's enormous undertaking. Ford's own career by then was on the decline, so the veteran director no longer stayed as busy as he had been in former years, and he became restless with enforced leisure. "I hope to go to Texas and cast a paternal eye on Duke Wayne," Ford wrote a few days before filming on *The Alamo* began. "This young and ambitious lad of fifty-six years [sic] is writing, producing, acting, and directing *The Alamo* with the excessive budget of five million bucks." The great director arrived in Brackettville a week or so later and announced that he planned to spend considerable time there. The following afternoon he appeared on the set and devoted the rest of the day to peering over Wayne's shoulder. At one point Ford seated himself in the director's chair, stopped Wayne in the middle of a scene, and growled, "Jesus Christ, Duke, that's not the way to do it."

For several days Ford remained on the set, advising Duke on how work should proceed. The old director had been the engine driving the machine for so long that his powerful personality knew no compromise. Duke respected Ford and did not want to hurt his feelings, but he realized that his authority as director was at stake. He couldn't ask his mentor to leave, but neither did he want Ford to take over his picture. "What the hell am I going to do?" Wayne asked cameraman William Clothier.

"Look," Clothier said, "I've got a big crew here and an extra first cameraman who's not doing a damn thing. Let's give the Old Man a second unit." Duke thought that a splendid idea. He assigned Ford a cameraman, a couple of camera operators, and his son Michael as assistant director, giving Michael firm instructions to keep Ford away from the principal actors. "It was a rough position that my father put me in," Michael Wayne recalled. "I was to try to keep Mr. Ford happy, but I wouldn't let him talk to Laurence Harvey or Richard Widmark or any of the guys who were playing major roles. He always wanted to get them in the scene and do something with them, so there were rubs between Mr. Ford and myself."

Hundreds of Mexican extras were brought across the border in buses each morning and taken back across the Rio Grande in the evening to avoid immigration problems. Ford worked mainly with them, filming scenes of Santa Anna's soldiers marching with bayonets along a river, their images reflected in the water. "I had something like 200 Mexican extras out there," Michael Wayne remembered, "and I didn't speak Spanish. I would have them come in phalanxes. It made an effective shot and is in the film."

Most of the footage Ford shot did not make the finished picture, but Wayne convinced his esteemed friend that Cliff Lyons couldn't possibly handle all the second unit work assigned to him without his expert assistance. Ford accepted the ruse and left Texas happy. Wayne wrote the director shortly after Ford's return to Hollywood, maintaining a pretense of gratitude. "I've had a helluva cold," Duke said. "If you had stayed, I'd have gone to bed for a night. Am good for about four hours, then start folding. Well, anyway, I can make it until Saturday, then I'll sleep for thirty hours. There's a light and a camera in the window waiting for your return. Sure appreciate having your shoulder to lean on."

Later Ford was hurt that so little of his work actually appeared in the finished film, but Wayne had made certain that the scenes he shot had little or nothing to do with the basic story. "I don't think we used three cuts that the Old Man did," William Clothier said. "I would estimate that it cost Duke over $250,000 to give Ford that second unit." But Wayne accepted the added expense rather than damage a thirty-year relationship with the man who had started him in the business.

As work on *The Alamo* progressed, many of the actors and crew members grew bored with the isolated location. "I'm a street kid from the neighborhoods of south Philadelphia," said Frankie Avalon. "When I got to the wide-open spaces of Texas, I didn't know where I was. To be exposed to the elements of scorpions and skunks and rattlesnakes, I didn't know what to do." Having grown up in Montana and worked on many Western locations, Hank Worden was better equipped to handle south Texas, but even he found Brackettville an adjustment. "I never saw so many rattlesnakes in my life," said Worden. On Saturday nights members of the company crossed over into Mexico. "I was Chill Wills's banker," Happy Shahan said of the character actor who played the Beekeeper in the film. "Every Saturday night Chill would come to me and say, 'Cuz, let me have a couple hundred.' So I'd give him $200 and Monday morning he'd pay me back."

During the week Jack Pennick, who had fought in the battle of Belleau Wood during World War I and was a veteran in John Ford's stock company, drilled the extras as if they were actually going into combat. Playing cards, sometimes for considerable money, became a popular diversion with some actors between takes. During lulls on the set Wayne instructed Danny Borzage to play the accordion, a trick he borrowed from Ford. "It's easy to talk an actor into a scene that way," Duke explained.

A pretty young Texas woman named LaJean Ethridge and her boyfriend, Chester Smith, read about the making of *The Alamo* and showed up in Brackettville eager to work in the movie. Batjac hired them as extras and assigned them to quarters in nearby Spofford. LaJean turned out to be a fair actress. "Once the camera was turned on her, she lit up," Happy Shahan declared. "Wayne saw it and assigned her a part." Since LaJean was to receive actor's pay instead of extra's pay, she was told she could move into better lodging at Fort Clark. "That made the girl's boyfriend mad," Shahan recalled. "That night when she went to Spofford to get her clothes, he knifed her and killed her." Chester Smith pleaded guilty to the stabbing and was eventually sentenced to twenty years in prison.

Work on *The Alamo* seemed to drag on forever, and with each passing week Wayne's temper grew shorter. James Henaghan, one of the writers on the picture, got drunk in Brackettville one night and began to make derogatory comments about Duke. When his remarks were relayed to Wayne, Duke sent for the complaining writer. Henaghan informed the messenger that if Wayne wanted to see him, he knew where to find him. Since Duke also had been drinking, the two ended up in a bitter quarrel. "Wayne likes to believe that he is relentlessly honorable and that his word is his bond," said Henaghan. "This is not true, anymore than it is true that any man is entirely honorable. He would like to be in life a John Wayne character in a movie, but he has never quite made it."

Many felt that the picture became too long and too talky. "I think Duke made a mistake on *The Alamo* when he didn't let Ford direct it," said Hank Worden. "There are places where there's an awful lot of dialogue, and Jimmy Grant kept adding dialogue here and there. I think Ford would have devised more action." Screenwriter-director Burt Kennedy was working for Wayne at the time and liked portions of the movie but felt that Duke ran into trouble in several areas. "Three hours is a long time to tell the story of the Alamo," Kennedy said. "It would be a good 110-minute movie. It's a story that's been told so many times that it's hard to keep interest in it."

Other members of the company came to believe more strongly in the project as filming continued. "At first I thought those lines were really corny," Chuck Roberson said, "but they worked out rather well." Nearly everyone in Brackettville was impressed by Duke's dedication. "Wayne's a strong man, a very strong character, and he's very professional," said stuntman Dean Smith, who broke into movies on *The Alamo*. "I came to love Duke like I would my father; he did an awful lot for me."

Wayne understood the hazards that stunt performers faced and tried never to ask them to do anything he wouldn't do himself, which created a bond between them. Still, stunt work was a difficult job. "For months we had rearing horses, falling horses, saddle falls, and falls off the fort," Gil Perkins said of his work on Wayne's picture. Most of the eighteen stuntmen employed on *The Alamo* understood Duke, knew that he didn't realize how angry he sounded at times, and accepted that Wayne was not capable of giving an order without sounding like a drill sergeant.

Duke was determined to finish the picture before Christmas, yet the logistics were so difficult that the production moved slowly. Hours were wasted in rounding up everybody for another take. Finally on December 20, 1959, principal photography on *The Alamo* ended, fourteen days behind schedule. Wayne was exhausted from three months of perpetual motion and weighed thirty pounds less than he had when shooting on the picture began.

After the holidays Wayne went to work with a film editor and held conferences with Dimitri Tiomkin, who scored the movie. Duke was convinced that he had photographed a noble statement of Americanism, a story of men who loved liberty enough to go down in defeat. "How can you measure such men?" Wayne said of the defenders of the Alamo. "How can you measure courage and human dignity and the desire for freedom?" Besides recording an inspiring segment of American history, Duke also felt that he had created movie entertainment on a grand scale. John Ford saw an early cut of *The Alamo* and pronounced it the greatest picture he had ever seen. "It will last forever, run forever, for all peoples, all families everywhere," Ford said.

But Duke was soon to face the greatest disappointment of his career. He had hired Russell Birdwell to head publicity on the film. Birdwell had enjoyed singular success advertising David O. Selznick's *Gone With the Wind* (1939) and had turned Jane Russell into a Hollywood sex symbol with his marketing of Howard Hughes's *The Outlaw* (1943). But the publicist miscalculated in his campaign for *The Alamo* by making his notices sound as though liking the movie was a patriotic duty. The presidential election of 1960 was about to take place, and Birdwell got the notion of contrasting the deceit of politicians with the purity of the heroes who had fought against Santa Anna. "There were no ghostwriters at the Alamo," an advertising slogan proclaimed. "Only men."

Birdwell's publicity efforts hit the public wrong. The excessive ballyhoo for the picture and the conservative jingoism that accompanied it created antipathy even before the film was released. "Russell Birdwell was Wayne's doom," Happy Shahan maintained, "he was the guy who caused all the problems."

Public reaction to *The Alamo* sparked a final outburst from the Motion Picture Alliance for the Preservation of American Ideals. Screenwriter Borden Chase, a founding member of the alliance and cohort of Wayne's, became indignant when the picture wasn't given a better reception. "When *The Alamo* was coming out, the word of mouth on it was that it was a dog," Chase said. "This was created by the Communists to get at Wayne. Then there were bad reviews inspired by the Communists."

The movie's premiere was held on October 24, 1960, at the Woodlawn Theater in San Antonio, with most of Wayne's family in attendance. The original version of the film ran 192 minutes, counting the overture and exit music. Nearly everyone agreed that the picture should be cut. "The day after the premiere I sat in Duke's suite from eleven in the morning until 3:30 P.M., with everyone from United Artists," Charles Feldman noted. "I spent the entire morning and afternoon going into every phase of the picture and made practically every recommendation for the cutting of the picture. I talked Duke and Birdwell out of cutting the cattle stampede on which Duke fought me and later gave in to me; and it is still in the picture. All the long drawn-out speeches in the first part of the picture and the birthday scene in the second half are now deleted from the picture. At least 40 minutes have been taken out."

Critics still found the first two hours of the movie long-winded and sluggish. Most reviewers thought that James Edward Grant's script was unimaginative and mawkish. Newspapers from coast to coast lambasted the film, claiming that it was trite, overdone, and pretentious. A few critics liked the picture, praising mainly its battle scenes and panoramic views of the Mexican army, and fans lined up to see it. But *The Alamo* was nowhere near the blockbuster John Wayne had anticipated. Later the critical appraisal would soften, yet at the time of its release Duke's pet project was considered a failure.

Wayne was devastated; he cared far more about the critics' opinions than he cared to admit. He felt that people who disliked *The Alamo* were laughing at him. Duke had voiced views in the movie that were sacrosanct to him. He believed the lines he spoke as Davy Crockett: "Republic . . . I like the sound of the word. It's one of those words that makes me tight in the throat." Decked out in buckskin, John Wayne at that moment was more than a symbol of frontier individualism; he was voicing what he considered the creed of every true American. When audiences snickered and critics called such sentiments flag-waving, Duke was wounded. "There's right and there's wrong," he said in *The Alamo*. "You gotta do one or the other. You do the one and you're living. You do the other and you may be walking around, but in reality you're dead as a beaver hat." When liberal friends pointed out that not everything in life is so black and white, Duke usually answered, "Why the hell isn't it?"

"My politics interfered with the fucking critics on that one," Wayne said of *The Alamo*'s tepid reception. He continued to believe that the movie was "a damned good picture," with "nothing in it political at all." He claimed that reviewers failed to understand that he wasn't for Travis and Houston and the rest of the Texans; it was *freedom* he favored.

Yet even the movie colony seemed to turn against him. *The Alamo* received six Oscar nominations in 1961, including one for best picture of the year. Chill Wills was nominated for best supporting actor, and the movie received nominations for best cinematography, best sound, best score, and best song ("The Green Leaves of Summer"). As was usual in Hollywood, Chill Wills's publicist took out advertisements in the trade papers hyping the actor's chances of victory. The electioneering for Wills was tasteless at best. A full-page ad in the *Hollywood Reporter* showed the cast and crew of the picture standing in front of the movie's replica of the Alamo. "We of *The Alamo* cast are praying harder than the real Texans prayed for their lives in the real Alamo for Chill Wills to win the Oscar," the copy read. "Cousin Chill's acting was great!" The notice was signed, "Your Alamo cousins."

Academy voters resented the ploy, as did segments of the general public. "It was like taking a bucket of fecal matter and throwing it over a beautiful red rose," Russell Birdwell said. Wayne was incensed by Wills's campaign for the Oscar, but he compounded the blunder by telling the press, "This is not the first time the Alamo has been the underdog. We need defenders today just as they did 125 years ago." Some representatives of the Hollywood establishment resented the power Wayne seemed to be exercising. "I have great affection for Duke Wayne," said 20th Century–Fox mogul Darryl Zanuck, "but what right has he to write, direct, and produce a motion picture? Everyone is becoming a corporation."

The Alamo won only one Academy Award—for best sound. The Oscar for best picture went that year to Billy Wilder's *The Apartment*, a movie Wayne hated. Over the years, thanks to worldwide distribution, *The Alamo* earned substantial profits. The movie proved an enormous success in Japan and did well in Europe. But by then Wayne had been forced to sell his share of the picture to United Artists to pay back the millions he had borrowed to complete the film. "I made a bad deal for myself on *The Alamo*," Duke affirmed. "United Artists made a great deal of money and I didn't make a cent. But I had it in my blood to do the picture."

The years after *The Alamo* were disturbing ones for Wayne. Financially he was on the brink. He had sunk everything he owned into one movie. "That picture lost so much money I can't buy a pack of chewing gum in Texas without a co-signer," he told a colleague. In time the film's investors were paid back, but Wayne remained overextended. Physically and mentally he was depleted. Everything seemed to go to pieces at once.

Duke discovered in 1960 that Bo Roos, who had been his financial adviser for seventeen years, had invested much of his money in ventures that proved unwise. The Trivoli Shrimp Company of Panama, in which Roos had invested heavily, went bankrupt. At one point Wayne and his partner, Tony Arias, had controlled over 70 percent of the shrimping business in the Central American country. Arias was killed in a plane crash on his way to Mexico City, and their company soon lost everything. A firm that imported whiskey, in which Wayne, actor Bruce Cabot, and Prince Bernhard of Holland were partners, also folded. Oil investments suffered a decline before Wayne dismissed his business manager. Duke, never an astute businessman except in the area of movie production, failed to keep accurate records and felt that Roos had betrayed him. "Bo cost me the first twenty years of my career," said Wayne. "I had just worked twenty years for no gain."

He kept Batjac's staff on at full salary, but the company remained inactive for several years after the *Alamo* debacle. Duke sold the standing set built on Happy Shahan's property to the ranch owner, who turned it into Alamo Village, a combination tourist attraction and Western movie street. Although Wayne had loaned thousands of dollars to friends and put hundreds of thousands more into friends' projects, he refused to ask them to return the money they owed him. "One of Duke's major faults was that he trusted too many people," Pilar said. "If he liked you, he put 100 percent confidence in you. That's why he got hurt so many times. He was a vulnerable person."

Duke's solution to his financial crisis was to work; over subsequent years he would star in picture after picture at a fatiguing pace. "It was a hard time," he admitted. "Before then, on paper, I was supposed to be worth $4 or $5 million." In 1961 he barely owned the clothes on his back.

Around the same time death began to claim members of Wayne's inner circle. Character actor Grant Withers was the first to go, taking his own life in 1959. An alcoholic who had repeatedly failed at recovery, Withers washed down an overdose of sleeping pills with a bottle of vodka. Duke was sad and shaken; he and Withers had been friends for thirty years. The following year Ward Bond died of a massive heart attack, shortly after the premiere of *The Alamo*. Bond was fifty-five, only two years older than Wayne. They had appeared in nineteen movies together, shared similar political persuasions, and been best friends since college. Duke delivered Bond's eulogy, and then went into a deep depression.

When Davy Crockett was run through the chest by a lance near the close of *The Alamo*, it seemed to bring John Wayne's own mortality into focus. "By the end of 1961," Aissa Wayne wrote, "death was more than a dismal abstract for my father. It had stolen his friends and darkened his world."

Regaining Financial Stability

As soon as *The Alamo* was finished, but before his services were needed to promote the film, John Wayne began work on *North to Alaska* under his three-picture deal with 20th Century–Fox. Shooting on the Fox comedy began in northern California on February 18, 1960. Already Duke sensed that his cinematic statement on Americanism was not the masterpiece he had hoped, yet he knew that he had given *The Alamo* his best effort. To add to the heartache, Wayne faced serious financial difficulties. He dealt with those, as he dealt with other problems, by plunging into work.

By 1960 Buddy Adler had replaced Darryl Zanuck as head of production at 20th Century–Fox, and under pressure from the company's president, Spyros Skouras, Adler instructed director Henry Hathaway to trim *North to Alaska*'s budget, which had initially been projected to cost $3.5 million. "This is ridiculous for a picture with John Wayne," said Skouras. "I'm not going to spend that kind of money." Hathaway cut $36,000 from the movie's budget, mainly by eliminating backgrounds and some of the locale shots, but agent Charles Feldman informed the studio that Wayne would not do the picture if any further cuts were made. "In this kind of comedy-farce," Duke's agent wrote, "it is very important to have the production values as are in the present script."

Since Feldman headed Famous Artists, a powerful talent agency, and Adler was a weaker production head than Zanuck had been, Feldman manipulated the executive into doing his bidding. Feldman's firm represented Adler himself and, according to director Richard Fleischer, the agent was "the shadow government" of the studio at the time, unofficially running Fox in conjunction with Adler. Hathaway was also represented by Feldman, as were *North to Alaska*'s writers, John Lee Mahin and Martin Rackin. But the agent's real interest in the picture was his current girlfriend, a beautiful French actress of limited ability named Capucine. Playing opposite John Wayne could mean an important step forward for the bland actress, and the crafty Feldman pushed Capucine's cause to fruition, winning for her the role of a spirited prostitute in an Alaskan brothel. "I knew my role was window dressing," the actress said. "It was not a splendid role," but it was the female lead.

During preproduction the writers ran into trouble with the script. Duke had agreed to make *North to Alaska* on the strength of its title. "We never told him the story," Feldman admitted. "He's been going along on good faith and trust." Busy with editing *The Alamo*, Wayne had not asked to read the screenplay for his upcoming movie but operated under the impression that the script was nearly finished. "We've been keeping him happy with reports about how well it's going," said Feldman. "If he finds out there isn't any screenplay, we'll lose him." The agent had no intention of letting that happen, and he pressed Adler and his writers to move ahead. "There was an edge to [Feldman's] voice that chilled me," said Fleischer, who eventually turned down the offer to direct the picture.

Stewart Granger, Duke's costar in the movie, remembered his first scene with Wayne as a nightmare. The British actor was so intimidated by the bullying direction of Henry Hathaway that he could not remember his lines. "The more I 'fluffed' the more Hathaway glared and chewed on his bloody cigar," Granger recalled. "I was terrified. I had lost all confidence and felt depressed and ill. . . . Somehow I managed to get through the slapstick comedy."

Capucine found Duke neither friendly nor aloof, simply businesslike. "It was a John Wayne picture," she said, "he knew it, and he expected everyone else to know it." Mainly Wayne seemed to be involved with himself and those attending him. "I had the feeling he was suspicious of me," Capucine said. "He wore lifts; everyone talked about it. And . . . he had a wig or toupee . . . [which] surprised me."

North to Alaska proved an uneven picture, but the film offers a couple of mass brawls that Hathaway handled in a rollicking silent picture style, with the action played for laughs. Duke portrayed a hard-drinking American adventurer with his familiar gusto, but reviews were tepid when the movie opened in November. Still, the lighthearted film set a pattern for Duke's later comedies and introduced a broader playing style that he developed in later years when working with rambunctious material.

While her husband was making *North to Alaska*, Pilar visited her family in Peru. She had been living in the United States for eight years and had started to feel homesick. Recently she had lost a baby and had grown emotionally anxious; doctors maintained that her problem was psychological.

Pilar arrived in Lima to find that most of her old friends had married and were involved with their own lives. Feeling like an outsider, she stayed only a few days. She returned home to a husband worried about *The Alamo,* alarmed over his financial situation, and busy with a stream of scripts that crossed his desk as possible projects. Duke rarely discussed finances with his wife, but she realized that he was more preoccupied with money than she had ever known him to be.

Still adjusting to American culture, not to mention to the narcissism of Hollywood, Pilar felt displaced and insecure. With her lack of formal education, she felt inadequate around Duke's celebrated acquaintances. Her faltering English did nothing to ease her discomfort. In an attempt to establish her own identity, she became involved with SHARE, a charity founded by Hollywood women to raise money for handicapped children. To most of the film colony, Pilar Wayne appeared gracious and friendly, yet a little mysterious—a cool Latin beauty with a classic face and huge brown eyes, dwarfed by her famous husband. When Duke was home, he continued to shower her with affection, and few doubted that theirs was a genuine love match. "I'll tell you why I love her," Wayne told a reporter. "I have a lust for her dignity."

With Aissa, his young daughter, Duke remained the adoring father. He inundated the child with toys and gifts yet sometimes treated her like a possession. Aissa grew up aware that her father was Hollywood royalty, but she was a painfully lonely child. The Waynes' San Fernando Valley mansion sat above five rolling acres, enclosed by ten-foot walls. Unless Aissa was with her parents or at school, she rarely left the estate, since there was constant fear of kidnapping. "Without other kids, our compound could feel like a prison," Wayne's daughter later wrote.

As deeply as Duke loved his wife and children, he continued to put his career above family obligations, insisting that he had to work to support two households. "I never quite knew if he was telling the truth when he pleaded poverty, or if we were really in trouble," Aissa said. She remembered her father's insisting, "If I don't make this movie, we're all gonna be hurting." Then he would buy a boat or an expensive dress for Pilar or exorbitant Christmas presents for the family. "For many years these messages were confusing," Aissa declared. But she later concluded that "it was his self-esteem that kept him working."

In 1960 Wayne's self-esteem and dedication to a zealous work ethic blended with economic necessity. To add to Duke's immediate anxiety, the Screen Actors Guild had joined the Writers Guild in a strike against studios and producers, and in March 1960 every Hollywood production shut down. Wayne, a devoted supporter of the Screen Actors Guild, attended a meeting in Janet Leigh's house during which the guild's president, Ronald Reagan, and his board explained the dilemma facing them. The major issue behind the strike was additional payments to actors and writers for television broadcasts of their earlier films. For Duke this would involve an important source of revenue, and at the moment he was out of work.

Wayne had been constantly critical of television, arguing that the medium's fast methods of production resulted in slipshod programs. "I'm a movie actor," he said, and fortunately Duke remained one of the few Golden Age stars to win followers among the younger generation. Time and again he turned down offers for work on television, claiming that to accept them "wouldn't be fair to the people who made my career." But in November 1960 he appeared in a cameo role on the *Wagon Train* series, hosted by Ward Bond and aired ten days after his friend's death. John Ford directed the segment, entitled "The Colter Craven Story," which featured a cast drawn from the Ford stock company. Billed as Michael Morris, Wayne played Gen. William Tecumseh Sherman, and the taping served as a happy final reunion for Bond and his dearest cronies.

In June 1961, with the strike over and promotional work for *The Alamo* behind him, Duke traveled to Moab, Utah, to begin location shooting on *The Comancheros*. The picture's starting date had been moved ahead because John Ford needed Wayne for *The Man Who Shot Liberty Valance* at Paramount toward the end of the summer. *The Comancheros* would complete Duke's three-picture commitment to 20th Century–Fox. He would soon sign an agreement with Paramount for ten movies at a fee of $600,000 per picture. Although the sum was less than his current price, the contract with Paramount would be nonexclusive, and the studio agreed to pay Wayne $6 million up front. The welcome cash meant that Duke could eliminate his debts, revitalize Batjac, and indulge his family in a superstar's lifestyle.

In *The Comancheros* Wayne played Jake Cutter, a duty-conscious, but softhearted Texas Ranger resolved to break up a band of outlaws. The script provided Duke's character no love interest but established a pattern for later roles. Duke was fifty-four, his hair had grown thin, and he was having trouble controlling his weight. His age bothered him, particularly when he had to submit to the indignity of wearing toupees. Studio executives urged him to consider plastic surgery, but the thought disgusted him. He later agreed to have his eyelids lifted, but only after continued pressure.

Wayne's screen image was shifting to that of a mature hero, one of enduring strength, who observed younger men's love affairs with understanding and a touch of humor. In *The Comancheros* he watched Stuart Whitman, twenty years his junior, romance Ina Balin. Curiously enough, it was Duke's mature roles—in which he played widowers and patriarchs—that more than any of his earlier roles made John Wayne a legend.

Michael Curtiz, a veteran filmmaker at the end of his career, directed *The Comancheros*. Curtiz was ill with cancer at the time and died shortly after the picture was completed. There were times when the director was so sick that Duke had to take over the set. Fortunately, William Clothier was on hand as the movie's cameraman, and the production resulted in a lively, pleasing entertainment, but it offered little that could be taken seriously.

By mid-July, Wayne had finished his commitment to 20th Century–Fox and was entitled to the full $2 million from the studio. "I am very concerned about you, Duke, and your not getting a holiday and working week after week practically for the past year," Charles Feldman wrote shortly before *The Comancheros* wrapped. But there was slim chance of a real vacation with so many demands on Wayne's time. He and Pilar usually got away on his yacht each year, somewhere off the coast of Mexico, but even then Duke spent much of his time discussing business over the telephone. Work had become a habit, and he couldn't stand being idle for long.

The Comancheros was not yet finished before John Ford began assailing Duke with memos about *The Man Who Shot Liberty Valance*. "For a change no locations," the director wrote on July 7. "All to be shot on the lot. . . . Seriously we have a great script in my humble opinion." *Liberty Valance* transforms the John Wayne hero into a poignant, fading figure. His character, Tom Doniphon, is a dogged frontier individualist, a man with a gun, but his day has passed. Civilization has come to the West and with it has come a respect for law and order. Ransom Stoddard, played in the picture by James Stewart, symbolizes both the new social system and a naive type of Western hero, who has the capacity to turn the wilderness into a garden. Liberty Valance, as played by Lee Marvin, is a flamboyant villain and an anachronism that threatens the changing frontier. It is Tom Doniphon who shoots Valance, but Doniphon allows Stoddard to take the credit and thereby gain the stature to usher in a new order.

"*Liberty Valance* was a tough assignment for me," Wayne said. Ford had Jimmy Stewart as the likable, innocent lawyer; Edmond O'Brien as the town's newspaper editor, gushing sophisticated witticisms; Andy Devine as the sheriff, adding clumsy humor; and Lee Marvin as the showy, un-tamed heavy. "There was no place for me," said Wayne. "I just had to wan-der around in that son of a bitch [Doniphon] and try to make a part for myself." Duke saw Tom Doniphon more as a tool than as a well-rounded character.

Ford wanted the picture to have a dark and claustrophobic look and therefore decided to shoot it in black and white. He argued that the cru-cial night scene in which Valance is shot would come across better if not filmed in color. Only four days of the entire movie were photographed outside the Paramount studio.

One of the picture's outdoor scenes occurs after Doniphon realizes that he has lost his woman to Stoddard. Wayne and black actor Woody Strode were called upon to rush back to Doniphon's ranch in a wagon at top speed, whereupon a drunken Tom Doniphon burns the place down. "John Wayne and I almost came to blows," Strode remembered. Duke was driving the team of horses and couldn't control them. "I was kneeling in the back of the wagon as we made our approach to the ranch," said Strode. "John was working the reins, but he couldn't get the horses to stop. I reached up to grab the reins to help him, and John swung and knocked me away." When the horses finally stopped, Duke fell out of the wagon, and Strode jumped off ready to fight him. Tension between Wayne and the former black athlete had built during the production, mainly because of Ford's teasing. "Duke," the director would yell, point-ing at Strode, "there's the real football player."

It was clear that Ford was miffed at Duke. Perhaps the director still har-bored hurt over his treatment in Brackettville and the fact that so few of his scenes were used in *The Alamo*. He accused Wayne of not accepting his telephone calls, although Duke vehemently denied the charge. "I talk to every Tom, Dick, and Harry who calls," Wayne wrote his mentor. "I cer-tainly would not be too tired to talk to a man whom I consider my best friend—that I have a feeling of blood kinship with." But Ford badgered his surrogate son more than usual during the making of *Liberty Valance*, pointing out that he, Jimmy Stewart, and Woody Strode had all served in the armed forces during World War II, whereas Duke had not. That "really pissed John Wayne off," said Strode. Ford's mood could also be explained by the fact that he was finding moviemaking increasingly taxing; he tired easily and his temper was even shorter than usual.

The Man Who Shot Liberty Valance was completed on November 7, 1961. It would be the last complete Western Wayne made for Ford. Critics at first failed to understand the film. Brendan Gill, writing for the *New Yorker*, found it a parody of Ford's best work. *Variety* dismissed the movie as "Model A 'Ford'" and suggested that the director was past his prime. Later the critical evaluation of *Liberty Valance* grew more positive, and it has since received its rightful share of attention. But Duke's performance in the picture was viewed as strong from the outset. "Wayne—taciturn, good-natured, tough, and supremely confident—is *the* John Wayne," DuPre Jones wrote for *Sight and Sound*.

Audiences in the early 1960s were unprepared for the nostalgia of *Liberty Valance* and not yet ready to mourn the demise of the machismo that Ford and Wayne had done so much to celebrate. Both men lamented the vanishing breed that Tom Doniphon represented. For Ford particularly, the days of all-night card games, heavy carousing, and tough assignments were coming to an end. With Ward Bond's death, Wayne and Ford saw less of each other. No longer were there the late-night drinking bouts in one another's homes, where the Ford gang spun tall tales, sang Irish songs, and cheated at poker. Weekends on the director's yacht were fewer, and the days when Duke poured vodka on a drunken Ward Bond's chest, lighted it, and set him ablaze had passed into memory.

Wayne loved such pranks and continued to drink too much, sometimes imbibing for days without showing ill effects, either to his health or his disposition. Duke's physical capacity for alcohol seemed limitless, and he was a happy drunk who enjoyed laughter and congenial friends. "Wayne believed you were not a man if you didn't drink," Dobe Carey said, and Duke freely admitted that he did not trust people who did not indulge. Mainly he drank as a release from the pressures of stardom. "I drink for comradeship," he said, "and when I drink for comradeship, I don't bother to keep count."

Sometimes he went for weeks at a time without touching alcohol and had no trouble disciplining himself. Wayne was a far more intelligent man than most people realized, and he valued his privacy. He was enormously literate and came to be an avid reader of nonfiction: history, military biographies, anything by Winston Churchill and by public figures he admired. He kept informed by reading *Time* and *Newsweek*. Although never a student, Duke enjoyed arguing about politics and current events yet shunned pomposity and didacticism of any sort. He did not believe in introspection or in talking issues to death. Basically his was a pragmatic mind; he saw situations in simplified terms that matched his uncomplicated vision of life.

In February 1962 Pilar gave birth to Duke's youngest son, John Ethan, named for Wayne's character in *The Searchers*. Duke was proud of his expanding second family and demonstrated love for his children with much hugging and kissing. "He was a great picker-upper," Maureen O'Hara observed; he gave "each and every one of these children an individual security blanket with his love." Yet he was also a controlling father who demanded constant displays of devotion. "My affection for him," said Aissa, "expressed so spontaneously when I was a little girl, sprung from fear and obligation as much as free will." As the girl grew older, she realized that her father had demons and fears of his own. What made living with him difficult was that he tended to suppress what was churning inside. "To his family, he rarely expressed his inner feelings, or even admitted he had them," Aissa said. "With all that bottled emotion, its release often came in the form of misdirected rage."

Wayne's quick temper, loudly voiced, could be frightening, but his rages generally dissipated as quickly as they came. Nonetheless, Duke's impatience and anger sometimes made for a stormy home life, and his wife and children were not always aware of what had set him off. With his fundamental mistrust of women, Wayne insisted on being the boss. "It is, I think, a common trait among men whose psyches crash back and forth between pride and insecurity," Aissa wrote. "My father lashed out when he felt himself getting weak."

Pilar recognized that her husband's tough exterior masked a fragile inner self and realized that he had an inordinate need for love and approval. She saw his gentle side and his underlying sentimentality. But she seldom heard him mention the doubts that anguished him most. "Duke and I had never communicated about things that really bothered us," said

Pilar. "Our life [was] lived at such a frantic pace that it [was] enough to talk about events rather than feelings."

On the surface their life together seemed drawn from the Hollywood storybook. "I knew that I could go out and buy anything I wanted," Pilar said, "and Duke gave me enough jewels to last me a lifetime. He loved to buy presents. One Christmas he bought me three fur coats." Reporters occasionally asked Wayne if the difference between his age and his wife's created problems. Duke always denied that any such difficulties existed. "If [age] ever gets to be a problem," he would answer with a smile, "I'll just have to find a younger woman." But the real plot was less comedic. The couple's major problems stemmed from Duke's inability to express vexing emotions, combined with his obsession with work. "For his entire adulthood," Aissa declared, "my father had felt a need to provide, to accomplish, to prove himself."

Although Wayne won a dispute with the Internal Revenue Service in March 1962, absolving him of $42,000 in taxes the government claimed he owed, Duke continued to insist that it was essential for him to keep making movies. "I never want to retire," he said. Work had long been his focus, and he had become a slave to his own energy. He awoke early, with his thoughts usually on forthcoming projects. A job well done brought him satisfaction, and he frankly did not understand people who lacked his motivation. "Duke couldn't be sensible or moderate when it came to his craft," said Pilar. He truly loved the picture business—everything except wardrobe fittings, posing for stills, and love scenes. "I can't stand those long, wet, drippy kisses," he said. Yet despite his enthusiasm for his profession, on another level Wayne felt embarrassment about being an actor. Most of Hollywood's male stars lacked depth, he claimed. "He called them decadent, weak-willed, effeminate," Aissa recalled. He preferred the company of physical types and respected the risks he knew it took for good action scenes. "He's ready to bust his ass," actor Strother Martin commented about Wayne's work habits. "And he expects everybody else to bust his ass." Those who didn't were soon in trouble with Duke; he tolerated no loafing on his pictures.

In January 1962 Duke flew to Paris for four days' work on Darryl Zanuck's *The Longest Day*, a lavish reconstruction of the Normandy invasion. For his comeback production Zanuck wanted an all-star cast and accepted that John Wayne was the top box-office attraction in the United

States. If he could sign Wayne for his picture, other big names would become available. Duke appears in *The Longest Day* for slightly more than twelve minutes, for which he was paid $250,000. Still mad at Zanuck for the mogul's snide remark about his decision to direct, produce, and star in *The Alamo,* Wayne pushed his price up to the limit, forcing Zanuck to double his initial offer. "It might be highway robbery," said Duke, "but it serves the bastard right."

The Longest Day employed four units working at the same time in three languages, with a different director on each one. No expense was spared, and the picture would result in Darryl Zanuck's return to 20th Century–Fox as production head. Wayne played Lt. Col. Benjamin Vandervoort of the Eighty-second Airborne Division in the film, a stern officer who breaks an ankle landing in France but continues his command using a rifle as his crutch.

Money was not a consideration when Duke accepted a cameo role in the $14.5 million epic *How the West Was Won.* The sprawling Western was filmed in the wide-screen Cinerama process and parceled between three veteran filmmakers—Henry Hathaway, George Marshall, and John Ford. Ford's segment, the Civil War sequence, is the shortest, and Wayne's involvement in it, again impersonating Gen. William Tecumseh Sherman, required a scant six days' work. His screen time is about three and a half minutes, and his role is little more than support in a scene centered around actor George Peppard. But Duke accepted the assignment as a courtesy to Ford.

Shortly after his son Ethan's birth, Wayne spent four months in Africa working with Howard Hawks on *Hatari!* for Paramount. Duke claimed that the time he spent in Tanganyika was the most fun he had had on any picture. "You wake up in the morning," Duke said, "and you hear the savage sounds of these animals, and your hair curls. You grab that gun and you take a different attitude than you did when you were at home." *Hatari!* was a lightweight adventure yarn with little or no character development, but Wayne liked working with Hawks and enjoyed the safari that making the picture required.

Hawks was an improvisational director, particularly on this film. "We never even worked from a script," cast member Red Buttons said. "We'd just talk each morning about what Hawks wanted us to do that day. Howard was the complete motion picture director; he was really able to open things up." The studio hired a trio of planes to spot interesting movements of wild game, and each morning at dawn the pilots would radio back to the crew what they had located and how to get to the various species. Hawks and his company would pack up their gear and rush to photograph the animals that seemed appropriate for their film.

Most of the picture's dialogue was ad-libbed. Hawks would shout "Gobble!" at Wayne and his supporting cast, which meant that they were to say whatever came into their minds. The director could put in whatever dialogue he needed after they had returned to the studio. "The boys got very good at it," said Hawks; "they'd turn around to one another and just say anything. . . . I think we chased nine rhinos and caught four to get the scenes in that part of the picture." The actors actually helped capture the animals, aided by a team of professionals, and on a few occasions Duke got himself into real trouble. A bull rhinoceros charged the Land Rover the star was riding in and dented its metal, yet Wayne insisted that the whole experience was more of a romp than serious filmmaking.

Hawks affirmed that Duke was an underrated actor. "He holds a thing together," the director said, "he gives it a solidity and honesty, and he can make a lot of things believable. If he's kind of grousing around in a scene, you know that there's something wrong with the scene. He maybe can't tell you, but you can find out what's bothering him. He has a very true sense of cinema. . . . Wayne is like a big cat on his feet; he thinks quickly and he thinks right. Also he contributes to what other people do."

Friends noticed that Duke had become more compulsive about his smoking than ever, lighting one cigarette after another. "So maybe it's six months off the end of my life," Wayne said in his cavalier manner, "they're not going to kill me." But his coughing spells had grown worse, and his family worried.

A few months after completing *Hatari!* Duke was in Hawaii with John Ford filming *Donovan's Reef* for Paramount. It was the last movie Wayne would make with the great director, and it was not a pleasant assignment. "Ford never should have used me in that picture," said Duke. "He should have picked some young guy. It didn't require much of [the actor]. All he had to be was a good-looking young guy, and I wasn't young enough."

Wayne's writer, James Edward Grant, had written the initial script for *Donovan's Reef*, but Ford hated what Grant turned in and hired his own writer, Frank S. Nugent, to redo it. The finished picture was heavy-handed, far from subtle in its humor. Ford's direction was perfunctory, mainly because of his age and failing health. The director seemed more crotchety than usual and his judgment not the best. He insulted actress Dorothy Lamour on the set, which embarrassed the cast and crew, but he quickly went to Lamour's dressing room to apologize. "As the days went by," the actress said, "I slowly began to realize that Pappy was not a well man."

Duke protected Ford during the making of the picture, at times serving as his assistant. "Wayne helped a great deal," said actor Cesar Romero. "He loved John Ford and had great respect for this man. . . . Ford was like a father to Wayne." But Duke saw that the aging director's thinking was not as sharp as it should have been and knew that his eyesight had grown poor. "Every day Duke had to go in and check the rushes to make sure everything was all right," Dorothy Lamour said. "Sometimes the strain got to him, and . . . he blew his stack."

The production was a sad experience for everyone concerned. Lee Marvin was extremely funny, but he drank heavily and it was evident to colleagues that he was a confused person. Wayne's coughing spells grew so severe that Pilar became frightened. What should have been a breezy comedy turned into pure contrivance, an anticlimax to Ford and Wayne's fourteen pictures together since the introduction of sound. "Those were great days," Duke recalled of their years together. "You're not supposed to look back, but it's pretty hard not to when there were guys like Ward and Jack. You don't meet them everyday."

With *Donovan's Reef* finished in early October, Wayne was free under his Paramount contract to make an outside picture. Two weeks after the Ford movie wrapped, Duke was in Arizona working on *McLintock!* for Batjac. The Western comedy was Wayne's first venture into production since *The Alamo*, and he turned the project into another family affair. Michael Wayne coproduced the film; Duke's brother, Robert, functioned as production supervisor; and Patrick and Aissa played featured roles. James Edward Grant wrote the script, which the author intended as an adaptation of Shakespeare's *The Taming of the Shrew* set in the Old West, but the movie turned out to be more like a Western version of *The Quiet Man*. To direct, Wayne chose Andrew V. McLaglen, the son of his old friend Victor McLaglen.

McLintock! was McLaglen's first feature film after a substantial apprenticeship in television, and would be one of five pictures he directed for

Wayne. The six-foot-seven director, whom the crew called "Big A," had known Wayne since childhood. Duke was fond of the budding moviemaker, liked his mild manner, and respected him. Although McLaglen was a competent director, Wayne himself supervised the picture closely. "Duke was always looking through the camera," stuntman Neil Summers remembered, "he was always talking over McLaglen's shoulder." Wayne devised the brawls in *McLintock!*, gave instructions to younger members of the cast, and sometimes flew into a rage and shouted obscenities at workers who were slow to do his bidding. "Duke was the man who had the final say on everything," Chuck Roberson concurred. "In reality, he was the man who made *McLintock!* the great picture that it was."

McLaglen deferred to Wayne's strength as a filmmaker and let the star shape his own performance. "Duke was really a hell of a guy," the director said. "He had total belief in himself and what he was doing. He'd acquired complete knowledge about who John Wayne was and what people expected him to be. He had such honesty as a performer."

As his costar Duke selected his most successful leading lady, Maureen O'Hara, who played McLintock's independent wife with gusto. "Maureen is kind of like a lady John Wayne," said stunt performer Dean Smith, "she's got a lot of character to her." Although Wayne and O'Hara admired one another and enjoyed working together, he showed her no mercy when it came to rough action. "Duke treated her an awful lot like I used to treat my little brother back on the ranch," Chuck Roberson maintained. Not overly concerned about her appearance, O'Hara willingly did whatever was required of her. In lusty action she gave as good as she got, much to Duke's amusement.

On one rare occasion Wayne did not like the way his costar was doing a scene. "C'mon, Maureen," he said, "get going. This is your scene." O'Hara replied that she was trying to go fifty-fifty with him. "Fifty-fifty, hell," he roared. "It's your scene, steal it." Then under his breath he added, "If you can." That was more than enough to inflame O'Hara to full power. "I stole it," she said with a satisfied smile. "His kids say that I was the only one who could stand toe to toe with their dad and be equal to him."

One night after work Duke decided he wanted to go out drinking with the stuntmen. Pilar didn't want him to go, but Wayne announced that he was going anyway and wanted O'Hara to go along, as one of the guys.

The actress thought, "Oh, Holy God, I don't want to go out with the cowboys and be out all night." So she told Duke that she had to go to the bathroom. She ran to her room in the Ramada Inn where the company was housed and hid on the floor under a picture window that looked into her quarters, pressing herself against the wall. In a few minutes Duke banged on her door and shouted, "Where are you? Come on, we gotta go." Then he came to the window and peered into her room. "I could see him," O'Hara recalled, "and I thought 'Oh, God, if he looks down, I'm gonna be killed.'" But he didn't see her, and the guys went off without her. "That's the kind of relationship we had," O'Hara said. "So many people think that there was a great romance between Duke and me. There wasn't. We had tremendous respect and love for one another and knew that we were good for each other on the screen."

Yvonne DeCarlo, whose husband, stuntman Bob Morgan, had lost a leg in an accident during the making of *How the West Was Won*, played Wayne's housekeeper in the movie, her first picture in four years. Duke was a friend of Morgan's and went out of his way to find a part that suited DeCarlo's talent and had the part expanded, rescuing the actress from the nightclub circuit. *McLintock!* "was a class production," DeCarlo said, "and I enjoyed every second of it."

The most memorable sequence in the film is a spectacular mud fight that ends up with Wayne, O'Hara, and half of the cast in an outrageous mud bath. "I think the whole thing took six days to shoot," Neil Summers declared. "What everybody remembers is how cold it was." The mud fight was filmed in November, and the weather on the Arizona desert—the sequence was filmed at a slag pit near Old Tuscon—had turned windy and cold. Smudge pots had to be set out each morning to thaw the ice that had formed during the night. Some of the stuntmen had asked for hazard pay for going down into the mud puddle, until Duke and O'Hara volunteered to do it themselves. O'Hara went down the slide first, instructed by Chuck Roberson to go down on her back and keep her head up. Wayne had no choice but to follow suit. "He couldn't let me win," said O'Hara. So they both slid down, yelling all the way, much to the amazement of some Indians gathered on a hill above. "The Indians were so thrilled," the actress recalled, "that they knelt down and bowed to me." Then the stars had to stand covered in movie mud (actually bentonite, which made for a better slide) while the scene was finished. "It was

249

awful stuff," O'Hara remembered, "and the wind was blowing." A prop man finally put a blanket around the two stars, which pressed the slimy substance next to their skin. "Good God, Duke," O'Hara exclaimed standing next to him with her arms out from her body. "This bloody stuff is like bird shit!" Wayne turned to her and said, "What do you mean *bird shit*? It's like snot!"

Although Duke was determined to produce a commercial movie that would restore Batjac to the good graces of United Artists, *McLintock!* suffered from lack of sustained action, aside from the slapstick mud slinging and Wayne's spanking O'Hara, who was dressed in her underdrawers. *McLintock!* cost less than $2 million, and Duke's salary was applied to the $700,000 debt Batjac still owed United Artists from the cost of *The Alamo*. Fortunately, the farce was a popular success, even though critic Judith Crist and others labeled it simpleminded. *McLintock!* remains a favorite among Wayne fans and ranked high with Duke himself.

John Wayne's son-in-law, Don LaCava, was working in the Batjac office during the early 1960s, having taken over the responsibility of managing Duke's investments after the dismissal of Bo Roos. Michael Wayne had assumed much of the burden of Batjac's day-to-day operation, and Duke kept his brother, Bobby, on the company's payroll, although he occasionally persuaded friends to give his unambitious brother jobs on movies they were making.

All in all Wayne had a raft of people reliant on him for their livelihood, yet Duke encouraged their dependence, found comfort in their companionship, and trusted that his family and friends would not take undue advantage of him. He hated nothing more than being alone and surrounded himself with sycophants who bolstered his sense of personal worth. Even though Duke had a secure knowledge of who John Wayne was, he was less sure about Marion Morrison. The team at Batjac and the regulars who worked on his pictures formed a cocoon within which Duke could find the assurance he needed.

The confidence he conveyed in work was never as great in private situations. Ashtrays overflowing with crumpled cigarette butts testified to the driven, uncertain man inside. Duke had struggled long and hard to rise to the top, but already he felt that he was working on borrowed time. He had watched the disappearance of other Hollywood legends and knew that popularity eventually ran out. Ward Bond and so many others of his crowd were dead, and John Ford was on the decline. The Duke knew that even America's personification of manhood could not endure forever.

Wayne relaxed best when he was at sea on his yacht. He loved the ocean, and most of his vacations were spent either off Catalina Island or aboard the *Nor'wester*, which he bought first, or later the *Wild Goose*, a converted minesweeper that became Duke's proudest possession. On shipboard he seemed less preoccupied and not so easily irritated. He owned half interest in a hillside estate overlooking Acapulco, which he and Pilar visited every year, but sometimes his family spent long weekends with friends anchored near Avalon, going ashore in a speedboat named *The Apache*. John Ford's grandson Dan remembered such excursions from his own childhood. "Duke was very spontaneous with kids," Dan Ford recalled, "and very warm with them. He enjoyed them and they enjoyed him. He wasn't really a movie star to us as kids; he was just a fun guy."

Duke bought the *Wild Goose* for $110,000 in 1962, and the ship quickly became his sanctuary. The 136-foot, former navy vessel had seen service in the Aleutian Islands during the final six months of World War II and, as remodeled by Wayne, became a commodious craft whose wheelhouse rose three stories above the waterline. The oak-paneled main salon contained a wood-burning fireplace, a poker table, a motion picture projector and screen, and a built-in wet bar. In addition to the master suite, there were three guest staterooms, each with its own bath, and a dining room that accommodated ten. A crew of eight had their quarters, and the most sophisticated navigation equipment had been installed.

Wayne oozed charisma aboard the *Wild Goose*, and he played cards or chess for hours on its sixty-foot afterdeck. He also swam, fished, and read, but much of his time at sea was spent drinking—usually tequila or brandy on the rocks. He seemed to enjoy the crew's company and conversed easily with the men. Each summer he would sail around the San Juan Islands in the Pacific Northwest and sometimes up to Alaska. "Duke was usually far too busy to join the boat for an entire voyage," Bert Minshall, the vessel's last skipper declared, "but when free he'd fly in by private plane to wherever the ship might be, stay a few days or a few weeks, then fly back to California."

In May 1963 Wayne reported to work for a cameo role in George Stevens's spectacle *The Greatest Story Ever Told*. Duke played the Roman centurion who accompanies Jesus to the cross, and it is unquestionably

251

the most ludicrous performance of his mature years. Wayne was ill equipped to deliver his one line—"Truly this man was a son of God." Audiences laughed when they heard those solemn words coming from Duke's mouth after Christ's death. Stevens had rightly opted for an unknown actor to play Jesus, but the director needed to bolster the film's box-office appeal with as many Hollywood stars as he could manage in trivial roles. Duke's services were required for only three days, for which he was well compensated. But appearing in the biblical epic was a misguided decision on Wayne's part. "There are actors who can do period roles and there are actors who can't," said Charlton Heston after considerable experience in historical films. "God knows Duke Wayne couldn't play a first-century Roman."

In June 1963 Wayne was scheduled to make *Circus World* in Spain for Paramount. Anxious to put the *Wild Goose* to the supreme test, he flew to Bermuda, boarded his yacht, and planned to make a transatlantic crossing aboard the vessel. Duke's brother went along on the adventure, but Pilar and their two children met Duke and his crew on the coast of Portugal. The dangerous Atlantic crossing proved to be a high point in the many months Wayne spent aboard the *Wild Goose*, but it was an experience Pilar was not eager to share.

Upon reaching Portugal, the boat was sent around to Barcelona, while Wayne and his family flew to Madrid, where the star had rented a villa that belonged to Ava Gardner. Duke arrived in Spain during July to find that Frank Capra, whom Paramount had hired to direct *Circus World*, had quarreled with screenwriter Jimmy Grant. "What I didn't realize was that when you took on Duke Wayne you took on a small empire," said Capra. "And part of that empire was a personal writer by the name of James Edward Grant." Grant represented a new experience for the veteran director—as Capra described him, "a writer who attached himself to a male star and functioned as that star's confidant, adviser, bosom playpal, baby sitter, flatterer, string-puller, and personal Iago to incite mistrust between his meal ticket and film directors, especially name directors."

Although Capra respected Wayne, he came to dislike and question the braggadocio Grant, who insisted that when Duke arrived, he and the actor would knock out a satisfactory screenplay for *Circus World* within a week's time. "All you gotta have in a John Wayne picture," Grant told Capra, "is a hoity-toity dame with big tits that Duke can throw over his knee and spank and a collection of jerks he can smack in the face every five minutes. In between you fill in with gags, flags, and chases. That's all you need. His fans eat it up."

While Jimmy Grant played golf and laughed at the director's concerns, Capra worked on a script of his own. "Wayne won't like it," Grant warned, and sure enough Duke didn't. Ultimately the producer, Samuel Bronston, had to choose between Wayne and Capra. The director made his decision easy by suggesting that Bronston hire Henry Hathaway, who had just quit a picture in England and was on good terms with Wayne. When Hathaway arrived in Spain, he asked Capra why he was walking out on Duke. "Hank, I'm not walking, I'm running," the disgruntled director said.

The script problems on *Circus World* were never solved, although Henry Hathaway hired Ben Hecht to rewrite the material submitted by Grant. Production on the picture started with a storyline full of clichés. "That was a terrible job," remembered actor Lloyd Nolan, who played a supporting role in the movie. Duke did not relish his part as a sullen circus boss and came to detest his costar, Rita Hayworth, who frequently arrived on the set late without knowing her lines. In private, Hayworth was surly with peers and belligerent after a few drinks. As the work dragged on, Wayne began to show signs of exhaustion. "We've been working nights for a month," he wrote his agent, "and I haven't done anything but say 'yes sir' to Hathaway and fall into bed at five in the morning."

The movie's big climax is a menacing fire in the circus tent, with animals trapped inside. Duke insisted on doing his own stunt work for the sequence, and for five straight days he inhaled smoke. On the final day of shooting he worked close to the flames, wearing fireproof underwear and a fireman's helmet under his hat. As Wayne swung an ax at the tent's seats and poles to create a firebreak, a sudden breeze fanned the blaze dangerously close behind him. With the fire out of control, Hathaway and his crew fled, while Duke was left working amid choking smoke and swirling pieces of burning wood. The fumes irritated his lungs, and he narrowly escaped more severe injury. "I was shocked by Duke's condition when he got home that night," Pilar recalled. "His eyes were red-rimmed, and he could barely tell me, between prolonged coughing spasms, what had gone wrong."

When shooting finished in Spain, the company moved to England for interior scenes that were filmed in a London studio. The cold, damp weather there did nothing to ease Wayne's vicious cough. "You've got to see a doctor," Pilar argued, but Duke dismissed her caution and continued chain-smoking upwards of five packs of cigarettes a day.

Wayne's coughing persisted after he flew from London to Acapulco, where he rejoined the *Wild Goose* on its return voyage home. Duke contended that he was just suffering a bad case of smoker's hack, even though he had begun to cough up blood. "God," he said with a shake of the head, "it's awful to grow old."

The following spring, with *Circus World* behind him, Wayne, Pilar, and their children boarded the *Wild Goose* near the small Mexican fishing village of La Paz. A few nights later, in the dark waters off Palmilla, tragedy struck. Crew members had heard about a local fiesta, and four of the younger men went ashore in a small boat for an evening's frolic. The next morning those aboard the yacht awoke to find that the men had failed to return. "We weren't overly alarmed," the *Wild Goose*'s skipper maintained. "They might have partied a little too hard and decided to sleep it off and return to the boat after daylight." But by midmorning the four still had not returned, and their delay seemed cause for alarm.

Shock and sadness settled over the *Wild Goose* when it was discovered that all but one of the missing crew members had drowned attempting to return to the anchored craft the night before. Coming across a stretch of open sea, one young man, full of tequila, had tripped over a line in the skiff's bottom and had tumbled overboard. When the others tried to pull him back in, the boat flipped over, pitching them all into the choppy water. "The boys fought to stay afloat," the *Goose*'s skipper wrote. "They clung to the overturned skiff, gulping seawater as the waves broke over them." As the hours went by and they struggled to hang onto the bobbing boat, their arms and legs began to ache. Three of the men attempted to swim to shore and were lost. The survivor, the son of Duke's valet, clung to the upturned skiff, since he could not swim, and was rescued.

Wayne felt responsible for the death of his crew members and became ill with self-reproach. Visibly shaken, Duke and his family cut their holiday short and flew back to Los Angeles under a cloud of gloom. It was clear that Duke was distraught. His smoker's hack sounded uglier, and crumpled tissues, stained with phlegm and blood, littered his nightstand once they were home. "When you get older and you realize I'm not as strong as you think I am, will you still love me?" he asked Aissa shortly after their return to Encino.

John Wayne, the heroic figure who gave a nation and the world reassurance, was a sick man. For millions he stood for strength, commitment, and courage. Now his time of private testing had come. He had risen to be the biggest movie star in Hollywood history, had made more money for his studios than any other actor, had become a symbol of America to millions, and had spent his life pleasing others. Soon the genial man of action would face his greatest personal challenge, one that could easily shatter his larger-than-life image among ordinary people. In the twilight of middle age Marion Morrison confronted John Wayne in a solitary battle over which had the greater claim to the mantle of Duke. For the sensitive lad from Iowa, it was a time when the dreamer, the scrappy rebel, and the goal-oriented realist must of necessity unite. For John Wayne it was a dramatic showdown that would force the popular champion to reveal his humanity and grain.

Licking the Big C

After *Circus World* Paramount insisted on another picture from John Wayne before the studio would consent to his appearing in a movie for his own company. "They are doing me a favor," said Duke. "I want time off after *McLintock!*" Although he had not stopped coughing since he left Spain and needed a rest, Wayne agreed to make *In Harm's Way* for Paramount during the summer of 1964, appearing opposite Kirk Douglas and Patricia Neal. The picture would be filmed in Hawaii, and Duke was scheduled to report for work there in late June.

Before leaving California, he stopped by Scripps Clinic in La Jolla for the compulsory physical movie stars have to pass before qualifying for the insurance studios carry on them while they are making a film. The staff at the clinic pronounced him healthy, and Duke, Pilar, and their children departed for Honolulu, where they stayed at the newly opened Ilikai Hotel on Waikiki Beach.

In Harm's Way is a military drama set against the bombing of Pearl Harbor. The picture benefits from an incisive script, a strong cast, and the firm direction of Otto Preminger. For John Wayne the film was a strenuous assignment, since it is filled with battle sequences and difficult action. "My father . . . never really stopped coughing," Aissa Wayne remembered. "Even in the crystalline air of Hawaii, it became so torturous that some days he had to stop shooting his scenes." Pilar insisted on Duke's seeing a doctor, but he stubbornly refused.

Patricia Neal had not seen Wayne since they had worked together on *Operation Pacific*, and the self-assured actress found him more relaxed and generous than he had been on their earlier picture together. "We had both been through a lot since then," Neal said. "He was certainly a better man for it. . . . This time we got along splendidly." The two stars had the right chemistry on the screen, and Neal and her husband, writer Roald Dahl, proved amusing company for Duke and Pilar during the weeks on location.

In Harm's Way was the first of three pictures Duke would make with Kirk Douglas, and although the two actors were never close friends, they got along well enough, considering the differences in their personalities and political viewpoints. "He was a strange fellow," said Douglas, one of the few people who called his costar John rather than Duke. "We would usually have dinner together only once or twice during the entire shooting of a movie. . . . We were two completely different kinds of people, but there was a mutual respect. Wayne liked to hunker down with the crew—the stuntmen and special-effects guys. I was much more of a loner."

More surprising is the fact that Wayne and the often ill-tempered Otto Preminger worked compatibly together. "There is probably no star whose politics are more at variance with mine than John Wayne's," the liberal director said. On the first day of shooting, Preminger's driver handed the filmmaker a reactionary magazine that he said Wayne wanted him to read. "Look, John," the director told his star when he arrived on the set, "let's agree not to talk politics, and we'll get along very well." Not only did they get along, they developed an affection for one another. "Wayne is an ideal professional," Preminger declared later, "always prompt, always prepared. He is also humorous." Duke in turn appreciated the director's craftsmanship and authority.

Their major point of disagreement came over Preminger's fascination with photographing miniatures for the picture, which Duke felt undermined the reality of the naval battle scenes. Yet a crew of forty did go to sea on the USS *St. Paul* to film much of the script, and $1 million was spent on the final combat sequence, which lasts only five minutes on the screen.

When production on the movie ended, ten days ahead of schedule, the governor of Hawaii gave a party for the cast. Otto Preminger and his wife were included in the receiving line, and the director gave each guest a lei of red flowers as he greeted them. When Preminger presented Wayne with his lei, the actor noted its redness and quipped, "Now at last you are showing your true colors." Those standing nearby joined in a laugh, aware that the two men had maintained harmony on the set by suppressing their strong differences of opinion. "Keep the guns well oiled," Kirk Douglas wrote Wayne a few weeks later. "You never know when we'll need them for another Preminger production."

Paramount executives anticipated that *In Harm's Way* would return box-office receipts to equal Columbia's success with *From Here to Eternity* (1953). But upon its release, the Preminger picture proved a disappointment. Critics found the movie shallow and glib, even though Duke's reviews were favorable. "John Wayne is the best he has ever been in his career," the *Hollywood Reporter* stated. "His tremendous masculinity, his massive physical strength, his ability to be an admiral are rare qualities. His acting, so often discounted, is at its casual best."

In truth Wayne's strength was in jeopardy. Something inside his massive frame had gone out of control. Duke and his family returned to California during the broiling heat of August 1964 with Wayne's cough persisting. Pilar nagged her husband into returning to the Scripps Clinic for a checkup. Duke drove to La Jolla alone. The staff at the clinic kept him there for five days, during which they examined and probed and reviewed the X-rays that had been taken twelve weeks earlier. When Wayne returned home, he met Pilar with downturned eyes. "I've got a little problem," he said. "The doc says I've got a spot on my lung."

He was scheduled for exploratory surgery two weeks later at Good Samaritan Hospital in Los Angeles. "I was never sick in my life," Duke said. "I had the flu back in the First World War, when I was about eight. I had an appendicitis operation, and a six-month bout with an ulcer when I was in my early thirties." But late one night he confessed to his wife that his continual hacking had reawakened childhood memories of his father's tubercular cough. Nonetheless, in his anxiety Duke's smoking appeared to increase. "I never saw my dad without a cigarette in his hand," Aissa said of the days before Wayne's surgery.

Duke was admitted to Good Samaritan Hospital on September 16, 1964. The next morning a malignant growth was removed from his left lung. The tumor, about the size of a golf ball, was sufficiently large that the surgeon had to enter through the patient's back. The six-hour operation was successful, but Wayne lost the upper lobe of his left lung and two ribs from his left side. He awoke to discover that he had only one functioning lung.

The following day his face, throat, and hands began to swell. Duke's coughing had ripped open some stitches, allowing air from his impaired lung to seep into the surrounding tissue. "I was in intensive care," Wayne remembered, "and every time I coughed I thought I would die." The doctors decided that another operation was necessary.

Five days after his cancer surgery Wayne was back on the operating table, where doctors treated his torn stitches and damaged tissue and drained the accumulation of fluid. John Ford kept a terrified Pilar company while she awaited results at the hospital. "I love that damn Republican," said Ford. "He is like a son to me." As they waited, the director ruminated over the past, speaking with pride about the work he and Wayne had done together. But the Duke they had both known and loved disappeared that day. "He'd reappear for weeks or months at a time," Pilar wrote, "but he'd never be back to stay. The operations had changed him forever."

Wayne hated the hospital, with its lack of privacy and odor of sickness. A two-foot-long incision, raised and inflamed, encircled his left side. His body was hooked to machines, and his breathing sounded heavy. For several days he lay in bed, mostly looking at the ceiling, trying to grasp what had happened to him. He was fifty-seven years old, with two young children to support and four more already grown. He might not live through the crisis at hand, and if he did, he might be left an invalid. He could not abide the thought of his loved ones feeling pity for him. "I'll never forget that black day the doctors told me I had 'the big C,'" Wayne said later. "Ever since I heard those words I haven't quite gotten over the feeling that I'm pretty much living on borrowed time."

While still in the hospital, Duke learned that his brother, Robert, another heavy smoker, also had lung cancer. Earlier that year Robert and Wayne's son Michael had been involved in an automobile accident in Burbank after a night of barhopping. Both had gone to the hospital with broken bones and severe injuries. Bobby Morrison drank heavily and was a womanizer, sometimes to Duke's anger and embarrassment. Yet Wayne had done his best for his brother, as he had for his aging mother and grown family.

Duke continued to feel that the children from his first marriage had never forgiven him for divorcing their mother, and he still suffered guilt over not being able to spend more time with them. He had demonstrated his love for them in every way he knew, yet he sensed that Michael, particularly, harbored resentment. He had opened doors for Michael in the movie business and had made him a vital part of Batjac, even though he was not always pleased with Michael's behavior. In fact, the two seldom talked about anything except business and then they often fought. Wayne did not approve of the way Michael dealt with Batjac employees and for a time took to calling him "Khrushchev." Sometimes when Michael called, Duke would instruct Pilar to say that he was out. The relationship with Patrick was friendlier, and Duke was proud of his second son's acting career and early screen popularity. Patrick was more easygoing than Michael and strikingly handsome—"a lot better looking than his old man," said Duke.

Duke sought in every way he could to bridge the gap between his two families, but tensions inevitably surfaced. Melinda, like Toni, had made a point of not inviting Pilar to her wedding. The bride "went on to explain her personal belief that Duke and I weren't married in the eyes of God," Pilar wrote. "My dad told me to love the older kids as brothers and sisters," Pilar's daughter Aissa wrote. "I tried to, but I never knew if their warmth was real or merely a show to placate my dad. It was all very cordial between us, and superficial."

Part of the problem was the difference in ages; Duke had grandchildren older than his youngest son and daughter. Michael and his wife, Gretchen, eventually had five children; Toni had seven. Melinda, who married attorney Gregory Munoz in 1964, would add two grandchildren. Patrick, who married socialite Peggy Hunt in 1965, fathered two more. When Pilar was expecting her third child, both Toni and Melinda were pregnant as well; all three children were born within two months of each other.

Wayne took satisfaction in knowing that none of his children had ever gotten into trouble with the law or had become involved with drugs or developed problems with alcohol. He consistently credited Josephine with raising their children right and imparting solid values to them as they were growing up. After his messy divorce from Chata, Duke had managed to establish a wholesome family-man image and give his younger children the stable upbringing he believed essential. With Pilar he was able to lead a life more consistent with his all-American image.

While Duke believed in God, he remained skeptical of organized religion. When asked his religious preference, he usually grinned and announced that he was a "Presby-goddamn-terian." He considered himself too pragmatic to take any organized church seriously, yet he considered himself a believer who had faith in God, faith in his country, faith in his fellow human beings, and faith in the homespun philosophy he had absorbed from his father. "For me, the stayer is basic art and simplicity," said Wayne. "Love. Hate. Everything right out there without much nuance." This fundamental credo had served him well enough during his youth and middle age. But accepting that he was a cancer victim proved more of an ordeal than Duke was prepared for, and his surgery marked a watershed.

"It was around this time," Aissa declared, "and increasingly over the next several years as sickness ravaged his patience, that it became harder and harder to salve his insecurities, avoid his temper, and sate his urgent need for his family's attention and love."

In late September, before his release from Good Samaritan Hospital, Duke suffered a setback from a respiratory ailment, and doctors had to remove an obstruction from his chest. Pale and still short of breath, he left the hospital on October 19, surrounded by a crowd of reporters. The public had not been informed that the surgeons had removed a malignancy, only that Wayne had developed lung congestion after suffering pain from an old football injury. Sensing more, the press hungered for details. "I was amazed when he managed to stand up before we reached the ground floor," Pilar said of his dismissal from the hospital. "The elevator door whooshed open to reveal Duke, standing straight and proud." He stepped forward, shook a few hands, chatted with reporters, smiled for the cameras, assured the press that he was fine, and walked without faltering to a waiting car. "Once safely inside, hidden by the limousine's dark windows, he groaned and asked for oxygen," Pilar recalled.

Duke was forty pounds lighter than before his surgery, but his willpower remained stronger than ever. Doctors had told him that he must remain inactive for at least six months, but he soon grew restless, despite congestion and continued difficulty in breathing. The better he felt, the more fretful he became. After three weeks at home he insisted on boarding the *Wild Goose* for a trip to Catalina. Then he took a cruise down the Mexican coast, where he did some fishing and started to drink again. To ease his craving for cigarettes, he began chewing tobacco. Always his oxygen tank and breathing mask were kept in readiness.

Duke was astonished at the number of letters of sympathy that poured in from all over the world. After fifty thousand he stopped counting. He was genuinely touched by the understanding acquaintances showed him. "It was Pilar who talked me into getting that routine physical examination," he told friends. "She probably saved my life." But he preferred not to talk about his illness and seemed convinced that he had won his fight with cancer and would soon return to full health.

After his operation Pilar urged her husband to retire, but Duke would have no part in such talk. "He didn't want, couldn't tolerate a wife who questioned his actions," Pilar declared. As the weeks went by, Duke seemed changed, mentally and physically. From 1965 on, his voice developed a huskier quality, but his family also noted a change in his eyes. "They held a world-weary wisdom," Pilar said. "He would never forgive himself for not being superhuman."

In his frustration Duke often became unreasonably angry. There were times when Aissa was actually afraid of her father. While Pilar talked of his slowing down, Duke steadily grew more impatient and rancorous. "Every day is precious to me now," he said. "I have to work." Instead of discussing his impaired health with family members openly, he pretended that his life had returned to normal. Rather than cross him, Aissa and Ethan feigned agreement, anything to avoid his rages. "We were all making believe," Aissa maintained.

Then on December 29, 1964, Wayne held a press conference in the living room of his Encino home. His agent and advisers at Batjac had implored him to hide the real reason for his September hospitalization, contending that the truth would destroy his image. "You'll never work again once the studios hear you've got cancer," Charles Feldman told him. But Wayne was aware that rumors were circulating, and he insisted that the time had come to explain the facts to reporters, his fans, and Hollywood producers. "I always believe in facing everything directly," he said.

But Duke's concept of veracity was built on himself as the hero. Not only did he admit to the media that he had had a malignancy removed, he said he wanted to give courage to other cancer victims by publicizing his illness and his speedy recovery. "I licked the big C," Wayne announced to the world. "I know the man upstairs will pull the plug when he wants to, but I don't want to end up my life being sick. I want to go out on two feet—in action."

His words were brave, his stance typical of the intrepid John Wayne towering above celluloid hazards. "I'm not the sort to back away from a fight," he said. "I don't believe in shrinking away from anything. It's not my speed. I never flinched before in my life, so I see no reason to do so now. I'm a guy who meets adversities head-on." His tone sounded like Sergeant Stryker in *Sands of Iwo Jima*; again he was the seasoned campaigner bolstering the spirits of reluctant followers.

During the press conference Duke managed to suppress his cough and joke with reporters. Immediately afterwards he vanished upstairs to his bedroom in a state of exhaustion. The following day his triumphant story appeared in newspapers around the world. "He'd vanquished every screen foe," Pilar said, "and he had to believe he'd beaten cancer too. He just didn't know any other way to live."

Duke counted on his fans embracing this brave image of a beleaguered warrior, and he assessed their loyalty correctly. Most of his public, including a host of converts, viewed Wayne's disclosure as a noble action. "His courage and fighting spirit made him an even greater hero in real life than he had been on screen," producer Hal Wallis observed. John Wayne in real life had battled a deadly foe, beaten the odds, and emerged victorious, and Duke acted the part to perfection. Fans were awed by his energy and renewed appetite for life. "I want to spend more time with my family and doing the things that are really important to me," he told the press. "I don't want to waste a minute."

Later Duke would be awarded a citation for his role in combating the public's cancer phobia. He campaigned extensively for the American Cancer Society, and doctors reported that hundreds of patients requested the kind of operation that John Wayne had undergone. "He handled his fight against cancer as he handled the other challenges in his life," actor Robert Stack said, "with a courage and simple faith that's consistent with the heroes he played in films. Even with one lung . . . , he was more man than anyone I know."

Yet the private Duke could not ignore his feet of clay. He ended 1964 still sleeping in a hospital bed and dependent on tanks of oxygen. Sometimes he gasped for breath. At sea on the *Wild Goose* any major exertion meant that he stayed in his cabin most of the following day. Still he refused to admit defeat, and his adoring public applauded him as indestructible. His celebrity took on new dimensions. Trapped in his own legend, Duke insisted on playing the valiant, at whatever price to himself. Always a driven man, he became all the more so. If he could not stay active, he had no interest in living. "Work is the only thing I know," he said.

On January 4, 1965, less than four months after his operation, Wayne packed his bags and left for Durango, Mexico, where his next picture, *The Sons of Katie Elder*, would be filmed. "I figured I had loafed around long enough," he said. "I wanted to get The Wound off my mind. . . . Hell, I can't stand being idle." Duke confessed later that he had started back to work too soon, but he knew that producer Hal Wallis had postponed *Katie Elder* until he could play the lead. The part of the eldest son had been written for Wayne, and Wallis insisted that no one else would do. The star maintained that he could not hold up production any longer; he had an obligation to Wallis and he intended to meet it.

Durango was an isolated location, high in the Sierra Madre range and cold during the winter. The thin air meant that Wayne would tire easily and be more dependent than ever on bottled oxygen. *The Sons of Katie Elder* is an action movie and a physically demanding one. When reporters asked Wayne if he was ready for such a tough assignment, he answered, "I'd better be. I didn't get famous for making drawing room comedies!"

Pilar and Duke battled over his going back to work so soon. "I was furious," she said. "Few people realize what he went through making that picture. He was in agony." Pilar herself hung on the edge of a nervous breakdown. "I went down to 80-something pounds," she recalled. "I was that upset."

Wallis, who liked Duke enormously, appreciated his star's consideration, even though he had offered to wait longer to begin production if need be. Wayne "represented the American folk hero at his best," the producer said. "On location in Durango, Mexico, he amazed me. Even though he was functioning on one lung and had a terrible scar running down his back, he showed no signs of illness or weakness. He did his own riding, roped steers, rounded up cattle, and handled the fight scenes without a double."

Paramount had bought *The Sons of Katie Elder* years before, but the story had sat on a shelf. Writer Harry Essex read it and suggested that the title character be eliminated from the script. Essex's idea was to let the audience only hear about Katie, allowing viewers to imagine what she was like. "It's a good film," said Essex. "You had to be able to write a certain way for Wayne. It had to be simple and basic. But there he was with one lung, just as powerful as ever. He was a very genuine character. If he liked you, you were in business; if he didn't like you, he would ignore you."

Pilar knew that Duke was in no condition to film an outdoor movie, particularly one that required riding and performing stunts in high altitudes and frigid temperatures. In private Wayne was irritable and short-tempered. Oxygen was never far from his reach, and he frequently fought to catch his breath. In the mountains of Mexico his coughing became horrendous, as he struggled to clear mucus from his remaining lung. Mounting a horse caused excruciating pain on his left side, but Duke knew that the press would be on hand to report any faltering. "Duke had something to prove to himself," Pilar wrote, "and Durango was the place where he planned to do it. He had to know if he could be the same man he'd been before cancer struck."

Director Henry Hathaway had undergone surgery himself for cancer of the colon, and he reassured Duke by reminding him that for twelve years now there had been no sign of its recurrence. But Hathaway was tough on actors. The director's approach to Westerns was relatively simple; he believed in a straightforward narrative that emphasized action and shied away from psychological nuances. "Henry could be so insensitive," said Earl Holliman, who played the youngest of Katie Elder's sons, "yet he was a very sensitive man. He covered it over with a lot of macho crap. He would forget that anybody else was around and say terrible things. And his descriptions could be the grossest."

In one sequence of *Katie Elder* Duke was to be pulled from a horse, fall into a mountain stream, and engage in a lengthy brawl. The river was ringed with ice the morning the scene was shot, the temperature near ten degrees. Duke fell waist-deep into the freezing water, felt his body weaken, yet was determined to perform the scene as planned. After an exchange of blows that seemed to go on forever, Wayne came out of the stream chilled to the bone, his face ashen. An aide wrapped a blanket around him, but Duke could not stop coughing. He grabbed his inhalator and placed the mask over his nose. As the press moved toward him, a photographer snapped a picture of Duke holding the oxygen mask to his face. Wayne snatched the camera from the reporter and angrily threw it to the ground. Hathaway shouted at the newsmen, "Get away, you sons of bitches. Can't you see he needs air?"

As the production proceeded, Wayne tried to be part of everything. He insisted on doing his own fights, and he rode a horse downhill at full tilt. For the benefit of the press he threw a couple of pills into his mouth, washed them down with a swig from a half-gallon jug of mescal, and proclaimed, "I'm the stuff that men are made of!" His exaggerated tone and the twinkle in his eye suggested that Wayne was making fun of himself, but the prank was also meant to demonstrate that being cut open had not slowed the Duke down much.

Earl Holliman arrived on the set of *Katie Elder* a John Wayne aficionado, but the young actor soon experienced disappointment. Holliman found Duke "a wonderful persona" and lots of fun. "But he had to be the macho man," the actor said, "he had to have more drinks than the next guy." Holliman was frankly disillusioned to find Wayne "a bit of a bigot in conversation," petty in certain areas, and not always as straightforward as he had expected. "I couldn't call him Duke," the younger actor said. "I called him John. He was very peculiar to me on the set, and it hurt me that he didn't like me very much. I was disappointed in that because I had grown up in awe of him. He wasn't mean to me or anything, but he treated me as if I was somebody there to report to the front office."

Holliman was under contract to Hal Wallis at the time and not part of Duke's regular gang. Dean Martin, who played another of the Elder boys, had worked with Wayne earlier on *Rio Bravo* and the two men had remained friends. Duke liked Martin's casual way, and during the making of *Katie Elder* they spent most of their free time together. Wayne and Martin often played cards after dinner and drank together on weekends. "Late one night the week I was in Durango," Aissa recalled, "I was jolted awake by a racket outside our hotel room. Stumbling outside I saw the cast, crew, writers, and paparazzi standing outside their own rooms waving and grinning. Down below in the dirt street, my father and Dean Martin marched arm-in-arm, singing their booze-soaked lungs out."

Martha Hyer, Duke's leading lady in the picture, played an unglamorous country schoolmarm who wore little makeup, old clothes, and a homely hairstyle. "Wayne felt that he was older," Hyer said, "and he didn't want anyone too young playing opposite him. He was very sensitive about this. So I tried to stay very much in character." From this point on the age factor was permanent in Duke's mind, gnawing at a self-esteem founded on physical attributes.

Durango in 1965 was a mountain village, with unnamed streets, one horseshoe-shaped hotel, and a diner. Mexican extras who appeared in *Katie Elder* had to get up at three o'clock in the morning to be transported to Hathaway's set, then faced a return trip after work. Some nights were so cold that exterior scenes had to be postponed. After nine weeks in Durango the company moved to Churubusco Studios outside Mexico City, where interior sequences were filmed. Much of Wayne's dialogue had to be dubbed in the studio. Yet despite a multitude of problems, *The Sons of Katie Elder* emerged as a leisurely, unpretentious Western that fared well at the box office. "Not a rare film," Howard Thompson wrote in the *New York Times*, "but lean, gory, and well served."

With *Katie Elder* finished, Pilar became a "virtual zombie, just going through the motions." She suffered from depression and felt that her husband had become a stranger in Durango. "I couldn't share my feelings with anyone, certainly not Duke," she said. "A part of me, a part of our marriage, died in that icy mountain stream." But Wayne assured her that everything was all right. All they needed was a change of scenery.

Duke had announced shortly after his surgery that he planned to sell their home in Encino, much to Pilar's surprise. He complained that the smog in Los Angeles made him cough, that the interior of the house was too dark, that he felt imprisoned on its spacious grounds, and that the isolated estate was an easy target for robberies. The truth was that the home had come to represent bygone days that Wayne wished to put behind him. No longer did the house ring with masculine laughter the way it had when John Ford and his gang were younger. Duke and his wife rarely attended parties in Hollywood any longer, and they knew few of their neighbors.

Without telling Pilar, Wayne impulsively put the house on the market, and a few days before Christmas 1964, he informed his wife that their home had been sold to Walt Disney's daughter. The couple returned from Mexico the following March to begin packing their belongings. Since Duke loved the California coastline, he decided that they should buy a house down at Newport Beach, where he kept the *Wild Goose*. Newport, sixty miles south of Los Angeles, had been one of the haunts of Duke's youth, and he felt it was an attractive place to start life anew. Los Angeles had increasingly come to represent illness, alcoholism, and death to him. With Wayne's inner circle decimated, Hollywood represented little for him except work.

In May 1965 he and his second family moved to Newport, living first on the *Wild Goose*, then in temporary quarters at the Newporter Inn, while a house was found and remodeled. Wayne charged his wife with selecting their new home, insisting only that it be on waterfront property. "Duke made all our major decisions," Pilar said. "I couldn't believe he wanted me to be responsible for this one." She chose a ten-room, seven-bath ranch house at 2686 Bayshore Drive, overlooking the harbor.

The front of the house could be reached only by passing through a guarded entrance to a colony of expensive homes. The Waynes' back patio afforded a spectacular view of Balboa Island as well as yachts and sailboats that plied the bay. Since the couple liked to watch their favorite evening television shows in bed, the house's master suite contained a viewing

267

screen in the ceiling which descended at the push of a button. Pilar's fondness of oriental art was evident in the decor, as was Duke's preference for a western motif. His wood-paneled den was the showroom of the house; it contained Wayne's western paintings and sculpture, his collection of kachina dolls, his antique guns, and a lifetime of awards and mementos.

Newport is only an hour away on the freeway from most Hollywood studios, so Duke could drive to work or take a helicopter from the Orange County Airport. Wayne considered himself a superb driver, even though he zipped through traffic at a speed that sometimes frightened passengers. Newport seemed to provide him with a freedom that Encino had not. He could go for early morning walks around the Bayshore enclave, drive to local stores in his green Pontiac (vaulted to accommodate his size) to pick up items for the house or the boat, and spend afternoons playing poker or chess at the Big Canyon Country Club with an assortment of friends who had no connection with the world of movies.

Newport Beach was still a small community when the Waynes settled there. Duke and Pilar were amazed when neighbors arrived with food the day they moved into their house. Although the locals treated Wayne like a celebrity at first, they soon got used to him. He could go and come relatively undisturbed. The community was rich, white, and politically conservative, and Duke immediately felt comfortable there. Aissa and Ethan had no trouble finding playmates, since neighborhood children frolicked on the street outside their door. "I came down here fifteen years ago and completely changed," Wayne said later. "The [movie] business had changed, and I was working my ass off. There were so many people hanging on."

He missed some of his old friends, whom he saw infrequently after the move to Newport, but Claire Trevor and her husband, Milton Bren, lived nearby and Duke's mother was still in Long Beach. Wayne eventually cut down on his drinking, although he and Pilar mixed with local denizens who occasionally motored over in their boats for an evening cocktail. Pilar soon became involved in a tennis club, while Duke entertained himself with cards or chess. "I remember going to his house at Newport," Dan Ford said. "Whenever you'd go there, there were always stacks and stacks of cards. Wayne was a shrewd card player."

Newport harbor had been dredged and developed into an exclusive berth for luxury craft. The dock where Duke kept his yacht was one of the largest in the channel, yet the *Wild Goose* jutted out beyond everything around it. When Wayne was not on location or working on a project in the Batjac office, he spent many of his happiest hours aboard ship. At sea, time stood still for him; he could ignore the aging process and fancy life on escapist terms.

Throughout his career Duke had trouble handling boredom and expected his family and friends to help fill his empty hours. But as Pilar became more absorbed with tennis and Aissa and Ethan developed friendships with playmates their own age, they were less willing to stay within Duke's orbit. Many of Wayne's friends in Newport were businessmen with hectic schedules of their own. Yet Duke needed to be surrounded by adulators who would dutifully put aside everything else for him. When none were available, he took little pleasure in solitude and became petulant. His career had not allowed him much time for monotony, and when he experienced it in later years, he could become a monster, imperious and easily provoked.

The move to Newport involved many adjustments. Within a six-month period he had undergone a cancer operation, sold his home, and uprooted his family. His world and theirs had been turned upside down; they all needed time to get their bearings. Yet Duke, needing activity, became restless and seemed loath to share his innermost thoughts with those around him.

Even before the family had moved into the new house, Duke was off to Rome on another movie assignment, leaving Pilar and the children in rented quarters. Writer-director Melville Shavelson had been trying to make a picture about the formation of modern Israel, but he could not secure the necessary backing. Shavelson told the story he had in mind to Wayne, who wanted to know what the problem with funding was. "That's the most American story I ever heard," said Duke, "an American army officer who helps a little country fight for its independence. Why can't you get it made?" Shavelson explained that he had been told by every studio in Hollywood that no one wanted to see a movie about a Jewish general. Wayne voiced surprise and volunteered his support. "I just want to make the picture Gentile by association," Shavelson told him. "If your name is attached to it, they can't say it's a Jewish movie anymore."

Wayne asked to see the first thirty pages of the script, which Shavelson had written himself, although he was primarily a comedy writer. Duke read them and phoned to say that he would appear in the picture in a subordinate role on one condition—that Shavelson write the entire screenplay. Casting Wayne in the role of Gen. Mike Randolph was a ploy. "If I could persuade this Rock of Gibraltar of Gentile culture to agree to appear in the movie," Shavelson said, "it would be equivalent to circumcising the entire Israeli army." The writer took his script to United Artists and said, "John Wayne," and the film was made. "It wouldn't have been done without him and his kind of Americanism," said Shavelson.

Though Duke was working hard at the time to rejuvenate Batjac, he soon became enthusiastic about helping Shavelson make his picture, entitled *Cast a Giant Shadow.* "Everybody's knocking the United States these days," said Wayne, "claiming we're sending in troops all over the world to hurt little countries where we have no right to be. They've forgotten who we are and what we've done. At a time like this, we need to remind the whole world how we helped this little country of Israel get its independence and how a goddamn American army officer gave his life for it." *Cast a Giant Shadow* became a Llenroe-Batjac-Mirisch-Bryna production, with Michael Wayne serving as Melville Shavelson's associate producer.

Kirk Douglas played the lead in the picture, the role of Col. Mickey Marcus, the American West Point graduate and lawyer who helped Israel gain its freedom. Wayne waxed so effusive about the Americanness of the picture that the director had to remind him that Mickey Marcus was Jewish. "Don't give me that crap," said Duke. "Jesus Christ was Jewish, too, and he didn't even go to West Point."

Most of the film's exteriors were shot in Israel, its interiors at Cinecitta Studios in Rome. Wayne wasn't needed in Israel and worked only four days on the picture in Rome. He appears in six sequences, totaling eleven minutes on the screen. During his evenings in Rome, Duke made the rounds of the nightclubs with Frank Sinatra, who was also in the cast. While filming a sniper sequence, Wayne jumped out of a jeep too fast and incurred a slipped disc. He was hospitalized for three days and forced to rest.

Although Duke frequented the clubs again afterwards, he continued to be a dedicated professional. When Kirk Douglas showed up on the set late one morning, Wayne bawled him out. "In Rome he was perfect as far as doing his part," Shavelson said. "He knew that the picture was being made because he had agreed to be in it."

Shavelson recalled having only one argument with Duke during the making of the movie. They were shooting in one of the airports in Rome at the time of the Watts riots in Los Angeles. Wayne began making statements like, "Those blacks got what they deserved," until the director and members of the company became infuriated. "You can't look at it that way," Shavelson told him, but Duke contended that the rioters had disturbed the peace and needed to be brought to order. "Whatever prejudices he had were based on his Americanism," Shavelson later remarked. "The important thing to him was, is it good or bad for the country."

Wayne returned to Newport in August 1965 to face both bad news and good. *Cast a Giant Shadow* would make less of an impact than he and Melville Shavelson had hoped. Also Duke was embroiled in a half-million-dollar litigation against his former financial adviser, Bo Roos, a suit that grew long and tiresome before its final resolution. Then Wayne discovered that his friend and former writer James Edward Grant was dying of cancer. Grant had not been a member of Wayne's team since the *Circus World* debacle, but the writer had played a pivotal role in Duke's career. "If there had not been a John Ford and a James Edward Grant," publicist Russell Birdwell said, "we would not today be enjoying the image known as John Wayne." Grant's death in February 1966 was slow and painful and served to remind Duke again of his own mortality.

On the positive side, the public appeared to accept John Wayne's image as the stalwart chieftain who had wrestled "the big C" and come away victorious. In the late 1960s he commanded $1 million per picture plus a percentage of the profits. Best of all, at age fifty-nine Duke had fathered his seventh and last child. His youngest daughter, Marisa, was born in February 1966 and looked more like her father than any of the other Wayne children. Her birth symbolized a new lease on life for Duke. He made a gallant effort to adopt a more mature outlook and savor his blessings. "Suffering gives you a better perspective," he said. "You even gaze at the sunrise with a little more enjoyment."

Duke would live another fifteen years after his cancer surgery, make eighteen more movies, and see his second family enter early adulthood. The gap between John Wayne the movie star and John Wayne the person had narrowed. Despite his bloated face and expanding paunch, Duke had fulfilled his destiny. In his twilight years Hollywood's lone horseman soared off the screen to become an enduring icon in world culture.

Reactionary Patriarch

By the mid-1960s John Wayne's roles had become stereotyped, tailored to fit his image as the indestructible hero. Duke exercised absolute control over the pictures produced by his own company; he worked with writers to fashion scripts that befitted his persona, surrounded himself with friends he had worked with for years, and selected directors who allowed him to be in charge. With Batjac's financial condition gaining strength, nourished as it was by diversified holdings outside the motion picture business, Duke was eager to make movies that expressed his personal philosophy.

In September 1966 he returned to Durango, Mexico, to begin shooting *The War Wagon*, a joint production for Batjac and Universal. Based on Clair Huffaker's book *Badman*, the film was directed by writer Burt Kennedy and cast Kirk Douglas in his third appearance opposite Wayne. Douglas remembered that Duke had trouble breathing in the plane flying to Durango. "We had to put an oxygen mask on him," the actor said. In Mexico the company lived in a modest motel overrun with scorpions. But Durango was a place where Duke could relax and regain his perspective, and he welcomed the temporary isolation and chance to socialize with old acquaintances. Working in Mexico also allowed his company to avoid the Hollywood unions and keep costs down.

Although Wayne continued to experience physical problems, he refused to let those limitations impinge on his professionalism. "He was always the first one on the set," Kirk Douglas recalled, "usually checking out what the special-effects guys were doing. He butted into everything." Without question Duke was the dominant force during the making of *War Wagon*, and he bullied Burt Kennedy shamelessly. "Burt was a very talented director," said Douglas, "but gentle. Wayne was a less talented director, and far from gentle. I tried to get Burt to stand up to him. It wasn't easy." If Duke was in a scene with a couple of cowboys on either side, he would turn to the left and give instructions, turn to the right and give instructions, then indicate to Kennedy that he was ready to begin.

"Duke was tough on directors," Kennedy admitted, "especially when it was his own company. He felt responsible for everything. Of course he was a frustrated director himself." Kennedy regarded Wayne as a fine actor, with a gift for making his performances seem natural. "Kirk and Duke respected each other," the director said, "but they didn't really like each other. It worked well on the screen, because they kept that wonderful conflict going. There was great chemistry between those two guys."

Between takes the costars had spirited exchanges about politics. Wayne made statements in favor of Republican candidates, and Douglas countered with praise for the Democrats. Their off-camera rivalry became a running gag in the picture. In one scene Wayne and Douglas shoot two scoundrels at the same time. Douglas looks proudly at Duke and says, "Mine hit the ground first." Wayne answered, "Mine was taller."

Abrasive though Duke could be, most of his crew and associates liked and admired him because of his forthright honesty and genuine moments of caring. It was not unusual for Wayne to walk up to a truck driver or grip working on a picture, call him by name, and ask after the fellow's new baby. "He remembered that sort of thing," character actor Hank Worden said, "and his crew remembered him for his courtesy and his kindness in remembering."

Duke celebrated his sixtieth birthday at the premiere of *The War Wagon*, held at the Majestic Theater in Dallas on May 27, 1967. Although the Western was judged an above-average horse opera, much of its humor failed to come off, even in the adept hands of its two veteran performers, and its plot bordered on the cliché. The *New York Times* branded the movie "pretty flabby prairie stuff."

But Wayne still believed in Westerns and felt that their waning popularity stemmed from overexposure on television. The video cowboy, he said, "is introverted and oversensitive. The real cowboy loved, hated, had fun, was lusty. He didn't have mental problems." John Wayne's Westerns continued to stress an older approach—action, excitement, and the triumph of virtue. "I try to make pictures that are like folklore," said Duke. "Stories of the West are in my opinion the best vehicles for the motion picture medium." Good Westerns to him were art. "Sure, they're simple," he acknowledged. "But simplicity is art."

Wayne denied that he ever set out to make a classic. He simply aimed for the best picture possible with the material he had available. Consciously arty films were not for him. "I am not a man of words and nuances," he said. "I relish action, which is an essential part of motion pictures." He favored strong personal stories, but liked the beauty of the western landscape and the excitement created by galloping horses. "In the Western you can still tell stories about people," said Duke, "but as an added attraction, you know you have a little platinum to put in the setting." While Wayne wanted conflict in his movies, he disapproved of excessive violence. "The violence in my pictures is lusty and a little bit humorous," he said. "I believe that humor nullifies violence." Above all, he believed that filmmakers must keep entertainment as their goal. "We're in the business of magic," he said.

Through the years Duke demonstrated a dependable sense of what roles were right for him. "I wouldn't play a mean or a small character," he said. "I try not to let the audience down about the type of fellow they expect me to be." In a John Wayne Western toughness is part of manhood, pride an essential ingredient in the American character, and fear something strong characters have only for God. Heroes must be true to their word and fast with a gun. "The day film companies think that a Western is a place for weaklings, I'll go," he said. Duke accepted that his films appealed more to men than to women, but he appreciated fans of both sexes. "Those are my customers," he said. "They're the people that pay my bills."

El Dorado, his last film for Paramount under their $6 million contract, cast Wayne as an older, less assured gunfighter. Shot in Old Tucson, *El Dorado* was Duke's one hundred and thirty-eighth picture. It had actually been filmed before *The War Wagon*, but its release was delayed so that the studio's *Nevada Smith* (1966) would not have to compete with a John Wayne movie at the box office. *El Dorado* finally reached the theaters in June 1967, a month after *The War Wagon* had opened.

Director Howard Hawks had grown as disturbed about recent changes in the motion picture business as Wayne had. Both objected to the nudity and foul language that had infiltrated contemporary movies, along with explicit sex and violence. Uncertain about the future direction of his career, Hawks went to Wayne and said, "Do you want to make a couple of Westerns till I can make up my mind what to do?" Duke accepted the offer, aware that the director was his kind of filmmaker and would adhere to the pattern he believed in.

Hawks worked closely with screenwriter Leigh Brackett to shape the script of *El Dorado*, essentially reversing the situations they had concocted for *Rio Bravo*. In the earlier Western the collaborators had Ricky Nelson as a teenage gunman; in *El Dorado* they created a young man (played by James Caan) who couldn't shoot at all. In *Rio Bravo* Wayne was a sheriff with an alcoholic deputy, whereas in *El Dorado* the drunk was the sheriff himself (portrayed by Robert Mitchum). Since Wayne was reaching the end of his career as a romantic lead, Hawks and Brackett focused on Duke's relationship with the inebriated sheriff. "I'm much more interested in the story of a friendship between two men than I am about a range war or something like that," the director said. "There's probably no stronger emotion than friendship between men. When it comes to Wayne and his relationships, that's better than the story."

Wayne and Mitchum were well matched, since each man projected a powerful image. Casting a male lead opposite Duke could be difficult. "If you get somebody who's not pretty strong," Hawks said, "he blows them right off the screen. He doesn't do it purposely; that's just what happens." With Robert Mitchum, as with Kirk Douglas, a satisfactory balance was struck.

Hawks wanted to keep *El Dorado* from becoming a tragedy, but he did retain one somber scene in which Wayne shoots a boy on top of a boulder. The director's intent was to begin the picture with this catastrophe, then turn it into a story with more humor. "We were lucky working it out," Hawks said, "because we were working with characters instead of a story."

Howard Hawks was a brilliant director, but tough like John Ford and Henry Hathaway. If actors muffed lines, he would bark belittling comments. Duke sometimes gave suggestions to newcomers in private, but he never dominated the production as he did those made by Batjac. Some of the younger performers resented his interference, but others realized how smart Wayne was about screen acting and listened to him. Although *El Dorado* was not produced by his own company, Duke was surrounded by wranglers and stunt performers he had known for years. "We'd travel around following these movies," said stuntman Neil Summers, "like cowboys who go on the rodeo circuit. We caravaned and took off to Old Tucson to see if there was any work on *El Dorado*." Summers managed to get two or three days' employment on the picture, then he and some cohorts returned to Kanab, Utah, where they had been working on *Duel at Diablo* (released in 1966).

Reviewers did not find *El Dorado* a spectacular Western, simply a crisp diversion with some amusing moments. Its two leathery stars meshed and established the tone and pace of the picture. James Caan scored laughs by playing his inept gunman with complete earnestness. "He didn't know he was playing comedy . . . until he went to see the preview," Howard Hawks maintained. When Caan voiced surprise at how humorous he was, the director told him, "Had you tried to be funny, you'd have spoiled it."

Duke was feeling progressively more uncomfortable with prevailing values in late-twentieth-century America. As he grew older, his determination to play characters who were courageous and honorable intensified. He felt that it was essential for him to set an example for a society racing toward permissiveness. He became convinced that the country's youth were being led astray by a radical minority. He was appalled at the widespread use of drugs and the counterculture's defiance of society's conventions. "There doesn't seem to be respect for authority anymore," he said, "these student dissenters act like children who have to have their own way on everything. They're immature and living in a little world all their own. Just like hippie dropouts, they're afraid to face the competitive world."

Duke remained vitally concerned about the image of America. He was alarmed by expanding welfare programs for minorities and popular acceptance of the notion that the government should take care of its citizens from the cradle to the grave. "This country was made available for individuals," he said, "and each individual would get a certain respect from his government. He would express his gratitude with responsibility toward his work and his behavior toward his neighbor."

Wayne continued to believe in the importance of the individual rather than pressure groups. In addition to providing entertainment, he thought it his duty as a filmmaker to project a consistent role model for fans. He wanted his younger audiences to consider him an older friend—"somebody believable and down-to-earth," he said, who exemplified human dignity, hard work, individual attainment, upward mobility, patriotism, and a pride in personal success. "I hope that I appeal to the more carefree times in a person's life rather than to his reasoning adulthood," Duke said. "I'd just like to be an image that reminds someone of joy rather than of the problems of the world."

Wayne had been among Hollywood's conspicuous Republicans since the late 1940s. He had supported Dwight Eisenhower, backed Richard Nixon, and in 1964 voted for Barry Goldwater. Long after the Motion Picture Alliance for the Preservation of American Ideals had disbanded,

Duke continued to boast of its achievements and express strong anti-Communist views. His political beliefs, like his movies, were oversimplified. Basically he mistrusted bureaucracy and considered government a necessary evil—"like motion-picture agents," he said. But few of his detractors doubted the sincerity of his love for America. "I am proud of every day in my life I wake up in the United States of America," he said. "We are the greatest sociological experiment that the world has ever known. If we fail our trust, democracy fails."

In the late 1960s John Wayne showed little sympathy for the changing world around him and refused to accept that his thinking was obsolete. An outspoken defender of traditional American values, he denied that he was a political animal, but stated time and again how important it was to voice an opinion on issues. "The world used to have an image of America as a bunch of right-thinking, rough but straightforward people who took a stand," said Duke. "The last bastion of that image is in Western pictures."

Over the years Wayne's work and his political views meshed; one simply dramatized the other. He disagreed that he was a reactionary; he was merely a concerned American who believed in his country's basic compact, he said. "I can't understand why our national leadership isn't willing to take the responsibility of leadership instead of checking polls and listening to the few that scream," he offered. "Why are we allowing ourselves to become a mobocracy instead of a democracy? When you allow unlawful acts to go unpunished, you're moving toward a government of men rather than a government of law; you're moving toward anarchy. And that's exactly what we're doing."

Duke had pulled himself up by his bootstraps, toiled to attain an elevated economic plateau, and earned his place of prominence. He saw no reason why others could not do the same. As his country moved toward a corporate society, he felt like a stranger in his own land. He believed in self-reliance, objected to the government's assuming a paternalistic role, and lamented the death of personal initiative and responsibility. Rather than letting special interest groups or political parties or powerful institutions sway judgments and determine policy, citizens must be guided by their own conscience. "It takes a long time to develop a philosophy that enables you to do that," said Duke. "It's like those old ranchers . . . in Texas. As they get older, facing the elements, they just get more straight-backed and take on a stronger attitude toward life."

Wayne prided himself on his headstrong personality, much as his movie heroes did. Rarely a joiner, he stood up for what he believed against critics of varied persuasions. "Mine is a personal rebellion," he said, "against the monotony of life, against the status quo." In the stormy 1960s Duke became a high-profile supporter of the shrinking establishment and apologized to no one. "There is only one point that I'm a reactionary about," he argued. "The motion picture business was intended to be a medium of illusion and all these young directors are trying to take the illusion out of it. . . . They want a realism that I think is unnecessary. Their attitude is realism versus illusion; it's that goddam simple." An eternal romantic, Duke's credo was that the individual must emerge and lead a troubled society back to national health, return America to international prominence.

In the summer of 1966 Wayne flew to Tokyo, then to Tan Son Nhut Air Base for a three-week tour entertaining American troops in Vietnam. "I promised . . . when I licked cancer that I'd go to Vietnam and shake hands with those kids," Duke told writer-producer Paul Keyes. "I did it with their fathers, and I'll do it for them. My debt has come due." He spent a few days in a village outside Saigon, talked, shook hands, joked with the men in marine outposts, and got near enough to the fighting that bullets from Vietcong rifles tore the turf a few yards away from him. "I didn't stop signing autographs," Duke claimed. He put in twenty-hour days, answered questions the men asked, and visited an American destroyer and an aircraft carrier. Outside Da Nang he was made an honorary soldier and given a bracelet some servicemen had made from a piece of wire. Wayne wore it from then on.

During the trip Duke came down with an eye inflammation, which had to be treated in a hospital. He returned home a stalwart defender of the Asian war and vowed that the American pubic owed unconditional allegiance to the armed forces fighting there. He attached a bumper sticker to his station wagon that read, "The Marines are looking for a few good men," and had no truck with questioning the policy that sent them into an impossible war. He showed draft dodgers and protesters no patience, objected to the barriers liberal members of Congress put before the military, and favored an all-out offensive in Vietnam. "Once you go over there you won't be middle-of-the-road," he said. "All those 'let's-be-sweet-to-our-enemies' guys are doing is helping the Reds and hurting their own country." Duke contended that it was a patriotic duty for Americans to support a conflict in which thousands of the nation's young men were sacrificing their lives. "We've lost too much blood and money by pussy-footing around," he said.

Home from the tour, Wayne decided that he had to make a movie about his country's fighting force in Vietnam. "I owe it to them," he said. Hollywood friends tried to dissuade him, and the prospect aroused controversy even before the picture went into production. But Duke clung to his convictions. "I get mad these days," he said, "when I see our boys getting killed and maimed and people back home aren't behind them. . . . I honestly believe that there's as much need for us to help the Vietnamese as there was to help the Jews in Germany." For Wayne the issue was clear: "If you fight, you fight to win."

Duke became a man with a mission, compelled to make the first movie about America's fighting men in Vietnam. "I want to show the folks back home just what they're up against out there," he said, "their heroism against tremendous odds." He secured for Batjac the rights to a novel by Robin Moore called *The Green Berets*, negotiated for the cooperation of the Defense Department, and went from studio to studio looking for backing. Paramount turned him down flat, maintaining that his defense of the Asian war was too controversial. Executives at Universal agreed to release the picture, then changed their minds, saying that the Vietnamese war was unpopular and Wayne's picture likely to be box-office poison. "What war was ever popular?" Duke asked. "Those boys in the U.S. Special Forces over there are doing the most dangerous work any soldiers have ever undertaken. . . . They patrol behind enemy lines and can only be protected from the air." Finally he made a deal with Warner Bros.–Seven Arts. At Jack Warner's urging, the studio agreed to invest $7 million in the project if Wayne would lower his fee as actor and director.

As with *The Alamo*, Duke had a burning need to make a statement; he went all out to film *The Green Berets*. "It was quite obvious that no one would tell the truth of why we were in Vietnam," he said. "I'd been over there. I knew that the people of South Vietnam were being treated badly and that we had a goddamn good right to be there. I tried to put that in the picture." Later Duke maintained that his purpose in filming *The Green Berets* was "to make an exciting motion picture about the bravery of the men in the Special Forces, not to make a controversial film about the war." But the movie would be received as blatant hawk propaganda, and critics denounced it roundly.

Wayne decided to direct the picture himself rather than trust Andrew

McLaglen or Burt Kennedy, who by then were Batjac's principal directors. *The Green Berets* "was something I was interested in," Duke said, "and I wanted it told the way I saw it over there." When Kennedy, still recovering from difficulties with Duke over the making of *The War Wagon*, was asked if he intended to participate in Wayne's defense of the questionable war, the director shook his head and replied, "I'd rather *join* the Green Berets."

Duke would have preferred to shoot the picture in Vietnam, but instead the Defense Department offered him facilities at Fort Benning, Georgia. Wayne spent five months at the base toward the latter part of 1967 working on the film. The weather in Georgia that fall was damp and cold, and heavy rains put the production behind schedule. Duke had trouble breathing, suffered spasms of coughing, and his back and legs ached with pain, yet his determination drove him on. Finally Warner Bros. insisted on bringing in veteran director Mervyn LeRoy to help move the picture along.

Directing and starring in *The Green Berets* had clearly become too much, even for John Wayne. Mervyn LeRoy worked on the movie for five and a half months but did not put his name on it. "Duke and I had a long talk and straightened out the question of how I could help him," LeRoy said. "Then I took over and assisted Duke with the directing whenever he felt he needed me." Unlike Clint Eastwood, Wayne was never at his best directing himself; he needed an objective eye to pull a superior performance from him. LeRoy, who was Harry Warner's son-in-law, lacked the authority of Ford, Hawks, or Hathaway, and Duke resented his interference. But Warner Bros. insisted that a studio representative be on hand to protect their investment.

By the time Mervyn LeRoy reached Georgia, altercations between Wayne and the military had already taken place. In a drunken rage Duke had tangled with one of Fort Benning's top-ranking officers, placing his production in jeopardy. At that point Warner threatened to close down the picture unless Duke accepted LeRoy as an assistant. There was criticism that Wayne had secured the use of a military post, its personnel, planes, helicopters, trucks, rifles, machine guns, and other equipment to make a film that distorted crucial facts about the war in Asia. Later the charge would be levied that the army had subsidized *The Green Berets* by contributing men and equipment equal to $1 million plus thirty-eight hundred days in time from army personnel. Wayne contended that Batjac had been charged by the Pentagon for everything the company used. But Democratic representative Benjamin Rosenthal of New York argued, "The glorified portrayal of the Vietnam war, which is the heart of the film, raises serious questions about the Defense Department's role in using tax funds for direct propaganda purposes."

Work in Georgia was nearly finished when an early frost turned the green woods the crew had been using to simulate the Vietnamese jungle yellow and orange. Consequently, in the middle of November, production on *The Green Berets* moved to Hollywood, where the jungle scenes were completed on a hastily constructed set, adding another $1 million to the cost of the picture.

The edited film bore slight resemblance to the Robin Moore novel. *The Green Berets* essentially became an old-fashioned war movie modeled after John Wayne's earlier successes. Scenes with Vera Miles, who played Duke's wife in the uncut version, ended up on the editing room's floor. What remained was a glorification of American soldiers under fire, with less mercy shown the Vietcong than Wayne's Westerns conferred on the Apache and Comanche. Full of platitudes, the film's attitude toward American involvement in the controversial war approximated that of a lynch mob that executes first and seeks justification afterwards.

The Green Berets has the dubious distinction of being the only major prowar picture made in Hollywood during the 1960s. When the movie opened at the Rivoli Theater in Manhattan on June 19, 1968, critics blasted it. Renata Adler said in her review for the *New York Times*: "*The Green Berets* is a film so unspeakable, so stupid, so rotten and false in every detail that it passes through being fun, through being funny, through being camp, through everything and becomes an invitation to grieve, not for our soldiers or for Vietnam . . . but for what has happened to the fantasy-making apparatus in this country. . . . It is vile and insane. On top of that, it is dull."

Other judgments were almost as harsh. The *New Yorker* called it "a film best handled from a distance and with a pair of tongs." *Commonweal* branded *The Green Berets* "a glossy piece of pro-intervention propaganda and intellectually disreputable." Film critic Pauline Kael quipped, "It never Waynes, but it bores." With the antiwar movement gaining momentum in the United States, protesters at some New York theaters where the picture was shown waved the Vietcong flag in front of the screen.

Hate mail poured into the Batjac office, and even some ardent John Wayne fans voiced anger.

Duke seemed unperturbed. "A little clique back in the East has taken great satisfaction in reviewing my politics instead of my picture," he said. "Renata Adler . . . almost foamed at the mouth because I showed a few massacres on the screen. She went into convulsions. She and other critics wouldn't believe that the Vietcong are treacherous—that the dirty sons of bitches are raping, torturing gorillas."

Despite the reproaches, *The Green Berets* proved a success at the box office, grossing $7 million within the first three months. Wayne contended that the carping merely ensured the movie's popularity. "*The Green Berets* would have been successful regardless of what the critics did," he argued, "but it might have taken the public longer to find out about the picture if they hadn't made so much noise about it." In private Duke brooded about the public attack on his film. Underneath the bravado, his self-esteem remained delicate; he hungered for acceptance and for manifestations of love, which were again becoming tentative in his personal life.

Not long after moving to Newport Beach, Duke and Pilar came to live separate lives. As her self-confidence grew, Pilar became dissatisfied with her exclusive role as Mrs. John Wayne. For years she had supported her husband's persona, accompanied him to far-off locations, stayed in the background while hordes of strangers monopolized his attention, and yielded to the demands of a superstar's career. Gradually she realized how shattering life with a famous person can be to an ordinary ego. She began devoting less time to the whims of the man she dearly loved. She wanted a life of her own and proof that Duke valued her opinions. She demanded time alone with her husband, and not always on his terms.

Pilar spent more time playing tennis, started going to out-of-town tournaments, and became interested in Christian Science. Her eventual conversion to that faith meant that she no longer could join her husband for a drink or a smoke. She enjoyed time alone, often reading books on positive thinking. She went to a marriage counselor in an effort to discover why two people who loved one another could cease to communicate.

Duke viewed the change in his wife as a betrayal. He took her refusal to go on trips with him as a lack of interest in their marriage. When she found excuses for not spending as much time as she once had aboard the *Wild Goose*, he considered it disloyalty. Pilar retorted that she had nothing to do while he fished and drank with his friends, but Duke failed to understand her change in attitude. More and more he went on cruises without her; at home their disagreements increased. Duke found fault with his wife's tennis outfits and seemed to pick on her any time she left home. "He doesn't know how to treat a woman," Pilar said. "Do you know that he's never once taken me out to dinner?" Gradually the house on Bayshore Drive fell silent; closed doors became more common. "One day when I was twelve," Aissa wrote, "without any confrontation or visible anger, my mother and father stopped sleeping together."

In public Duke would assert, "What I really like to do when I'm not working is be with my kids. It's wonderful to have a family all over again." He meant that, and he did give his children and grandchildren as much attention as possible. Yet there were so many distractions in his life. John Wayne's world was a fishbowl; his stardom eclipsed everything else, even his family. "A man pays a high price for fame," Duke said. "He surrenders his private life, and often his happiness."

Wayne loved holding little Marisa on his lap like a doll, petting her, and rambling on about how pretty she was. He came back from trips loaded down with teddy bears and stuffed animals for her. He liked to go shopping for gifts to bring to the children and spent hours browsing through mail-order catalogs, marking items for his secretary to order as presents. At Christmas he delighted in the trappings of the season, loved the decorations and gift giving, and welcomed expressions of good cheer. "He would go through the house with a can of spray and spray snow," Pilar remembered, "and you could hardly walk into the house for all the packages. Duke just adored Christmas. He was like a little boy."

But those around him often felt smothered. Duke's insatiable need for love resulted in a tendency for him to possess the people closest to him. His tenderness was accompanied by an urge to control. As his children became older, they found it almost impossible to escape his larger-than-life image and establish an identity of their own. "I could never outdistance John Wayne," Aissa said.

While Wayne's children grew up pampered and privileged, they were never sure whether they were liked for themselves or because they were a superstar's son or daughter. "Making self-discovery even murkier," Aissa said, "my childhood was filled with artifice." In the Wayne household no one said what they thought or felt; they pretended, keeping their emotions hidden. The children were taught responsibility and independence, but they were denied an opportunity to deal with personal problems openly. They were expected to be an all-American family, ready to meet the press on all occasions. "I worked fifty years for my reputation," Duke told Aissa. "I worked damn hard. If you get caught doing something wrong, or if you're with other kids who are doing things wrong, it will go right in the papers. You'll ruin fifty years of my hard work. You'll ruin my name."

The Wayne children felt loved at home, but grew up nervous and fearful. They dared not disobey their father's dictates and adjusted themselves to his schedule. With the approach of adolescence, Aissa became embarrassed by her dad's obstinate views on public issues. Her long-haired schoolmates ridiculed her about her father's conservatism to a point that she disclaimed the name Wayne. Reluctant to join the open rebellion of her peers, she started to sneak around. By the early 1970s, as the recklessness of the counterculture heightened, she became more brazen. "Unknown to the press or my dad," Aissa said, "I experimented with diet pills, marijuana, and getting arrested."

Ethan, on the other hand, did not develop into a man fast enough to suit his father. Even as a child, the boy was not allowed to cry. Duke rode Ethan hard, unleashing his temper on him for slight misdemeanors. Wayne's sheer size proved intimidating to his children, yet he thirsted for their love until there was no room for them to breathe—not even when he was away from home.

Duke's itinerary remained hectic. When he was not making a movie, he was off some place to accept an award, give a speech, or look after assorted business interests. Despite earning $1 million a picture, plus 10 percent of the gross, Duke complained about taxes, his exorbitant medical costs, the expense of owning a boat, his receding cash flow, and the mismanagement of his finances.

In 1968 he left for Gillette, Wyoming, to film *Hellfighters* for Universal. The picture was an uninspired attempt at an action movie suited to Wayne's present age. A fictionalized account of firefighter Red Adair's life, the picture offered more challenges to the special effects department than to Duke, who could have walked through the part in his sleep. The production required oil-well fires and the use of explosives to check damages. Director Andrew McLaglen tried to bring together the ingredients of a classic John Wayne movie, but the results were easily forgotten.

Duke's attitude toward the production was perfunctory; he spent a great deal of his time on the set off in a corner playing chess. When *Hellfighters* was released in December, critics were not kind.

Duke needed fresh material and thought he had found it in Charles Portis's novel *True Grit*. The author's agent had sent copies of the book in galleys to all the major studios. Wayne read it, became fascinated with Portis's central character, Rooster Cogburn, and recognized that the part was an ideal vehicle to pump vitality into his flagging career. "Rooster was the kind of marshal the screen had never seen before," said Duke. "An old sloppy-looking, hard-drinking, disreputable one-eyed son-of-a-gun who'd been around long enough to know that you don't mess around with outlaws, but you use every trick in the book, fair or foul, to bring them to justice."

Wayne offered $300,000 for the film rights to the novel for Batjac, only to discover that producer Hal Wallis had already acquired the rights. Wallis had devoured the book in one night and also found Rooster an engaging character. The next day he called director Henry Hathaway and said, "I've got this book and by five o'clock I have to say whether I'll buy it." Wallis sent the book over to Hathaway, who gave it a quick reading and counseled Wallis to buy the rights posthaste.

The producer assigned Hathaway to direct the picture, and preparation on a script began. Most of the completed screenplay was taken directly from Portis's novel, including its delicious dialogue. Wallis then offered the role of Rooster Cogburn to John Wayne, even though the author argued that Wayne was wrong for the part. But Hathaway agreed with Wallis that no one could play Rooster better than Wayne, and Duke eagerly accepted the part. Here was a chance to poke fun at his own image without destroying the integrity of the character. He grew convinced that *True Grit* was the perfect vehicle to cap his reputation as a man in control of his destiny and have fun in the process.

Duke's Rooster Cogburn emerged as a swaggering braggart, burly, tough, a paladin past his prime, yet with a rude dignity that alternated between warmth and humor. "He feels the same way about life that I do," Wayne said. "He doesn't believe in pampering wrongdoers, which certainly fits into the category of my thinking. He doesn't believe in accommodation. Neither do I." Like many of Wayne's earlier screen heroes, Rooster is an outsider; he doesn't belong to his generation and is a relic of the past. Duke approached the role with as much zest as he had shown for *The Alamo* and *The Green Berets*.

As appealing as Rooster Cogburn is, his nature is made sharper by his relationship with spunky Mattie Ross, a fresh-faced girl who is as stubborn as he is. "The way that girl talked was sensational," said Hathaway. "The idea of a mere girl dominating such a man was irresistible." Hal Wallis first cast Mia Farrow in the part, but Farrow went to England to make a movie with Joe Losey before production on *True Grit* began. While she was there, she mentioned to her costar, Robert Mitchum, that Henry Hathaway would be directing her next picture. Mitchum advised her not to work with the cantankerous Hathaway, and Farrow heeded his warning. She told Wallis that she would prefer to work with Roman Polanski, who had directed her in *Rosemary's Baby* (1968). When the producer ignored her suggestion, Farrow cabled him that she had changed her mind about making his picture. She was replaced by Kim Darby.

Although the story is set in Arkansas, Wallis wanted *True Grit* to be filmed in Colorado to take advantage of the autumn foliage there. Darby arrived on location with a brusque attitude. She was often rude and seemed determined to show that she was not impressed by working with John Wayne. Duke considered her a spoiled brat and quickly realized that they had little in common. "I went over and tried to get some rapport," he said, "but I didn't have much luck. Mr. Hathaway did everything but lay down green bows, that she might walk on them, to try to get some kind of a sympathetic relationship. But it didn't matter. The part was beautiful, and she was beautiful in it."

True Grit was singer Glen Campbell's first movie. Campbell was diligent and eager to learn, but Henry Hathaway grew difficult under pressure and gave the inexperienced actor a hard time. Stuntman Dean Smith said that working with Hathaway was "like having a pet rattler in your pocket," and the cast, with the possible exception of Duke, would probably have agreed. "Henry is a tough, rugged, old coot," said Hal Wallis, "but he's a hard worker and he makes good pictures."

Over the years Wayne had developed an affection for the surly old director and respected his talent. "In *True Grit*," Duke said, "he took what was a fantasy and put it in a background that kept that fantasy alive. There was a kind of beauty that was different from most Westerns. My part was as beautifully written a thing as I've ever read. And the girl's part was the best part I ever read in my whole life. That left poor Glen out there on the limb all by himself, which is too bad because a lot of the critics picked on him."

Charles Portis thought that Rooster Cogburn should have a handlebar mustache, but Duke differed. "Picture yourself as an actor," Wayne said. "You've got a big hat on. That cuts down on part of your expression. Now they put a patch over your left eye. That cuts out more. Now they put a walrus mustache on you. How in the name of God are you going to react so that the audience knows how you're feeling? It was just too much to have all that on. I think the patch did the job."

The script called for Rooster and Mattie to eat corn dodgers, but no one at Paramount knew what corn dodgers looked like or how to make them. The problem was solved in the studio's commissary. "Henry Hathaway was very particular to have everything just right," said Pauline Kessinger, longtime head of Paramount's dining facilities, "and we finally wound up with corn dodgers that pleased him. We made them out of corn meal and rolled them in corn meal and cooked them in deep fat. We had to put red color on some of them because they were supposed to have blood on them." Around six hundred corn dodgers were made in the studio's kitchen and sent by air to Hathaway's location. "They tasted pretty good," Kessinger said.

Most of *True Grit* was filmed around Montrose, Colorado. "We watched the changing of the aspen trees," Dean Smith recalled, "they went from green to yellow to red. That's why we went there. John Wayne was the most professional person I've ever worked with. He'd sit there made up as Rooster, and you'd damn well better know what you were doing. He was just massive in that character, but I loved him."

Duke had difficulty breathing in the mountain altitude, but he remained dauntless. *True Grit* was special for him, and he rose to the challenge. The morning that the gunfight in the meadow was to be shot, the company gathered before dawn. Wayne spent the entire day in the saddle rehearsing and filming the tricky action. It was a cold day, but the sky was clear blue. Red and golden aspen trees bordered the valley, creating an amphitheater of color. There Rooster Cogburn faces the villainous Ned Pepper (played by Robert Duvall), and they have a salty exchange. "I call that bold talk for a one-eyed fat man," yells Pepper. "Fill your hand, you son of a bitch!" Rooster shouts back, as he takes the horse's reins in his teeth, grabs his six-shooter in one hand, and pulls his rifle from its scabbard with the other. Enraged, he drives his spurs into the flanks of his horse and charges toward Pepper and his henchmen. It is the most exhilarating shoot-out Wayne was ever in. Outnumbered, he took the whole pack on and triumphed. "I like those bigger-than-life characters," Dean Smith said. "Duke knew that person. That was him doing all of that, and he was tremendous."

Sixty-one years old at the time, Wayne repeated the ride until he was certain that Hathaway had captured the moment on film in all its glory. Pilar watched from the sidelines, worried about her husband's condition, but Duke would not stop. The picture contained the first profanity to appear in a John Wayne movie, but Duke felt the language was justified in this instance. The script was so rich that to remove one piece of it might weaken the whole. "What a remarkable movie that is," Pilar Wayne said years later.

Hal Wallis knew when he saw the rushes that the picture was a winner. Wayne was extraordinary, and Kim Darby matched him with precision. When *True Grit* opened at Radio City Music Hall on July 3, 1969, the reviews were glowing. "When the John Wayne retrospectives are in full swing," William Wolf wrote in *Cue*, "this will loom as one of his finest movie triumphs." Duke was proud of Rooster Cogburn, and even John Ford praised his performance. The picture proved a huge success at the box office, and there was immediate talk of an Academy Award for its star.

Pilar again tried to talk her husband into retiring, but Duke insisted that they could not afford for him to quit working. Although Wayne hadn't accumulated the fortune that Bob Hope or Gene Autry had, he was comfortably a multimillionaire. But Duke needed to keep busy; he enjoyed the roar of the crowd. Probably no one in Hollywood knew how to handle the public better than John Wayne did. He gave out lithographed signature cards, which he always carried, treated his fans with consideration, yet was skilled at not letting them hassle him. Duke seemed in person much like he was on the screen, with none of the temperament of a star. Offscreen he looked and acted exactly like John Wayne, pleasant and polite, but a real presence. "It was amazing," director Richard Fleischer said, "how people identified with this man. This was true stardom. This was Power with a capital P. Without even being aware of it, he could influence lives."

Wayne had become the unofficial spokesman for provincial America, giving sanction to traditional attitudes in a time of raging conflict. Duke came forward as a vehement foe of gun control and admitted that he always kept several weapons around the house for security purposes. He disdained hippies, long hair on men, and left-wing writers and eggheads who questioned the conservative principles on which the United States had taken root. "The disorders in the schools are caused by immature professors who have encouraged activists," he said. "I don't want somebody like Angela Davis inculcating an enemy doctrine in my kids' minds." Despite his marriages to three Hispanic women, Duke would have no part of multiculturalism. "No, we're not encouraging our children to adopt a dual culture," he said. "They're all-American."

He remained convinced that blacks had a better life in America than anywhere else in the world. "I believe in white supremacy until the blacks are educated to a point of responsibility," Duke declared. "I don't believe in giving authority and positions of leadership and judgments to irresponsible people." When director Martin Ritt's *Sounder* was released in 1972, Wayne wrote the filmmaker that his picture's romantic portrait of Negro sharecroppers during the Great Depression would "do more for the blacks than all the phony liberals and Black Panthers could do in twenty years."

As the Native American movement gained force in the early 1970s, Duke adamantly denied that the continent had been stolen from the Indians. "There were great numbers of people who needed new land, and the Indians were selfishly trying to keep it for themselves," he said. "What happened between their forefathers and our forefathers is so far back—right, wrong, or indifferent—that I don't see why we owe them anything." He asserted that he had always been careful to see that Native Americans lost none of their dignity in the movies he made.

While the Westerns made during the 1970s tended to idealize outlaws and glorify antiestablishment figures, John Wayne's movies continued to center on heroes with allegiance to conventional causes. Wayne's characters were seldom pure heroes, for they had their share of human frailties, but his aging champions remained hardy and laconic, with a fixed concept of right and wrong. Above all, they were fighting for the land they cherished. "This is my country, the country that I love," Duke said with typical innocence. "I can't figure out why we're always pulling ourselves down these days and kowtowing to everyone else."

In October 1969, Wayne began work on *Chisum* for Batjac. The movie tells the story of the Lincoln County War in New Mexico, which made a folk hero of Billy the Kid. Duke plays cattle baron John Chisum, a self-made man who gained the respect of his community. Directed by Andrew McLaglen, the Western has the viewpoint of a picture made twenty years earlier. Wayne portrays the frontier patriarch with conviction, although his face looks puffy and his belt penetrates his girth.

After a cruise on the *Wild Goose* and a brief visit to his ranch near Springerville, Arizona, for the annual cattle sale, Duke went back to Durango, Mexico, to make *The Undefeated* for 20th Century–Fox. Batjac had built a film complex in Durango, and Wayne exercised firm control over the picture, which cast him as a former Civil War officer who vigorously defends private enterprise against bureaucratic intrusion. Andrew McLaglen again directed, and Duke was supported by character actors of his own selection, among them Paul Fix, Harry Carey, Jr., Ben Johnson, John Agar, and Bruce Cabot.

The novel member of the company was Duke's costar, Rock Hudson. A serious professional who had learned his craft by working on routine action features, Hudson got along well with Wayne, despite the younger actor's homosexuality. After dinner on location Hudson played bridge with Duke, Pilar, and a fourth, then spent the rest of the night with a noted player on the Los Angeles Rams football team. "What Rock does in the privacy of his own room is his business," Duke said. "I don't care what they say; I think Rock's a hell of a guy." When he liked someone, Wayne could be unusually tolerant. "It never crossed my mind that Rock was gay," said Pilar. "Duke knew it all the time, but he never told me about it."

In February 1969 Wayne fell, fractured two ribs, and was not able to work for ten days. He also tore some ligaments in his shoulder, which robbed him of complete use of one arm. "It makes me look like an idiot when I'm getting on a horse," he complained. "Goddammit, I hate getting old. You just can't do what you used to anymore." Before filming finished in Durango, he and Pilar had an argument that caused her to return to California early. Tension within the marriage had grown steadily worse. But it was on the set of *The Undefeated* that Wayne learned that he had been nominated for an Academy Award as best actor for his performance in *True Grit*.

The Undefeated was a mediocre film, yet critics seemed to be taking

Duke's work more seriously. "All of a sudden they're saying that he's an actor," Andrew McLaglen said. "Well, he always was." Wayne showed unusual wisdom in his choice of mature roles, and he became a virtuoso at playing strong, older types who stood for integrity and justice. "Duke realized that he was getting old," director Budd Boetticher said, "but he did it with great dignity. He was smart. Very few actors have that kind of ego. I think he handled his career better than anybody in pictures." Many critics who had been hostile to Wayne earlier did an unexpected reversal and said that Duke, like vintage wine, was improving with age. "I'd still like to play romantic leads," Wayne admitted, "but hell, how can I at my age? I long ago gave up roles where I win beautiful women. A man has to know when to stop."

He was making *Rio Lobo* in Old Tucson when time came to present the 1969 Academy Awards. Duke flew to Los Angeles for the event and met Pilar and his children at the Beverly Hills Hotel, where they had reserved a bungalow. Wayne considered himself the underdog in the best actor race, since he faced competition from Richard Burton, Peter O'Toole, Dustin Hoffman, and Jon Voight. When Barbra Streisand called out his name as the winner, Duke jumped up and dashed to the podium. When he turned to speak, tears filled his eyes. "Wow!" he said. "If I'd known what I know now, I'd have put a patch on my eye thirty-five years ago."

His was one of the most popular awards ever given. He received a standing ovation as well as his Oscar. "I've got to admit I wanted that Oscar so bad I could taste it," Wayne later confessed. "The Oscar meant a lot to me—even if it took them forty years to get around to it." He returned to the *Rio Lobo* location the morning after the awards ceremony, having gotten little or no sleep. When he arrived on the set in Old Tucson, the entire cast and crew—even Duke's horse—were wearing patches over their left eyes.

Rio Lobo was Howard Hawks's last picture. "I don't know what to make nowadays except Westerns," the director told Wayne. But Hawks had lost his touch, and the movie's deficiencies are glaring. Neither Wayne nor Hawks was satisfied with it. "That film was all done on a yellow tablet," said stuntman Neil Summers. "Every morning Hawks and Wayne and a woman who took care of Hawks would sit down and write the dialogue out on a yellow pad of paper. It was a mishmash."

Hawks claimed that the studio undercut the picture by refusing to spend the money for another forceful actor besides Wayne. "So I threw out the story and wrote a new one quickly," the director said. Jorge Rivero, who was hired as Duke's costar, was a good-looking former Olympic swimmer from Mexico. "But in order to do anything, he had to think it in Spanish, and then transfer his lines mentally to English," Hawks said. "He was really too slow, and he didn't have any authority at all."

Rio Lobo was Wayne's one hundred and forty-fourth movie. "He doesn't move as much as he did," the picture's director observed, but "he's got a quality that nobody else has." Duke continued to do most of his own stunts and could still deliver a persuasive punch. "He had a fist as big as a ham," stunt performer Hal Needham said. "When he threw it, it looked like it knocked the man's head off." Younger workers looked up to Wayne, learned from him, and tried to emulate his strengths. "He did more to excite me, to generate me to aspire to things, and gave me more enjoyment than anybody in my whole life except for my father," Neil Summers declared. "To be on the Wayne shows was the epitome. . . . Even the most hardened grips to the biggest beer-bellied trunk drivers standing around Old Tucson with tattoos all over them wanted a handshake from this man."

When Duke would arrive on a set, every eye, every head turned toward him. "I've never seen people on crews get pictures with any star as these hardened crew members did with John Wayne," said Summers. "All these old boys with their shirts off or their cigarettes rolled up in their sleeves would pull out a Kodak sometime during the production and get a picture with him." Duke was loud, he would cuss, he would spit tobacco juice, and he could be brutal to people who came into a scene unprepared. But he would stay late and do off-camera dialogue with young actors who had had only a few days' experience, and his crews loved him for it.

Old Tucson offered moviemakers one of the best Western streets available, although planes flying into the city caused a company to lose at least ten minutes every hour. A big part of *Rio Lobo*, including the hijacking of a train, was filmed outside Cuernavaca, Mexico, with Yakima Canutt supervising the second-unit action. Interiors were finished in June 1970 on the old Republic lot, which had been taken over by CBS. While working in the studio, Duke stayed at the nearby Sportsman's Lodge, but without Pilar. He admitted to Dave Grayson, his personal makeup man, that they were having serious marital problems.

Wayne was feeling alone, conscious that age was catching up with him.

During the time he was in Cuernavaca making *Rio Lobo*, Duke learned that his mother's health was failing. He returned to Los Angeles just before her death. She was eighty-one years old and had suffered a long illness. Then, soon after the picture for Hawks wrapped, Duke's brother, Robert, died of lung cancer. The news came as a terrific shock. In spite of their differences, Wayne loved Bobby and had enjoyed their testy relationship. Now his nuclear family was gone, and his marriage crumbling.

Nor was all well at Batjac. Duke's son-in-law, Donald LaCava, left the company in almost a replay of the Bo Roos affair. To recoup the resultant financial losses, Wayne plunged into new projects, resolved to make as many films as he could before work became impossible. He had recently been voted "the Superstar of the Decade," but time was running out. "I'll never retire," he told reporters, "until the public just doesn't want me any more."

Between pictures Duke began spending more time at his 26-Bar Ranch in Arizona, one of his family's most successful business ventures. With a partner, Louis Johnson, Wayne owned about sixty-five sections, including a feedlot that held eighty thousand head of cattle. He also had an irrigated farm near Stanfield, Arizona, where cotton and grain were raised. "I'm about as big a rancher as there is in Arizona," Duke said shortly after the LaCava incident, "so I have outside interests other than my motion picture work. The turning point was the moment I decided to watch what was being done with my money."

Duke developed a passion for his ranch and loved to attend the annual bull sale, which attracted cattle dealers from across the country. But Wayne seldom got on a horse when he visited his ranch. "He had eighty-five horses," Duke's son Michael said, "and not one of them did he ride." When asked why, Wayne generally grinned and replied, "They pay me a lot of money when I get on a horse."

Popular tastes in entertainment were changing. The 1970s witnessed a tremendous decline in Western movies, yet the public's appetite for John Wayne remained hearty. Duke continued to view the traditional Western as part of America's central myth. "They deal in life and sudden death and primitive struggle," he said, "and with basic emotions—love, hate, anger. In other words, they're made of the same raw material Homer used. . . . Westerns are folklore, just the same as the *Iliad* is."

Yet Duke's Westerns no longer had the strong hand of John Ford or Howard Hawks or Henry Hathaway. On his later pictures Wayne tended to be the controlling force; he was quick to step in and tell others how to play scenes, not always with beneficial results. "Duke wanted everybody to be real 'ballsy,'" said Dobe Carey, "and sometimes the character wasn't supposed to be 'ballsy.' Duke didn't have a great deal of tact when he thought a guy wasn't doing a scene right."

Wayne insisted that good Westerns embodied the country's best qualities. Repeated embodiment of frontier virtues had made him a star and later a national symbol. Duke's public looked upon him as a constant in a morass of change. They reveled in Wayne's victories, in his refusal to compromise, and in his ability to suggest sorrow beneath his heroic demeanor.

Duke's appeal to younger generations sustained his reputation, yet in many of his later movies his characters are challenged by children or adolescents. In his most revered roles in the 1970s, Wayne played widowers, mature men estranged or divorced from their wives, and even grandfathers. Some of his most memorable scenes are those between a father and son or those in which a rugged savant passes on wisdom and gives focus to an adolescent boy. Seldom comfortable with domesticity, Duke's heroes dote on family more than marriage and assume a leadership role in coaching young males in their search for manhood. "They talk about a generation gap," said Wayne, "but it's never easy for a young man to talk to an old man unless the old man paves the way." It was a relationship he knew well from his own boyhood.

In *Big Jake* the title character hunts for his grandson (played by Duke's young son Ethan) and gives the boy a lesson in growing up when he discovers him in a dangerous situation. The movie, set in 1909, mirrored Wayne's concern with age; his hero is less self-assured than those he had played earlier. Like Wayne himself, Big Jake is a man who has outlived his era. He stands apart from society, yet protects it with his personal code of honor.

Produced by Batjac, *Big Jake* went before the cameras in October 1970 in Durango, Mexico. The Western reunited Duke with Maureen O'Hara for the last time on the screen, a move calculated to ensure the picture's appeal at the box office. Through the years Wayne and O'Hara had remained close friends, and in many ways they were alike. He admired her frankness; she respected the boldness and consistency of his beliefs. "He'll always stand up and be counted," O'Hara said. "There's no bull about Duke. There's no kowtowing and there never has been. He has security in himself and in whatever he does, and he passes that feeling to everyone around him." O'Hara remembered Wayne on the set surrounded by his children and grandchildren. "They were up on his shoulder, under his arm, and hanging onto his leg," she said. "They were almost permanently attached to him."

Big Jake's director, George Sherman, had made scores of low-budget Westerns and action movies during the 1930s, including several with Wayne, but by the early 1970s he was having trouble finding work. Duke hired him to direct *Big Jake*, although there was never any question about who was in charge. "George Sherman was about the size of a popcorn kernel," Gene Autry declared, "but he was an artist. Like Howard Hawks, he had a taste for give-and-take dialogue and the tongue-in-cheek approach to making films." But Sherman's major talent was getting the job done without wasting time and money. Duke frequently disagreed with the director's approach and took control of the set himself, even to the extent of writing dialogue. But he insisted that younger actors pay attention to Sherman and look at the director while he was talking to them. "Like Henry Hathaway, Wayne would lose his temper," said Dobe Carey. "He'd bawl the hell out of the cameraman, which made things kind of tense."

On *Big Jake* Duke was again surrounded by his own team, most of whom had served their apprenticeship under John Ford. Michael Wayne produced the picture, Patrick Wayne played an important role, Cliff Lyons headed second-unit work, and Chuck Hayward and Chuck Roberson—Good Chuck and Bad Chuck, as Ford called them—were among the stuntmen. Duke even rode his trusty horse Dollar, which he did time and again in his later pictures. "We're all together at the final shoot out," Dobe Carey wrote Ford from Durango.

Big Jake, one of the bloodiest of Wayne's Westerns, cast Harry Carey, Jr., as a scroungy and mean old man. "I didn't think Wayne would go for that," Carey said, "because he always thought of me as a kid. . . . was only about forty-five at the time, and my character was supposed to be around seventy. But I enjoyed working on that picture; it went very well." Critics, however, were less enthusiastic, and the picture did suffer when some of the footage establishing the Wayne-O'Hara relationship was cut. "Originally," the actress said, "Duke looked at a cameo, and the audience got a glimpse of what their marriage had been like. But that was deleted because the movie was too long."

Wayne had tried to do most of his own stunts on *Big Jake*, but he performed them with great effort. "God, Maureen," Duke said to his costar one day, "they get harder every time." "You're telling me," replied O'Hara, who did everything except her own horseback riding. "You're just a pair of old Rolls Royces," the actress's stunt double remarked, "and mileage never hurt a Rolls Royce."

But the years were showing. "I don't know what it was that drove Wayne to work so hard," said Dan Ford, "and make so many of the same bad movie. The *Big Jakes* . . . they're all the same stupid movie. I think he enjoyed the work, as my grandfather did. They just liked the process, whether the pictures were good or bad. They just wanted to be on a set and be involved; there is a camaraderie in it. Making a movie is such a difficult, grinding process, and it feels so good when you get it done. Why do generals go to war? Because that's what they do. John Wayne and my grandfather made movies."

Duke did take a four-month break before he began filming *The Cowboys* in April 1971. That picture marked a departure from the typical Wayne formula. Duke was simply an actor in the movie, under the direction of the talented, New York–trained Mark Rydell. For the first time in years Wayne was isolated from his familiar colleagues, working with a new director, new writers, a new cameraman, and an unfamiliar supporting cast and crew. "I hired only Actors Studio people," said Rydell. "That was necessary . . . because I didn't want him to be comfortable doing his old kind of John Wayne thing. . . . The woman who played his wife, Sarah Cunningham, was a left-wing, blacklisted actress, but he didn't know that." None of Duke's old drinking partners were in the company, but he rose to the challenge. "He *knew* that he was in alien territory," Rydell said. "He watched everybody work. He insisted that he and Gary Cooper had been doing Actors Studio stuff all their lives and nobody had to teach them how to do it . . . , and it's true."

Wayne claimed that he enjoyed every minute of his association with Rydell. "He's bright and awake, although he's never made a Western before," Duke said. "He's surrounded himself with men who have done them and men who know their technical jobs." Wayne also worked agreeably with the eleven boys in the cast and spoke admiringly of their conduct and talent. "He's just like John Wayne on the screen," said thirteen-year-old Mike Pyeatt, who played a role in the picture. "He doesn't do anything different. And when he finds out you're having trouble, he gets in there and helps you."

In *The Cowboys,* Duke is an elderly rancher whose hired hands abandon him right before they are to drive fifteen hundred head of cattle to market. In desperation the old man enlists the aid of a passel of young boys, whom he fathers and guides to manhood. When the rancher is killed, the youngsters draw upon his discipline to wreak havoc on the outlaw band responsible for his death. "He takes these kids," Duke said of his role, "and by their association with him, they are better able to face the world."

To attract contemporary audiences, *The Cowboys* includes a Jewish cowboy and a black cook among its characters. Wayne's presence enlarged the Western's budget to $6 million, a sizable amount at that time for a movie made within the United States. Most of the picture was shot on the San Cristobal Ranch near Santa Fe, New Mexico, where work was dusty and arduous.

Duke hurt his shoulder during the production and had difficulty protecting it. "I am in such misery," he said. "Yesterday . . . I had to roll into a scene and be drug out by a rope." In filming the scene, the crew got excited, forgot about his injured shoulder, and gave the rope a spirited yank. "They just drove my shoulder into the ground!" Wayne said. He had so little strength left in his arm after that that he could barely control his horse.

Dan Ford went with his grandfather to visit Duke on the *Cowboys* location. Much to their surprise they found him living in a house with two hippie girls he had seen hitchhiking on his drive to New Mexico. "Wayne was not known for being a particularly tolerant man," the director's grandson said, "but he hired these two good-looking hippie girls to take care of the house and cook for him. Two hippie girls with a satchel full of pot! They were great, and they were funny, and he enjoyed them."

The Cowboys opened at Radio City Music Hall in January 1972, but it was moved to a smaller theater before the end of its appointed run because of poor attendance. Reviews, however, were favorable. "In *The Cowboys,*" Rex Reed wrote in the New York *Daily News,* "all the forces that have made [John Wayne] a dominant personality as well as a major screen presence seem to combine in an unusual way, providing him with the best role of his career. Old Dusty Britches can act."

By the early 1970s John Wayne was the best-known movie star in the world. *Photoplay* readers voted him the most popular male actor of 1971, and the *Motion Picture Herald* named him that year's top box-office personality. More than Hollywood's most durable moneymaker, Duke had become a national monument. Whether his pictures were good or bad, Wayne's roles were consistent with his image. "I look for an interesting character," he said. "I have a businessman's approach to motion pictures. My output is two pictures a year. One of them I might do because I think it'll be commercially successful, and the other one I might do because I really want to play that part." His number one rule about acting was that his role must be played truthfully. "I have to identify with something in the character," he said. "A good actor can play all kinds of parts. But in any dramatic situation I react just as I would in real life. So any roles have to be tailored to fit me. . . . The big tough boy on the side of right—that's me. Simple themes. Save me from the nuances. I stay away from psychoanalyst's couch scenes."

Duke wanted people to know what they were getting when they bought tickets to a John Wayne movie. He wanted them to leave the theater comfortable and satisfied. While other filmmakers of the decade were spicing their pictures with explicit sex and graphic violence, Wayne continued to make the old-fashioned features that had earned him his singular reputation. "He brings to each new movie," future director Peter Bogdanovich observed, "a resonance and a sense of the past."

Virile man though he was, Duke's allure was never primarily sexual, and the older he got, the more that aspect of his appeal lessened. "He was powerful," Budd Boetticher said. "I think that's why he had this great image. It was a father image, it was a big brother image, it was a tough guy. Young women felt that he was powerful enough to take care of them." Yet his biggest audience remained men, some of whom went to John Wayne movies from habit.

For many of his fans Wayne had become an old friend, and they often approached him in public as such. On one occasion in Mexico an inebriated American tourist staggered over to Duke and with a telltale slur said, "I know who you are." Duke thought, Here we go again, but said, "You do?" The man said, "Yeah, you're Tom White, the bank manager from my hometown." Wayne shook his head. "Wait a minute." the man said. "You're Matthew Green, who runs the local hotel." Wayne smiled and said, "Wrong again." The man came up with a third try, and Wayne again shook his head. "Well then," the drunk said, "you have to be somebody else," and he walked off. Duke loved to tell the story.

In the summer of 1971 Duke appeared in *The American West of John Ford*, a documentary that Dan Ford produced for television. "Because I was in Monument Valley and we were making a Western, I finally felt that I had joined the human race," the legendary director's grandson remarked. John Ford himself was there, and Wayne flew into the landing strip below Goulding's lodge in his private twin-engine prop plane. Dan Ford drove down to pick his star up, thrilled at the chance to establish himself in his grandfather's profession. When Wayne came down the steps of the plane, young Ford rushed to greet him. "Duke, this is just the greatest moment of my life," he said. "I'm really just so glad to be with you in Monument Valley." "Yeah," Wayne said, unzipping his fly, "it's really good to see you, kid," and he began to urinate. "He pissed on my foot, he pissed on the tire," Dan Ford recalled. "He'd been in that little plane, bumping across clouds, and he had to take a leak. So he did—all over my foot!"

Despite his immense popularity, Duke remained a modest, unassuming man who never lost his common touch. "I have no time for pseudo-sophisticates," Wayne said. The older he got, the more he detested flashiness. "Not too far below the surface," Bert Minshall, the skipper of the *Wild Goose* said, "was the little boy waiting to leap out." Sometimes the simplest things gave Duke great delight. Gadgets and novelties fascinated him, and he was especially fond of flashlights, which he bought in abundance for the house, the family's cars, and his boat.

His closest friend in Newport Beach was Porsche dealer Chick Iverson, but he also saw a great deal of Claire Trevor Bren and her husband. Duke and Milton Bren, a small, caustic yachtsman who took pleasure in poking fun at Wayne, shared many interests, and Wayne enjoyed the teasing. The Brens lived only three minutes away from Bayshore, and Duke frequently played chess with their young son. When the boy was killed, Wayne wrote Claire Trevor a letter that she treasured. "He was a man of deep feelings," the actress said, "much deeper than one would expect of John Wayne."

Duke also liked to visit Maureen O'Hara and her husband, Charles Blair, at their home in the Virgin Islands. Wayne and Blair spent hours playing chess and flying in a private plane to surrounding islands. Blair was a pioneer in aviation and Wayne was drawn to strong, spirited types whom he did not intimidate and who liked him for himself. On one trip, the two men flew in a four-engine seaplane to Puerto Rico without an assistant pilot. When they landed, the Federal Aviation Administration was there to meet them, demanding to know why a second pilot was not aboard. "You know John Wayne," Blair offered in explanation, "and you've seen *The High and the Mighty*." At that, the FAA representatives backed down and let the two men take off, convinced that if John Wayne was aboard, all was well.

Underneath the glitter and despite all the activity, Duke was a lonely person. He read thousands of books during his later life, four newspapers a day when he wasn't busy with a movie, and endless magazines and catalogs. As he grew older and became less active physically, he battled weight. Between pictures Duke ballooned up to 250 or 260 pounds. For breakfast he wanted a huge New York steak—rare—and he freely admitted that he ate more than he should. Pilar, on the other hand, was relentless about keeping herself trim. As their estrangement widened, Duke maintained the facade of domestic bliss—in part for his public, in part for self-esteem. "Twilight years?" he thundered. "If this is twilight, then hell, give me more."

Those who knew him best detected a hollow note. Wayne grew depressed about his country's failure in Vietnam, angry over the rise of militant feminism, and disturbed by the violence perpetrated by the nation's disaffected. He actively campaigned for Richard Nixon's second election, became an early champion of Ronald Reagan's rising political star, and spoke out on patriotism at every opportunity. In July 1971 the Marine Corps League named John Wayne as the man who best exemplified the word "American." After he won the Oscar, many who despised Duke's political convictions admitted their admiration for the courageous manner in which he expressed his opinions.

Yet despite the awards, Wayne felt that he was unpopular within the film industry, since his conservative philosophy was at odds with prevailing attitudes. He disliked what had happened in Hollywood. He deplored the use of profanity in pictures, took a strong stand against nudity, and hated the contemporary trend toward antiheroes, whom he dismissed as "psychotic weaklings." Regardless of his celebrity, Wayne had become an anachronism in the movie business. "I haven't seen many films lately that appeal to me," he said. "They're so corrupt, or the approach is so cheap that I walk out after the first reel." He abhorred *Midnight Cowboy* (1969), *Easy Rider* (1969), and *Myra Breckinridge* (1970) and turned down an offer to play the ruthless title role in *Dirty Harry* (1971), which Clint Eastwood undertook with tremendous success. "I've been in pictures all my life," Duke said, "and I deplore the garbage now being flashed on the screen."

By the 1970s the fundamental structure of the motion picture industry had changed. Most of the old giants were gone, and Duke disliked or mistrusted the new breed. "The men who control the big studios today are stock manipulators and bankers," he said. "They know nothing about our business. They're in it for the buck. . . . Some of these guys remind me of high-class whores." He complained about the lack of integrity within the industry, the misrepresentation, the lying, and the out-and-out fraud. "Whenever I signed a contract for five years or for a certain amount of money," he said, "I've always lived up to it." He insisted that movies should still be family entertainment and should exert a positive influence on public morals. "Sex is not a spectator sport," he said.

Increasingly Duke came to feel that there was no place for him in the modern world. He was uncomfortable in a structured society, unwilling to compromise his stalwart individualism. "The last vestiges of heroics," Frank Capra said of motion pictures in the early 1970s, "are the gaspings of tired, bloated, aged John Wayne." Predictable and simplistic though Duke's movies were, they embodied his beliefs and fulfilled his fans' expectations. "The producers don't want me to play any roles but the one people seem to like," Wayne said, "and I wouldn't want to do anything different anyway."

By producing his own pictures Duke could oversee the ingredients he felt made for a successful recipe and escape the confinement of an industry he no longer fully understood. *The Train Robbers*, which went before the cameras in early 1972, was Batjac's second consecutive Western released through Warner Bros. The picture was written and directed by Burt Kennedy and produced by Michael Wayne. What resulted was an undemanding divertissement sure to please Duke's fans. "It was John Wayne in all his glory," Kennedy said, "but I didn't get the casting I wanted. I ended up with about three actors that I didn't want, and it hurt the picture. If you've got a bunch of scenes that require talk, you'd better have good actors or the picture can go right down the toilet." But Kennedy was working for Batjac, and it was John Wayne who dictated terms.

The Train Robbers was filmed in Durango and cast Ann-Margret as the female lead. "Duke was still a strong, rugged, formidable man, larger-than-life and incredibly personal," the actress said. "He was a big teddy bear, and we got along famously. Duke gave me the confidence I lacked." Ann-Margret had been frightened of horses since childhood. For three weeks before shooting began on the picture, she had taken riding lessons from stuntman Chuck Hayward, an expert horseman, and with Duke's reassurance she overcame her fear. Actor and actress developed an amiable relationship, but when Ann-Margret's character lets Duke's know that she is attracted to him, Wayne discourages her by saying, "I've got a saddle older than you are." The implication is that Duke still exudes romantic appeal but is sensible enough not to act on it with a woman a fraction of his age.

Duke broke two ribs a few days before shooting on *The Train Robbers* began. The fractures caused him excruciating pain. He even had trouble sleeping. Perfectionist that he was, Wayne wanted his action scenes to look believable. "He was forever getting scratched, bruised, or otherwise battered during a film," Pilar said. But his movement was restricted during the making of *The Train Robbers*, so that the movie ended up stressing characterization more than action. To calm his nerves on the set, Duke allowed himself two cigarettes a day despite doctors' warnings and over his wife's protests.

During the film's production Wayne's friend Ben Johnson was nominated for an Academy Award for his supporting role in *The Last Picture Show*. Johnson was working with Duke in Durango when time came for the awards ceremony in April. Wayne loaned the actor his private plane, wished him luck, and sent him to Los Angeles. Johnson returned with the Oscar in hand, and Wayne's faith in unaffected acting was again confirmed.

Although Duke denied that he simply played himself in pictures, he saw no reason to spend days discussing the motivation behind a part. "I read what's in the script and then I go out there and deliver my lines," he said. "There's no way of being natural on the screen. . . . You have to act natural because you have to keep the scene going and still keep your own personality in it. But if you were really natural, your scene would drop clear off the deck!" Duke had developed the ability to perform as spontaneously on the fifth take as he had on the first. He had an intuitive sense of where the camera was and knew how to place himself for maximum effect. "I've always felt that if a scene is handled with simplicity—and I don't mean simple—it'll be good," he maintained. "The best script to have is a script where you're a bystander, where you're reacting to what other people are doing."

A quick study, Duke wanted to get a scene worth printing within the first three takes, unless it was a complicated setup involving several actors. His concentration was exemplary, and he could study himself on the screen and dissect his own performance. He knew instantly when he had been good and where he had gone wrong. "I learned that if *you* cry, the audience won't," he said. "A man can cry for his horse, for his dog, for another man, but he cannot cry for a woman. It's a strange thing. Where he's supposed to be boss, with his child or wife, he'd better hold back his tears and let *them* cry."

Wayne understood that a picture had slim chance of becoming better than its script. He was aware from the outset that *Cahill, United States Marshal*, shot in late 1972, lacked the requisites for a distinguished movie. "It just wasn't a well-done picture," Duke admitted. "It needed better writing. It needed a little better care in the making." Wayne himself was so debilitated by emphysema that he had to use a stepladder to mount his horse. Visitors to the set were shocked at the gyrations necessary to keep the ladder out of the eye of the camera. Produced for Batjac by Michael Wayne and directed by Andrew McLaglen, *Cahill, United States Marshal* was a tedious film to make and followed a stale formula.

The picture was shot in Durango, where Duke rented a house for himself and Michael. Pilar did not join them, and her absence set off a rash of gossip in Hollywood. Wayne appeared to be jovial, often playing jokes on crew members he loved and respected. But *Cahill* seemed a lost cause, and privately Duke grieved. "He was not as peppy as earlier," actress Marie Windsor declared, "but he was down to earth and wanted everything done right." Windsor found Duke a consummate stylist, considerate on the set and off. As the holiday season approached, Wayne gave the actress a day off and had his driver take her into town to do some Christmas shopping.

During the making of *Cahill* the company received word that John Ford was dying of cancer in Palm Desert. Duke flew to California to see his mentor one last time and came away sad and depressed. Ford looked gaunt and unwashed, and Wayne knew that the master filmmaker had reached the end. Duke returned to Durango and a movie he knew was in trouble. Harry Carey, Jr., who played a supporting role in *Cahill*, met him and inquired about Ford's condition. "He's down there in that goddamned Palm Desert dying, Dobe," Wayne replied. "And we need him. We need him real bad!"

When Ford died on August 31, 1972, Duke was devastated. He said it was like losing his father again. "It's the end of a goddamn era," Wayne said. "No one's ever been able to equal him. No one ever will." Duke felt alone and vulnerable. Ford's death was another gloomy reminder of his own mortality. Suddenly the indomitable John Wayne became plagued with doubts—about his industry, about his relationships, about life. "I haven't quite gotten over the feeling," he told reporters, "that I'm pretty much living on borrowed time."

Return of the Big C

Wayne was in Seattle, Washington, in 1973 making *McQ* when Warner Bros. held the premiere of *Cahill, United States Marshal* in the city to take advantage of the star's presence there. The event was marred by the critics' cool reception of the picture and by a group of Native American protesters who gathered outside the theater, claiming that *Cahill* was unfair to Indians.

By then, even John Wayne wondered if perhaps the traditional Western movie had run its course. With *McQ* Batjac tried to capitalize on the recent success of *Dirty Harry* and a spate of urban detective films by casting Wayne for the first time as a police investigator. "I felt like a bit of change," said Duke, "but I had to stick to action movies, of course, and the tough cop thriller is where a lot of action is these days." In truth he wasn't ecstatic about making *McQ* and felt that there was too much stilted dialogue and too many loose ends in the script. Wayne worked on a short fuse early in the production, unhappy about what he knew was a hackneyed story, coupled with the knowledge that his marriage was falling apart.

Duke lived aboard the *Wild Goose* during the making of *McQ* and spent weekends sailing around the nearby islands. As the pressures of filming multiplied, he became more and more dispirited. He was working with a strong new director, John Sturges, and was unfamiliar with most of the cast and crew. "Wayne didn't try to take over," said Julie Adams, who played Duke's former wife in the picture. "He appeared to have a great deal of respect for John Sturges, and they seemed to get along well. Since I played his ex-wife, my biggest acting problem was to erase John Wayne, this figure of such importance and power, [and think of him as] this big guy that I used to be married to. But Wayne was charming and made it all very easy."

Since Duke went back to his boat at the Seattle Yacht Club every evening, the company had little opportunity to socialize with him after working hours. "He was extremely un-iconish in his manner," Adams recalled. "He told a couple of self-deprecating jokes and didn't seem to be self-conscious at all. I only worked with him one day, but he didn't seem to be acting at all, just there. It was a bit of an uncomfortable scene. There was not a lot of lines, so we were just sort of playing with awkward pauses. He seemed to enjoy it that way. I think John Wayne became more and more John Wayne as the years went by. It's as though this particular image became more highly polished, which is probably one reason that he became this strong figure to America, because people didn't have to think of him as an actor. I think he had mastered that art of portraying his inner self as well as any screen actor ever has."

Midway through the making of *McQ*, Pilar and Marisa arrived in Seattle. Duke was delighted to see his wife and angry when he discovered that she did not plan to stay. Marisa remained on location with her father for several days while Pilar went to Carmel, California, to play in a tennis tournament. When that was over, Marisa rejoined her mother. As filming on the picture progressed, Duke became friendly with his new secretary, Pat Stacy, whom he had hired when Mary St. John retired. "Our relationship [became] considerably more informal than it had been in Newport," said Stacy. "There [was] a lot more time for jokes and chats, and for the first time, we [began] to feel really comfortable with each other."

By the time the company moved to Ocean Shores, Washington, for additional shooting, Duke appeared to be relaxed. He ate dinner with members of the cast and crew, invited some of the fellows over for card games, and occasionally stayed up too late and drank too much. "It was not always easy to get to the set the next morning," Stacy wrote, "but we always did." Observers noticed that Wayne and Pat Stacy grew more intimate as work on the picture progressed.

Principal photography on *McQ* ended in Seattle, but Wayne was aware that the movie was mediocre. Upon its release in February 1974, audiences found seeing John Wayne in a contemporary urban setting anachronistic. As Duke anticipated, critics roasted the film. "Somehow or another we lost our contact," he said. "Everybody lost their contacts with each other, and it became a series of action shots rather than a motion picture." The movie's best scene pairs Duke in an unlikely combination with Broadway actress Colleen Dewhurst. "That's about the only scene that had a chance to play," Wayne said. "The rest of it was pretty pedestrian." The sequence with Dewhurst allowed Duke to show sensitivity yet still maintain a strong macho image. His later prototype relies less on phony masculine struts and more on a quiet resolve that proves itself in action.

After *True Grit,* Duke's image was so fixed in the American consciousness that even a succession of dull pictures could not tarnish it. With advancing age came a barrage of honors and awards. The University of
Southern California had awarded Wayne an honorary doctorate of fine
arts degree in 1968, and five years later he was Grand Marshal of the Rose
Bowl Parade. In December 1973 Duke went to New York to accept an
award from the National Football Hall of Fame. "He would have been a
successful guy in any business," Dan Ford maintained, "because he was a
people person. He was good with crowds, and he liked to be around people. He enjoyed the whole promotional aspect of being a celebrity. He
seemed to revel in it. If he'd gone into the car business, he would have
wound up owning five dealerships, because he was a charismatic guy who
could attract able people around him."

But when Duke returned home from New York on December 6, 1973,
he found Pilar and her belongings gone. The tension between them had
become agony for both, and the stress had begun to affect their children.
"I felt so guilty about leaving," Pilar wrote, "knowing how deeply I'd disappointed him, shattering his expectations of a serene and peaceful old
age. Yet I couldn't live with the angry, unyielding man he'd become." She
moved into a condominium five miles away, in the exclusive Big Canyon
section of Newport. Their children began dividing their time between the
two households. "Duke would have given the children and me anything
money could buy," Pilar said. "What he couldn't grant us was some degree of independence."

The couple's parting was dignified, quiet, and amicable. Hollywood
reporters voiced surprise when the Waynes' nineteen-year-old marriage
resulted in separation, but close friends had seen the split coming for
months. Pilar insisted that she still loved Duke, and they became friendlier once she moved out. Yet Wayne was deeply wounded. "He never cried
in front of me until their marriage was crumbling," Aissa said. "His health
was slipping away, and my father knew there was no time left for striking
poses."

In public Duke remained the steadfast chauvinist and master of his
emotions. "She can have a divorce anytime she wants one," he told the
press. "There will be no more marriages for me." When asked how he had
managed not to learn more than a few words of Spanish, having married
three Hispanic women, Duke replied without apology, "I guess I never

listened to what they were saying." But his self-assurance had become a masquerade.

Suddenly the nation's hero faced old age with everything success could buy and a shattered personal life. Aside from his movie work, he owned oil wells, apartment houses, hotels, taxi franchises, two ranches, mining interests, and investments in a variety of other businesses. He had made a phenomenal amount of money, but he spent it recklessly. "I watched him lose $11,000 on one roll of the dice in Vegas one night," said Happy Shahan. In many respects Duke was still a naive man, and he often committed huge amounts of his earnings, with catastrophic results, to ventures that friends fancied. Work could eradicate most financial losses, but the feeling of loneliness and abandonment that accompanied Pilar's departure was permanent. While they continued to see each other and for a while talked of reconciliation, Pilar knew that to live with Duke meant doing so on his terms. "At sixty-seven he was too old to change," she said. "Our separation had changed me irrevocably. I'd finally become my own person."

The final break came during the summer of 1974, while Wayne was filming *Brannigan* in England. Pilar and the children visited him in London, but their visit was cut short when Pilar discovered that Duke had gone to Paris for a weekend with Pat Stacy. "My mother left in a rage," Aissa recalled, "certain her husband had started romancing his thirty-two-year-old secretary."

Pilar described a more poignant scene. She and Duke had shared a bedroom during her brief visit to London, she claimed, and one night, after the children were asleep, they talked about their future. Eventually Duke took his wife's hand and said with a grieved expression, "Pilar, you know I love you very much. But there's something you have to know. I'm old and tired. I don't feel well, and I'm taking a lot of medication. I just can't be a real husband to you any more." Pilar sensed his pain. "We both have to face it," he said. "Our marriage is over."

They never divorced, and each continued to speak highly of the other. Pilar opened the Fernleaf Cafe and an interior decorating business in Newport. Duke occasionally stopped by her restaurant for a chat and frequently called about the children, but his life was empty. "I'd never seen him so torn up, nor so lonely," Aissa declared.

Duke continued to work hard, but picture offers came less often and with far less satisfaction. In *Brannigan* he played a tough Chicago cop ordered to England to retrieve a fugitive racketeer. "It's the same old Western plot brought up to date," Wayne said. His son Michael served as executive producer and Douglas Hickox directed. Critics viewed the film with minimum enthusiasm, much as Duke had expected. "*Brannigan* is an okay John Wayne actioner," *Variety* reported.

The Watergate scandal broke during the summer Wayne spent in England, yet Duke never vacillated in his support of Richard Nixon. "The President is too great a man to be mixed up in anything like Watergate," he said. In the stormy weeks that followed, Duke blamed a hostile press for smearing Nixon's reputation and placed the guilt on those around the chief executive. It was an unhappy time in the country's history and it resonated in Wayne's own despondency.

Duke spent most of his holidays with friends aboard the *Wild Goose*, making weekend trips to Catalina and longer excursions to Mexico and the Pacific Northwest. He still loved to drink and gamble and stay up late, but now his health forced him to be more moderate. His relationship with Pat Stacy deepened, as the attractive brunette became his companion and lover as well as a secretary. Stacy claimed that they first had sex aboard the *Wild Goose* in June 1973, while Wayne was on location for *McQ*. From then on she customarily shared his stateroom when he was on his yacht, and they developed an earnest affection for one another. "Certainly she was company for Duke," Bert Minshall, the skipper of the *Wild Goose* wrote, "someone who would help lessen the loneliness I know he felt after his separation from Pilar."

Stacy later insisted that Wayne made no secret of their affair, even demonstrating his love for her in front of his children. "In truth, he was standoffish toward Pat when I was around," wrote Aissa, who argued that Stacy's book exaggerated the romance with her father. "An aging Hollywood star with a younger woman," Wayne's daughter contended, "was good for his image."

Duke could not bear to be alone, and Stacy was there and willing to fill the void in his personal life. They spent many hours together in deep conversation, discussing the dearth of good scripts that came his way, Duke's concerns over money and his children's future, and his precarious health. With Stacy he could forget his toupee and be himself. "I do know she was later the target of Duke's frustrations when he was sick and an outlet for his pain," wrote Minshall. "She took it, and I suppose she genuinely loved him in spite of it."

In September 1974 Stacy accompanied Wayne to Oregon, where he was slated to film *Rooster Cogburn* opposite Katharine Hepburn. By then rumors of a romance between Duke and Pat Stacy had made the Hollywood gossip columns, and his attitude toward his young secretary on location seemed to substantiate the reports.

Rooster Cogburn had been concocted as a commercial postscript to *True Grit*, and the film sparked a great deal of publicity since it paired Wayne and Hepburn for the first time. The two legends had not met until Hepburn introduced herself to Wayne in Piccadilly Circus while he was in London making *Brannigan* and she was there filming *Love among the Ruins*. The initial draft of *Rooster Cogburn* had been put together by producer Hal Wallis and his wife, actress Martha Hyer, but neither thought that they had fashioned a shootable script. Later Charles Portis, the creator of the Cogburn character, polished their work, and Wayne and Hepburn rewrote much of their dialogue themselves. When Wallis and Duke met for a script conference in Newport Beach, both were conscious of the story's deficiencies, but they felt those limitations could be offset by spirited performances. Wayne and Wallis agreed that Henry Hathaway should direct the sequel, but Hathaway turned down the project. "When I read the script, I thought the combination of Hepburn and Wayne would be absolutely sensational," the director said. "But the script was ridiculous."

Wallis next approached Richard Fleischer, who agreed to direct the Western mainly because of the potential of the Wayne-Hepburn combination. Duke, however, had directorial approval, and he refused to sanction Fleischer. "Hal Wallis couldn't understand it," said Fleischer. "He tried over and over to get him to change his mind. Wayne wouldn't budge." The rejected filmmaker sensed that Duke still harbored a grudge over Fleischer's turning down an offer to direct *North to Alaska* fourteen years before. "I had broken an unwritten law," Fleischer declared. "No varmint turns down a John Wayne picture. When you do that, pard, you're hurtin' his feelin's and woundin' his pride. And there's no forgivin' that." Fleischer learned that Wayne was not a person one wanted to offend. "He could be petty, small, and mean," the director said.

Ultimately, *Rooster Cogburn* was placed in the hands of Stuart Millar, who had directed only one other film. Wayne did not get along with Millar, and he and Hepburn essentially directed themselves. More than once Duke complained that the inexperienced Millar overshot scenes. "Goddammit," Wayne thundered, "we can say these lines just so many times before they stop making sense." The situation degenerated to a point that Wallis threatened to replace Millar, but Wayne said no. Instead, Duke persisted in referring to the director as a "six-foot-six, no-talent son of a bitch." Irritable and feeling his age, Wayne was determined to have things his way. "To be fair," Pat Stacy said, "Duke never got along with any of his directors during the time I was with him."

Since Hepburn and Wayne were both perfectionists, they respected one another's work and developed a personal rapport that nourished the characters they played. Hepburn found Duke a confident man of enormous charisma. "He's quick," she said; "he's sensitive. He knows all the techniques. I think he's an awfully good actor and a terribly funny man." The two enjoyed many laughs on the set, and Hepburn was struck by Duke's naturalness and the reality he brought to his performance. "He has an extraordinary gift," the actress observed, "a very subtle capacity to think and express and caress the camera . . . with no apparent effort."

Although Hepburn had made *The Sea of Grass* in 1947, in which she portrayed a rancher's wife, *Rooster Cogburn* was her first real Western. In the movie she played Eula Goodnight, the spinster daughter of a preacher ministering to a remote village of Indians. In effect, the film juxtaposed Wayne's role in *True Grit* with elements of Hepburn's character in *The African Queen* (1951). While Duke tended to ad-lib during takes, Hepburn delivered the lines agreed upon during rehearsals. When he overacted, she calmly informed him, "You're tippin' your mitt, old boy." He became fascinated with her honesty. At lunch one day Hepburn remarked, "I love working with Duke, but he tells everyone what to do, bosses everyone around, and I'm the one who usually gets to do that. Now I don't get to."

Photography on *Rooster Cogburn* began in Grants Pass, Oregon, where the company stayed in a small motel. The surrounding scenery was magnificent, the fall weather perfect. The picture's river footage was filmed on the Rogue, with Wayne and Hepburn refusing to use doubles in shots of a raft going through the rapids. In mid-October the location shifted to a forest outside Bend, Oregon; then the company finished their work near the Sunriver Ranch Resort.

On a day off, Duke gave golf lessons to his seven-year-old daughter at

Sunriver. As he stood behind her, demonstrating a swing, Marisa struck him under the eye with the end of her club. An ugly bruise developed, which on another picture might have delayed the shooting schedule. "It's just your luck," Wayne told Hal Wallis. "The eye she hit is the one with the patch on it!"

Toward the end of production Duke gave a birthday party for Wallis in the house the producer had rented for him. Food was flown in, and champagne flowed freely. As the guests relaxed, Hepburn began to tease Duke. "I'm glad I didn't know you with two lungs," she said. "You really must have been a bastard. Losing a hip has mellowed me—but *you*!" Wayne understood that the gibes were her way of expressing affection, and with a knowing grin he fired back, "I can't bully you, because I promised Jack Ford I'd be nice to you."

Wayne worked on the picture without serious breathing problems until the last night. On Halloween, Wallis gave a wrap party, and the bitter cold and altitude finally got the best of Duke. "During the evening," Wallis remembered, "he started wheezing and gasped, 'I can't breathe.' We rushed oxygen to him and he rallied." But Duke had trouble sleeping in Oregon, was upset that his medication interfered with his drinking, and often seemed cross. Mainly he was unhappy about advancing age and the breakup with Pilar.

Hepburn referred to herself as "Miss Kissinger" and got along with her costar despite his impatience. Underneath his image, she found him an uncomplicated man, "simple in his enjoyment of his own success." To Hepburn, Duke possessed a childlike, naive quality that resulted in openness. His reactionary politics, she felt, were an outgrowth of his own experience. "He was surrounded in his early years in the motion picture business by people like himself," the actress wrote. "Self-made. Hardworking. Independent. Of the style of man who blazed the trails across our country. Reached out into the unknown. People who were willing to live or die entirely on their own independent judgment."

Wayne's inflexible views had become so much a part of him that to understand the man was to accept his conservatism. Duke's candor won wide respect, even among those who disagreed with his principles. When Wayne went to Massachusetts early in 1974 to receive the Harvard *Lampoon*'s "Brass Balls Award," students there were ready to crucify him as "the biggest fraud in history." The crowd outside the auditorium where he spoke had to be held back by police. Duke rode into Harvard Square atop a thirteen-ton tank, manned by members of the Fifth Armored Cavalry. Some students, dressed as cowboys, fired toy guns at him, while others threw snowballs. But more were amused by the mockery of his arrival.

Inside the theater, Wayne announced that he was happy to be invited to "the pseudo-intellectual swamps of Harvard Square" and seemed relaxed as he began to answer questions from the floor. "Where did you get that phony toupee?" one student asked. "It's not phony," Duke answered. "It's real hair. Of course, it's not mine, but it's real." The assemblage laughed in spite of themselves. "What are your views on women's lib?" another student wanted to know. Said Duke, "I think they have a right to work anyplace they want to . . . as long as they have dinner on the table when you come home." Hoots joined applause as he began to win over his audience by sheer force of personality.

"They were such refreshing young men, goddammit, and they appreciated the fact that I had accepted their humor," Wayne later maintained. "I had the best damn time. . . . They thought I was a horse's ass, but when they saw I was as honest about what I thought as they were about their beliefs, they came around. . . . We stayed up all night drinking. I guess I was the father they never had."

As the controversy over America's involvement in Vietnam diminished during the mid-1970s, admiration for the strength of John Wayne's convictions came more frequently from the media, and even liberals seemed to embrace him as the last of the frontier heroes. Duke liked to think of himself as an independent in politics, and although he remained an ardent supporter of Ronald Reagan, he backed Jimmy Carter's treaty to turn the Panama Canal over to Panama in 1977, which was viewed as a liberal measure, even among some Democrats. For the first time in his life Wayne received hate mail from the right wing. "Man, I sure caught hell on that one," he claimed. "The new treaties modernize an outmoded relationship with a friendly and hospitable country."

Socially and politically Wayne appeared to be mellowing. He claimed to understand the current youth, since he had gone through some of the same experiences they were going through. "The average young man or woman or child of today is quite a bit ahead of our generation because of the technology and improved communications which have made them so much more knowledgeable," he said. "I think many of them admire me because I haven't been afraid to say that I drink a little whiskey, that I've done a lot of things wrong in my life, that I'm as imperfect as they are." He even admitted that he had once tried marijuana.

But in 1975, for the first time in twenty-five years, John Wayne was not listed among Hollywood's top ten stars at the box office. His films had grossed a total of $700 million, yet problems related to insurance, as a result of Duke's failing health, made hiring him precarious for feature filmmakers. Nor was it easy to find suitable roles for a folk hero who had outlived his time. Duke made an occasional guest appearance on television, including on Norman Lear's controversial sitcom *Maude* in 1974, as well as on several variety programs and talk shows. "This is not my racket," he said of the experience. "I prefer movies."

Despite fifty years in the film business Wayne had not tired of making pictures. "The only reason I hate age is that I love this work so much," he said. "A person who is eager to go to his job every day is a happy man, and that's success." No longer did he churn out two or three movies a year, even though money remained an obsession with him. In May 1975, at sixty-eight, he agreed to an operation to raise his drooping eyelids, but feature film offers were still few and far between. "I know I'm a good actor," said Wayne, and there is no question that he had improved with age. He had entertained three generations of moviegoers, learned his craft before their eyes, and mastered the art of creating images in a rare and forceful way.

As the years passed, Duke continued to wage a losing fight with his protruding paunch; his face became more craggy, his nose more bulbous. "I want to get on a picture as quickly as I can," he said in late 1975, "because that's the only time I really have any definite pattern—when I'm on a regular and sane daily program. I've made it a practice when I'm on a picture to devote all my energies to the part I am portraying. . . . When I finish my work for the day, all I have to do is go home, get out of my clothing, have a shower, get some hot food, and think of the next day's work." Work gave him a sense of purpose, a focus, and an interlude when life made sense and he was again in control.

On January 8, 1976, Wayne left for Carson City, Nevada, where he would start *The Shootist* five days later. He was excited about the new movie, lost ten pounds and grew a mustache before filming began, and arrived on location early to acclimatize himself and let townspeople get used to seeing John Wayne in their midst. "This is the kind of picture you wait for," Duke said. "They don't come by often."

Photography on *The Shootist* began with Wayne in high spirits. "He'd have breakfast in a busy coffee shop," Pat Stacy recalled, "talk to everyone who came over, sign autographs, observe all the amenities." But the weeks in Nevada soon became a physical nightmare for him. He had difficulty breathing, riding, and walking; finally even talking tired him. His body protested, his voice grew weak. Emotionally the story proved wrenching for him, since it dealt with an aging gunfighter who is dying of cancer. "Sometimes the irony of this film gets to me," Duke admitted to a reporter.

The plot of *The Shootist* seemed to come from his own life. The picture's central character, J. B. Books, arrives in town on the day in 1901 when Queen Victoria died. He is told by a local physician that he has terminal cancer, and while the discovery mellows Books, he is determined not to submit to a painful, undignified death. Instead he chooses to die in a final gun battle, aware that an epoch ends with his death.

"I think my father had similar apprehensions," Aissa Wayne declared, and the similarity between Duke and J. B. Books is unmistakable. "I won't be wronged, I won't be insulted, I won't be laid a hand on," the aging gunman vows in the movie. "I don't do these things to others, and I require the same of them." Books is psychologically out of step with a changing world, yet like John Wayne he endures as a vision of what many Americans wish their past had been.

The Shootist became the most difficult experience of Wayne's long career. His confrontations with director Don Siegel became so heated that producer Mike Frankovich grew alarmed. Siegel's background was in film editing, and his approach seemed rigid and unnatural to Duke. "There were arguments, conferences, compromises," Pat Stacy recalled. But Wayne found other irritants and subjected coworkers to endless outbursts. Dave Grayson, Duke's makeup man, suddenly realized how out of shape and old the star looked, and the realization pained him.

During the making of the picture Wayne stayed in a suite at the Ormsby Hotel in Carson City, but he did little socializing after work because of his fragile health. "Most nights, he was so tired all he wanted to do was have an early dinner, maybe play some cards, and go to bed," Stacy said. Duke's breathing seemed to grow worse as filming progressed. Location shooting finished on January 23, when the production moved to the Warner Bros. lot in Burbank, which Paramount had leased. Duke moved into an apartment at the nearby Oakwood Gardens, with Pat Stacy across the hall from him. In March, he became so sick with an ear infection that the movie had to shut down for a few days.

Wayne's costar, Lauren Bacall, claimed that Duke was ornery during the making of *The Shootist*, but insisted that he had always been ornery. "I knew he felt rotten all the time," Bacall wrote, "but he never complained. Once he said, 'God, I can't smoke anymore, can't drink anymore, all the fun's gone.'" The actress sensed that Duke was struggling with his own mortality. One day while they were waiting for a set to be lighted, Wayne took Bacall's hand and held it. "Boy, it's a beautiful day!" a crew member said as he walked by. "Every day you wake up is a beautiful day," Duke retorted.

Ron Howard played Bacall's adolescent son in the picture, and Wayne pronounced him the most talented young actor he had ever encountered. The two developed mutual admiration for one another as work on *The Shootist* progressed, and their scenes together are particularly effective. In the concluding sequence Howard's character avenges Books's death by using his dead hero's gun, then throws the weapon away, rejecting further violence as an acceptable route to manhood. The scene, which Books lingers long enough to sanction, serves as a haunting denouement to John Wayne's image as a Western hero.

The Shootist wrapped behind schedule on April 5. Despite its melancholy theme, it proved an eloquent finale to Wayne's august career. Although the picture did not fare well at the box office, critics ranked Duke's performance among his finest. "It's a film to remember," Arthur Knight wrote for the *Hollywood Reporter*. "Wayne had courage," director Melville Shavelson said, "and he carried that over into the roles he played. *The Shootist* was the story of his cancer, and that takes guts to have the courage to do that."

No one knew that the Western would be Duke's last picture. "I didn't see how he could go on working much longer," Pilar said, although Wayne still insisted that he had no intention of retiring. Soon after *The Shootist* wrapped he boarded the *Wild Goose* for a cruise down the Mexican coast, and his health showed an improvement. In July, Duke embarked on a twelve-day personal appearance tour to publicize the movie, but the film's theme was too grim for his fans' liking. Many were uncomfortable watching their hero in such a debilitated condition.

Duke filled his time with friends. "In the twilight of our lives," he wrote Maureen O'Hara in the Virgin Islands, "when are you going to invite me to St. Croix?" She called him immediately to arrange a visit. Wayne spent hours out on the patio talking politics and aircraft with O'Hara's husband, Charles Blair. Rather than wearing his toupee, Duke wore an old hat and ordered steak for breakfast, lunch, and dinner. Because of his size, he didn't fit into an ordinary car, so the Blairs rented a big red truck for him to drive. One day Duke was sitting in a big armchair, and O'Hara was standing behind her husband's chair. Duke looked at his costar, then at Blair, and said, "You really do love him, don't you?" O'Hara replied, "Yes, I do." Duke said, "All right then, isn't it time you quit movies and stayed home?" The actress looked down at her husband and back at Wayne and said, "Okay, fine." Later she remarked, "The two of them were quite a pair. I'm sure they thought they were going to get one helluva fight from me. Instead, I quit."

With the approach of fall Wayne stepped up his work schedule by agreeing to appear on a number of television specials. "It was as if he were driven to pack in as much activity as he could," Pat Stacy maintained, "to make every week count." In the three years that followed the filming of *The Shootist,* Duke was sick most of the time. Pneumonia, influenza, prostate surgery, lung congestion, gallstones—Wayne suffered them all. "There's no such thing as growing old gracefully," he said. "It's all deterioration, decay. You just can't give in to it." Work remained his lifeline. "As long as a man has a project—*something* to look forward to—there'll always be something important to him. He'll never really get old. If I had nothing to look forward to, I might as well be dead."

Yet Duke became grouchier than ever, mad that he could not do the things he had always done. Minor incidents infuriated him, and he could be cruel at times. He seemed jealous of younger men, even his sons. In private Duke admitted that he was filled with anxieties and dared not give in to his weaknesses. Instead, he was determined to live out his life as though he were not afraid, when in fact he was terrified.

By 1977 Wayne's health would not permit the rigors of moviemaking. For income he made television commercials—first for Datril pain relievers, then for Great Western Savings and Loan Association. The Datril commercials were filmed in Monument Valley, and it was there that he was forced to face how much he missed John Ford and the camaraderie of the old gang. "All gone," he murmured. "Never to return. That was yesterday; nothing remains the same."

Even his voice began to fail. By February 1978 it was almost unrecognizable. He checked into a local hospital in Newport Beach for what was thought to be bronchitis. Then in late March he flew to Boston for open heart surgery. A defective mitral valve in his heart had to be replaced with a valve from a pig's heart. Wayne ate dinner with his family the night before his surgery. Doctors had agreed that he could have one drink at the restaurant, so Duke ordered the biggest martini the bartender could make. When the drink came, he rose, toasted his children, and said, "To the last supper."

During a twelve-hour operation Duke's heart was removed from his chest and placed on a pump while surgeons made the substitution of valves. Afterwards, as he lay in bed recuperating at Massachusetts General Hospital, Wayne tried to joke about his condition, saying that he could now "oink with the best of them," but his mood fluctuated between depression and petulance. Michael, Patrick, Aissa, and Pat Stacy stayed near him; Pilar waited in Newport for her daughter's report. Wires and flowers poured in during Duke's three weeks in Boston, and so many bags of mail arrived at the hospital each day that Wayne had to hire three secretaries and buy a computer to answer all of the cards and letters.

During his hospitalization, the 1978 Academy Awards ceremony took place in Los Angeles. Toward the end of the telecast Bob Hope unexpectedly looked into the camera and said, "We want you to know, Duke, we miss you tonight. We expect you to amble out here in person next year, because there is no one who can fill John Wayne's boots." Three weeks after Duke left Massachusetts he taped a segment for a Bob Hope television special.

Wayne returned to Newport Beach an angry man. His tirades knew no bounds. He was disgusted with the Carter administration and outraged at talk of gun control. In sweat clothes and white gym shoes he walked a lap around the Bayshore complex each morning and spent evenings on the patio watching the sun sink over the bay. During Newport's annual boat parade in late April, an entire flotilla sailed past Wayne's house with whistles blowing and a giant banner proclaiming, "Welcome Home, Duke." A grin creased his face as he watched the spectacle.

Although he suffered a bout with hepatitis, Wayne began talking about making another movie. At seventy-one, he needed work to forget his illness and loneliness. He had bought the rights to a novel, *Beau John*, which he hoped to film with Ron Howard. By July he felt strong enough to host a television special for General Electric, and in November he was in Williamsburg, Virginia, to tape a spot for Perry Como's Christmas show.

Shortly before the holidays Duke began complaining of stomach pains. His disposition was terrible. Nothing pleased him, and he had trouble sleeping. He began losing weight and he couldn't tolerate the smell of food. On Christmas morning he didn't feel well enough to dress and went back to bed before all the presents were opened. He said he felt as if jagged glass had been raked across the inside of his stomach.

Duke had agreed to a television interview with Barbara Walters on January 8, and that week his spirits seemed to lift. He admitted to Walters that he did not look forward to death, but claimed that he had what he had always had—"deep faith that there is a Supreme Being." He failed to mention that he was scheduled to enter the UCLA Medical Center for exploratory surgery two days later.

When Duke arrived at the Westwood campus on the afternoon of January 10, 1979, Michael and Patrick Wayne were at the medical center waiting for him. An operation two days later revealed that he had developed cancer of the stomach. In a nine-hour ordeal Duke's entire stomach was removed. While his children anxiously awaited the results, hordes of reporters jammed the hospital's lobby.

Wayne spent a full month in recovery. He could not eat much and had no appetite. Once he was able to, he walked up and down the halls of the UCLA Medical Center wearing his USC cap, much to everyone's amusement. He returned home on February 11, determined to be well enough to attend the Academy Awards ceremony in April.

He was scheduled to begin daily radiation treatments at Hoag Hospital in Newport. Duke was painfully thin, and the look of death filled his eyes. "I knew that Duke suffered badly," Pat Stacy said, "not only from the physical pain but from the mental agony of dying and the frustration of losing control." Dignity had always been important to Duke, but his world was slipping from his grasp. He spent a few days on his ranch in Arizona, managed a weekend or two near Catalina, and continued to talk of new projects. Once again the press boasted that John Wayne had beaten "the big C." A spokesman at the UCLA Medical Center was quoted as saying, "You can't keep a good old cowboy tied down for long."

Duke's spirits started to rise as time for the annual Academy Awards ceremony approached. He spent more time outside and planned to resume his career during the coming summer. On the morning of April 9, Duke drove to Hoag Hospital for his daily radiation treatment. Then he, Pat Stacy, and his daughter Marisa were taken in the motor home he frequently used as a dressing room to the Music Center in Los Angeles, where a dress rehearsal for the Oscars ceremony was underway. "We were told they'd run through Duke's segment as soon as he arrived," said Stacy, "there'd be no tedious waiting around." Wayne balked at being treated like an invalid, but he declined to sit through the rehearsal. Instead, he went to the Bonaventure Hotel a few blocks away, where Stacy had reserved accommodations.

Duke took a nap and began preparing for the show, which was to begin at 7 P.M. "Our plan was to dine in our room and watch the show until it was time for us to leave," Stacy remembered. "Duke hadn't eaten all day; he barely touched the soft food we had ordered for him." Shortly before 8 o'clock Dave Grayson arrived at the hotel to make Wayne up for the telecast. An hour and a half later Duke's driver pulled up in back of the Dorothy Chandler Pavilion with his party inside. Wayne emerged from the motor home and was ushered into a private waiting room until time for him to present the award for best picture of the year.

Despite Grayson's artistry, Duke looked emaciated. Under his tuxedo he wore a thick wetsuit to make him look heavier, but he had trouble standing for any prolonged period. When master of ceremonies Johnny Carson introduced him, the crowd at the Music Hall rose in a standing ovation. Duke was perspiring and looked ashen. When the clapping stopped, he said in an unsteady voice: "That's just about the only medicine a fella'd ever really need. Believe me when I tell you that I'm mighty pleased that I can amble down here tonight. Oscar and I have something in common. Oscar came to the Hollywood scene in 1928—so did I. We're both a little weather-beaten, but we're still here, and plan to be around a whole lot longer."

He had only two more months to live. The 1979 Oscars ceremony would be John Wayne's last public appearance. Ironically, the award for best picture of 1978 went that night to *The Deer Hunter*, a forceful film that opposed the war in Vietnam and questioned much that Duke stood for. Afterwards Wayne made his way to the press room, stayed only a few minutes, slipped unnoticed out the back door, and was driven back to Newport. "In retrospect," Pat Stacy wrote, "I believe Duke was there to bid a glorious and fond farewell—to the industry, to his friends, to the world."

Thirteen days later, in a fit of despair, he asked Stacy to bring him the Smith and Wesson .38 he kept beside his bed. "I want to blow my brains out," he said. Duke was haunted by the knowledge that his friend Pedro Armendariz had put a gun to his head and pulled the trigger after doctors told him that he had terminal cancer. There were moments when Wayne thought the Mexican actor had taken the only reasonable course.

Duke's radiation treatments continued, but so did his despondency. "Christ," he told director Peter Bogdanovich, "everybody's gone." Physically Wayne appeared to be melting away. When friends came to visit, he made an effort to be cheerful. Maureen O'Hara spent three days at his house in Newport, during which she entertained Duke with her wit and lively banter, but left knowing that she would never see her friend again. Milton and Claire Bren arrived on a Sunday afternoon and were dismayed at how much their friend had deteriorated. "He had a time just walking up a slight incline," Claire Trevor said.

Every few days Duke called Olive Carey, whose down-to-earth wisdom he respected. "I didn't go down to visit him," Ollie's son Dobe Carey said, "because I just couldn't stand to see him like that." Hank Worden drove to Newport for frequent visits, and others sent notes. "It appears to me that you're doing that which makes you happy," Duke wrote in response to a letter from Budd Boetticher, "and that's a mighty important niche to find in life. I hope our paths cross before we are too old to walk them."

Pilar kept her distance, although the children kept her informed about her husband's condition. In one of their last meetings, Duke said to his estranged wife, "Promise that you'll take care of the kids. They're going to need you." He continued to speak fondly of Pilar and, in his own way, understood why she had left him. "She's a fine woman," he told Barbara Walters. "She's the mother of my children. We just lost contact. Completely lost contact." Years later Pilar dedicated her book to Duke, referring to him as "the most admirable human being I have ever met."

On the evening of May 2, 1979, Wayne was sitting next to the kitchen stove when he suddenly fell over. "I have got to go to the hospital," he said to his children. "I'm in such pain." The next morning Ethan drove him to the UCLA Medical Center. "My father's pain was so severe he couldn't sit up," Aissa remembered, "so we folded down his station wagon's back seat, spread out some blankets, and laid him gently back there." By the time they reached Westwood, television cameras and newspaper photographers were waiting for Duke outside the hospital. "If I can't get well, I just want to die," he told his family.

Doctors discovered new cancer cells in his body, and surgeons removed a considerable portion of his colon. Tests revealed that the malignant cells had multiplied and spread throughout his lymph system. Duke had promised to cooperate with the doctors and nurses who attended him, but his outbursts grew angrier as his condition was pronounced terminal. "He fought them like a tiger," Aissa said, "a man with a lifelong need for control. Most of all he resisted his powerful drugs." Doctors admitted on May 17 that their celebrated patient was declining. Ten days later, X-rays showed that his intestines were almost completely blocked. Doctors ordered Wayne to be given intravenous morphine. "After that," Aissa said, "my father mostly floated."

Michael became the family's spokesman. Doctors talked mainly to him, and he issued the necessary instructions. Tension mounted within the family, particularly between the two sets of children, who went in to see their father in shifts. Meanwhile the hospital was bombarded with phone calls and visitors. Too numb to fight nurses over needles and medication, Duke seemed unable to focus on anything for long. Late one afternoon Aissa sat at his bedside. "With his eyes open wide," she recalled, "he said he had just returned from a wonderful parade. He said he marched in the middle of many majestic horses, and the drummers drummed and the streets were lined by children." He spoke of other visions in the days that followed.

On June 9, in a surprise move, Wayne received the archbishop of Panama. "He was baptized a Catholic just before he died," Duke's son Michael said. "I think he did it for the family. My mother was a Catholic, and all of us kids were. Every wife of his was a Catholic, although my father was not a religious man in a formal way. He was very moral, but he hated groups. He loved individuals and felt that when groups of people get together bad things happen."

His conversion mystified most of his friends and relatives. "Knowing my father, how he felt about religion, I couldn't believe it," Aissa declared. "Frankly, I think he was too drugged up to know a conversion was even being attempted." Although Aissa had been raised a Catholic, Duke never attended church with her nor had he ever shown any inclination toward organized religion of any sort. "By the day the archbishop came to see him," Wayne's daughter insisted, "my father was heavily drugged on intravenous morphine."

Toward the end Duke was in and out of a coma, and his breathing became tortured. Friends tried to see him, but most were turned away. President Carter was granted permission to enter Wayne's hospital room, and Henry Fonda was admitted after the actor swore he would wait all night if necessary. Frank Sinatra, with whom Wayne had fought over politics, stepped into Duke's room and left a shaken man, tears clouding his eyes.

On the morning of Friday, June 11, 1979, John Wayne lay in a semi-coma. By late afternoon all his children, except for Michael, who was with lawyers, had gathered at his bedside. Aissa held her father's hand. Duke took a breath, but never exhaled. "Good-bye, Dad," Patrick said faintly; then the room grew still. Wayne died at 5:23 P.M., Pacific Daylight Time. He was seventy-two years old.

Soon Michael arrived and told the family to conceal their grief on their way out. They were to pretend that nothing had happened, lest Duke's death be turned into a media sideshow. "The facade went up even before we shuffled out of my father's ninth-floor room," Aissa remembered. "Michael had hired a security guard to sit at the door and fend off the press and visitors, so we cleared up our tears and nonchalantly walked out by the guard one at a time, smiling."

The next day headlines in the Los Angeles *Herald Examiner* announced, "The Duke Is Dead." Halfway around the world, a Tokyo newspaper proclaimed, "Mr. America Passes On." Wayne himself often said, "I have tried to live my life so that my family would love me and my friends respect me. The others can do whatever the hell they please." Over the years he frequently quoted a Mexican saying—"*Feo, fuerte, y formal,*" which he translated as, "He was ugly, he was strong, but he had dignity." That, Duke proclaimed, was epitaph enough for him.

When Ward Bond died, Wayne had said, "God, how I hate solemn funerals! When I die, take me into the room and burn me. Then my family and a few friends should get together, have a few belts, and talk about the crazy old times we had together." To Duke the burial ceremony was medieval and primitive. He had made it clear that he wanted to be cremated—"anything rather than be buried in a box," he'd instructed. He told Pilar that he wished to have his ashes scattered over the sea between Newport Beach and Catalina Island. "I don't want to miss the ocean," he said. "I want to stay here."

But Michael had his father's body taken to the Laguna Hills Mortuary. Because "he died a Catholic," his eldest son maintained, "he had a traditional Christian burial." Pilar and her children learned only the day before the funeral that Duke would be buried, not cremated

On June 15, the flag outside the patio of John Wayne's Newport Beach home was lowered. To ensure privacy, a Catholic service was held for him in Newport at 5:45 in the morning. Shortly after daybreak Duke was buried in a hilltop plot in Pacific View Memorial Park, overlooking the ocean. The group of onlookers was small, consisting of Pilar, the seven Wayne children, Pat Stacy, and a few of Duke's closest friends. Josephine Wayne, of her own choice, was not there. "I merely stood back and fumed," Aissa wrote, "watching my father denied a fitting farewell."

After the funeral the mourners gathered for breakfast and a reception at Pilar's home. It was a subdued, awkward gathering that quickly dispersed. The grave would remain unmarked for fear that vandals might steal the body. A second fresh grave was dug nearby and flowers were placed there in an effort to make sure that Wayne's final resting place would not be discovered and disturbed.

Wayne left an estate worth $6.8 million. He had provided for Pilar in a trust fund, although she was excluded from his will. He had set up generous trusts for his heirs, which included all of his children and Josephine. Yet the rift between Duke's two families widened after his death. "Since Duke passed away," Pilar wrote, "his oldest son, Michael, has seemed to grow much colder toward me, and I have felt excluded from all events commemorating my husband's memory. . . . It seemed to me that Michael pretended I didn't exist."

Although Pilar never met Josephine, Duke's first four children had been in and out of their father's home through the years, and Pilar had felt close to them. "We did everything possible to be a family," she said, "I never thought we would ever part. But the minute that Duke was buried they all turned on me like snakes. I don't think they ever accepted the fact that Duke had a second family."

In 1981 a new wing was dedicated in John Wayne's name at the UCLA Medical Center, which specialized in cancer research. Shortly before Duke's death Congress voted to mint a special gold medal honoring him. The bill had been introduced by Wayne's friend Barry Goldwater, and Maureen O'Hara and Elizabeth Taylor, then married to Sen. John Warner, testified in behalf of its passage. The inscription on the congressional medal read simply, "John Wayne—American."

In 1979 the Orange County Airport was renamed John Wayne Airport by the county's board of supervisors, and three years later a nine-foot statue of Duke in cowboy garb was installed at the entrance. In 1983 a twenty-one-foot bronze of John Wayne on horseback was unveiled before the Wilshire Boulevard offices of Great Western Savings and Loan, a tawdry effort to capitalize on Duke's identification with the American West.

Fans from all over the world continue to visit the cemetery where Wayne is buried, but they find no gravestone bearing his name. Those who bring flowers are told to leave them at the base of the cemetery's flagpole. The largest arrangement left there was a four-foot cowboy boot, decorated with red and white roses in the form of an American flag.

Michael Wayne still heads Batjac and has remained the principal keeper of Duke's flame. In the years since his father's death, Michael has commissioned prints, sculptures, plates, and other memorabilia bearing Duke's likeness. He also formed John Wayne Enterprises to control the use of his father's name and image. "Michael's biggest problem is that he can't accept that his father is gone," one Hollywood veteran maintained.

In 1984 Pilar married Stephen Stewart, a municipal judge in Newport Beach, but the union proved a mistake. With the passage of time the financial situation of Wayne's widow has become less secure, although she still draws income from the trust fund Duke created for her before his death. His image is prominent in her home, and she has taken up commercial painting, mainly reproductions from Duke's pictures. She frequently dreams of him and their life together. "We're either with the kids or talking about the kids or packing to go to a location," she explained. "But he's always there. I guess twenty-seven years is a long time to be together."

Like Patrick, Ethan Wayne became an actor, although he did stunt work for feature films and television first. He appeared in a number of low-budget movies, won a recurring role on the soap opera *The Bold and the*

Beautiful, and played in the television series *Adam-12.* In 1989 he eloped to Prescott, Arizona, with his longtime girlfriend, flight attendant Gina Rivadeneyra, but the marriage lasted only a brief while. Later that year Ethan and two of his friends rescued a nineteen-year-old woman who apparently had been kidnapped, tied up, and dumped over a cliff in upper Newport Bay. An acrobatic pilot, Ethan often flies over his mother's house and spends weekends there whenever he is not busy with an assignment.

Marisa was married to former Olympic skier Jack Romick for four years, during which she lived on a ranch outside Steamboat Springs, Colorado. Later she became a country and western singer. "She's the image of John Wayne," Pilar declared. "That's her face in Duke's early Westerns."

After divorcing tennis player Lornie Kuhl, Aissa married Thomas A. Gionis, an orthopedic surgeon, but became embroiled in a bitter custody dispute over their daughter, Anastasia, when the couple separated in 1988. In October of that year Aissa and her boyfriend, millionaire Roger Luby, were attacked by two gunmen inside the garage of Luby's Newport Beach home. Gionis was accused of ordering the attack, was arrested, and was convicted after a mistrial. In 1992 he was sentenced to five years in prison. Aissa became a prosecutor and moved to Pacific Palisades.

"I can't picture Duke alive in the 1990s," Pilar said, "with all the bombings and killings and threats that are part of life today. He would go berserk. If he'd been alive when Aissa was attacked, he would have been out in the streets with a gun. Whether he was right or wrong, I admired his stance very much. He loved his country; nobody was going to harm it in his presence. He was gong to protect it all over the world."

For most of his adult life John Wayne loomed larger than life, a throwback to the previous century. By the end of his screen career Duke's image was about all that was left of the Old West, and he had become the most powerful personality in film history. The older he got, the more Wayne personified America's past. His performances and his real-life behavior merged into a mythic figure of global consequence. An emblem of American resourcefulness, John Wayne came to represent the rugged male—tough, aggressive, competitive, a man against the elements, yet loyal to his comrades and full of moral certainty. In Wayne's world there was little room for conciliation; his was an absolutist viewpoint oriented toward conquering adversity with speed and efficiency.

"To the people of the world," Maureen O'Hara testified for the *Con-*

gressional Record, "John Wayne is not just an actor . . . John Wayne *is* the United States of America. He is what they believe it to be; he is what they hope it will be; and he is what they hope it will always be. . . . He is a man who has a code of beliefs. . . . He believes in individual responsibility and honor. He believes also in the adherence to the American dream—enterprise, hard work, and reward. . . . He's just the same at home. He doesn't change. That's the wonderful thing about Duke; you can depend on him."

Yet Wayne's Hollywood career was a prolonged battle to reach the top. He had no major studio behind him the way Clark Gable, Errol Flynn, and Tyrone Power did. In his early years Duke worked mainly for Republic and lesser Poverty Row companies. He lacked the executive support and expansive publicity campaigns that boosted other screen stars to fame. Wayne pulled himself up through sheer determination and hard work. He developed a personal style of acting and put his signature on the better movies he made as much or more than the writers, directors, producers, and cinematographers did.

Duke enjoyed his success, basked in the fruits of capitalism, was grateful when strangers rushed to greet him like an old friend, and relished every aspect of the celebrity he attained. "I love making pictures," he said. "I get a charge out of reading a script or watching the day's rushes in the projection room." Endlessly fascinated with moviemaking, Wayne grew proficient in his craft and added dimension to his screen persona. "I know my trade as well as the next man in Hollywood," Duke said. "When I begin to creak at the hinges and take on the appearance of a tired water buffalo, I'll play character parts. . . . No matter what, I'll always be part of the motion picture industry, for it has been my life."

Like other masterful screen performers, John Wayne learned the knack of delivering dialogue so that his lines had no hint of acting, and he acquired unfailing finesse in courting the cinematographer's lens. With great economy Wayne could layer his performances so that his thoughts could be read in his face. His ability to project the eternal American yet still remain an old friend made him a box-office champion. Duke defined such a performer as "a non-actor that people who have never heard of the Theatre Guild or Stanislavsky will pay hard-earned cash to watch non-act." With that as his credo he won lasting fame. "There'll never be another John Wayne," Harry Carey, Jr., declared.

Wayne may have epitomized the all-American male in looks, yet neither his image nor his life represented a fully actualized man. Emotionally he was incomplete, too underdeveloped for sustained intimacy, too much the combatant to tolerate concessions or reveal his inner self, too external, restless, and impatient for deep personal growth. Yet for a society that placed image over reality, John Wayne became a champion.

More accurately he became a summation of vanishing American ideals, a symbol of the strengths and limitations of the national character, a walking embodiment of the American dream. An anachronism energized by boldness and familiarity, John Wayne remains the quintessential Western hero, yet one more commendable in legend than in life. For the contemporary world Duke's militarism and bigotry make him a hazardous model, yet the sincerity of his convictions stands as a beacon in troubled times.

During his last years even Wayne appeared to modify certain views. "Our country thrives on change," he said shortly before his death. "In nature nothing is permanent. So it stands to reason that as laws change, ideologies and mores change so that society changes, and that is good." He preferred slow changes, allowing time to test what was solid and real, but he never doubted that his country, with all of its problems and uncertainties, made the good life possible.

The American way had served him well; he had no doubt it would serve others as well. Even when the swagger and punch had gone out of his life, he voiced gratitude for a system that afforded him success. "The American people have been awfully good to me for a long time," he often said. With the heart of a child, John Wayne eulogized an America that gave people like him a chance to turn aspirations and ambition into reality. That was the America he envisioned, the only America he understood.

Filmography

Films are listed in chronological order within each year.

1928

Mother Machree. Fox Film Studio. *Director:* John Ford. *Screenplay:* Gertrude Orr. *Camera:* Chester Lyons. *Cast:* Belle Bennett, Neil Hamilton, Victor McLaglen, Ted McNamara, Ethel Clayton, Constance Howard, Eulalie Jensen, William Platt, Philippe De Lacy, Pat Somerset, Jacques Rollens, John Wayne (an unbilled extra).

Hangman's House. Fox Film Studio. *Director:* John Ford. *Screenplay:* Marion Orth. *Camera:* George Schneiderman. *Cast:* Victor McLaglen, June Collyer, Hobart Bosworth, Larry Kent, Earle Fox, Eric Mayne, Belle Stoddard, Marion Morrison (John Wayne).

1929

Salute. Fox Film Studio. *Director:* John Ford, David Butler. *Screenplay:* John Stone. *Camera:* Joseph H. August. *Cast:* George O'Brien, Helen Chandler, Stepin Fetchit, William Janney, Frank Albertson, Joyce Compton, Lumsden Hare, David Butler, Rex Bell, John Breeden, Ward Bond, Marion Morrison (John Wayne).

Words and Music. Fox Film Studio. *Director:* James Tinling. *Screenplay:* Frederick Hazlitt Brennan, Jack McEdward. *Cast:* Lois Moran, David Percy, Helen Twelvetrees, William Orlamond, Elizabeth Patterson, Duke Morrison (John Wayne), Frank Albertson, Tom Patricola, Bubbles Crowell, The Biltmore Quartet.

1930

Men without Women. Fox Film Studio. *Director:* John Ford. *Screenplay:* Dudley Nichols. *Camera:* Joseph H. August. *Cast:* Kenneth MacKenna, Frank Albertson, Paul Page, Pat Somerset, Walter McGrail, Stuart Erwin, Warren Hymer, J. Farrell McDonald, Roy Stewart, Warner Richmond, Harry Tenbrook, Ben Hendricks, Jr., Marion Morrison (John Wayne), Robert Parrish.

Rough Romance. Fox Film Studio. *Director:* A. F. Erickson. *Screenplay:* Kenneth B. Clark. *Camera:* Daniel B. Clark. *Cast:* George O'Brien, Helen Chandler, Antonio Moreno, Noel Francis, Eddie Borden, Harry Cording, Roy Stewart, Marion Morrison (John Wayne).

Cheer Up and Smile. Fox Film Studio. *Director:* Sidney Lanfield. *Screenplay:* Richard Cornell. *Camera:* Joe Valentine. *Cast:* Arthur Lake, Dixie Lee, Olga Baclanova, Whispering Jack Smith, Johnny Arthur, Charles Judels, John Darrow, Sumner Getchell, Franklin Pangborn, Buddy Messinger, Marion Morrison (John Wayne).

The Big Trail. Fox Film Studio. *Director:* Raoul Walsh. *Screenplay:* Hal G. Evarts. *Camera:* Lucien Androit, Arthur Edeson. *Cast:* John Wayne, Marguerite Churchill, Ian Keith, El Brendel, Tully Marshall, Tyrone Power, Sr., David Rollins, Frederick Burton, Russ Powell, Ward Bond, Marcia Harris, Andy Shufford, Helen Parrish.

1931

Girls Demand Excitement. Fox Film Studio. *Director:* Seymour Felix. *Screenplay:* Harlan Thompson. *Camera:* Charles Clarke. *Cast:* Virginia Cherrill, John Wayne, Marguerite Churchill, Helen Jerome Eddy, William Janney, Eddie Nugent, Terrance Ray, Marion Byron, Martha Sleeper, Addie McPhail, Ray Cooke.

Three Girls Lost. Fox Film Studio. *Director:* Sidney Lanfield. *Screenplay:* Robert D. Andrews. *Camera:* L. William O'Connell. *Cast:* Loretta Young, John Wayne, Lew Cody, Joyce Compton, Joan Marsh, Katherine Clare Ward, Paul Fix, Bert Roach.

Men Are Like That (also called ***Arizona***). Columbia Pictures. *Director:* George B. Seitz. *Screenplay:* Robert Riskin, Dorothy Howell. *Camera:* Teddy Tetzlaff. *Cast:* John Wayne, Laura LaPlante, June Clyde, Forrest Stanley, Nena Quartaro, Susan Fleming, Loretta Sayers, Hugh Cummings.

Range Feud. Columbia Pictures. *Director:* D. Ross Lederman. *Screenplay:* Milton Krims. *Camera:* Ben Kline. *Cast:* Buck Jones, John Wayne, Susan Fleming, Ed Le Saint, William Walling, Wallace MacDonald, Harry Woods.

Maker of Men. Columbia Pictures. *Director:* Edward Sedgwick. *Screenplay:* Howard J. Green, Edward Sedgwick. *Camera:* L. William O'Connell. *Cast:* Jack Holt, Richard Cromwell, Joan Marsh, Robert Allen, John Wayne, Walter Catlett, Natalie Moorhead, Ethel Wales, Richard Tucker.

1932

Haunted Gold. Warner Bros. *Director:* Mack V. Wright. *Producer:* Leon Schlesinger. *Screenplay:* Adele Buffington. *Camera:* Nick Musuraca. *Cast:* John Wayne, Sheila Terry, Erville Alderson, Harry Woods, Otto Hoffman, Martha Mattox, Blue Washington.

The Shadow of the Eagle. Mascot Pictures Corporation. *Director:* Ford Beebe. *Screenplay:* Ford Beebe, Colbert Clark, Wyndham Gittens. *Camera:* Ben Kline, Victor Scheurich. *Cast:* John Wayne, Dorothy Gulliver, Edward Hearn, Richard Tucker, Lloyd Whitlock, Walter Miller, Edmund Burns, Pat O'Malley, Little Billy, Ivan Linow, James Bradbury, Jr., Ernie S. Adams, Roy D'Arcy, Bud Osborne, Yakima Canutt.

The Hurricane Express. Mascot Pictures Corporation. *Director:* Armand Schaefer, J. P. McGowan. *Screenplay:* Colbert Clark, Barney Sarecky, Wyndham Gittens. *Camera:* Ernest Miller, Carl Wester. *Cast:* John Wayne, Shirley Grey, Tully Marshall, Conway Tearle, J. Farrell MacDonald, Matthew Betz, James Burtis, Lloyd Whitlock, Edmund Breese, Al Bridge, Ernie Adams, Charles King, Glenn Strange.

Texas Cyclone. Columbia Pictures. *Director:* D. Ross Lederman. *Screenplay:* William Colt MacDonald. *Camera:* Benjamin Kline. *Cast:* Tim McCoy, Shirley Grey, John Wayne, Wheeler Oakman, Wallace MacDonald, Harry Cording, Vernon Dent, Walter Brennan, Mary Gordon.

Lady and Gent. Paramount Pictures. *Director:* Stephen Roberts. *Screenplay:* Grover Jones, William Slavens McNutt. *Camera:* Harry Fischbeck. *Cast:* George Bancroft, Wynne Gibson, Charles Starrett, James Gleason, John Wayne, Joyce Compton, Charles Grapewin, Frank McGlynn, Sr.

Two-Fisted Law. Columbia Pictures. *Director:* D. Ross Lederman. *Screenplay:* William Colt MacDonald. *Camera:* Benjamin Kline. *Cast:* Tim McCoy, Alice Day, Wheeler Oakman, Tully Marshall, Wallace MacDonald, John Wayne, Walter Brennan, Richard Alexander.

Ride Him, Cowboy. Warner Bros. *Director:* Fred Allen. *Screenplay:* Kenneth Perkins. *Camera:* Ted McCord. *Cast:* John Wayne, Ruth Hall, Henry B. Walthall, Harry Gribbon, Otis Harlan, Charles Sellon, Frank Hagney.

The Big Stampede. Warner Bros. *Director:* Tenny Wright. *Screenplay:* Marion Jackson. *Camera:* Ted McCord. *Cast:* John Wayne, Noah Beery, Mae Madison, Luis Alberni, Berton Churchill, Paul Hurst.

1933

The Telegraph Trail. Warner Bros. *Director:* Tenny Wright. *Screenplay:* Kurt Kempler. *Camera:* Ted McCord. *Cast:* John Wayne, Marceline Day, Frank McHugh, Otis Harlan, Yakima Canutt, Albert J. Smith, Clarence Gelbert.

Central Airport. First National Pictures. *Director:* William A. Wellman. *Screenplay:* Jack Moffitt. *Camera:* Sid Hickox. *Cast:* Richard Barthelmess, Sally Eilers,

Tom Brown, Glenda Farrell, Harold Huber, Grant Mitchell, James Murray, Claire McDowell, Willard Robertson, John Wayne.

His Private Secretary. Showmen's Pictures. *Director:* Philip A. Whitman. *Screenplay:* Lew Collins. *Camera:* Abe Schultz. *Cast:* John Wayne, Evalyn Knapp, Alec B. Francis, Natalie Kingston, Arthur Hoyt, Al St. John, Mickey Rentschler.

Somewhere in Sonora. Warner Bros. *Director:* Mack V. Wright. *Screenplay:* Will Levington Comfort. *Camera:* Ted McCord. *Cast:* John Wayne, Shirley Palmer, Henry B. Walthall, Paul Fix, Ann Faye, Billy Franey, Ralph Lewis, Frank Rice, J. P. McGowan.

The Life of Jimmy Dolan. Warner Bros. *Director:* Archie Mayo. *Screenplay:* Bertram Milhauser, Beulah Marie Dix. *Camera:* Arthur Edeson. *Cast:* Douglas Fairbanks, Jr., Loretta Young, Aline MacMahon, Guy Kibbee, Fifi D'Orsay, Shirley Grey, Lyle Talbot, Farina Harold Huber, George Meeker, David Durand, Dawn O'Day (Anne Shirley), Arthur Hohl, Mickey Rooney, John Wayne.

The Three Musketeers (released as ***Desert Command*** in 1946). Mascot Pictures Corporation. *Director:* Armand Schaefer, Colbert Clark. *Screenplay:* Norman S. Hall, Colbert Clark, Wyndham Gittens, Barney Sarecky. *Camera:* Ernest Miller, Ed Lyons. *Cast:* John Wayne, Ruth Hall, Jack Mulhall, Raymond Hatton, Francis X. Bushman, Jr., Noah Beery, Jr., Creighton Chaney, Al Ferguson, Hooper Atchely, Edward Peil, George Magrill, Gordon DeMain, William Desmond, Robert Frazer, Emile Chautard, Robert Warwick, Rodney Hildebrandt, Wilbur Lucas.

Baby Face. Warner Bros. *Director:* Alfred E. Green. *Screenplay:* Mark Canfield. *Camera:* James Van Trees. *Cast:* Barbara Stanwyck, George Brent, Donald Cook, Margaret Lindsay, Henry Kolker, John Wayne, Douglass Dumbrille, Arthur Hohl, Theresa Harris, Harry Gribbon, Robert Barrat.

The Man from Monterey. Warner Bros. *Director:* Mack V. Wright. *Screenplay:* Leslie Mason. *Camera:* Ted McCord. *Cast:* John Wayne, Ruth Hall, Nena Quartaro, Luis Alberni, Francis Ford, Donald Reed, Lillian Leighton, Lafe McKee.

Riders of Destiny. Monogram Pictures. *Director:* Robert N. Bradbury. *Producer:* Paul Malvern. *Screenplay:* Robert N. Bradbury. *Camera:* Archie Stout. *Cast:* John Wayne, Cecilia Parker, George "Gabby" Hayes, Forrest Taylor, Al St. John, Heinie Conklin, Earl Dwire, Lafe McKee.

Sagebrush Trail. Monogram Pictures. *Director:* Armand Schaefer. *Producer:* Paul Malvern. *Screenplay:* Lindsley Parsons. *Camera:* Archie Stout. *Cast:* John Wayne,

Nancy Shubert, Lane Chandler, Yakima Canutt, Wally Wales, Art Mix, Robert Burns, Earl Dwire.

West of the Divide. Monogram Pictures. *Director:* Robert N. Bradbury. *Producer:* Paul Malvern. *Screenplay:* Robert N. Bradbury. *Camera:* Archie Stout. *Cast:* John Wayne, Virginia Brown Faire, Lloyd Whitlock, Yakima Canutt, George "Gabby" Hayes, Earl Dwire, Lafe McKee.

1934

The Lucky Texan. Monogram Pictures. *Director:* Robert N. Bradbury. *Producer:* Paul Malvern. *Screenplay:* Robert N. Bradbury. *Camera:* Archie Stout. *Cast:* John Wayne, Barbara Sheldon, George "Gabby" Hayes, Lloyd Whitlock, Yakima Canutt, Earl Dwire, Edward Parker.

Blue Steel. Monogram Pictures. *Director:* Robert N. Bradbury. *Producer:* Paul Malvern. *Screenplay:* Robert N. Bradbury. *Camera:* Archie Stout. *Cast:* John Wayne, Eleanor Hunt, George "Gabby" Hayes, Ed Peil, Yakima Canutt, George Cleveland, George Nash.

The Man from Utah. Monogram Pictures. *Director:* Robert N. Bradbury. *Producer:* Paul Malvern. *Screenplay:* Lindsley Parsons. *Camera:* Archie Stout. *Cast:* John Wayne, Polly Ann Young, George "Gabby" Hayes, Yakima Canutt, Ed Peil, Anita Campillo, George Cleveland, Lafe McKee.

Randy Rides Alone. Monogram Pictures. *Director:* Harry Fraser. *Producer:* Paul Malvern. *Screenplay:* Lindsley Parsons. *Camera:* Archie Stout. *Cast:* John Wayne, Alberta Vaughn, George "Gabby" Hayes, Earl Dwire, Yakima Canutt, Tex Phelps, Arthur Ortega.

The Star Packer. Monogram Pictures. *Director:* Robert N. Bradbury. *Producer:* Paul Malvern. *Screenplay:* Robert N. Bradbury. *Camera:* Archie Stout. *Cast:* John Wayne, Verna Hillie, George "Gabby" Hayes, Yakima Canutt, Earl Dwire, George Cleveland, Arthur Ortega, Edward Parker.

The Trail Beyond. Monogram Pictures. *Director:* Robert N. Bradbury. *Producer:* Paul Malvern. *Screenplay:* Lindsley Parsons. *Camera:* Archie Stout. *Cast:* John Wayne, Verna Hillie, Noah Beery, Iris Lancaster, Noah Beery, Jr., Robert Fraser, Earl Dwire, Edward Parker.

'Neath Arizona Skies. Monogram Pictures. *Director:* Harry Fraser. *Producer:* Paul Malvern. *Screenplay:* B. R. Tuttle. *Camera:* Archie Stout. *Cast:* John Wayne, Sheila Terry, Jay Wilsey, Yakima Canutt, Jack Rockwell, Shirley Rickert, George "Gabby" Hayes.

1935

Lawless Frontier. **Mo**nogram Pictures. *Director:* Robert N. Bradbury. *Producer:* Paul Malvern. *Screenplay:* Robert N. Bradbury. *Camera:* Archie Stout. *Cast:* John Wayne, Sheila Terry, George "Gabby" Hayes, Earl Dwire, Yakima Canutt, Jack Rockwell, Gordon D. Woods.

Texas Terror. Monogram Pictures. *Director:* Robert N. Bradbury. *Producer:* Paul Malvern. *Screenplay:* Robert N. Bradbury. *Camera:* Archie Stout. *Cast:* John Wayne, Lucille Browne, LeRoy Mason, George "Gabby" Hayes, Buffalo Bill, Jr., Bert Dillard, Lloyd Ingraham.

Rainbow Valley. Monogram Pictures: *Director:* Robert N. Bradbury. *Producer:* Paul Malvern. *Screenplay:* Lindsley Parsons. *Camera:* William Hyer. *Cast:* John Wayne, Lucille Browne, LeRoy Mason, George "Gabby" Hayes, Buffalo Bill, Jr., Bert Dillard, Lloyd Ingraham.

Paradise Canyon. Monogram Pictures. *Director:* Carl Pierson. *Producer:* Paul Malvern. *Screenplay:* Lindsley Parsons. *Camera:* Archie Stout. *Cast:* John Wayne, Marion Burns, Yakima Canutt, Reed Howes, Perry Murdock, Gino Corrado, Gordon Clifford.

The Dawn Rider. Monogram Pictures. *Director:* Robert N. Bradbury. *Producer:* Paul Malvern. *Screenplay:* Robert N. Bradbury. *Camera:* Archie Stout. *Cast:* John Wayne, Marion Burns, Yakima Canutt, Reed Howes, Denny Meadows, Bert Dillard, Jack Jones.

Westward Ho! Republic Pictures. *Director:* Robert N. Bradbury. *Producer:* Paul Malvern. *Screenplay:* Lindsley Parsons. *Camera:* Archie Stout. *Cast:* John Wayne, Sheila Mannors, Frank McGlynn, Jr., Jack Curtis, Yakima Canutt, Mary McLaren, Dickie Jones, Hank Bell.

Desert Trail. Monogram Pictures. *Director:* Collin Lewis. *Producer:* Paul Malvern. *Screenplay:* Lindsley Parsons. *Camera:* Archie Stout. *Cast:* John Wayne, Mary Kornman, Paul Fix, Edward Chandler, Lafe McKee, Henry Hull, Al Ferguson.

The New Frontier. Republic Pictures. *Director:* Carl Pierson. *Producer:* Paul Malvern. *Screenplay:* Robert Emmett. *Camera:* Gus Peterson. *Cast:* John Wayne, Muriel Evans, Mary McLaren, Murdock MacQuarrie, Warner Richmond, Sam Flint, Earl Dwire, Alfred Bridge.

Lawless Range. Republic Pictures. *Director:* Robert N. Bradbury. *Producers:* Trem Carr, Paul Malvern. *Screenplay:* Lindsley Parsons. *Camera:* Archie Stout. *Cast:*

John Wayne, Sheila Mannors, Earl Dwire, Frank McGlynn, Jr., Jack Curtis, Yakima Canutt, Wally Howe.

1936

The Lawless Nineties. Republic Pictures. *Director:* Joseph Kane. *Producer:* Paul Malvern. *Screenplay:* Joseph Poland. *Camera:* William Nobles. *Cast:* John Wayne, Ann Rutherford, Lane Chandler, Harry Woods, Snowflake, George "Gabby" Hayes, Etta McDaniel, Charles King, Sam Flint, Al Taylor, Cliff Lyons.

King of the Pecos. Republic Pictures. *Director:* Joseph Kane. *Producer:* Paul Malvern. *Screenplay:* Bernard McConville. *Camera:* Jack Martin. *Cast:* John Wayne, Muriel Evans, Cy Kendall, Jack Clifford, Frank Glendon, Herbert Heywood, Arthur Ayelsworth, John Beck, Mary McLaren, Bradley Metcalfe, Jr., Yakima Canutt.

The Oregon Trail. Republic Pictures. *Director:* Scott Pembroke. *Producer:* Paul Malvern. *Screenplay:* Lindsley Parsons, Robert Emmett. *Camera:* Gus Peterson. *Cast:* John Wayne, Ann Rutherford, Yakima Canutt, E. H. Calvert, Fern Emmett, Gino Corrado, Marian Farrell, Frank Rice, Joe Girard, Harry Harvey.

Winds of the Wasteland. Republic Pictures. *Director:* Mack V. Wright. *Producer:* Nat Levine. *Screenplay:* Joseph Poland. *Camera:* William Nobles. *Cast:* John Wayne, Phyllis Fraser, Yakima Canutt, Lane Chandler, Sam Flint, Lew Kelly, Bob Kortman, Douglas Cosgrove, W. M. McCormick.

The Sea Spoilers. Universal Pictures. *Director:* Frank Strayer. *Producer:* Trem Carr. *Screenplay:* George Waggner. *Camera:* Archie Stout, John P. Fulton. *Cast:* John Wayne, Nan Grey, Fuzzy Knight, William Bakewell, Russell Hicks, George Irving, Lotus Long, Harry Worth.

The Lonely Trail. Republic Pictures. *Director:* Joseph Kane. *Producer:* Nat Levine. *Screenplay:* Bernard McConville. *Camera:* William Nobles. *Cast:* John Wayne, Ann Rutherford, Cy Kendall, Snowflake, Etta McDaniel, Bob Kortman, Sam Flint, Yakima Canutt, Bob Burns, Lloyd Ingraham.

Conflict. Universal Pictures. *Director:* David Howard. *Producer:* Trem Carr. *Screenplay:* Charles A. Logue, Walter Weems. *Camera:* Archie Stout. *Cast:* John Wayne, Jean Rogers, Tommy Bupp, Eddie Borden, Ward Bond, Harry Woods, Frank Sheridan, Bryant Washburn, Frank Hagney.

1937

California Straight Ahead. Universal Pictures. *Director:* Arthur Lubin. *Producer:* Trem Carr. *Screenplay:* Herman Boxer. *Camera:* Harry Neumann. *Cast:* John

Wayne, Louise Latimer, Robert McWade, Tully Marshall, Theodore Von Eltz, LeRoy Mason, Grace Goodall.

I Cover the War. Universal Pictures. *Director:* Arthur Lubin. *Producer:* Trem Carr. *Screenplay:* George Waggner. *Camera:* Harry Neumann. *Cast:* John Wayne, Gwen Gaze, Don Barclay, James Bush, Pat Somerset, Charles Brokaw, Arthur Aylesworth, Earl Hodgins, Jack Mack.

Idol of the Crowds. Universal Pictures. *Director:* Arthur Lubin. *Producer:* Trem Carr. *Screenplay:* George Waggner, Harold Buckley. *Camera:* Harry Neumann. *Cast:* John Wayne, Sheila Bromley, Billy Burrud, Russell Gordon, Charles Brokaw, Virginia Brissac, Clem Bevans, George Lloyd.

Adventure's End. Universal Pictures. *Director:* Arthur Lubin. *Producer:* Trem Carr. *Screenplay:* Ben Ames Williams. *Camera:* Gus Peterson, John Fulton. *Cast:* John Wayne, Diana Gibson, Moroni Olsen, Montague Love, Ben Carter, Maurice Black, George Cleveland, Glenn Strange, Britt Wood.

1938

Born to the West (also called *Hell Town*). Paramount Pictures. *Director:* Charles Barton. *Screenplay:* Stuart Anthony, Robert Yost. *Camera:* J. D. Jennings. *Cast:* John Wayne, Marsha Hunt, John Mack Brown, John Patterson, Monte Blue, Lucien Littlefield, Alan Ladd, James Craig, Nick Lukats.

Pals of the Saddle. Republic Pictures. *Director:* George Sherman. *Screenplay:* Stanley Roberts, Betty Burbridge. *Camera:* Reggie Lanning. *Cast:* John Wayne, Ray Corrigan, Max Terhune, Doreen McKay, Frank Milan, Jack Kirk, Ted Adams, Harry Depp.

Overland Stage Raiders. Republic Pictures. *Director:* George Sherman. *Screenplay:* Luci Ward. *Camera:* William Nobles. *Cast:* John Wayne, Louise Brooks, Ray Corrigan, Max Terhune, Fern Emmett, Frank LaRue, Anthony Marsh, Gordon Hart.

Santa Fe Stampede. Republic Pictures. *Director:* George Sherman. *Producer:* William Berke. *Screenplay:* Luci Ward, Betty Burbridge. *Camera:* Reggie Lanning. *Cast:* John Wayne, June Martel, Ray Corrigan, Max Terhune, William Farnum, LeRoy Mason, Martin Spellman, Tom London.

Red River Range. Republic Pictures. *Director:* George Sherman. *Producer:* William Berke. *Screenplay:* Stanley Roberts, Berry Burbridge, Luci Ward. *Camera:* Jack Marta. *Cast:* John Wayne, Ray Corrigan, Max Terhune, Polly Moran, Kirby Grant, William Royale, Perry Ivins, Stanley Blystone, Lenore Bushman, Roger Williams, Olin Francis.

1939

Stagecoach. United Artists. *Director:* John Ford. *Producer:* Walter Wanger. *Screenplay:* Dudley Nichols. *Camera:* Bert Glennon. *Cast:* John Wayne, Claire Trevor, Thomas Mitchell, John Carradine, Andy Devine, Louise Platt, George Bancroft, Berton Churchill, Donald Meek, Tim Holt, Tom Tyler, Elvira Rios, Francis Ford, Marga Ann Deighton, Kent Odell, Yakima Canutt, Chief Big Tree, Florence Lake.

The Night Riders. Republic Pictures. *Director:* George Sherman. *Screenplay:* Betty Burbridge, Stanley Roberts. *Camera:* Jack Marta. *Cast:* John Wayne, Ray Corrigan, Max Terhune, Doreen McKay, Ruth Rogers, Tom Tyler, Kermit Maynard, George Douglas.

Three Texas Steers. Republic Pictures. *Director:* George Sherman. *Screenplay:* Betty Burbridge, Stanley Roberts. *Camera:* Ernest Miller. *Cast:* John Wayne, Carole Landis, Ray Corrigan, Ralph Graves, Max Terhune, Colette Lyons, Roscoe Ates, Lew Kelly, David Sharpe.

Wyoming Outlaw. Republic Pictures. *Director:* George Sherman. *Screenplay:* Jack Netteford. *Camera:* Reggie Lanning. *Cast:* John Wayne, Adele Pearce (Pamela Blake), Ray Corrigan, Donald Barry, Raymond Hatton, LeRoy Mason, Yakima Canutt, Charles Middleton, Elmo Lincoln, David Sharpe.

New Frontier (also called ***Frontier Horizon***). Republic Pictures. *Director:* George Sherman. *Producer:* William Berke. *Screenplay:* Betty Burbridge, Luci Ward. *Camera:* Reggie Lanning. *Cast:* John Wayne, Ray Corrigan, Raymond Hatton, Phylis Isley (Jennifer Jones), Eddy Walker, Sammy McKim, LeRoy Mason, Harrison Greene, Dave O'Brien, Jack Ingram, Bud Osborne.

Allegheny Uprising. RKO Radio Pictures. *Director:* William Seiter. *Producer:* P. J. Wolfson. *Screenplay:* P. J. Wolfson. *Camera:* Nicholas Musuraca. *Cast:* Claire Trevor, John Wayne, George Sanders, Brian Donlevy, Wilfrid Lawson, Robert Barrat, John F. Hamilton, Moroni Olsen, Eddie Quillan, Chill Wills, Ian Wolfe, Wallis Clark, Monte Montague, Eddy Walker, Olaf Hytten, Clay Clement.

1940

Dark Command. Republic Pictures. *Director:* Raoul Walsh. *Producer:* Sol C. Siegel. *Screenplay:* Grover Jones, Lionel Houser, F. Hugh Herbert. *Camera:* Jack Marta. *Cast:* John Wayne, Claire Trevor, Walter Pidgeon, Roy Rogers, George "Gabby" Hayes, Porter Hall, Marjorie Main.

Three Faces West (also called ***The Refugee***). Republic Pictures. *Director:* Bernard Vorhaus. *Producer:* Sol C. Siegel. *Screenplay:* F. Hugh Herbert, Joseph Moncure

March, Samuel Ornitz. *Camera:* John Alton. *Cast:* John Wayne, Sigrid Gurie, Charles Coburn, Spencer Charaters, Helen MacKellar, Roland Varno, Sonny Bupp, Wade Boteler, Trevor Bardette, Russell Simpson, Charles Waldron, Windell Niles.

The Long Voyage Home. United Artists. *Director:* John Ford. *Producer:* Walter Wanger. *Screenplay:* Dudley Nichols. *Camera:* Gregg Toland. *Cast:* John Wayne, Thomas Mitchell, Ian Hunter, Barry Fitzgerald, Wilfrid Lawson, Mildred Natwick, John Qualen, Ward Bond, Arthur Shields, Joseph Sawyer, J. M. Kerrigan, Rafaela Ottiano, Carmen Morales, Douglas Walton, Billy Bevan, Cyril McLaglen.

Seven Sinners. Universal Pictures. *Director:* Tay Garnett. *Producer:* Joe Pasternak. *Screenplay:* John Meehan, Harry Tugend. *Camera:* Rudoplph Maté. *Cast:* Marlene Dietrich, John Wayne, Broderick Crawford, Mischa Auer, Albert Dekker, Billy Gilbert, Anna Lee, Oscar Homolka, Samuel S. Hinds, Reginald Denny, Vince Barnett, Herbert Rawlinson, James Craig, William Bakewell, Antonio Moreno, Russell Hicks, William Davidson, Richard Carle, Willie Fung.

1941

A Man Betrayed (also called *Wheel of Fortune*). Republic Pictures. *Director:* John A. Auer. *Producer:* Armand Schaefer. *Screenplay:* Isabel Dawn. *Camera:* Jack Marta. *Cast:* John Wayne, Frances Dee, Edward Ellis, Wallace Ford, Ward Bond, Harold Huber, Alexander Granach, Barnett Parker, Ed Stanley, Tim Ryan, Harry Hayden, Russell Hicks, Pierre Watkin, Ferris Taylor.

Lady from Louisiana. Republic Pictures. *Director:* Bernard Vorhaus. *Producer:* Bernard Vorhaus. *Screenplay:* Vera Caspary, Michael Hogan, Guy Endore. *Camera:* Jack Marta. *Cast:* John Wayne, Ona Munson, Ray Middleton, Henry Stephenson, Helen Westley, Jack Pennick, Dorothy Dandridge, Shimen Ruskin, Jacqueline Dalya, Paul Scardon, James H. MacNamara, James C. Morton, Maurice Costello.

The Shepherd of the Hills. Paramount Pictures. *Director:* Henry Hathaway. *Producer:* Jack Moss. *Screenplay:* Grover Jones, Stuart Anthony. *Camera:* Charles Lang. *Cast:* John Wayne, Betty Field, Harry Carey, Beulah Bondi, James Barton, Samuel S. Hinds, Marjorie Main, Ward Bond, Marc Lawrence, John Qualen, Fuzzy Knight, Tom Fadden.

Lady for a Night. Republic Pictures. *Director:* Leigh Jason. *Producer:* Albert J. Cohen. *Screenplay:* Isabel Dawn, Boyce DeGaw. *Camera:* Norbert Brodine. *Cast:* Joan Blondell, John Wayne, Ray Middleton, Philip Merivale, Blanche Yurka, Edith Barrett, Leonid Kinskey, Hattie Noel, Montague Love, Carmel Myers, Dorothy

Burgess, Guy Usher, Ivan Miller, Patricia Knox, Lew Payton, Marylin Hare, Dewey Robinson.

1942

Reap the Wild Wind. Paramount Pictures. *Director:* Cecil B. DeMille. *Producer:* Cecil B. DeMille. *Screenplay:* Alan LeMay, Charles Bennett, Jesse Lasky, Jr. *Camera:* Victor Milner, William V. Skall. *Cast:* Ray Milland, John Wayne, Paulette Goddard, Raymond Massey, Robert Preston, Susan Hayward, Lynne Overman, Walter Hampden, Louise Beavers, Elizabeth Risdon, Hedda Hopper, Martha O'Driscoll, Victor Kilian, Monte Blue, Charles Bickford, Janet Beecher, Barbara Britton, Mildred Harris, Victor Varconi, Julia Faye, Oscar Polk, Ben Carter, Lane Chandler, Keith Richards, Milburn Stone.

The Spoilers. Universal Pictures. *Director:* Ray Enright. *Producer:* Frank Lloyd. *Screenplay:* Lawrence Hazard, Tom Reed. *Camera:* Milton Krasner. *Cast:* John Wayne, Marlene Dietrich, Randolph Scott, Margaret Lindsay, Harry Carey, Richard Barthelmess, William Farnum, George Cleveland, Samuel S. Hinds, Marietta Canty, Robert W. Service, Russell Simpson, Jack Norton, Charles Halton, Ray Bennett.

In Old California. Republic Pictures. *Director:* William McGann. *Producer:* Robert North. *Screenplay:* Gertrude Purcell, Frances Hyland. *Camera:* Jack Marta. *Cast:* John Wayne, Binnie Barnes, Albert Dekker, Helen Parrish, Patsy Kelly, Edgar Kennedy, Dick Purcell, Harry Shannon, Charles Halton, Emmett Lynn, Bob McKenzie, Milt Kibbee, Paul Sutton, Anne O'Neal.

Flying Tigers. Republic Pictures. *Director:* David Miller. *Producer:* Edmund Grainger. *Screenplay:* Kenneth Gamet, Barry Trivers. *Camera:* Jack Marta. *Cast:* John Wayne, John Carroll, Anna Lee, Paul Kelly, Gordon Jones, Mae Clarke, Addison Richards, Edmund McDonald, Bill Shirley, Tom Neal, James Dodd, Gregg Barton, John James, Chester Gan, David Bruce.

Reunion in France. Metro-Goldwyn-Mayer. *Director:* Jules Dassin. *Producer:* Joseph L. Mankiewicz. *Screenplay:* Jan Lustig. *Camera:* Robert Planck. *Cast:* Joan Crawford, John Wayne, Philip Dorn, Reginald Owen, Albert Bassermann, John Carradine, Ann Ayars, Moroni Olsen, J. Edward Bromberg, Henry Daniell, Howard Da Silva, Charles Arnt, Morris Ankrum, Edith Evanson, Ernest Dorian, Margaret Laurence, Odette Myrtil, Peter Whitney, Ava Gardner.

Pittsburgh. Universal Pictures. *Director:* Lewis Seiler. *Producer:* Charles K. Feldman. *Screenplay:* Kenneth Gamet, Tom Reed. *Camera:* Robert de Grasse. *Cast:* Marlene Dietrich, John Wayne, Randolph Scott, Frank Craven, Louise Allbritton,

Thomas Gomez, Ludwig Stossel, Shemp Howard, Sammy Stein, Paul Fix, John Dilson, Samuel S. Hinds, Douglas Fowley, Virginia Sale, Bess Flowers, Mira McKinney.

1943

A Lady Takes a Chance (also called *The Cowboy and the Girl*). RKO Radio Pictures. *Director:* William A. Seiter. *Producer:* Frank Ross. *Screenplay:* Robert Ardrey. *Camera:* Frank Redman. *Cast:* Jean Arthur, John Wayne, Charles Winninger, Phil Silvers, Mary Field, Don Costello, John Philliber, Grady Sutton, Grant Withers, Hans Conreid, Peggy Carroll, Ariel Heath, Sugar Geise, Joan Blair.

War of the Wildcats (also called *In Old Oklahoma*). Republic Pictures. *Director:* Albert S. Rogell. *Producer:* Robert North. *Screenplay:* Ethel Hill, Eleanore Griffith. *Camera:* Jack Marta. *Cast:* John Wayne, Martha Scott, Albert Dɛĸ George "Gabby" Hayes, Marjorie Rambeau, Dale Evans, Grant Withers, Sidney Blackmer, Paul Fix, Cecil Cunningham, Irving Bacon, Anne O'Neal.

The Fighting Seabees. Republic Pictures. *Director:* Howard Lydecker, Edward Ludwig. *Producer:* Albert J. Cohen. *Screenplay:* Borden Chase, Aeneas MacKenzie. *Camera:* William Bradford. *Cast:* John Wayne, Susan Hayward, Dennis O'Keefe, William Frawley, Adele Mara, Addison Richards, Leonid Kinskey, Paul Fix, J. M. Kerrigan, Ben Welden, Grant Withers, Duncan Renaldo.

Tall in the Saddle. RKO Radio Pictures. *Director:* Edwin L. Marin. *Producer:* Robert Fellows. *Screenplay:* Michael Hogan, Paul J. Fix. *Camera:* Robert de Grasse. *Cast:* John Wayne, Ella Raines, Ward Bond, George "Gabby" Hayes, Audrey Long, Elizabeth Risdon, Don Douglas, Paul Fix, Russell Wade, Emory Parnell, Raymond Hatton, Harry Woods, Wheaton Chambers, Frank Puglia, Bob McKenzie.

1945

Flame of the Barbary Coast. Republic Pictures. *Director:* Joseph Kane. *Producer:* Joseph Kane. *Screenplay:* Borden Chase. *Camera:* Robert de Grasse. *Cast:* John Wayne, Ann Dvorak, Joseph Schildkraut, William Frawley, Virginia Grey, Russell Hicks, Jack Norton, Paul Fix, Manart Kippen, Eve Lynne, Marc Lawrence, Butterfly McQueen, Rex Lease, Hank Bell, Al Murphy.

Back to Bataan. RKO Radio Pictures. *Director:* Edward Dmytryk. *Producer:* Robert Fellows. *Screenplay:* Ben Barzman, Richard Landau. *Camera:* Nicholas Musuraca. *Cast:* John Wayne, Anthony Quinn, Beulah Bondi, Fely Franquelli, Leonard Strong, Richard Loo, Philip Ahn, "Ducky" Louie, Lawrence Tierney, Paul Fix, Abner Biberman, Vladimir Sokoloff, J. Alex Havier.

Dakota. Republic Pictures. *Director:* Joseph Kane. *Producer:* Joseph Kane. *Screenplay:* Lawrence Hazard. *Camera:* Jack Marta. *Cast:* John Wayne, Vera Hruba Ralston, Walter Brennan, Ward Bond, Ona Munson, Hugo Haas, Mike Mazurki, Olive Blakeney, Paul Fix, Nicodemus Stewart, Grant Withers, Robert Livingston, George Cleveland, Jack LaRue, Bobby Blake, Robert Barret, Sarah Padden, Claire DuBrey, Ward Bond.

They Were Expendable. Metro-Goldwyn-Mayer. *Director:* John Ford. *Producer:* John Ford. *Screenplay:* Lt. Comdr. Frank Wead. *Camera:* Joseph H. August. *Cast:* Robert Montgomery, John Wayne, Donna Reed, Jack Holt, Ward Bond, Marshall Thompson, Paul Langton, Leon Ames, Arthur Walsh, Donald Curtis, Cameron Mitchell, Jeff York, Murray Alper, Harry Tenbrook, Jack Pennick, Alex Havier, Charles Trowbridge, Robert Barrat, Bruce Kellog, Tim Murdock, Louis Jean Heydt, Russell Simpson, Vernon Steele.

1946

Without Reservations. RKO Radio Pictures. *Director:* Mervyn LeRoy. *Producer:* Jesse L. Lasky. *Screenplay:* Andrew Solt. *Camera:* Milton Krasner. *Cast:* John Wayne, Claudette Colbert, Don Defore, Anne Triola, Phil Brown, Frank Puglia, Dona Drake, Thurston Hall, Fernando Alvarado, Charles Arnt, Louella Parsons.

1947

Angel and the Badman. Republic Pictures. *Director:* James Edward Grant. *Producer:* John Wayne. *Screenplay:* James Edward Grant. *Camera:* Archie Stout. *Cast:* John Wayne, Gail Russell, Harry Carey, Bruce Cabot, Irene Rich, Lee Dixon, Tom Powers, John Halloran, Stephen Grant, Joan Barton, Paul Hurst, Craig Woods, Marshall Reed.

Tycoon. RKO Radio Pictures. *Director:* Richard Wallace. *Producer:* Stephen Ames. *Screenplay:* Borden Chase, John Twist. *Camera:* Harry J. Wild. *Cast:* John Wayne, Laraine Day, Sir Cedric Hardwicke, Judith Anderson, James Gleason, Anthony Quinn, Grant Withers, Paul Fix, Fernando Alvarado, Harry Woods, Michael Harvey, Charles Trowbridge.

1948

Fort Apache. RKO Radio Pictures. *Director:* John Ford. *Producer:* John Ford, Merian C. Cooper. *Screenplay:* Frank S. Nugent. *Camera:* Archie Stout. *Cast:* John Wayne, Henry Fonda, Shirley Temple, Pedro Armendariz, Ward Bond, Irene Rich, John Agar, George O'Brien, Anna Lee, Victor McLaglen, Dick Foran, Jack Pennick, Guy Kibbee, Grant Withers, Mae Marsh, Miguel Inclan, Movita, Mary Gordon, Francis Ford, Frank Ferguson.

Red River. United Artists. *Director:* Howard Hawks. *Producer:* Howard Hawks. *Screenplay:* Borden Chase, Charles Schnee. *Camera:* Russell Harlan. *Cast:* John Wayne, Montgomery Clift, Walter Brennan, Joanne Dru, Harry Carey, Sr., John Ireland, Coleen Gray, Harry Carey, Jr., Noah Berry, Jr., Paul Fix, Tom Tyler, Lane Chandler, Shelley Winters.

Three Godfathers. Metro-Goldwyn-Mayer. *Director:* John Ford. *Producer:* John Ford, Merian C. Cooper. *Screenplay:* Laurence Stallings, Frank S. Nugent. *Camera:* Winton C. Hoch, Charles Boyle. *Cast:* John Wayne, Pedro Armendariz, Harry Carey, Jr., Ward Bond, Mae Marsh, Mildred Natwick, Jane Darwell, Guy Kibbee, Dorothy Ford, Ben Johnson, Charles Halton, Hank Worden, Jack Pennick, Fred Libby, Michael Dugan, Don Summers.

1949

Wake of the Red Witch. Republic Pictures. *Director:* Edward Ludwig. *Producer:* Edmund Grainger. *Screenplay:* Harry Brown, Kenneth Gamet. *Camera:* Reggie Lanning. *Cast:* John Wayne, Gail Russell, Gig Young, Adele Mara, Luther Adler, Eduard Franz, Grant Withers, Henry Daniell, Paul Fix, Dennis Hoey, Jeff Corey, Erskine Sanford, Duke Kahanamoku, Harry Brandon, John Wengraf, Myron Healey, Fred Libby.

She Wore a Yellow Ribbon. RKO Radio Pictures. *Director:* John Ford. *Producer:* John Ford, Merian C. Cooper. *Screenplay:* Frank S. Nugent, Laurence Stallings. *Camera:* Winton C. Hoch. *Cast:* John Wayne, Joanne Dru, John Agar, Ben Johnson, Harry Carey, Jr., Victor McLaglen, Mildred Natwick, George O'Brien, Arthur Shields, Harry Woods, Chief Big Tree, Noble Johnson, Cliff Lyons, Tom Tyler, Michael Dugan, Mickey Simpson, Frank McGrath, Don Summer, Fred Libby, Jack Pennick, Billy Jones, Fred Graham, Fred Kennedy, Rudy Bowman, Ray Hyke, Lee Bradley.

The Fighting Kentuckian. Republic Pictures. *Director:* George Waggner. *Producer:* John Wayne. *Screenplay:* George Waggner. *Camera:* Lee Garmes. *Cast:* John Wayne, Vera Hruba Ralston, Philip Dorn, Oliver Hardy, Marie Windsor, John Howard, Hugo Haas, Grant Withers, Odette Myrtil, Paul Fix, Mae Marsh, Jack Pennick, Mickey Simpson.

Sands of Iwo Jima. Republic Pictures. *Director:* Allan Dwan. *Producer:* Edmund Grainger. *Screenplay:* Harry Brown, James Edward Grant. *Camera:* Reggie Lanning. *Cast:* John Wayne, John Agar, Adele Mara, Forrest Tucker, Wally Cassell, James Brown, Richard Webb, Arthur Franz, Julie Bishop, James Holden, Peter Coe, Richard Jaeckel, Bill Murphy, George Tyne, Hal Fieberling, John McGuire, Martin Milner, Leonard Gumley, Willliam Self, Dorothy Ford, Dick Jones, David Clarke.

1950

Rio Grande. Republic Pictures. *Director:* John Ford. *Producer:* John Ford, Merian C. Cooper. *Screenplay:* James Kevin McGuiness. *Camera:* Bert Glennon. *Cast:* John Wayne, Maureen O'Hara, Ben Johnson, J. Carrol Naish, Victor McLaglen, Chill Wills, Harry Carey, Jr., Claude Jarman, Jr., Grant Withers, and The Sons of the Pioneers.

1951

Operation Pacific. Warner Brothers. *Director:* George Waggner. *Producer:* Louis F. Edelman. *Screenplay:* George Waggner. *Camera:* Bert Glennon. *Cast:* John Wayne, Patricia Neal, Ward Bond, Scott Forbes, Philip Carey, Martin Milner, Jack Pennick, Paul Picerni, Bill Campbell, Kathryn Givney, Virginia Brissac.

Flying Leathernecks. RKO Radio Pictures. *Director:* Nicholas Ray. *Producer:* Edmund Grainger. *Screenplay:* James Edward Grant. *Camera:* William E. Snyder. *Cast:* John Wayne, Robert Ryan, Don Taylor, Janis Carter, Jay C. Flippen, William Harrigan, James Bell, Barry Kelley, Maurice Jara, Adam Williams, James Dobson, Carleton Young, Steve Flagg, Brett King, Gordon Gebert.

1952

The Quiet Man. Republic Pictures. *Director:* John Ford. *Producer:* John Ford, Merian C. Cooper. *Screenplay:* Frank S. Nugent. *Camera:* Winton C. Hoch. *Cast:* John Wayne, Maureen O'Hara, Barry Fitzgerald, Ward Bond, Victor McLaglen, Mildred Natwick, Francis Ford, Eileen Crowe, May Craig, Arthur Shields, Charles FitzSimons, James Lilburn, Sean McGlory, Jack McGowran, Joseph O'Dea, Eric Gorman, Kevin Lawless, Paddy O'Donnell, Webb Overlander, Patrick Wayne, Michael Wayne, Ken Curtis, Melinda Wayne, Antonia Wayne.

Big Jim McLain. Warner Bros. *Director:* Edward Ludwig. *Producer:* John Wayne, Robert Fellows. *Screenplay:* James Edward Grant. *Camera:* Archie Stout. *Cast:* John Wayne, Nancy Olson, James Arness, Alan Napier, Gayne Whitman, Hans Conreid, Veda Ann Borg, Hal Baylor, Robert Keys, John Hubbard, Sarah Padden, Dan Liu.

1953

Trouble along the Way. Warner Bros. *Director:* Michael Curtiz. *Producer:* Melville Shavelson. *Screenplay:* Melville Shavelson, Jack Rose. *Camera:* Archie Stout. *Cast:* John Wayne, Donna Reed, Charles Coburn, Tom Tully, Marie Windsor, Sherry Jackson, Tom Helmore, Dabbs Greer, Leif Erickson, Douglas Spencer, Chuck Connors.

Island in the Sky. Warner Bros. *Director:* William A. Wellman. *Producer:* John Wayne, Robert Fellows. *Screenplay:* Ernest K. Gann. *Camera:* Archie Stout. *Cast:* John Wayne, Lloyd Nolan, Walter Abel, James Arness, Andy Devine, Allyn Joslyn, James Lydon, Harry Carey, Jr., Hal Baylor, Sean McGlory, Wally Cassell, Gordon Jones, Frank Fenton, Robert Keys, Sumner Getchell, Regis Toomey, Paul Fix, Jim Dugan, George Chandler, Bob Steele, Darryl Hickman, Touch Connors, Carl Switzer, Cass Gidley, Guy Anderson.

Hondo. Warner Bros. *Director:* John Farrow. *Producer:* John Wayne, Robert Fellows. *Screenplay:* James Edward Grant. *Camera:* Robert Burks, Archie Stout. *Cast:* John Wayne, Geraldine Page, Ward Bond, Michael Pate, Lee Aaker, James Arness, Rodolfo Acosta, Leo Gordon, Tom Irish, Paul Fix, Rayford Barnes.

1954

The High and the Mighty. Warner Bros. *Director:* William A. Wellman. *Producer:* John Wayne, Robert Fellows. *Screenplay:* Ernest K. Gann. *Camera:* Archie Stout. *Cast:* John Wayne, Claire Trevor, Laraine Day, Robert Stack, Jan Sterling, Phil Harris, Robert Newton, David Brian, Paul Kelly, Sidney Blackmer, Julie Bishop, Pedro Gonzales-Gonzales, John Howard, Wally Brown, William Campbell, Ann Doran, John Qualen, Paul Fix, George Chandler, Joy Kim, Michael Wellman, Douglas Fowley, Regis Toomey, Carl Switzer, Robert Keys, William DeWolf Hopper, William Schallert, Julie Mitchum, Karen Sharpe, John Smith, Doe Avedon.

1955

The Sea Chase. Warner Bros. *Director:* John Farrow. *Producer:* John Farrow. *Screenplay:* James Warner Bellah, John Twist. *Camera:* William H. Clothier. *Cast:* John Wayne, Lana Turner, David Farrar, Lyle Bettger, Tab Hunter, James Arness, Richard Davalos, John Qualen, Paul Fix, Lowell Gilmore, Luis Van Rooten, Alan Hale, Wilton Graff, Peter Whitney, Claude Akins, John Doucette, Alan Lee.

Blood Alley. Warner Bros. *Director:* William A. Wellman. *Screenplay:* A. S. Fleischman. *Camera:* William H. Clothier. *Cast:* John Wayne, Lauren Bacall, Paul Fix, Joy Kim, Berry Kroeger, Mike Mazurki, Anita Ekberg, Henry Nakamura, W. T. Chang, George Chan.

1956

The Conqueror. RKO Radio Pictures. *Director:* Dick Powell. *Producer:* Dick Powell. *Screenplay:* Oscar Millard. *Camera:* Joseph LaShelle. *Cast:* John Wayne, Susan Hayward, Pedro Armendariz, Agnes Moorehead, Thomas Gomez, John Hoyt, William Conrad, Ted de Corsia, Leslie Bradley, Leo Gordon, Lee Van Cleef, Peter Mamakos, Fred Graham, Richard Loo, George E. Stone, Jeanne Gerson, Lane Bradford, Sylvia Lewis.

The Searchers. Warner Bros. *Director:* John Ford. *Producer:* Merian C. Cooper, Patrick Ford. *Screenplay:* Frank S. Nugent. *Camera:* Winton C. Hoch. *Cast:* John Wayne, Jeffrey Hunter, Vera Miles, Natalie Wood, John Qualen, Olive Carey, Henry Brandon, Ken Curtis, Harry Carey, Jr., Ward Bond, Antonio Moreno, Hank Worden, Lana Wood, Walter Coy, Dorothy Jordan, Pippa Scott, Patrick Wayne, Beulah Archuletta.

1957

The Wings of Eagles. Metro-Goldwyn-Mayer. *Director:* John Ford. *Producer:* Charles Schnee. *Screenplay:* Frank Fenton, William Wister Haines. *Camera:* Paul C. Vogel. *Cast:* John Wayne, Dan Dailey, Maureen O'Hara, Ward Bond, Ken Curtis, Edmund Lowe, Kenneth Tobey, James Todd, Barry Kelley, Sig Ruman, Henry O'Neill, Willis Bouchey, Dorothy Jordan, Peter Ortiz, Louis Jean Heydt, Tige Andrews, Dan Borzage, William Tracy, Harlan Warde, Jack Pennick, Bill Henry, Mimi Gibson, Evelyn Rudie, Mae Marsh.

Jet Pilot. RKO Radio Pictures. *Director:* Josef von Sternberg. *Producer:* Jules Furthman. *Screenplay:* Jules Furthman. *Camera:* Winton C. Hoch. *Cast:* John Wayne, Janet Leigh, Jay C. Flippen, Paul Fix, Richard Rober, Roland Winters, Hans Conreid, Ivan Triesault, John Bishop, Perdita Chandler, Joyce Compton, Denver Pyle.

Legend of the Lost. United Artists. *Director:* Henry Hathaway. *Producer:* Henry Hathaway. *Screenplay:* Robert Presnell, Jr., Ben Hecht. *Camera:* Jack Cardiff. *Cast:* John Wayne, Sophia Loren, Rossano Brazzi, Kurt Kasznar, Sonia Moser, Angela Portaluri, Ibrahim El Hadish.

1958

I Married a Woman. RKO Radio Pictures. *Director:* Hal Kanter. *Producer:* William Bloom. *Screenplay:* Goodman Ace. *Camera:* Lucien Ballard. *Cast:* George Gobel, Diana Dors, Adolphe Menjou, Jessie Royce-Landis, Nita Talbot, William Redfield, Steve Dunne, John McGiver, Steve Pendleton, Cheerio Meredith, Kay Buckley, Angie Dickinson, John Wayne.

The Barbarian and the Geisha. 20th Century–Fox. *Director:* John Huston. *Producer:* Eugene Frenke. *Screenplay:* Charles Grayson. *Camera:* Charles G. Clarke. *Cast:* John Wayne, Eiko Ando, Sam Jaffe, So Yamamura, Norman Thomson, James Robbins, Movita, Kodaya Ichikawa, Hiroshi Yamato, Tokujiro Iketaniuchi, Fuji Kasai, Takeshi Kumagai.

1959

Rio Bravo. Warner Bros. *Director:* Howard Hawks. *Producer:* Howard Hawks. *Screenplay:* Jules Furthman, Leigh Brackett. *Camera:* Russell Harlan. *Cast:* John

Wayne, Dean Martin, Ricky Nelson, Angie Dickinson, Walter Brennan, Ward Bond, John Russell, Pedro Gonzales-Gonzales, Estrelita Rodriquez, Claude Akins, Malcolm Atterbury, Harry Carey, Jr., Bob Steele, Myron Healey, Fred Graham.

The Horse Soldiers. United Artists. *Director:* John Ford. *Producer:* John Lee Mahin, Martin Rackin. *Screenplay:* John Lee Mahin, Martin Rackin. *Camera:* William H. Clothier. *Cast:* John Wayne, William Holden, Constance Towers, Althea Gibson, Hoot Gibson, Anna Lee, Russell Simpson, Stan Jones, Carleton Young, Basil Ruysdael, Strother Martin, William Henry, William Leslie.

1960

The Alamo. United Artists. *Director:* John Wayne. *Producer:* John Wayne. *Screenplay:* James Edward Grant. *Camera:* William H. Clothier. *Cast:* John Wayne, Richard Widmark, Laurence Harvey, Richard Boone, Frankie Avalon, Patrick Wayne, Linda Cristal, Joan O'Brien, Chill Wills, Joseph Calleia, Ken Curtis, Carlos Arruza, Jester Hairston, Veda Ann Borg, John Dierkes, Denver Pyle, Aissa Wayne, Hank Worden, Bill Henry, Bill Daniel, Wesley Lau, Chuck Roberson, Guinn Williams, Olive Carey, Rubin Padilla, Carol Berlin, Tom Hennesy, Cy Malis, Rojelio Estrada.

North to Alaska. 20th Century–Fox. *Director:* Henry Hathaway. *Producer:* Henry Hathaway. *Screenplay:* John Lee Mahin, Martin Rackin, Claude Binyon. *Camera:* Leon Shamroy. *Cast:* John Wayne, Stewart Granger, Ernie Kovacs, Fabian, Capucine, Mickey Shaughnessy, Karl Swenson, Joseph Sawyer, Kathleen Freeman, John Qualen, Stanley Adams, Stephen Courtleigh, Douglas Dick, Jerry O'Sullivan, Ollie O'Toole, Frank Faylen, Esther Dale, Richard Deacon, Kermit Maynard, Lilyan Chauvin, Joey Faye, Arlene Harris, James Griffith.

1961

The Comancheros. 20th Century–Fox. *Director:* Michael Curtiz. *Producer:* George Sherman. *Screenplay:* James Edward Grant, Claire Huffaker. *Camera:* William H. Clothier. *Cast:* John Wayne, Stuart Whitman, Ina Balin, Nehemiah Persoff, Lee Marvin, Michael Ansara, Patrick Wayne, Bruce Cabot, Joan O'Brien, Jack Elam, Edgar Buchanan, Henry Daniell, Richard Devon, Steve Baylor, John Dierkes, Roger Mobley, Bob Steele, Luisa Triana, Iphigenie Castiglioni, Aissa Wayne, George Lewis.

1962

The Man Who Shot Liberty Valance. Paramount Pictures. *Director:* John Ford. *Producer:* Willis Goldbeck. *Screenplay:* James Warner Bellah, Willis Goldbeck. *Camera:* William H. Clothier. *Cast:* John Wayne, James Stewart, Vera Miles, Lee

Marvin, Edmond O'Brien, Andy Devine, Woody Strode, John Qualen, Jeanette Nolan, Lee Van Cleef, Strother Martin, Ken Murray.

Hatari! Paramount Pictures. *Director:* Howard Hawks. *Producer:* Howard Hawks. *Screenplay:* Leigh Brackett. *Camera:* Russell Harlan. *Cast:* John Wayne, Hardy Kruger, Elsa Martinelli, Red Buttons, Gerard Blain, Michele Girardon, Bruce Cabot, Valentin De Vargas, Eduard Franz, Queenie Leonard.

The Longest Day. 20th Century–Fox. *Director:* Ken Annakin, Andrew Marton, Bernhard Wicki. *Producer:* Darryl F. Zanuck. *Screenplay:* Cornelius Ryan. *Camera:* Jean Bourgoin, Henri Persin, Walter Wottiz. *Cast:* John Wayne, Robert Mitchum, Henry Fonda, Robert Ryan, Rod Steiger, Robert Wagner, Richard Beymer, Mel Ferrer, Jeffrey Hunter, Paul Anka, Sal Mineo, Roddy McDowall, Stuart Whitman, Steve Forrest, Eddie Albert, Edmond O'Brien, Fabian, Red Buttons, Tom Tryon, Alexander Knox, Richard Burton, Kenneth More, Peter Lawford, Richard Todd, Leo Genn, John Gregson, Sean Connery, Curt Jurgens, Werner Hinz, Paul Hartmann, Gert Frobe, Hans Christian Blech, Wolfgang Preiss, Peter Van Eyck, Arletty, Jean-Louis Barrault, Bourvil, Pauline Carton, Ray Danton, Irina Demich, Henry Grace, Peter Helm, Donald Houston, Karl John, Fernand Ledoux, Christian Marquand, Dewey Martin, Michael Medwin, Richard Munch, Leslie Phillips, Ron Randell, Madeleine Renaud, Georges Riviere, Norman Rossington, Tommy Sands, George Segal, Jean Servais, Richard Wattis, Georges Wilson.

How the West Was Won. Metro-Goldwyn-Mayer. *Director:* Henry Hathaway, John Ford, George Marshall. *Producer:* Bernard Smith. *Screenplay:* James R. Webb. *Camera:* William H. Daniels, Milton Krasner, Charles Lang, Joseph LaShelle. *Cast:* Carroll Baker, Lee J. Cobb, Henry Fonda, Carolyn Jones, Karl Malden, Gregory Peck, George Peppard, Robert Preston, Debbie Reynolds, James Stewart, Eli Wallach, John Wayne, Richard Widmark, Brigid Bazlen, Walter Brennan, David Brian, Andy Devine, Raymond Massey, Agnes Moorehead, Henry (Harry) Morgan, Thelma Ritter, Mickey Shaughnessy, Russ Tamblyn, Lee Van Cleef, Rodolfo Acosta, Jay C. Flippen, Joseph Sawyer. *Narrator:* Spencer Tracy.

1963

Donovan's Reef. Paramount Pictures. *Director:* John Ford. *Producer:* John Ford. *Screenplay:* Frank S. Nugent. *Camera:* William H. Clothier. *Cast:* John Wayne, Lee Marvin, Jack Warden, Elizabeth Allen, Cesar Romero, Dorothy Lamour.

McLintock! United Artists. *Director:* Andrew V. McLaglen. *Producer:* Michael Wayne. *Screenplay:* James Edward Grant. *Camera:* William H. Clothier. *Cast:* John Wayne, Maureen O'Hara, Patrick Wayne, Stefanie Powers, Yvonne DeCarlo, Jack

Kruschen, Chill Wills, Jerry Van Dyke, Edgar Buchanan, Bruce Cabot, Perry Lopez, Michael Pate, Strother Martin, Gordon Jones, Robert Lowery, H. W. Gin, Aissa Wayne.

1964

Circus World. Paramount Pictures. *Director:* Henry Hathaway. *Producer:* Samuel Bronston. *Screenplay:* Ben Hecht, Julian Halvey, James Edward Grant. *Camera:* Jack Hildyard, Claude Renoir. *Cast:* John Wayne, Claudia Cardinale, Rita Hayworth, Lloyd Nolan, Richard Conte, John Smith, Henri Dantes, Wanda Rotha, Katharyna, Kay Walsh, Margaret MacGrath, Katherine Ellison, Miles Malleson, Katharine Kath, Moustache.

1965

The Greatest Story Ever Told. United Artists. *Director:* George Stevens. *Producer:* George Stevens. *Screenplay:* James Lee Barrett, George Stevens. *Camera:* William C. Mellor, Loyal Griggs. *Cast:* Max von Sydow, Dorothy McGuire, Robert Loggia, Charlton Heston, Michael Anderson, Jr., Robert Blake, Burt Brinckerhoff, John Considine, Jamie Farr, David Hedison, Peter Mann, David McCallum, Roddy McDowall, Gary Raymond, Tom Reese, David Sheiner, Ina Balin, Janet Margolin, Michael Tolan, Sidney Poitier, Joanna Dunham, Carroll Baker, Pat Boone, Van Heflin, Sal Mineo, Shelley Winters, Ed Wynn, John Wayne, Telly Savalas, Angela Lansbury, Johnny Seven, Paul Stewart, Harold J. Stone, Martin Landau, Nehemiah Persoff, Victor Buono, Robert Busch, John Crawford, Russell Johnson, John Lupton, Abraham Sofaer, Chet Stratton, Ron Whelan, José Ferrer, Claude Rains, John Abbott, Rodolfo Acosta, Michael Ansara, Philip Coolidge, Dal Jenkins, Joe Perry, Marian Seldes, Donald Pleasence, Richard Conte, Frank De Kova, Joseph Sirola, Cyril Delevanti, Mark Lenard, Frank Silvera.

In Harm's Way. Paramount Pictures. *Director:* Otto Preminger. *Producer:* Otto Preminger. *Screenplay:* Wendell Mayes. *Camera:* Loyal Griggs. *Cast:* John Wayne, Kirk Douglas, Patricia Neal, Tom Tryon, Paula Prentiss, Brandon de Wilde, Jill Haworth, Dana Andrews, Stanley Holloway, Burgess Meredith, Franchot Tone, Patrick O'Neal, Carroll O'Connor, Slim Pickens, James Mitchum, George Kennedy, Bruce Cabot, Barbara Bouchet, Tod Andrews, Larry Hagman, Stewart Moss, Richard Le Pore, Chet Stratton, Soo Yong, Dort Clark, Phil Mattingly, Henry Fonda.

The Sons of Katie Elder. Paramount Pictures. *Director:* Henry Hathaway. *Producer:* Hal Wallis. *Screenplay:* William H. Wright, Allan Weiss, Harry Essex. *Camera:* Lucien Ballard. *Cast:* John Wayne, Dean Martin, Martha Hyer, Michael Anderson, Jr., Earl Holliman, Jeremy Slate, James Gregory, Paul Fix, George Kennedy, Dennis Hopper, John Litel, Strother Martin, Rhys Williams, John Qualen, Percy Kelton, Rodolfo Acosta, James Westerfield.

1966

Cast a Giant Shadow. United Artists. *Director:* Melville Shavelson. *Producer:* Melville Shavelson, Michael Wayne. *Screenplay:* Melville Shavelson. *Camera:* Aldo Tonti. *Cast:* Kirk Douglas, Yul Brynner, Senta Berger, Angie Dickinson, Luther Adler, Stathis Giallelis, James Donald, Gordon Jackson, Haym Topol, Frank Sinatra, John Wayne, Ruth White, Michael Shilo, Shlomo Hermon.

1967

The War Wagon. Universal. *Director:* Burt Kennedy. *Producer:* Marvin Schwartz. *Screenplay:* Clair Huffaker. *Camera:* William H. Clothier. *Cast:* John Wayne, Kirk Douglas, Howard Keel, Robert Walker, Keenan Wynn, Bruce Cabot, Valora Nolan, Gene Evans, Joanna Barnes, Terry Wilson, Don Collier.

El Dorado. Paramount Pictures. *Director:* Howard Hawks. *Producer:* Howard Hawks. *Screenplay:* Leigh Brackett. *Camera:* Harold Rossen. *Cast:* John Wayne, Robert Mitchum, James Caan, Charlene Holt, Michele Carey, Arthur Hunnicutt, R. G. Armstrong, Edward Asner, Paul Fix, Johnny Crawford, Christopher George, Robert Rothwell, Adam Roarke, Chuck Courtney, Robert Donner.

1968

The Green Berets. Warner Bros.–Seven Arts. *Director:* John Wayne, Ray Kellogg, Mervyn LeRoy (uncredited). *Producer:* Michael Wayne. *Screenplay:* James Lee Barrett. *Camera:* Winton C. Hoch. *Cast:* John Wayne, David Janssen, Jim Hutton, Aldo Ray, Raymond St. Jacques, Bruce Cabot, Jack Soo, George Takei, Patrick Wayne, Irene Tsu, Edward Faulkner, Jason Evers, Mike Henry, Craig Jue, Luke Askew.

Hellfighters. Universal Pictures. *Director:* Andrew V. McLaglen . *Producer:* Robert Arthur. *Screenplay:* Clair Huffaker. *Camera:* William H. Clothier. *Cast:* John Wayne, Katharine Ross, Vera Miles, Jim Hutton, Jay C. Flippen, Bruce Cabot, Edward Faulkner, Barbara Stuart, Edmund Hashim, Valentin De Vargas.

1969

True Grit. Paramount Pictures. *Director:* Henry Hathaway. *Producer:* Hal B. Wallis. *Screenplay:* Marguerite Roberts. *Camera:* Lucien Ballard. *Cast:* John Wayne, Glen Campbell, Kim Darby, Jeremy Slate, Robert Duvall, Dennis Hopper, Alfred Ryder, Strother Martin, Jeff Corey, Ron Soble, John Fielder, James Westerfield, John Doucette, Donald Woods, Edith Atwater, Carlos Rivas, Isabel Boniface, H. W. Gim, John Pickard, Elizabeth Harrower, Ken Renard, Jay Ripley, Kenneth Becker.

The Undefeated. 20th Century–Fox. *Director:* Andrew V. McLaglen. *Producer:* Robert L. Jacks. *Screenplay:* James Lee Barrett. *Camera:* William H. Clothier.

Cast: John Wayne, Rock Hudson, Antonio Aguilar, Roman Gabriel, Marian Mc-Cargo, Lee Meriwether, Merlin Olsen, Melissa Newman, Bruce Cabot, Michael Vincent, Ben Johnson, James Dobson, Edward Faulkner, Harry Carey, Jr., Paul Fix, Royal Dano, Richard Mulligan, Carlos Rivas, John Agar, Guy Raymond, Don Collier, Big John Hamilton, Dub Taylor, Henry Beckman, Victor Junco, Robert Donner, Pedro Armendariz, Jr., Rudy Diaz, Richard Angarola, James McEachin, Gregg Palmer, Juan Garcia, Kiel Martin, Bob Gravage.

1970

Chisum. Warner Bros. *Director:* Andrew V. McLaglen. *Producer:* Michael Wayne, Andrew J. Fenady. *Screenplay:* Andrew J. Fenady. *Camera:* William H. Clothier. *Cast:* John Wayne, Forrest Tucker, Christopher George, Ben Johnson, Glenn Corbett, Andrew Prine, Bruce Cabot, Geoffrey Deuel, Pamela McMyler, Patric Knowles, Richard Jaeckel, Lynda Day, John Agar, Lloyd Battista, Robert Donner, Ray Teal, Edward Faulkner, Ron Soble, John Mitchum, Glenn Langan, Alan Baxter, Alberto Morin, William Bryant, Pedro Armendariz, Jr., Christopher Mitchum, Abraham Sofaer, Gregg Palmer.

1971

Rio Lobo. National General Pictures. *Director:* Howard Hawks. *Producer:* Howard Hawks. *Screenplay:* Leigh Brackett, Burton Wohl. *Camera:* William H. Clothier. *Cast:* John Wayne, Jorge Rivero, Jennifer O'Neill, Jack Elam, Victor French, Susana Dosamantes, Christopher Mitchum, Mike Henry, David Huddleston, Bill Williams, Edward Faulkner, Sherry Lansing, George Plimpton.

Big Jake. National General Pictures. *Director:* George Sherman. *Producer:* Michael Wayne. *Screenplay:* Harry Julian Fink, R. M. Fink. *Camera:* William H. Clothier. *Cast:* John Wayne, Richard Boone, Maureen O'Hara, Patrick Wayne, Christopher Mitchum, Bobby Vinton, Bruce Cabot, Glenn Corbett, Harry Carey, Jr., John Doucette, Jim Davis, John Agar, Gregg Palmer, Robert Warner, Jim Burke, Dean Smith, Ethan Wayne, Virginia Capers, William Walker, Jerry Gatlin, Tom Hennesy, Don Epperson, Everett Creach, Jeff Wingfield, Hank Worden.

1972

The Cowboys. Universal Pictures. *Director:* Mark Rydell. *Producer:* Mark Rydell. *Screenplay:* Irving Ravetch, Harriet Frank, Jr., William Dale Jennings. *Camera:* Robert Surtees. *Cast:* John Wayne, Roscoe Lee Brown, Bruce Dern, Colleen Dewhurst, Slim Pickens, Lonny Chapman, Charles Tyner, A. Martinez, Alfred Barker, Jr., Nicolas Beauvy, Steve Benedict, Robert Carradine, Norman Howell, Jr., Stephen Hudis, Sean Kelly, Clay O'Brien, Sam O'Brien, Mike Pyeatt, Sarah Cunningham, Allyn Ann McLerie, Matt Clark.

1973

The Train Robbers. Warner Bros. *Director:* Burt Kennedy. *Producer:* Michael Wayne. *Screenplay:* Burt Kennedy. *Camera:* William H. Clothier. *Cast:* John Wayne, Ann-Margret, Rod Taylor, Ben Johnson, Christopher George, Bobby Vinton, Jerry Gatlin, Ricardo Montalban.

Cahill, United States Marshal. Warner Bros. *Director:* Andrew V. McLaglen. *Producer:* Michael Wayne. *Screenplay:* Harry Julian Fink, R. M. Fink. *Camera:* Joseph Biroc. *Cast:* John Wayne, George Kennedy, Gary Grimes, Neville Brand, Clay O'Brien, Marie Windsor, Morgan Paull, Dan Vardis, Royal Dano, Scott Walker, Denver Pyle, Jackie Coogan, Rayford Barnes, Dan Kemp, Harry Carey, Jr., Walter Barnes, Paul Fix, Pepper Martin, Vance Davis, Ken Wolger, Hank Worden, James Nusser, Murray MacLeod, Hunter von Leer.

1974

McQ. Warner Bros. *Director:* John Sturges. *Producer:* Jules Levy, Arthur Gardner. *Screenplay:* Lawrence Roman. *Camera:* Harry Stradling, Jr. *Cast:* John Wayne, Eddie Albert, Diana Muldaur, Colleen Dewhurst, Clu Gulager, David Huddleston, Jim Watkins, Al Lettieri, Julie Adams, Robert E. Mosley, William Bryant, Joe Tornatore, Richard Kelton, Richard Eastham, Dick Friel.

1975

Brannigan. United Artists. *Director:* Douglas Hickox. *Producer:* Jules Levy, Arthur Gardner. *Screenplay:* Christopher Trumbo, Michael Butler, William P. McGivern, William Norton. *Camera:* Gerry Fisher. *Cast:* John Wayne, Richard Attenborough, Judy Geeson, Mel Ferrer, John Vernon, Daniel Pilon, John Stride, James Booth, Del Henney, Anthony Booth, Brian Clover, Ralph Meeker, Arthur Batanides.

Rooster Cogburn. Universal Pictures. *Director:* Stuart Millar. *Producer:* Hal B. Wallis. *Screenplay:* Martin Julien. *Camera:* Harry Stradling, Jr. *Cast:* John Wayne, Katharine Hepburn, Anthony Zerbe, Richard Jordan, John McIntire, Paul Koslo, Jack Colvin, Jon Lormer, Richard Romancito, Lane Smith, Warren Vanders, Jerry Gatlin, Strother Martin.

1976

The Shootist. Paramount Pictures. *Director:* Don Siegel. *Producer:* M. J. Frankovich, William Self. *Screenplay:* Miles Hood Swarthout, Scott Hale. *Camera:* Bruce Surtees. *Cast:* John Wayne, Lauren Bacall, Ron Howard, James Stewart, Richard Boone, Hugh O'Brian, Bill McKinney, Harry Morgan, John Carradine, Sheree North, Richard Lenz, Scatman Crothers, Gregg Palmer, Alfred Dennis, Melody Thomas, Kathleen O'Malley.

Bibliographical Essay

The greatest barrier to current research and writing about John Wayne is the unavailability of the Wayne papers, which are still in possession of the actor's family, as are the records of his production company, Batjac. This void is in part filled by the Charles K. Feldman Papers in the Mayer Library of the American Film Institute in Los Angeles and the voluminous John Ford Collection in the Lilly Library at Indiana University in Bloomington. Since Feldman was Wayne's long-term agent, his files include pertinent letters, telegrams, business memos, contracts, and production material on the star's films. The Ford Collection consists of correspondence, scripts, production records, legal documents, photographs, and germane interviews taped by the director's grandson, Dan Ford.

Production files from Warner Bros., Metro-Goldwyn-Mayer, and 20th Century–Fox are available in the Doheny Library at the University of Southern California, as are Joseph Pasternak's scrapbook and the varied and useful Constance McCormick Collection. The Cecil B. DeMille Papers, housed at Brigham Young University, contain much information on the making of *Reap the Wild Wind*, whereas material on several of Wayne's films may be found in the Henry Hathaway Collection at AFI's Mayer Library. The Maurice Zolotow Collection in the Humanities Research Center of the University of Texas at Austin holds most of the research compiled by the New York critic for his 1974 biography of Wayne, including a supposed autobiography focusing on the star's early life and based on the biographer's conversations with the actor. Among the holdings of the Wisconsin Center for Film and Theater Research at the University of Wisconsin are the papers of Walter Wanger and Walter Mirisch, two of John Wayne's significant producers.

My own oral histories have been fundamental in the writing of *Duke: The Life and Image of John Wayne*. Expressly for this book I interviewed Julie Adams (Los Angeles, 1993), Budd Boetticher (Ramona, California, 1993), Red Buttons (Los Angeles, 1993), Diana Serra Cary (Hollister, California, 1996), Linda Cristal (Los Angeles, 1991), Dan Ford (Evanston, Illinois, 1993), Kathleen Freeman (Los Angeles, 1993), Coleen Gray (Los Angeles, 1993), Earl Holliman (Los Angeles, 1993), Roy Huggins (Los Angeles, 1993), Ben Johnson (Mesa, Arizona, 1992), Martin Jurow (Dallas, 1994), Janet Leigh (Los Angeles, 1993), Mary Anita Loos (Los Angeles, 1994), Adele Mara (Los Angeles, 1993), Maureen O'Hara (Los Angeles, 1996), Martha Scott (Los Angeles, 1993), James T. "Happy" Shahan (Brackettville, Texas, 1993), Melville Shavelson (Los Angeles, 1993), Robert

353

Stack (Los Angeles, 1993), Linda Stirling (Los Angeles, 1993), Claire Trevor (Los Angeles, 1994), Pilar Wayne (Laguna Beach, California, 1996), and Marie Windsor (Los Angeles, 1993).

As director of the SMU Oral History Program on the Performing Arts for twenty-five years, I taped numerous sessions with individuals who knew Wayne or contributed to some aspect of his career. Among these are Gene Autry (Los Angeles, 1984), Hall Bartlett (Los Angeles, 1985), Charles Bennett (Los Angeles, 1980), Steven Broidy (Los Angeles, 1988), Harry Carey, Jr. (Los Angeles, 1984), Donald Curtis (Dallas, 1988), Laraine Day (Los Angeles, 1979), Edward Dmytryk (Austin, Texas, 1979), Ann Doran (Los Angeles, 1983), Joanne Dru (Los Angeles, 1991), Harry Essex (Los Angeles, 1989), Dale Evans (Fort Worth, Texas, 1982), Douglas Fairbanks, Jr. (Dallas, 1982), Charles FitzSimons (Los Angeles, 1991), Leone "Mike" Goulding (Monument Valley, Utah, 1991), Henry Hathaway (Los Angeles, 1983), Marsha Hunt (Los Angeles, 1983), Martha Hyer (Los Angeles, 1982), John Ireland (Montecito, California, 1990), Burt Kennedy (Los Angeles, 1987), Pauline Kessinger (Los Angeles, 1976), Anna Lee (Los Angeles, 1981), James Lydon (Los Angeles, 1989), Andrew V. McLaglen (San Juan Island, Washington, 1992), Catherine McLeod (Los Angeles, 1983), Walter Mirisch (Los Angeles, 1986), Mildred Natwick (New York, 1979), Lloyd Nolan (Los Angeles, 1976), Darcy O'Brien (Tulsa, Oklahoma, 1992), George Peppard (Los Angeles, 1991), Gil Perkins (Los Angeles, 1986), Stefanie Powers (Dallas, 1991), Ella Raines (Los Angeles, 1983), Cesar Romero (Dallas, 1979), Dean Smith (Dallas, 1979), R. G. Springsteen (Coronado, California, 1986), Charles Starrett (Laguna Beach, California, 1983), Peggy Stewart (Los Angeles, 1985), Milburn Stone (Rancho Santa Fe, California, 1976), Marshall Thompson (Los Angeles, 1980), Hal B. Wallis (Los Angeles, 1982), Michael Wayne (Los Angeles, 1991), Patrick Wayne (Los Angeles, 1991), Elmo Williams (Brookings, Oregon, 1989), and Hank Worden (Los Angeles, 1981 and 1991). The transcripts and tapes of these interviews reside in the DeGolyer Library at Southern Methodist University. Oral reflections on John Wayne have been augmented by letters from Marsha Hunt (July 2, 1993), Catherine McLeod (August 10, 1983), and Darcy O'Brien (May 28, 1993). Budd Boetticher provided the author with a copy of Wayne's final letter to him, dated March 22, 1979.

Relevant interviews in the Columbia University Oral History Collection include sessions with Dana Andrews (1958), Gene Autry (1971), Walter Brennan (1971), Andy Devine (1971), Henry Fonda (1959), Henry Hathaway (1971), Howard Hawks (1971), George "Gabby" Hayes (1959), Geraldine Page (1959), Joseph Pasternak (1971), Rod Steiger (1959), and John Wayne himself (1971).

Transcripts of Maurice Zolotow's interviews on Wayne may be found in the Humanities Research Center at the University of Texas at Austin. Among them are Wayne's own reminiscences (1972), along with those of John Agar (1972), Russell Birdwell (1973), William Clothier (1973), Burt Kennedy (1972), Chuck Roberson (1972), Raoul Walsh (1972), and Michael Wayne (1972).

In the Arizona State Historical Society are interviews with Wayne, Yakima Canutt, William Clothier, Howard Hawks, and Chuck Roberson, all dating from 1970. The Ford Collection at Indiana University contains sessions with Harry Carey, Jr., Olive Golden Carey, William Clothier, Ken Curtis, Joanne Dru, Henry Fonda, John Ford, Mary Ford, Chuck Hayward, Winton Hoch, Ben Johnson, Anna Lee, Lee Marvin, James Stewart, and John Wayne, all taped in preparation for Dan Ford's book, *Pappy: The Life of John Ford* (Englewood Cliffs, N.J.: Prentice-Hall, 1979). Louis McMahon recorded a lengthy oral history with Yakima Canutt for the Directors Guild of America (1977), and Peter Bogdanovich conducted similar sessions with Allan Dwan for the American Film Institute (1968–69). Barbara Hall's interviews with agent Sam Jaffe (1991) and film executive Robert M. W. Vogel (1990) for the Academy of Motion Picture Arts and Sciences both contribute information on Wayne, as do film historian Scott Eyman's talk with William Clothier, writer Robert Nott's interview with Edmund Hartmann, and historian Ray White's conversations with Paul Malvern, which Eyman, Nott, and White generously shared with me.

Clipping files on the early life of John Wayne exist in the public libraries of Winterset, Iowa, and Glendale, California. The Madison County Historical Society houses a scrapbook that details the future actor's years in Winterset and Earlham, Iowa, and various newspaper accounts have been preserved in the John Wayne birthplace in Winterset. Material on Wayne is also available in the City of Lancaster Museum, Lancaster, California, and background information on his years there may be found in *Lancaster Celebrates a Century, 1884–1984* (Lancaster, Calif.: Centennial Committee of the City of Lancaster, 1983). The *Stylus*, the Glendale High School yearbook, for 1924–25 is available in special collections at the Glendale Library and reveals Duke's activities during his senior year. Worth noting are Ethel C. Scar, *The Great American: A John Wayne Biography* (Winterset, Iowa: John Wayne Birthplace, n.d.); Sue P. McKean and Kendall H. Williams, "John Wayne's Roots," *Heritage World: A Magazine of Family History and Genealogy* (1979), 31–44; and *The Life and Times of John Wayne* (n.p.: Harrison House, 1979).

Printed interviews with Wayne include Richard Warren Lewis, "Interview: John Wayne," *Playboy*, May 1971, 76–79; Joe McInerney, "John Wayne Talks Tough," *Film Comment*, September-October 1972, 52–55; "John Wayne Talking to Scott Eyman," *Focus on Film*, Spring 1975, 17–23; "An Interview with John Wayne," *Film Heritage*, Summer 1975, 11–28; Barbara Walters interview with Wayne on *The Barbara Walters Show* (aired on ABC, March 13, 1979). Portions of a transcript of the Walters interview are quoted in Pat Stacy, *Duke: A Love Story,* coauthored by Beverly Linet (New York: Atheneum, 1983), 151–57.

Among the published interviews with Duke's colleagues are observations from John Ford in Peter Bogdanovich's *John Ford* (Berkeley: University of California Press, 1978); Joseph Kane and Arthur Lubin in Todd McCarthy and Charles Flynn (eds.), *Kings of the Bs: Working within the Hollywood System* (New York: Dutton, 1975); Howard Hawks, Raoul Walsh, and William Wellman in Richard Schickel's *The Men Who Made the Movies* (New York: Atheneum, 1975); Charles Bennett, John Lee Mahin, and Niven Busch in Patrick McGilligan's *Backstory* (Berkeley: University of California Press, 1986); Howard Hawks in Joseph McBride's *Hawks on Hawks* (Berkeley: University of California Press, 1982), John Kobal's *People Will Talk* (New York: Knopf, 1985), and "Man's Favorite Director: Howard Hawks," *Cinema,* November-December 1963, 11, 12, 13; Gil Perkins in Bernard Rosenberg and Harry Silverstein's *The Real Tinsel* (London: Macmillan, 1970); Bert Glennon in "Photographing *Rio Grande*," *International Photographer,* September 1950, 4–5; Mark Rydell in John Andrew Gallagher's *Film Directors on Directing* (New York: Praeger, 1989); Geraldine Page in Joanmarie Kalter's *Actors on Acting* (New York: Sterling, 1979); Harry Fraser in Wheeler W. Dixon and Audrey Brown Fraser's *I Went That-a-Way: The Memoirs of a Western Film Director* (Metuchen, N.J.: Scarecrow, 1990); Capucine in Boze Hadleigh's *Hollywood Lesbians* (New York: Barricade, 1994); Paul Fix in Christopher Finch and Linda Rosenkrantz's *Gone Hollywood* (Garden City, N.Y.: Doubleday, 1979); numerous actors and stuntmen in Tim Lilley (ed.), *Campfire Conversations: Interviews with Some of John Wayne's Coworkers* (Akron, Ohio: Big Trail Publications, 1992); and an array of friends and coworkers in Herb Fagen's *Duke: We're Glad We Knew You* (Secaucus, N.J.: Birch Lane, 1996).

Of the several books on Wayne, the major primary source is Pilar Wayne's *John Wayne: My Life with the Duke* (New York: McGraw-Hill, 1987), written with Alex Thorleifson. Significant also is Aissa Wayne's *John Wayne, My Father* (New York: Random House, 1991), written with Steve Delsohn. Interesting, if exaggerated, is Pat Stacy's *Duke: A Love Story.* Of less importance is Bert Minshall's memoir with Clark Sharon of the actor at sea, *On Board with the Duke: John Wayne and the Wild Goose* (Washington, D.C.: Seven Locks Press, 1992), an account by the yacht's last skipper under Wayne's ownership.

Among the coworkers and associates to record their memories of John Wayne are Ann-Margret, *My Story* (New York: Putnam's, 1994), written with Todd Gold; Gene Autry, *Back in the Saddle Again* (Garden City, N.Y.: Doubleday, 1978), written with Mickey Herskowitz; Budd Boetticher, *When in Disgrace* (Santa Barbara, Calif.: Neville, 1989); Lauren Bacall, *Now* (New York: Knopf, 1994); Frank Capra, *The Name above the Title* (New York: Macmillan, 1971); Harry Carey, Jr.,

Company of Heroes: My Life as an Actor in the John Ford Stock Company (Metuchen, N.J.: Scarecrow, 1994); Iron Eyes Cody, *Iron Eyes: My Life as a Hollywood Indian* (New York: Everest House, 1982), written with Collin Perry; Yvonne DeCarlo, *Yvonne: An Autobiography* (New York: St. Martin's, 1987), written with Doug Warren; Cecil B. DeMille, *The Autobiography of Cecil B. DeMille* (Englewood Cliffs, N.J.: Prentice-Hall, 1959), edited by Donald Hayne; Marlene Dietrich, *Marlene* (New York: Grove, 1987); Edward Dmytryk, *It's a Hell of a Life but Not a Bad Living* (New York: Times Books, 1978); Kirk Douglas, *The Ragman's Son* (New York: Simon and Schuster, 1988); Douglas Fairbanks, Jr., *The Salad Days* (New York: Doubleday, 1988); Richard Fleischer, *Just Tell Me When to Cry: A Memoir* (New York: Carroll and Graf, 1993); Henry Fonda, *Fonda: My Life* (New York: New American Library, 1981), written with Howard Teichmann; Tay Garnett, *Light Up Your Torches and Pull Up Your Tights* (New Rochelle, N.Y.: Arlington House, 1973); Stewart Granger, *Sparks Fly Upward* (New York: Putnam's, 1981); Hedda Hopper, *The Whole Truth and Nothing But* (Garden City, N.Y.: Doubleday, 1963), written with James Brough; Katharine Hepburn, *Me: Stories of My Life* (New York: Knopf, 1991); John Huston, *An Open Book* (New York: Knopf, 1980); Dorothy Lamour, *My Side of the Road* (Englewood Cliffs, N.J.: Prentice-Hall, 1980), written with Dick McInnes; Jesse L. Lasky, *I Blow My Own Horn* (Garden City, N.Y.: Doubleday, 1957), written with Don Weldon; Janet Leigh, *There Really Was a Hollywood* (Garden City, N.Y.: Doubleday, 1984); Mervyn LeRoy, *Mervyn LeRoy: Take One* (New York: Hawthorn, 1974); Sophia Loren, *Sophia: Living and Loving* (New York: Bantam, 1979), written by A. E. Hotchner; Myrna Loy, *Myrna Loy: Being and Becoming* (New York: Knopf, 1987), written with James Kotsilibas-Davis; Tim McCoy, *Tim McCoy Remembers the West* (Lincoln: University of Nebraska Press, 1988), written with Ronald McCoy; Ray Milland, *Wide-Eyed in Babylon: An Autobiography* (New York: Morrow, 1974); Patricia Neal, *As I Am: An Autobiography* (New York: Simon and Schuster, 1988), written with Richard DeNeut; Robert Parrish, *Growing Up in Hollywood* (New York: Harcourt Brace Jovanovich, 1976); Otto Preminger, *Preminger: An Autobiography* (Garden City, N.Y.: Doubleday, 1977); Maria Riva (Dietrich's daughter), *Marlene Dietrich* (New York: Knopf, 1993); Chuck Roberson, *The Fall Guy* (North Vancouver, B.C.: Hancock House, 1980), written with Bodie Thoene; Melville Shavelson, *How to Make a Jewish Movie* (Englewood Cliffs, N.J.: Prentice-Hall, 1971); Robert Stack, *Straight Shooting* (New York: Macmillan, 1980), written with Mark Evans; Josef von Sternberg, *Fun in a Chinese Laundry* (New York: Macmillan, 1965); Woody Strode, *Goal Dust: An Autobiography* (Lanham, Md.: Madison, 1990), written with Sam Young; Lana Turner, *Lana: The Lady, the Legend, the Truth* (New York: Dutton, 1982); Hal Wallis, *Starmaker* (New York: Macmillan, 1980), written with Charles Higham; Martha Hyer Wallis, *Finding*

My Way: A Hollywood Memoir (New York: Harper, 1990); Raoul Walsh, *Each Man in His Time* (New York: Farrar, Straus, and Giroux, 1974); and William A. Wellman, *A Short Time for Insanity: An Autobiography* (New York: Hawthorn, 1974).

Garry Wills's *John Wayne's America* (New York: Simon and Schuster, 1997) is a highly interpretive study of Wayne's impact on social and political thought, more essay than biography. Wills has a talent for delving beneath the surface, but his analysis is often based on partial truths and selected data. While the author turns a dazzling phrase, Wills's treatment of John Wayne suffers from dreary attempts at film criticism and a captious attitude.

Randy Roberts and James S. Olson's *John Wayne: American* (New York: Free Press, 1995) is the most recent and exhaustive of previous Wayne biographies. For two decades Maurice Zolotow's *Shooting Star: A Biography of John Wayne* (New York: Simon and Schuster, 1974) ranked as the best treatment of the actor's life, although George Bishop's *John Wayne: The Actor, the Man* (Ottawa: Caroline House, 1979), Allen Eyles's *John Wayne* (Cranbury, N.J.: A. S. Barnes, 1979), Emanuel Levy's *John Wayne: Prophet of the American Way of Life* (Metuchen, N.J.: Scarecrow, 1988), Jean Ramer's *Duke: The Real Story of John Wayne* (New York: Charter, 1973), Donald Shepherd and Robert Slatzer's *Duke: The Life and Times of John Wayne* (Garden City, N.Y.: Doubleday, 1985), and Mike Tomkies's *Duke: The Story of John Wayne* (New York: Avon, 1972) each has merits. Useful are John Boswell and Jay David, *Duke: The John Wayne Album* (New York: Ballantine, 1979); Gene Fernett, *Starring John Wayne* (Cocoa, Fla.: Brevard, n. d.); Charles John Kieskalt, *The Official John Wayne Reference Book* (Secaucus, N.J.: Citadel, 1993); Judith M. Riggin, *John Wayne: A Bio-Bibliography* (New York: Greenwood, 1992); and Steve Zmijewsky, Boris Zmijewsky, and Mark Ricci, *The Complete Films of John Wayne* (Secaucus, N.J.: Citadel, 1993).

Articles on Wayne of exceptional insight are headed by Joan Didion, "John Wayne: A Love Song," *Saturday Evening Post*, August 14, 1965, 76–79; Terry Curtis Fox, "People We Like: The Duke of Deception," *Film Comment*, September-October 1979, 68–70; Molly Haskell, "What Makes John Wayne Larger Than Life?" *The Village Voice*, August 16, 1976, 69–70; Edwin Miller, "Do You Ever Think of Duke as Big Daddy?" *Seventeen*, October 1971, 122–23, 178–82; Clayton Riley, "John Wayne Dethroned," *Ebony*, September 1972, 127–36; David Sutton, "John Wayne: Image vs. Man," *Saturday Evening Post*, March 1976, 54–57, 117–18; and Maurice Zolotow, "John Wayne: What Makes Him an American Institution," *50 Plus*, October 1978, 12–17.

Worth consulting are Nancy Anderson, "On Location with *The Train Robbers*," *Photoplay*, August 1972, 34–38, 97–100; Jane Ardmore, "Cancer Doesn't Fight Fair," *Family Health*, September 1976, 30–33, 58; Fred Barrow, "The Duke Takes Harvard," *The Progressive*, March 1974, 51–52; Joseph N. Bell, "John Wayne's

Scrapbook," *Good Housekeeping*, June 1976, 116–19; Joseph N. Bell, "John Wayne's Very Private World," *Good Housekeeping*, February 1973, 72–73, 130–36; Peter Bogdanovich, "The Duke's Gone West," *New York*, June 25, 1979, 67–68; Diana Serra Cary, "From the Old Frontier to Film," *Wild West*, October 1994, 42–48; Fred Cavinder, "John Wayne: How He Won the West," *Saturday Evening Post*, July 1979, 57–64; Fred Cavinder, "John Wayne's Other Roles," *Saturday Evening Post*, October 1979, 32–35; John Deedy, "News and Views," *Commonweal*, June 28, 1968, 426; Lorraine Gauguin, "Duke in Durango," *National Review*, April 27, 1973, 472–73; John Gault, "A Metaphor for His Time," *Maclean's*, June 25, 1979, 26–27; Mark Goodman, "Full Ahead, Mr. Wayne," *Motor Boating and Sailing*, November 1978, 58–61, 98; Richard Grenier, "John Wayne's Image," *Commentary*, September 1979, 79–81; Jack Hamilton, "John Wayne: The Big Man of the Westerns," *Look*, August 2, 1960, 83–87; Arnold Hano, "John Wayne: A Man in Every Sense of the Word," *Good Housekeeping*, October 1965, 243, 252–54; Molly Haskell, "Wayne, Westerns, and Women," *Ladies Home Journal*, July 1976, 76–77, 88–94; Paul Hendrickson, "John Wayne: The Iron Duke," *Saturday Evening Post*, Spring 1972, 84–91; Herb Howe, "Duke in Coonskin," *Photoplay*, January 1950, 54–55, 88; Helen Itria, "Big John," *Look*, August 11, 1953, 67–71; Dean Jennings, "John Wayne," *Saturday Evening Post*, October 27, 1962, 28–35; Grady Johnson, "John Wayne: Star of Iron," *Coronet*, December 1954, 113–18; Stanley Kauffmann, "Stars in Their Courses," *The New Republic*, June 30, 1979, 24–25; P. F. Kluge, "First and Last, a Cowboy," *Life*, January 28, 1972, 42–46; Jack Knoll, "John Wayne: End as a Man," *Newsweek*, June 25, 1979, 76–79; Jim Liston, "At Home with John Wayne," *American Home*, April 1961, 13–18; Pete Martin, "The Ladies Like 'Em Rugged," *Saturday Evening Post*, December 23, 1950, 19, 73–74; Thomas B. Morgan, "God and Man in Hollywood," *Esquire*, May 1963, 74–75, 123–75; Ronald Reagan, "Unforgettable John Wayne," *Reader's Digest*, October 1979, 114–19; John Reddy, "John Wayne Rides Again . . . and Again. . . and Again," *Reader's Digest*, September 1970, 138–42; Margaret Ronan, "Two Screen Cowboys Talk about the Reel West and the Real West," *Senior Scholastic*, December 6, 1971, 10–11; Andrew Sarris, "John Wayne's Strange Legacy," *New Republic*, August 4, 1979, 33–36; Richard Schickel, "Duke: Image from a Lifetime," *Time*, June 25, 1979, 50–51; Martin Scott, "John Wayne," *Cosmopolitan*, November 1954, 26–33; Howard Sharpe, "John the Duke," *Photoplay*, January 1944, 47, 78–79; Andrew Sinclair, "The Man on Horseback: The Seven Faces of John Wayne," *Sight and Sound*, Autumn 1979, 232–35; Marvin Stone, "A Hero to Fit the Image," *U.S. News and World Report*, May 28, 1979, 80; Toni Wayne, "Our Hearts Belong to Daddy," *Movieland*, April 1952, 25, 66–67; and Steven Zmijewsky, "John Wayne: Greatest Cowboy of 'Em All," *Liberty*, Spring 1971, 22–23.

Articles attributed to Wayne's own authorship include "The Good Things: Duke on America," *Saturday Evening Post*, September 1979, 38–44; "Mistakes I've Made," *Movieland*, June 1954, 48–49, 73–75; "On the Level," *Movieland*, May 1950, 30–31, 78; and "The Turning Point in My Life," *Movieland*, October 1951, 46–47, 73.

Of secondary importance are "Big John," *Newsweek*, March 1, 1965, 86; Peter Bogdanovich, "Hollywood," *Esquire*, May 1972, 66,190; "Do I Get to Play the Drunk This Time?" *Sight and Sound*, Spring 1971, 97–100; "The Duke at 60," *Time*, June 9, 1967, 67; "Duke and Sister Kate Too," *Time*, November 18, 1974, 113; "Dusty and the Duke," *Life*, July 11, 1969, 38–41; "In Praise of Famous Men," *Saturday Review*, September 1, 1979, 8; "John Wayne Rides Again," *Life*, May 7, 1965, 69–75; "John Wayne as the Last Hero," *Time*, August 8, 1969, 53–56; "John Wayne's America," *Good Housekeeping*, November 1977, 138–41, 282–84; "John Wayne's Ordeal," *Newsweek*, July 25, 1960, 107; Todd McCarthy, "Back Talk," *Film Comment*, March-April 1979, 78–79; "United We Fall; Divided We Stand," *Saturday Review*, January 2, 1971, 59; and "The Wages of Virtue," *Time*, March 3, 1952, 64–66, 68–69.

Useful background information may be found in Joey Adams, *The God Bit* (New York: Mason and Lipscomb, 1974); Rudy Behlmer (ed.), *Memo from Darryl F. Zanuck* (New York: Grove, 1993); Kevin Brownlow, *The West, the War, and the Wilderness* (New York: Knopf, 1979); Ronald L. Davis, *John Ford: Hollywood's Old Master* (Norman: University of Oklahoma Press, 1995); George N. Fenin and William K. Everson, *The Western* (New York: Bonanza, 1962); Gene Fernett, *Next Time Drive off the Cliff!* (Cocoa, Fla.: Cinememories, 1968); Gene Fernett, *Poverty Row* (Satellite Beach, Fla.: Coral Reef Publications, 1973); Michael Malone, *Heroes of Eros: Male Sexuality in the Movies* (New York: Dutton, 1979); Charles Hamblett, *The Hollywood Cage* (New York: Hart, 1969); Richard Maurice Hurst, *Republic Studios: Between Poverty Row and the Majors* (Metuchen, N.J.: Scarecrow, 1979); Irving Lazar with Annette Tapert, *Swifty: My Life and Good Times* (New York: Simon and Schuster, 1995); John H. Lenihan, *Showdown: Confronting Modern America in the Western Film* (Urbana: University of Illinois Press, 1980); Kenneth Macgowan, *Behind the Screen* (New York: Delacorte, 1965); Frank Manchel, *Cameras West* (Englewood Cliffs, N. J.: Prentice-Hall, 1971); Rollo May, *The Cry for Myth* (New York: Delta, 1992); Archie P. McDonald, *Shooting Stars: Heroes and Heroines of Western Film* (Bloomington: Indiana University Press, 1987); Joan Mellen, *Big Bad Wolves: Masculinity in the American Film* (New York: Pantheon, 1977); Don Miller, *B Movies* (New York: Ballantine, 1988); James Robert Parish, *Great Western Stars* (New York: Ace, 1976); Danny Peary (ed.), *Close-Ups* (New York: Workman Publishers, 1978); William T. Pilkington and Don Graham (eds.), *Western Movies* (Albuquerque: University of New Mexico Press,

1979); J. A. Place, *The Western Films of John Ford* (Secaucus, N.J.: Citadel, 1974); Donald Spoto, *Camerado: Hollywood and the American Man* (New York: New American Library, 1978); Bette L. Stanton, *"Where God Put the West": Movie Making in the Desert* (Moab, Utah: Four Corners Publications, 1994); John Tuska, *The Filming of the West* (Garden City, N.Y.: Doubleday, 1976); John Tuska, *The Vanishing Legion: A History of Mascot Pictures, 1927–1935* (Jefferson, N.C.: McFarland, 1982); and Alexander Walker, *Stardom: The Hollywood Phenomenon* (New York: Stein and Day, 1970).

Quotations from reviews of Wayne's films have been drawn from *Cue*, *Hollywood Reporter*, *Los Angeles Examiner*, *Motion Picture Herald*, *Newsweek*, *New York Daily News*, *New York Herald Tribune*, *New York Times*, *New York World-Telegram*, *New Yorker*, and *Time*.

Index

369

373